Atlas of Florida

Edward A. Fernald
Elizabeth D. Purdum
Editors

James R. Anderson, Jr.
Peter A. Krafft
Cartographers

Institute of Science and Public Affairs
Florida State University

University Press of Florida

Atlas of Florida / editors, Edward A. Fernald [and] Elizabeth D.
  Purdum ; cartographers, James R. Anderson [and] Peter A. Krafft.
      p.   cm.
   Includes bibliographical references and index.
   Contents: Natural environment—History and culture—Population
—Economics—Recreation and tourism—Infrastructure and
planning—Origin of place names—Statistics.
   ISBN 0-8130-1131-0
   1. Florida—Maps.   I. Fernald, Edward A.   II. Purdum, Elizabeth D.
III. Anderson, James R.   IV. Krafft, Peter A.
G1315.A83   1992 <G&M>
912.759—dc20   92-822
                                                         CIP
                                                        MAP

The University Press of Florida is the scholarly publishing agency of the State
University System of Florida, comprised of Florida A&M University, Florida
Atlantic University, Florida International University, Florida State University,
University of Central Florida, University of Florida, University of North
Florida, University of South Florida, University of West Florida.

Orders for books should be addressed to:
University Press of Florida
15 NW 15th Street
Gainesville, FL 32611

Atlas Staff

Associate Cartographer
Becky Wilkes

Cartographic Assistants
Daniel C. Endrizzi
Daryl B. Huffman
James A. Reed
Thomas J. Richard
Traci A. Schultz
Christopher D. Wilkes

Art and Photo Editor
Assistant Editor
Laura Peck Thompson

Production Assistants
Charles P. Bilodeau
Tracey Helin
Scott E. Johnson

Contributors

James R. Anderson, Jr., Florida Resources and Environmental Analysis Center, Florida State University

Kenneth M. Campbell, Florida Geological Survey

David W. Crumpacker, Department of Environmental, Population, and Organismic Biology, University of Colorado, Boulder

Edward A. Fernald, Institute of Science and Public Affairs, Florida State University

Tory Grissom, Florida House of Representatives, Reapportionment Committee

Stephen M. Hodges, Homer Hoyt Center for Land Economics and Real Estate, Institute of Science and Public Affairs, Florida State University

C.J. Janus, Freelance illustrator

Randy Kautz, Florida Game and Fresh Water Fish Commission

James W. May, Homer Hoyt Center for Land Economics and Real Estate, Institute of Science and Public Affairs, Florida State University

George Meier, Florida House of Representatives, Reapportionment Committee

J. Barry Mittan, Florida Department of Health and Rehabilitative Services

Donald J. Patton, Department of Geography, Florida State University

Elizabeth D. Purdum, Institute of Science and Public Affairs, Florida State University

Thomas Scott, Florida Geological Survey

William F. Tanner, Department of Geology, Florida State University

Laura Peck Thompson, Institute of Science and Public Affairs, Florida State University

Frank A. Unger, Florida Resources and Environmental Analysis Center, Florida State University

Karen Walby, Budget and Tax Reform Commission

Morton D. Winsberg, Department of Geography, Florida State University

Acknowledgments

Nearly three years and the efforts of many people have gone into the production of this revision of the *Atlas of Florida*. The production of this atlas was made possible through the combined efforts of many talented individuals at Florida State University and throughout the state. The idea to revise and reissue the comprehensive *Atlas of Florida* was conceived by the staff of the Institute of Science and Public Affairs at Florida State University, endorsed by the offices of Florida State University President Dale Lick and Provost and Vice President for Academic Affairs Bob Glidden and approved as a project of the office of the State Geographer by the Secretary of State, the Honorable Jim Smith. We are especially grateful to the office of the Secretary of State for the partial funding of the cartographic development of the atlas. Beverly Burnsed and Hal Lynch of the Secretary of State's office deserve special thanks for their efforts on our behalf.

Faculty, students, and staff throughout the university participated in the planning, research, and production of the atlas. Our deepest appreciation goes to all of these individuals for their valuable contributions. The untiring efforts, enthusiasm, and ideas of Dr. Morton Winsberg, professor of geography, deserve special recognition. As noted in the table of contents he was a major contributor to the intellectual development of this work. Dr. Donald J. Patton, professor of geography, also made substantial contributions to the atlas beyond those noted in the table of contents. To all of the authors we give a special thanks.

Much of the staff of the Institute of Science and Public Affairs is due a word of thanks for the many hours spent in record-keeping, typing, and other functions necessary for the atlas production, including Susan Galloway, Sheila Williams, and Mac Hall. The University Press of Florida, under the direction of Dr. George Bedell, receives thanks for the major task of advertising and marketing the finished product. We are especially grateful to Lizbeth Kent, Larry Leshan, Walda Metcalf, and Lynn Werts of the press. Frank M. Reiber of the University of Kansas generously assisted us in the early phases of design of the book. We also acknowledge Leah DeMilly Smith and William R. Brueckheimer, contributors to the first atlas of Florida. Many of their ideas have been incorporated into this revision.

Thanks and appreciation also go to the many agency, university and private firm personnel who supplied data, maps, photographs, and ideas crucial to the successful completion of the atlas. These special people include: Charles D. Blume, Apalachee Regional Planning Council; Thomas Boswell, Department of Geography, University of Miami; Chris Bowley, Florida State University; Greg Brock, Florida Department of Natural Resources; George Fischer, Department of Anthropology, Florida State University; Florida Sugar Cane League, Inc.; Diane D. Greer, editor, *Florida Architect*; John Hann, Florida Department of State; Jim Harvey, South Florida Water Management District; Charles Hudson, Department of Anthropology, University of Georgia; Ann Johnson, Florida Natural Areas Inventory; Randy Kautz, Florida Game and Fresh Water Fish Commission; Steve Kimble, Executive Office of the Governor; Julia A. Magee, Florida Department of Community Affairs; Pat Marx, Metropolitan Dade County Art in Public Places; Jim Miller, Florida Department of State; Stewart Miller, Architect; Ed Montanaro, the Florida legislature; Joan Morris and Joanna Norman, Florida State Archives; Edward A. Mueller, Morales and Shumer Engineers, Inc.; Dixie Nims, Florida Department of Commerce; Joseph R. Orsenigo, Sci-Agra, Inc.; Jim Quinn, Florida Department of Community Affairs; David P. Reddy, Florida Department of State, Florida Folklife Programs; Thomas Scott, Florida Geological Survey; Janet Starnes-Smith, Northwest Florida Water Management District; William Serow and Robert Weller, Center for the Study of Population, Florida State University; John Stevely, Florida Cooperative Extension Service; Don Wood, Florida Game and Fresh Water Fish Commission; and Michael Zimny, formerly of the Florida Department of State.

Preface

This is the second comprehensive atlas of Florida produced by the Institute of Science and Public Affairs at Florida State University. The design and content of this atlas are so substantially changed from the first atlas, published in 1981, that it is issued as a new book rather than as a second edition. The major goal, however, of the two atlases is the same—to show, largely in graphic form, physical, historical, demographic, and economic patterns, trends, and conditions throughout Florida. We also wanted to give a sense of place as well as pattern and have added many photographs showing richness and variety in both natural and cultural landscapes. Virtually every page of the atlas has been redone and many new topics added, including land forms, ecosystems, sponge and cigar industries, the arts, and tourist attractions. In keeping with the trends in government in Florida in the 1980s a new section has been added on infrastructure and planning.

The atlas is intended as a basic reference volume on Florida for citizens, potential residents, and tourists as well as for students, researchers, policy makers, and planners. Although some of the information in the atlas is complex, every attempt has been made to clarify terms and concepts for the nonspecialist reader. In most cases, the graphics are self-explanatory.

The ideas and data for this atlas came from a variety of sources. The most up-to-date statistics available, primarily from state and federal agencies, were used to construct the maps and graphs. In some instances, particularly in the natural environment section, maps were adapted from existing maps produced by state and federal agencies. The majority of the data in the population section came from the recently released 1990 U.S. Census of Population. Much of the atlas is a product of the creative efforts of the authors. The authors extensively researched the topics for their pages and then worked with the cartographers to present the results in a visual form. The sources for both graphics and text are at the back of the book listed by section and page number. In the back of the atlas is also a section of statistical data by county.

Different types of maps and graphics were used to give the reader a visual perspective of various aspects of the state. County-level data are most commonly displayed in the atlas on choropleth maps. A computer program developed by George F. Jenks at the University of Kansas was used to determine class intervals for data on these maps. The program forms the classes by grouping areas that are statistically most similar. Although this program tends to create uneven intervals, it presents patterns more accurately.

As a basic reference volume, the *Atlas of Florida* should serve a wide variety of readers. Our major objective is to present the nature of Florida in a balanced way that will foster better understanding of this beautiful, fragile, and rapidly growing state as it exists in the 1990s.

Contents

BRICKELL AVENUE, Rafael Salazar

INTRODUCTION

On a map of the continental United States Florida is easily recognized as the southward jutting peninsula separating the Atlantic Ocean from the Gulf of Mexico. Florida is the exposed portion of the Floridan Plateau, a mass of rock nearly 500 miles long and from 250 to 400 miles wide. On top of a foundation of mostly igneous rock, assumed to be a continuation of the geologic base of the Piedmont region of Georgia, are more than 4,000 feet of highly porous sedimentary rock, chiefly limestone, formed over millennia by deposition of shells and bones of sea creatures as well as chemicals evaporated from the shallow seawater.

Over the millions of years of the Florida peninsula's geologic history, its size and shape have changed many times: 50 million years ago it was an island south of North America, 10 million years ago it was completely submerged, and since then peninsulas and islands of various sizes and shapes have been created and redrawn by fluctuating sea levels. Florida's abundance of ridges, sinkholes, springs, rivers, lakes, and plains is the result of these rises and falls of the sea and of the uplift and subsidence of land. The sea is also largely responsible for the state's many bays, inlets, wetlands, and islands. The Florida Keys, a gentle arc of islands extending 150 miles south of the peninsula to Key West, are composed of coral rock covered in most places with a thin layer of sand.

Florida's location between latitudes 24° 30' N and 31° N, the warming influence of the Gulf Stream, and its geologic history result in a climate and an array of plants and animals unlike any other state. The climate of Florida is basically humid subtropical with the exception of the southern tip of the peninsula and the Keys, which are tropical. Long, hot summers are separated from short, cool, and sometimes cold, winters by mild and pleasant days during spring and fall. The Gulf Stream moderates Florida's temperatures year-round. Sea breezes keep land along the coast slightly warmer in the winter and cooler in the summer than inland areas. Climatic differences are smallest in the summer when the state is almost continually under the influence of warm, moist air from the Gulf of Mexico and the Atlantic. During July, the warmest month, temperature differences are small throughout Florida: mean daily maximum values range from 88 to 91° F, and mean minimum values range from 72 to 75° F. In the

Florida Facts

Total area: 58,560 square miles
Total land area: 54,252 square miles
Total water area: 4,308 square miles
Rank among states in total area: 22nd
Length north and south (St. Marys River to Key West): 447 miles
Width east and west (Atlantic Ocean to Perdido River): 361 miles
Distance from Pensacola to Key West: 792 miles (by road)
Highest natural point: 345 feet near Lakewood in northeast Walton County
Geographic Center: 12 miles northwest of Brooksville, Hernando County
Coastline: 1,197 statute miles
Tidal shoreline (general): 2,276 statute miles
Beaches: 663 miles
Longest river: St. Johns, 273 miles
Largest lake: Lake Okeechobee, 700 square miles
Largest county: Palm Beach, 2,578 square miles
Smallest county: Union, 245 square miles
Number of lakes (greater than 10 acres): approximately 7,700
Number of first-magnitude springs: 27
Number of islands (larger than 10 acres): approximately 4,500
First permanent European settlement: 1565, St. Augustine, by Spanish
U.S. Territory: 1821
Admitted to union as state: March 3, 1845 (27th state)
Population 1990: 12,937,926
Population rank among states 1990: 4th
Population 1980: 9,739,992
Population growth rate 1980–90: 32.83%
Most populous metropolitan area 1990: Tampa–St. Petersburg–Clearwater, 2,067,959
Number of counties: 67
Form of government: Governor and independent cabinet consisting of secretary of state, attorney general, comptroller, treasurer, commissioner of agriculture, and commissioner of education
State sales tax: 6%
State income tax: none
Legislature: 120 house districts, 40 senate districts, 23 congressional districts

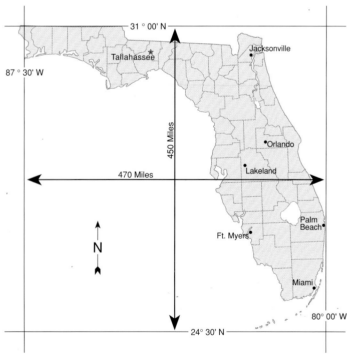

Virtually 100 percent of South America is east of Florida. The correct order from west to east of the Florida cities (remembering that Jacksonville includes all of Duval County) on the map is Tallahassee, Jacksonville, Lakeland, Ft. Myers, Orlando, Miami, and Palm Beach.

winter temperature differences are far greater across the state: mean daily maximum temperatures during January, the coldest month, range from 75° F in southern Florida to 60° F in the western panhandle, and mean daily minimum temperatures range from 60° F in the south to 40° F in the north.

With the exception of the north, where rain accompanies winter cold fronts, most of Florida receives the majority of its rain from summer showers and storms, a predictable and welcome afternoon relief from the heat and humidity. The Florida peninsula has been dubbed the "thunderstorm capital" of the northern hemisphere. Only in the heart of sub-Saharan Africa are thunderstorms more frequent than over the Florida peninsula.

Florida averages 54 inches of rainfall annually, more than any other state. Despite its high rainfall Florida has relatively few days when the sun fails to shine at least part of the day. So rare are these days that a St. Petersburg newspaper used to give away its evening edition on sunless days.

Great amounts of rain may fall within short periods of time: 38.7 inches in 24 hours in Yankeetown in 1950, 6 inches in 1 hour in Hialeah (near Miami) in 1947. The heaviest rainfall occurs in a strip 10 to 15 miles inland from the southeast coast and in the western panhandle, which averages 66 inches of rain each year. The Keys normally receive the smallest amount of rainfall—an average of 40 inches each year. Miami Beach averages 47 inches each year, and Miami, only 9 miles inland averages 58 inches. Rain may appear suddenly from a cloudless sky and may fall in one block and not another.

Although rainfall is abundant in Florida, it varies seasonally and annually as well as spatially, sometimes resulting in severe supply problems, particularly in south Florida. Geologist Garald Parker identified a line snaking across the peninsula from New Smyrna Beach to Cedar Key as the Florida Hydrologic Divide. The area south of this line, which supports over three-quarters of the state's population, is totally dependent on rainfall it receives for its water: virtually no net movement of either surface water or groundwater occurs across this line.

All of Florida is susceptible to hurricanes—tropical storms with wind in excess of 74 miles per hour—from June through November, with the greatest number occurring in September and October. Dade County and the Keys have the highest probability of experiencing a hurricane: 1 in 7 in any given year. Defying these odds, no major hurricane has directly hit the now densely developed south Florida since Betsy in 1965. Thousands of lives, however, were lost to hurricanes earlier in the century. Over 120 people were killed and 5,000 homes destroyed when a hurricane hit Miami in 1926. Two years later over 2,000 people—mostly migrant farm workers—drowned when a dike around Lake Okeechobee broke during a hurricane, an event vividly recounted in frightening detail by Zora Neale Hurston in her novel, *Their Eyes Were Watching God*. The Labor Day hurricane of 1935 killed over 400 in the Keys. Many were unemployed World War I veterans sent to work on public road projects. They were killed when the train sent from Miami to evacuate them was swept off the track by wind and water.

GREAT SEAL

STATE FLAG

STATE FLOWER

STATE ANIMAL

STATE BIRD

STATE SEA SHELL

STATE TREE

STATE MARINE MAMMAL

Motto: In God We Trust
Nickname: The Sunshine State
Bird: Mockingbird
Flower: Orange blossom
Song: "Old Folks at Home"
Tree: Sabal palm
Day: April 2
Beverage: Orange juice
Freshwater fish: Florida largemouth bass
Saltwater fish: Atlantic sailfish
Marine mammal: West Indian manatee
Saltwater mammal: Bottlenose dolphin
Animal: Florida panther
Shell: Horse conch
Gem: Moonstone
Gem: Agatized coral
Soil: Myakka fine sand

Even today after decades of intense development and thousands of years of human occupancy, Florida is still a biological wonderland and global hotspot of biodiversity, with a mixture of species derived from more temperate areas to the north and tropical Caribbean areas to the south. Travelling across north Florida and along the St. Johns River in 1777, naturalist William Bartram described large-mouth bass weighing 25 to 30 pounds, diamondback rattlesnakes 10 to 12 feet long, and live oaks with circumferences of 12 to 18 feet. He also identified 400 species of plants, 125 of which were previously unknown to him.

Contemporary biologists estimate that there are 300 species of native trees and 3,500 species of vascular plants in Florida. Today the predominant vegetative community throughout Florida is pine forests. One to three species of pine (longleaf, slash, pond) are found mixed with oak. Herbs, saw palmetto, shrubs, and small hardwood trees form an understory. A century ago, before large-scale drainage and development, as much as 60 percent of Florida's surface was wetlands. Now they occupy 15 to 20 percent. Today mangroves, swamps, and saltwater marshes are still found on the southern rim of the penin-

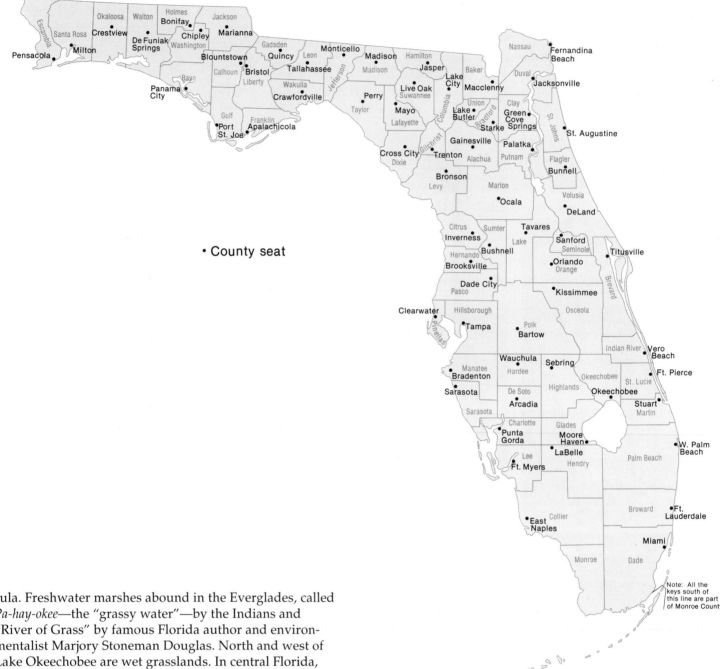

• County seat

Note: All the keys south of this line are part of Monroe County

sula. Freshwater marshes abound in the Everglades, called *Pa-hay-okee*—the "grassy water"—by the Indians and "River of Grass" by famous Florida author and environmentalist Marjory Stoneman Douglas. North and west of Lake Okeechobee are wet grasslands. In central Florida, pine flatwoods are interspersed with mixed forests of pine, xerophytic oak, and hardwoods. In the northern panhandle are forests of mixed hardwoods and pines. Where trees have been cut for lumber or pulp, secondary growth consists mostly of pines. Throughout the state, river valleys and large lakes are bounded by cypress forests. Most of the coastline is sandy beaches, saltwater marshes, or mangrove swamps.

Much of the vegetation in the panhandle and the northern part of the state is shared with the rest of the Gulf and the Atlantic coastal plains. Specialized assemblages of plants developed in the central portion of the state when the area was isolated by higher seas. Tropical and subtropical plants, many of Caribbean and South American origin, thrive in the hammocks of south Florida. Florida has over 150 native species of reptiles and amphibians, including the now-abundant alligator and the much rarer American crocodile, as well as over 200 native species of freshwater fish. Over 425 species of birds—approximately half the

bird species in the U.S.—may be observed in Florida. The only coral reefs off the continental United States are in the clear waters off the Florida Keys. Here more than 200 species of fish and 50 species of coral are found.

Humans have been drawn to this abundant and diverse natural environment for thousands of years. The first of Florida's many million residents were Indians who migrated into the peninsula more than 12,000 years ago when the land mass was larger and the climate drier than it is today. Mastodons, camels, mammoths, saber-toothed cats, giant sloths, bisons, and horses roamed vast grasslands. Florida's early inhabitants were nomadic, hunting big game and traveling in small family groups in response to availability of food and water.

JUAN PONCE DE LEÓN AT THE FOUNTAIN OF YOUTH

On April 3, 1513, searching for an island the Carib Indians called Bimini—reputed to be a paradise of pearls, silver, gold, and a fountain of youth—Juan Ponce de León landed at an unknown spot along the upper east coast of Florida. He named the land *La Florida* because it was *Pascua Florida* (the Easter season, literally translated as Feast of Flowers) and because from the sea the land appeared laden with flowers and trees. Ponce claimed every contiguous parcel of land for the Spanish crown, having no idea he was staking claim to virtually all of North America. Ponce de León was the first of a long series of European adventurers, explorers, and missionaries seeking gold and other precious metals, sites for settlements, and converts in *La Florida*.

At least 100,000 Indians—perhaps several times more—were living in Florida in the early 1500s. The Apalachee and Timucuan Indians in the north shared many cultural traits with other Indians of what was to become the southeastern U.S., including agriculture, chief-centered political organization, temple mounds, and elaborate burial rituals. The Calusa and other Indians in the southern peninsula ate large quantities of readily available fish and shellfish, and produced huge shell middens, elaborate earthworks, and delicately carved wooden figurines.

The Spanish admiral Pedro Menéndez de Avilés established the first permanent European settlement in Florida in 1565 and named it St. Augustine. Today St. Augustine is popular with tourists as the oldest continuously occupied settlement founded by Europeans in the United States. For nearly three centuries, Florida was a pawn in the European competition for the New World and fell under control of Spain (twice) and Britain before becoming a territory of the U.S. in 1821.

By the early 1700s all but a handful of the descendants of Florida's original Indian population had been eradicated by disease and war. Creeks and other southeastern Indians, displaced from their native lands by advancing colonists, began to move into the now nearly vacant land, establishing towns, raising cattle, and growing crops. In the 1800s as Florida became more and more attractive to the expanding United States three wars were fought to remove these Indians, who had become known as the Seminoles. When the Third Seminole War ended in 1858, only 100–300 Seminoles remained in Florida.

In 1830, when first federal census to include Florida was taken, 37,730 persons were counted in the territory. The only settlements of consequence were St. Augustine to the east and Pensacola to the west, each with populations of about 2,000. Tallahassee's growth was just beginning. The site—previously the center of Apalachee Indian culture and later the location a Seminole Indian town—was selected in 1823 as the territorial capital because of its location halfway between Pensacola and St. Augustine. By 1845, when Florida became a state, Tallahassee had become the center of a flourishing cotton plantation region.

Nearly all of Florida's population was in its northern tier, when in the 1850s the federal government gave two-thirds of Florida's land (24 million acres) to the state, declaring it "swamp and overflowed" and "unfit for civilization." The state sold at very low prices millions of acres to anyone promising to drain the land and to connect it by train to the North. By 1880, 60 percent of the entire state was owned by five railroad companies, one drainage enterprise, and one man—Hamilton Disston who bought 4 million acres for 25 cents per acre. In the 1880s Henry Flagler and Henry Plant built opulent hotels along the coasts of Florida linking them with their railroads to population centers in the North, attracting wealthy tourists to the state for the first time.

By 1900 the state's population exceeded one-half million, and Jacksonville, which had developed as the gateway to the peninsula from a cow town surrounded by scattered farms, was the most populous city, with around 28,000 persons. Pensacola, a thriving lumber port, and Key West, the home of a federal naval base, had populations around 17,000, and Tampa, originally the site of Ft. Brooke established during the Second Seminole War, had a population of almost 16,000.

Settlement patterns changed in the twentieth century as people moved into the central and southern parts of the peninsula, especially along the slightly elevated Atlantic Coastal Ridge and along the Gulf coast, away from interior swamps and marshes. Development first occurred along

Hello, Tampa!

We're coming, coming, coming, coming without fail,
We're pushing, pushing, pushing through
The Tamiami Trail!

Drilling, blasting, dredging, piling up the road bed, stopping for nothing every day or two moving camp to keep up with the drill and the dredge—here goes the Tamiami Trail.

In about one more month it will reach Pinecrest, that sight for sore eyes, a beautiful pine ride lying in the midst of the long, level meadow lands—the first high ground suitable for a townsite west of Miami on the Trail. Then the prices of town lots there will soar. NOW you can buy them at your own price at auction. W. J. WILLINGHAM.

Population, 1990

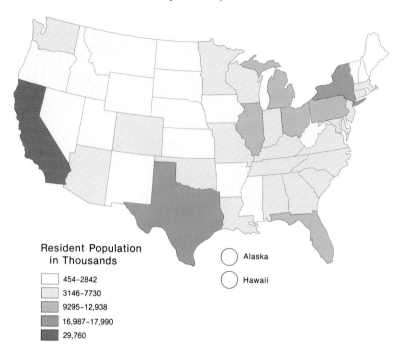

Resident Population
in Thousands

☐	454–2842
☐	3146–7730
☐	9295–12,938
☐	16,987–17,990
☐	29,760

○ Alaska

○ Hawaii

Population Change, 1980–1990

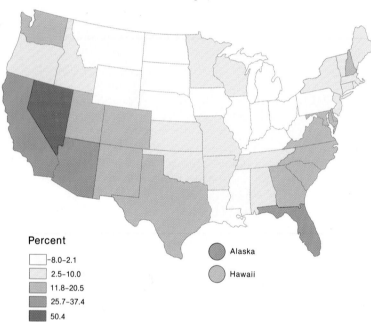

Percent

☐	-8.0–2.1
☐	2.5–10.0
☐	11.8–20.5
☐	25.7–37.4
☐	50.4

● Alaska

● Hawaii

the east coast, extending from Jacksonville south to Miami, then along the west coast from Tampa to St. Petersburg, Clearwater, Sarasota, and Ft. Myers. The space industry accelerated growth on the east coast, and Walt Disney World spurred growth in the central region. Today much of northern Florida is lightly populated. Much of the most heavily populated land in Florida is the least suitable environmentally for development. The largest amount of suitable land is in the still scarcely populated uplands of northern Florida.

During the early twentieth century, masses of land speculators converged on the state. Miami's population swelled from slightly less than 30,000 to over 110,000 between 1910 and 1920. At the height of the boom, land on

the Atlantic Coastal Ridge sold for $25,000 per acre and a foot of prime downtown commercial space was reputed to sell for $20,000. In 1925 alone 2.5 million people entered the state. A hurricane struck Miami in 1926, leveling tourist camps and tent cities, hastily constructed to house people during the boom. The Great Depression signaled the end of the first great land boom, but by 1930 Florida had become a predominantly urban state, with three-quarters of its population on 6 percent of its land. By 1950 the greatest boom in all of Florida history was underway and has continued unabated through the 1990s.

In 1987 Florida overtook Pennsylvania as the fourth most-populous state in the nation with an estimated 12 million persons, up from twentieth place in 1950 and tenth place in 1964. By 1990 Florida's population had risen to nearly 13 million. Over 90 percent of Florida's population resides within its twenty metropolitan statistical areas. Many of Florida's counties still retain their rural character, although new communities, many aimed at retirees, with names like Beverly Hills, El Ranchero Village, and Jasmine Estates are continuously springing up, particularly in once-rural counties adjacent to urban complexes. In culture and character north Florida remains more like its neighboring counties in Georgia and Alabama than like south and central Florida.

Florida's phenomenal growth since World War II has come from retirees and workers and their families from other states as well as from Cuban, Haitian, Vietnamese, and other refugees principally from the Caribbean and South and Central America. In 1980, almost 20 percent of Florida's residents had lived in another state during the preceding 5 years. Between 1978 and 1984, Florida gained nearly 200,000 residents a year, averaging nearly 4,000 each week, and over 500 each day: about 500,000 persons moved into the state each year, while 300,000 moved out of the state.

In 1990, 86 percent of Florida's population was white and 14 percent was nonwhite. The percentages of whites and nonwhites vary considerably across the state, with the highest percentages of nonwhites in Dade County and in rural north Florida counties with a legacy of plantation agriculture.

Florida's Hispanic population, comprised of people from many Latin American nations, has grown steadily since the 1959 Cuban Revolution. Between 1959 and 1966, 400,000 mainly middle-class Cubans settled in Miami. In 1980, 125,000 Cubans entered south Florida from the port of Mariel. Forced by Cuban authorities to depart were many of Cuba's mentally ill and criminals. In 1990, 12.2 percent of the state's population was Hispanic, an increase from 8.9 percent in 1980. Dade County was 49 percent Hispanic in 1990. The Miami metropolitan area contains the second largest concentration of Cubans in the world, behind only Havana. Over 50 percent of all Cubans in the U.S. now live in Miami.

Florida also has a large percentage of the aged in its population. In 1990, 18 percent of all Floridians were 65 years of age or older and 1.6 percent was 85 years of age or older. In some counties (Charlotte, Highlands, Pasco, Sarasota, and Citrus) the percentage of those 65 and over approaches 40 percent. The greatest percentages of young

Relief

Relief is the vertical distance between the highest and lowest points on the land surface within the study area. The entire continent, taken as a whole, obviously has more relief than any small part of it. Therefore the size of the study area must be specified. The map to the right was made by measuring the relief in squares 6 miles on each side (approximately 9.6 kilometers on each side), or 36 square miles in area. This size area was selected because topographic maps in the United States until recently were gridded by the township method, and each township by definition contains 36 square miles.

In general, maximum local relief is greatest within the panhandle and next greatest across the Central Florida Ridge, which runs north and south along much of the peninsula. Minimum relief is less than 2.0 meters (about 6.6 feet) and is widespread in southern Florida (south of Lake Okeechobee) and in the coastal strip along the Big Bend area (northeastern corner of the Gulf of Mexico). This almost featureless area owes its very gentle, uniform slope to wave action in the past. At one or more times in the latest million years or so, when sea level stood about 13 meters (about 43 feet) above its present position, breaking waves from the Atlantic smoothed this area. The wave-cut cliff that was made at that time can be seen now, north and northwest of Lake Okeechobee.

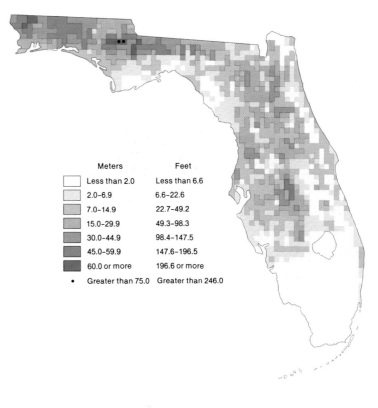

Meters	Feet
Less than 2.0	Less than 6.6
2.0–6.9	6.6–22.6
7.0–14.9	22.7–49.2
15.0–29.9	49.3–98.3
30.0–44.9	98.4–147.5
45.0–59.9	147.6–196.5
60.0 or more	196.6 or more
• Greater than 75.0	Greater than 246.0

Physiography

Compared with mountainous terrain, such as in the Andes or the Himalayas, Florida is almost featureless; but if Florida is studied without regard to other areas, many variations in the land surface can be seen. The coastal areas are subdivided, on the map to the right, into the following categories: barrier islands, Gulf coast estuaries (river mouth bays), swamps and marshes, lowlands, and the Florida Keys (limestone islands in a chain near the southern tip of the state). Swamps are poorly drained flatlands having a tree cover; in the coastal zone, this tree cover is commonly dominated by mangroves. Marshes are flatlands having poor drainage and basically a grass or low shrub cover. The coastal lowlands typically have better drainage than marshes and swamps. In addition, there are highlands and ridges, which stand well above adjacent areas, and which are well drained; upland plains, which are relatively featureless and not well drained; and transition areas. The transition areas are located between highlands and coastal lowlands and do not really have the characteristics of either.

This broad diversity within the state is complicated by smaller, more recent features, such as sinkholes, solution lakes, and solution marshes (all made by dissolving part of the underlying limestone), sand dunes (built by the wind), and modern river deltas (within estuaries in the panhandle).

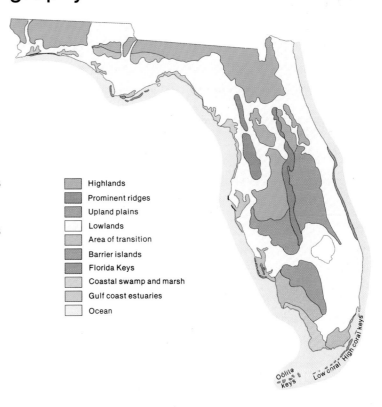

	Highlands
	Prominent ridges
	Upland plains
	Lowlands
	Area of transition
	Barrier islands
	Florida Keys
	Coastal swamp and marsh
	Gulf coast estuaries
	Ocean

Landforms

1. The Anastasia Formation, a sandy coquina of late Pleistocene age (approx. 125,000 years old), exposed along the east coast of Martin County at the Refuge.

2. View from Sugarloaf Mountain (elevation 302 feet) on the Central Highlands looking east toward Lake Apopka in the Central Valley.

3. Pleistocene sand dunes along the eastern side of the Lake Wales Ridge in Highlands County along State Road 70.

4. An aerial view of sinkhole lakes in the Central Highlands near Winter Haven, Polk County.

5. Middle miocene sediments (approx. 14 million years old) exposed along the Suwannee River in Hamilton County northeast of White Springs.

6. Hwy 270 in Liberty County, crossing Sweetwater Creek Valley.

7. A view of Alum Bluff on the Apalachicola River, Liberty County. Sediments exposed in the bluff range from approximately 15 million years old to present-day river sediments.

8. An aerial view of river meanders on the St. Marys River which separates Florida from Georgia.

9. Thunderstorm over the Osceola Plain (Coastal Lowlands), Okeechobee County.

10. Brooks Sink in Bradford County is one of the most spectacular examples of a sinkhole in Florida. Approximately 75 feet of sediments are exposed above the average water level. The sediments range from approximately 19 million years old to recent.

11. Lake Okeechobee occupies a broad, shallow depression in the Pleistocene-Holocene sediments of southern Florida.

Drainage Basins and Divides

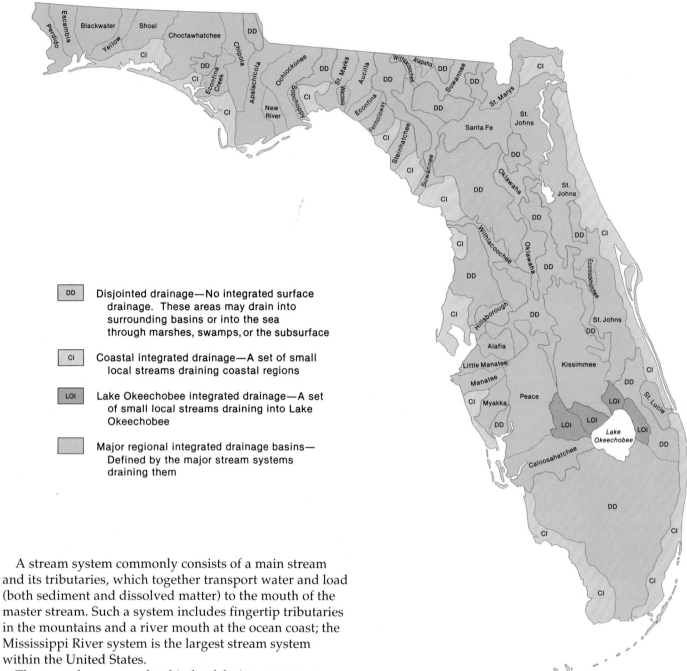

DD   Disjointed drainage—No integrated surface
       drainage. These areas may drain into
       surrounding basins or into the sea
       through marshes, swamps, or the subsurface

CI   Coastal integrated drainage—A set of small
       local streams draining coastal regions

LOI   Lake Okeechobee integrated drainage—A set
       of small local streams draining into Lake
       Okeechobee

       Major regional integrated drainage basins—
       Defined by the major stream systems
       draining them

A stream system commonly consists of a main stream and its tributaries, which together transport water and load (both sediment and dissolved matter) to the mouth of the master stream. Such a system includes fingertip tributaries in the mountains and a river mouth at the ocean coast; the Mississippi River system is the largest stream system within the United States.

There are, however, other kinds of drainage systems. Some drainage is disjointed, or not integrated; that is, many small streams occupy the area but are not connected with each other on the land surface. Karst drainage is commonly disjointed and can be found in many areas, such as peninsular Florida, which are underlain by easily soluble rocks (e.g., limestone). Individual streams in a karst area commonly flow into sinkholes, or sinkhole lakes, rather than into master streams. The water then drains from the sinkhole into the subsurface, where it flows through caves or smaller openings and emerges elsewhere as springs or seeps, either on land or under the sea. Still another kind of drainage system is referred to as poorly defined; that is, there are few or no channels, even though water flows across the surface. Extensive marsh or swamp area, where the surface is almost flat, has poorly defined drainage. Poorly defined drainage has been shown on the map in the same way as disjointed drainage; this is because in Florida the two types are commonly mixed and cannot be separated on a map this size. Divides are the margins of drainage basins; the land slopes away from each divide in opposite directions.

Monitoring Stations

We monitor many aspects of the natural world. The usefulness of the information however depends on how closely the monitoring (or measuring) stations are placed to each other. Not all data types require the same network density. Rainfall is, commonly, very erratic. Therefore many weather stations are needed; in fact, there are many more than 100 in the state. This is still not enough for certain highly technical work, but is adequate for everyday use. On the other hand, only a few tide gauges are needed.

Weather Stations

Pensacola
Tallahassee
Jacksonville
Apalachicola
Daytona Beach
Orlando
Tampa
Ft. Myers
West Palm Beach
Miami
Key West

- Precipitation only
- Precipitation and temperature
- Precipitation, temperature, and evaporation
- More detailed meteorological data

Coastal Information Stations

Pensacola
St. Marks River entrance
Mayport
Gainesville
St. Petersburg
Miami Harbor entrance
Key West

□ Tidal measurement stations
○ Coastal data network

The network is coordinated by the University of Florida Coastal and Oceanographic Engineering Department. Atlantic stations are .5 miles offshore at a depth of 30 feet; the Gulf station is 1.2 miles offshore at a depth of 18 feet. Water level and wave data are collected at these stations.

Stream Gauging Stations

National Stream Quality Accounting Network Stations (NASQAN)

▼ NASQAN Stations

1. Perdido River at Barrineau Park
2. Escambia River near Century
3. Yellow River at Milligan
4. Choctawhatchee River near Bruce
5. Chipola River near Altha
6. Apalachicola River at Chattahoochee
7. Ochlockonee River near Havana
8. Suwannee River at Branford
9. St. Johns River near Deland
10. Spruce Creek near Samsula
11. Withlacoochee River near Holder
12. Alafia River at Lithia
13. Main Canal at Vero Beach
14. Kissimmee River at S65E near Okeechobee
15. Peace River at Arcadia
16. Fisheating Creek near Palmdale
17. Caloosahatchee Canal at Ortona Lock near La Belle
18. Miami Canal at NW 36th Street, Miami
19. Tamiami Canal – Fortymile Bend to Monroe Station
20. Santa Fe River at Worthington Springs
21. Sopchoppy River near Sopchoppy (Hydrologic Benchmark Station)
22. Oklawaha River near Conner

These stations monitor temperature, specific conductance, important inorganic constituents, sediments, organic and minor inorganic constituents, bacterial content and other biological information. In addition the stream's ability to support biological life is monitored.

Groundwater Monitoring Stations
Number per county

1 1 8 15 0 1 0
0 1 0 0 0 0
1 1 1 0 0 0 70
1 3 6 0 0 2
2 0 1 0
3 39 0
16 11 2 0
12 28 0
25 4
64 57 10 1
24 3 1 1 2
70 4 1 30
7 1 4
163 29 12
134 92
0 83

Geologic Formations

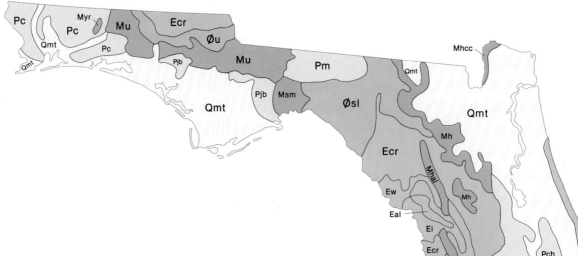

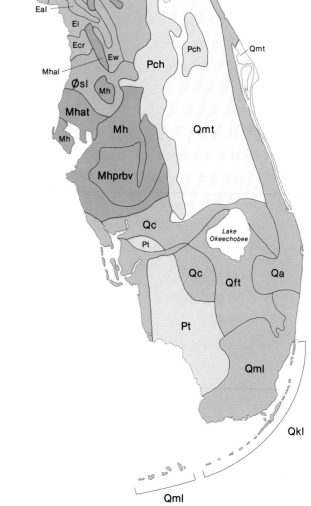

Youngest Rocks

Series	Symbol	Formation & Member	Description
Recent and Pleistocene	Qmt	Several lower marine and estuarine deposits	Freshwater marls, peats, sands, muds, now forming in stream valleys and freshwater lakes and marine sediments accumulating along shorelines and shelves of the Gulf of Mexico and the Atlantic Ocean
	Qlm	Lake Flint Marl occurs in Lake Flint area, Glades County (not shown at this scale)	
Pleistocene	Qa	Anastasia Formation	In south Florida the Pleistocene is represented by limestone, shell hash, clay and sand
	Qml	Miami Limestone	
	Qkl	Key Largo Limestone	
	Qft	Fort Thompson Formation	
	Qc	Caloosahatchee Formation	
Pliocene	Pch	Cypresshead Formation	Marine sand; clay and gravel in peninsula
	Pc	Citronelle Formation	Sand, gravels, and clays
	Pm	Miccosukee Formation	Silty clayey quartz sands
	Pjb	Jackson Bluff Formation	Argillaceous, carbonaceous sands and sandy shell marl
	Pt	Tamiami Formation	Creamy white limestones, greenish gray marls, silty sands and clay
Miocene	Mrb	Red Bay Formation	Gray sandy and clayey shell marl
	Myr	Yellow River Formation	Dark gray to bluish micaceous sands
	Mh	Hawthorn Group	Marine sands, clays, marls, and sandy limestones; contains commercial grade attapulgite (or fuller's earth) and economically important phosphate deposits
	Mhprbv	Bone Valley Member Peace River Formation Hawthorn Group	Phosphatic boulders and pebbles in matrix of phosphatic sandy clay; source of Florida's phosphate deposits
	Mhal	"Alachua Formation" Hawthorn Group	Clay, sand, sandy clay; in Gilchrist County contains a vertebrate fauna that is one of the most prolific Miocene faunas in the U.S. Residual sediments from the Hawthorn Group
	Mhcc	Charlton Member Coosawhatchie Formation Hawthorn Group	Phosphoritic clays and argillaceous and sandy limestones
	Mhat	Tampa Member Arcadia Formation Hawthorn Group	Sandy limestones with minor phosphate
	Msm	St. Marks Formation	Sandy chalky limestone
	Miocene undifferentiated Mu Includes: Shoal River Formation, Chipola Formation, Chattahoochee Formation, and local exposures of the Fort Preston Formation, Hawthorn Formation, and St. Marks Formation (see above)	Shoal River Formation	Fossiliferous, micaceous, slightly clayey and silty sand
		Chipola Formation	Bluish gray to yellowish brown fossiliferous marl
		Chattahoochee Formation	Argillaceous and silty, sandy chalky limestone
Oligocene	Øsl	Suwannee Limestone	Fossiliferous marine limestone
	Oligocene undifferentiated Øu Includes: Duncan Church Beds, "Bryam" Formation, Marianna Limestone	Duncan Church Beds	Fossiliferous shallow marine sediments consisting essentially of large foraminifers and mollusks
		"Bryam" Formation	Dolomitic limestones and clays and impure limestones
		Marianna Limestone	Shallow marine granular fossiliferous limestone

			Formation	Description
Eocene	Ecr	Jackson	Crystal River Formation	Shallow marine limestone composed of large foraminifers and mollusks. It is an important source of high calcium limestone and is chief supply of road stone in Florida
	Ew		Williston Formation	Shallow marine limestone; important source of road stone
	Ei		Inglis Formation	Shallow marine fossiliferous limestone and crystalline dolomite
	Eap	Claiborne	Avon Park Formation	Chalky, fossiliferous limestone, and crystalline dolomite, source of dolomitic limestone, agricultural stone and road stone

Oldest Rocks

Stratigraphic Nomenclature of Florida

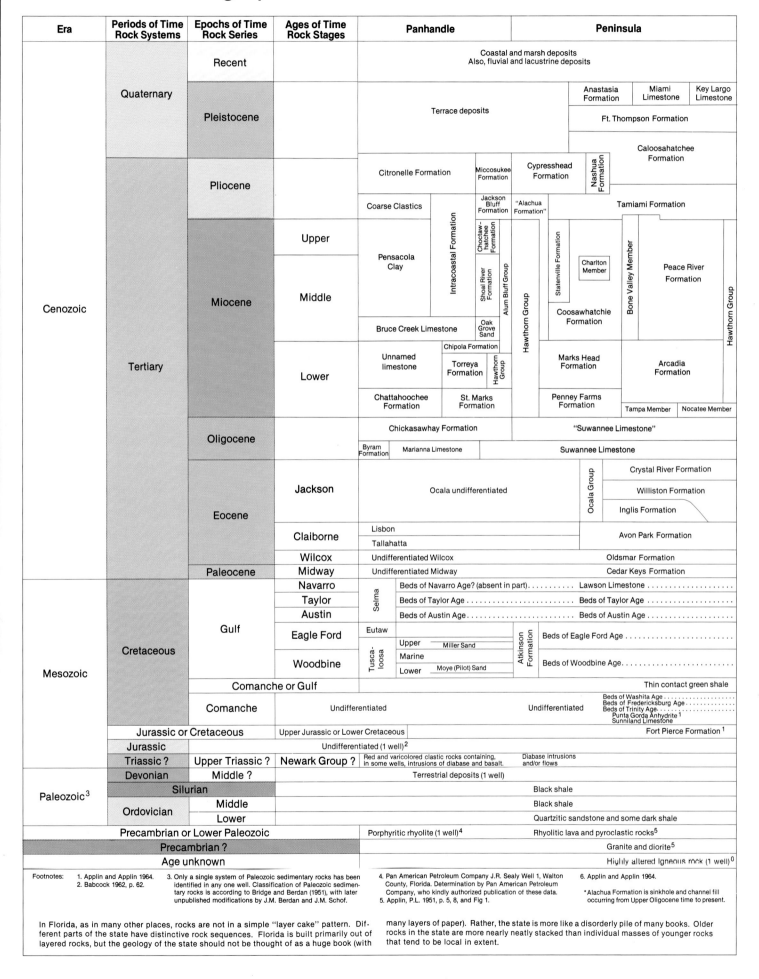

Footnotes:
1. Applin and Applin 1964.
2. Babcock 1962, p. 62.
3. Only a single system of Paleozoic sedimentary rocks has been identified in any one well. Classification of Paleozoic sedimentary rocks is according to Bridge and Berdan (1951), with later unpublished modifications by J.M. Berdan and J.M. Schof.
4. Pan American Petroleum Company J.R. Sealy Well 1, Walton County, Florida. Determination by Pan American Petroleum Company, who kindly authorized publication of these data.
5. Applin, P.L. 1951, p. 5, 8, and Fig 1.
6. Applin and Applin 1964.

*Alachua Formation is sinkhole and channel fill occurring from Upper Oligocene time to present.

In Florida, as in many other places, rocks are not in a simple "layer cake" pattern. Different parts of the state have distinctive rock sequences. Florida is built primarily out of layered rocks, but the geology of the state should not be thought of as a huge book (with many layers of paper). Rather, the state is more like a disorderly pile of many books. Older rocks in the state are more nearly neatly stacked than individual masses of younger rocks that tend to be local in extent.

Basement Geology

Two of the maps on this page, Basement Structural Geology and Basement Geology, display alternative geologic interpretations of the ancient, highly crystallized, deeply buried rocks that are collectively known as basement. The map in the lower right section of the page shows information both on rock type and structure; the map directly above it is more generalized and shows no structure. The third map, entitled Principal Structures, indicates major aspects of basement structure that have been inferred from surface and very shallow geological features. Interpretation of basement geology is difficult, because the shallowest of basement surface in Florida is some 3,000 feet below the ground surface, and most of the basement surface is far deeper. Only a very few wells are deep enough to reach the basement; therefore the nature of the basement surface must be inferred through various indirect means and is subject to alternative interpretations.

The basement structure map shows faults that in general cannot be seen at the surface. They represent rock deformation and breakage tens or hundreds of millions of years ago. The rock types shown on this map include continental deposits (Eagle Mills Formation) formed from materials derived directly from ancient land surfaces, and volcanic materials, both roughly 200 million years old, as well as various types of much older rock, including more volcanics. The index map and diagrams of geologic cross sections on the facing page should also be consulted for further information on type, depth, and age of basement rocks.

Basement Geology

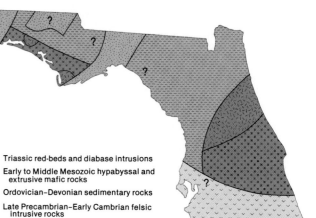

▦	Triassic red-beds and diabase intrusions
▦	Early to Middle Mesozoic hypabyssal and extrusive mafic rocks
⌄	Ordovician–Devonian sedimentary rocks
▦	Late Precambrian–Early Cambrian felsic intrusive rocks
▦	Late Precambrian–Early Cambrian felsic extrusive rocks
——	Approximate contact
?	Denotes areas for which there are conflicting descriptions or a lack of data

Principal Structures

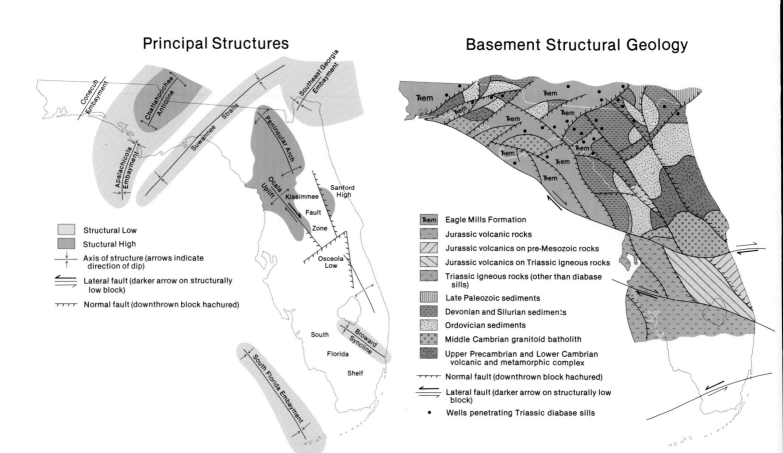

▦	Structural Low
▦	Stuctural High
↕	Axis of structure (arrows indicate direction of dip)
⇉	Lateral fault (darker arrow on structurally low block)
⊤⊤⊤	Normal fault (downthrown block hachured)

Basement Structural Geology

Ћem	Eagle Mills Formation
∧	Jurassic volcanic rocks
▨	Jurassic volcanics on pre-Mesozoic rocks
▨	Jurassic volcanics on Triassic igneous rocks
▦	Triassic igneous rocks (other than diabase sills)
▥	Late Paleozoic sediments
▦	Devonian and Silurian sediments
▦	Ordovician sediments
▦	Middle Cambrian granitoid batholith
▦	Upper Precambrian and Lower Cambrian volcanic and metamorphic complex
⊤⊤⊤	Normal fault (downthrown block hachured)
⇉	Lateral fault (darker arrow on structurally low block)
•	Wells penetrating Triassic diabase sills

Geologic Cross Sections

Florida cannot be cut with a giant knife to expose the rock layers below the surface. Geologists can use data from wells and from geophysical instruments, however, to construct cross sections, which show what would be seen if the state were cut open. Two such sections are shown. Note, first, that the scales of the two sections are quite different; Section C-C′ has been enlarged greatly and shows near-surface detail such as can be obtained from water wells, whereas Section NW-SE has been enlarged slightly and shows rocks to a greater depth. Note also that the vertical scale is not the same as the horizontal scale; the vertical measurements have been exaggerated in order to show data in more detail.

The upper section (C-C′) shows a history in the last 40 or 50 million years of gentle folding and minor faulting (near western end of section). The lower section (NW-SE) shows much more severe deformation roughly 150 to 200 million years ago. The C-C′ section is shallower and therefore required little interpretation. The NW-SE section is deeper and therefore required more inference. On the NW-SE section, the nearly vertical lines are inferred faults, showing breakage and displacement of the rocks, according to the best available geological thinking.

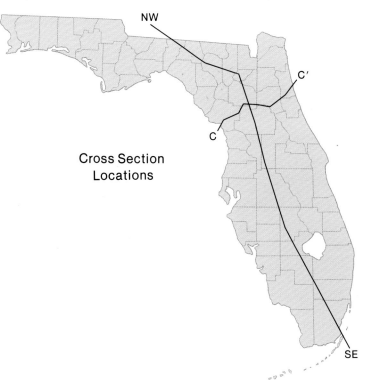

Cross Section Locations

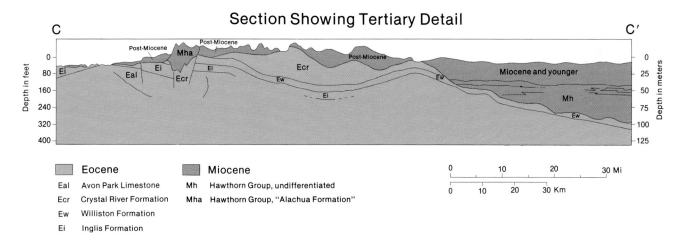

Section Showing Tertiary Detail

	Eocene		Miocene
Eal	Avon Park Limestone	Mh	Hawthorn Group, undifferentiated
Ecr	Crystal River Formation	Mha	Hawthorn Group, "Alachua Formation"
Ew	Williston Formation		
Ei	Inglis Formation		

Section Showing Generalized Basement Structure

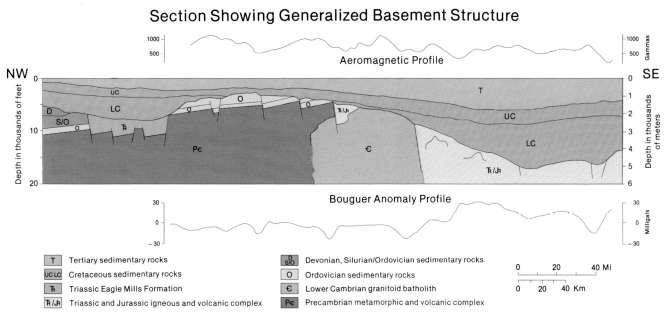

T	Tertiary sedimentary rocks	D S/O	Devonian, Silurian/Ordovician sedimentary rocks
UC LC	Cretaceous sedimentary rocks	O	Ordovician sedimentary rocks
Tr	Triassic Eagle Mills Formation	C	Lower Cambrian granitoid batholith
Tr/Jr	Triassic and Jurassic igneous and volcanic complex	Pc	Precambrian metamorphic and volcanic complex

Paleogeography

The Cretaceous Period
Approximately 110 million years ago

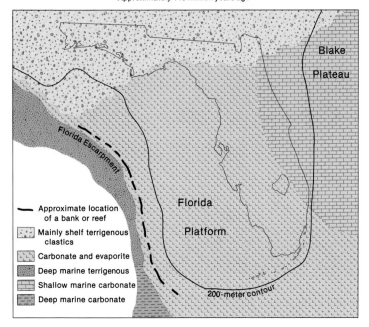

The Middle Miocene Period
Approximately 10–15 million years ago

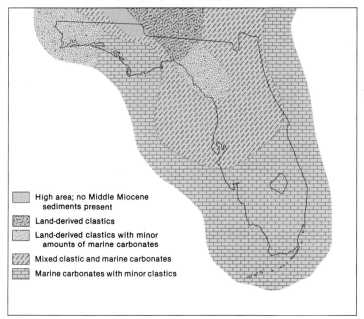

Paleogeography is the geography of the geological past. Paleogeographic maps commonly show two types of information: physical features, such as shorelines, deltas, and rivers; and sediment types, such as terrigenous (derived from the land) or marine. The Cretaceous map shows major features in the Florida area 70 to 110 million years ago. The terrigenous sediments were carried from the Appalachian mountains, which were more rugged than today. Most of what is now the Florida peninsula was the site of deposition of marine carbonate sediment (e.g., shell and shell fragments, largely microscopic in size); there was also deposition of evaporites (such as anhydrite), due to the high air temperature and very shallow water.

The Miocene map shows conditions 10 to 15 million years ago. A tongue of delta sediments was deposited in the north, representing one or more rivers which drained the Appalachian mountains. In the southern half of the peninsula, marine carbonates accumulated in shallow water.

The paleolatitude map shows the northward migration of what is now Florida, deduced from rock magnetism, during the last 250 million years. The latitude lines and values are valid for that entire time span; the longitude lines and values, only for the present. This difference between longitude and latitude looks strange, at first glance. However, the reasons are as follows: (1) Latitude is defined by the geometry of a spinning globe. (The polar axis is the axis of spin, and the equatorial plane is perpendicular to, and bisects, that axis.) Ancient latitudes can be obtained from measurements of magnetic mineral grains in the rocks that were formed at different times. (2) Longitude is measured from an artificial marker at Greenwich, in the London, England, area. Longitude numbers make up a man-made scheme and did not exist before Greenwich was

Paleolatitudes

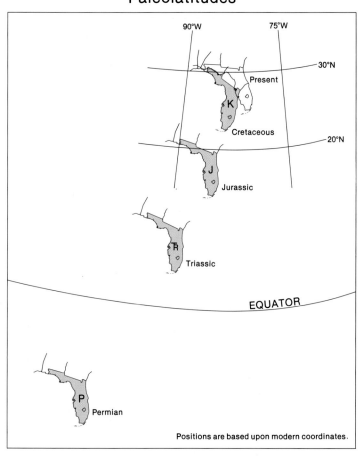

Positions are based upon modern coordinates.

chosen to mark zero longitude. Furthermore, longitude has been measured, over the years, by clocks showing real time, and this kind of measurement cannot be made for the past.

Environmental Geology

Human history unfolds on a platform of rocks, loose sediment, and soil. Planning and management decisions, in connection with highway construction and maintenance, water supply evaluation, waste disposal, geologic hazards, mining, reclamation, and land management in general, should be based on suitable geological information. The environmental geology map, a condensation of the Florida Bureau of Geology map series on environmental geology, shows a simplified scheme of rock and sediment types (regardless of age and nomenclature), which are, or may be, important in terms of environmental matters such as probable rainfall insoak, availability of construction materials, and strength of the rock or sediment foundation.

The economic geology map shows raw materials and processing plants. Areas not marked may be underlain by materials that are similar to valuable rocks or sediment, but that either do not meet industrial requirements or are not close enough to markets to be exploited commercially.

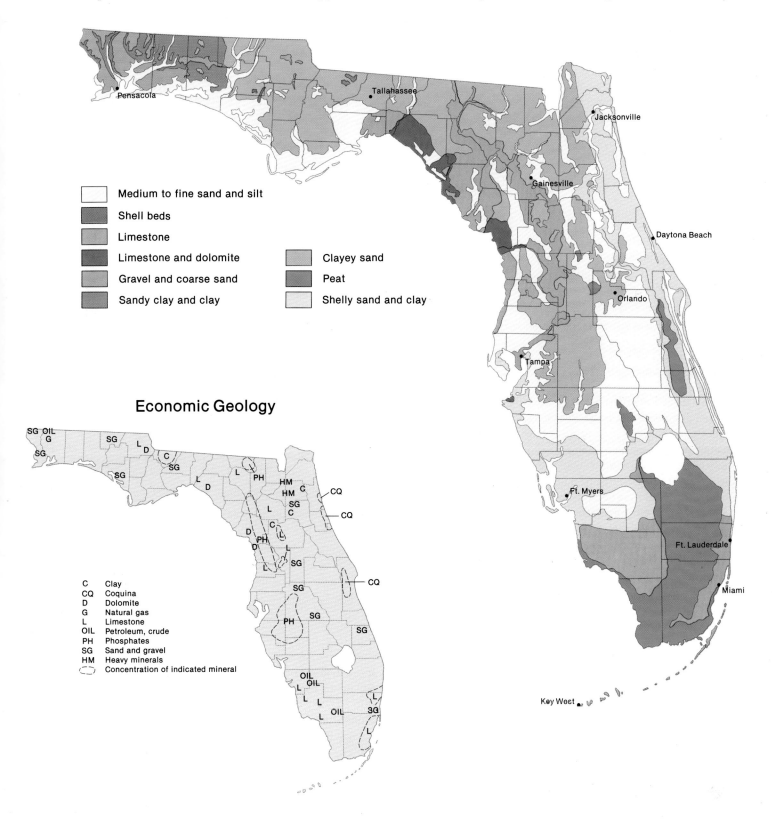

Medium to fine sand and silt

Shell beds

Limestone

Limestone and dolomite

Gravel and coarse sand

Sandy clay and clay

Clayey sand

Peat

Shelly sand and clay

Economic Geology

C   Clay
CQ   Coquina
D   Dolomite
G   Natural gas
L   Limestone
OIL   Petroleum, crude
PH   Phosphates
SG   Sand and gravel
HM   Heavy minerals
⌐⌐⌐   Concentration of indicated mineral

Regional Magnetics

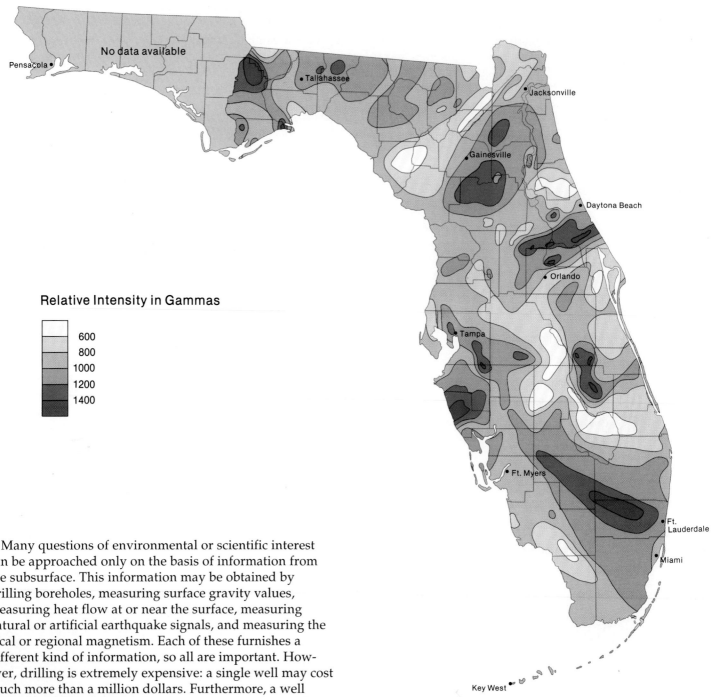

Relative Intensity in Gammas

600
800
1000
1200
1400

Many questions of environmental or scientific interest can be approached only on the basis of information from the subsurface. This information may be obtained by drilling boreholes, measuring surface gravity values, measuring heat flow at or near the surface, measuring natural or artificial earthquake signals, and measuring the local or regional magnetism. Each of these furnishes a different kind of information, so all are important. However, drilling is extremely expensive: a single well may cost much more than a million dollars. Furthermore, a well does not provide information about any other part of the state, and never extends deeper than 8–10 kilometers. Therefore a large part of our information about the subsurface comes from measurements of gravity, heat flow, earthquakes, and magnetism.

Aeromagnetic profiles have been combined with ground data to prepare the regional magnetic map of Florida (except the panhandle). North-south flights were made mostly at 1,500 feet, and ground surface profiles were run east-west. The aeromagnetic data were obtained in terms of total field intensity, and the ground data were used to tie the flight lines together and as the basis for interpolation between them.

The intensity of the magnetic field, at or not far above the surface, is generally between 24,000 and 68,000 gam-

mas. The field in Florida occupies only a very small part of that range, hence only relative values are shown on the map. The map shows clearly structural trends (at depth) in the north that parallel the southern Appalachian Mountains. In the south, a different trend appears resembling the Ouachita Mountains of Arkansas.

However, it is not now possible to explain in detail why there is so much variation in the magnetic field in Florida. Much of it may be due to differences in the mineral content of the rocks at depths of several kilometers.

Magnetic Anomalies

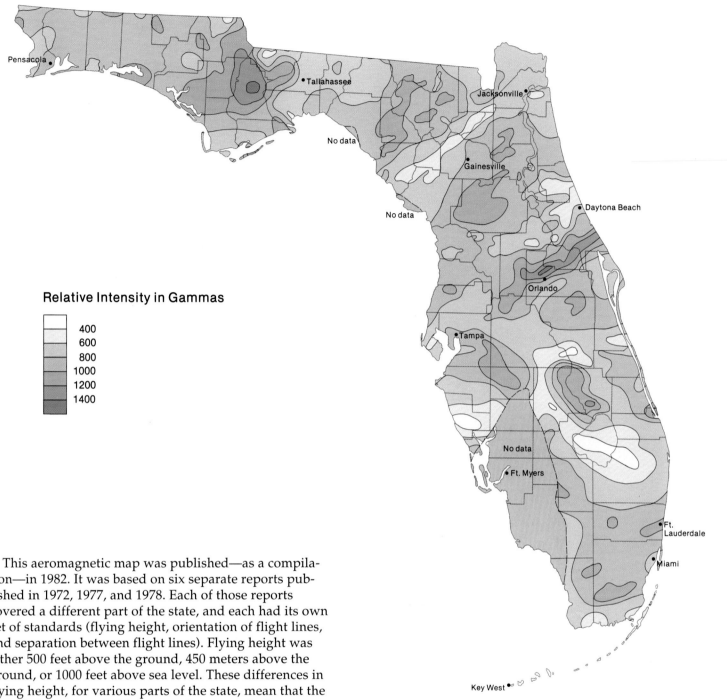

Relative Intensity in Gammas

400
600
800
1000
1200
1400

This aeromagnetic map was published—as a compilation—in 1982. It was based on six separate reports published in 1972, 1977, and 1978. Each of those reports covered a different part of the state, and each had its own set of standards (flying height, orientation of flight lines, and separation between flight lines). Flying height was either 500 feet above the ground, 450 meters above the ground, or 1000 feet above sea level. These differences in flying height, for various parts of the state, mean that the recorded magnetic field does not have exactly the same geological significance from point to point. Separation between flight lines was 1 mile, 5 nautical miles, or 8 kilometers. For the state of Florida, these differences in separation probably are not important.

The differences between this map and the one on the facing page are considerable. This is not necessarily a question of right versus wrong. Rather it is a matter of trying to show the features of the magnetic field by using two different methods. This newer map also provides coverage in the Florida panhandle, much of which was left blank on the facing page.

The new map shows the following general features: (1) there is no clear Southern Appalachian structural pattern in the panhandle; (2) structures parallel with the Appalachians are visible in northeastern Florida; and (3) trends like those in the Ouachita Mountains (Arkansas) may be present in the deep subsurface in southern Florida.

Bouguer Gravity Anomalies

The earth has a physical attraction for other objects reasonably close to it: gravity. It is gravity that keeps us from flying out into space. Gravity varies from point to point. It is zero at the center of the earth, increases to a maximum some hundreds of kilometers below the surface, then decreases to the surface and on into space. Even on the surface, it varies from place to place by a tiny amount.

In preparing a gravity map, corrections must be made for elevation above sea level, for latitude, for rock materials between the instrument and sea level, and for the effects of nearby hills and valleys. All of these are applied to the instrument reading; the corrected value is called the Bouguer anomaly (pronounced "boo-gay").

The standard unit of measure of gravity is the gal (after Galileo). One gal is the strength of attraction equal to

1 cm per second per second (that is, cm/sec^2). The milligal is $1/1000$ gal. Bouguer anomalies in the eastern United States are generally between -60 milligals and +40 milligals. Positive anomalies indicate unusually dense (i.e., heavy) rocks at depth. Negative anomalies indicate light rocks at depth.

In many cases heavy or light rocks (at depth) occur in bands, or stripes, perhaps indicating old mountain ranges, long ago worn flat by erosion and then buried by younger material. The gravity anomalies in south Florida appear to have the same pattern as the Ouachita Mountains of Arkansas. Can this be taken as evidence for a part of that old mountain system? Or does it mean that—at one time in the past—Florida was part of some other continent, perhaps South America, Africa, or Europe?

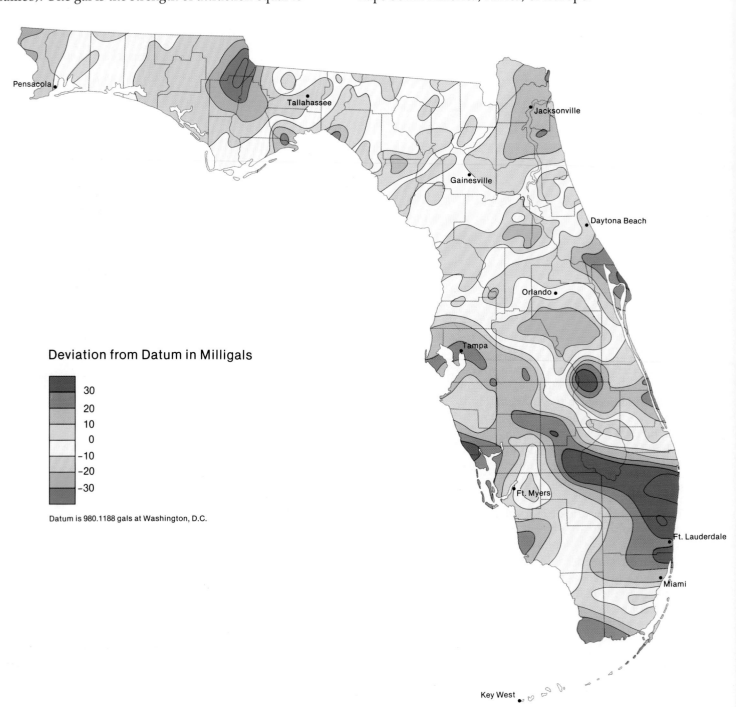

Deviation from Datum in Milligals

30
20
10
0
-10
-20
-30

Datum is 980.1188 gals at Washington, D.C.

Enhanced Gravity Anomalies

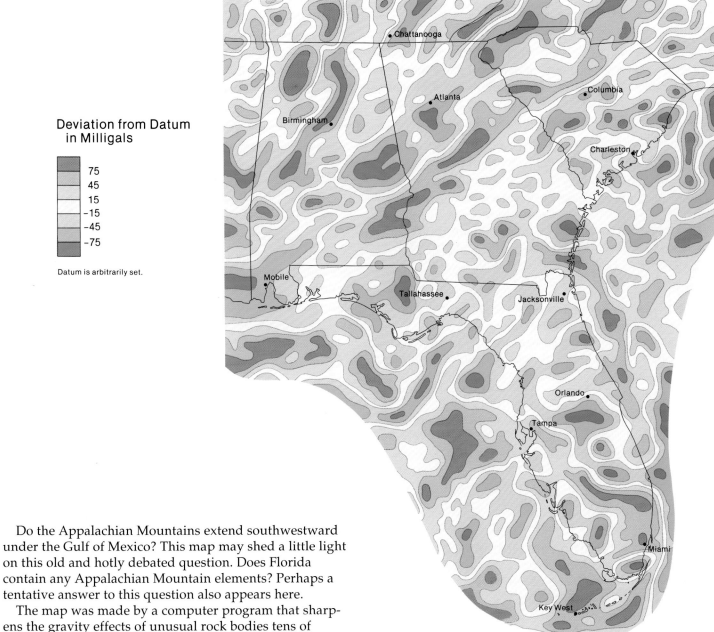

Deviation from Datum in Milligals

	75
	45
	15
	−15
	−45
	−75

Datum is arbitrarily set.

Do the Appalachian Mountains extend southwestward under the Gulf of Mexico? This map may shed a little light on this old and hotly debated question. Does Florida contain any Appalachian Mountain elements? Perhaps a tentative answer to this question also appears here.

The map was made by a computer program that sharpens the gravity effects of unusual rock bodies tens of kilometers down (too deep to drill). The red and orange colors indicate a heavier rock mass at such depths. The green and blue colors show a lighter rock mass. But the linear patterns may be more important than the actual colors.

Evidence for such differences at depths of tens of kilometers appears on various kinds of gravity maps, but this version makes the contrasts more obvious. On this map one can get a good picture of what major mountain and basin structures look like, at depths much too great for drilling.

The folded (western) part of the Appalachian Mountains extends along a southwest-northeast band through Birmingham and Chattanooga. The older (eastern) part extends along a southwest-northeast zone running through Atlanta. Most of Georgia, Alabama, eastern Tennessee, and western North Carolina are underlain by structures (visible on this map) within, or parallel with, the Appalachian Mountains. Southern Alabama appears to have a basement with a different pattern. Does this show the southwestern end of the Appalachian Mountains?

The Florida basement includes two different parts. The northern part appears to be organized like the Appalachian Mountains. The southern part looks quite different and must have had a different origin.

The correct name for this map is "First vertical derivative of the isostatic residual gravity." These words refer to various parts of the method used in calculating the gravity values for this map.

Earthquakes and Geothermal Measurements

Temperatures generally decrease from the soil surface downward for a short distance, such as 50 to 100 meters. Below that, temperatures rise, because the center of the earth is hotter than the surface. This increase in temperature with an increase in depth, at depths of a few hundred meters or a few kilometers, is commonly about 3.7°C per 100 meters (2°F per 100 feet). This means that at a depth of 1.0 km, the temperature is typically about 37°C (about 66°F) warmer than at the surface.

The geothermal gradient map shows that in Florida the temperature change is gentler than in most other places. A very steep gradient would be 4°C or more per 100 meters. In terms of geothermal energy, Florida is not a first-class source.

The isothermal map shows a constant temperature (in this case 100°C) at a variable depth. The depth to 100°C map shows how far you would have to drill to find water at the boiling point, if the water content were at atmospheric pressure. At most places in the state one would have to drill to depths of around 4.0 or 5.0 km (2.5 to 3 miles) to encounter water at the boiling temperature.

The seismic activity map shows recorded earthquakes in Florida large enough to be felt. "Instrument level" quakes, too weak to be noticed by people, are not indicated. If earthquake activity is taken as an index to deformation of large areas (such as in mountain-making activity), Florida clearly can be considered to be very stable. The Modified Mercalli intensity refers to the amount of damage done at the surface (XII=maximum damage).

Seismic Activity

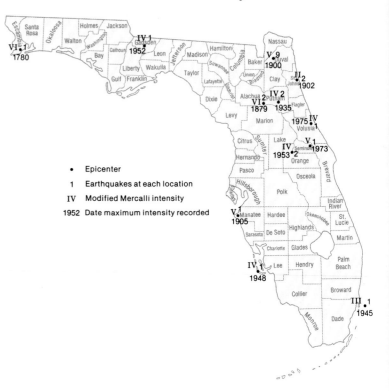

- •   Epicenter
- 1   Earthquakes at each location
- IV   Modified Mercalli intensity
- 1952   Date maximum intensity recorded

Geothermal Gradient

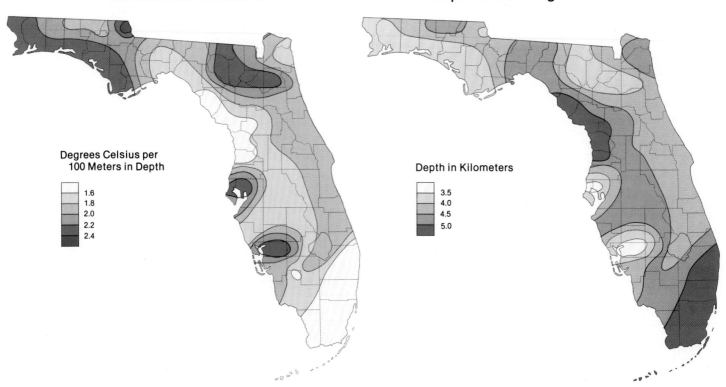

Degrees Celsius per
100 Meters in Depth

- 1.6
- 1.8
- 2.0
- 2.2
- 2.4

Depth to 100 Degrees Celsius

Depth in Kilometers

- 3.5
- 4.0
- 4.5
- 5.0

Gamma Ray Intensity

Gamma rays are produced by various natural substances in certain rocks and sediments. Gamma ray intensity, for the maps on this page, was obtained in 1976 and 1977 from a gamma ray spectrometer flown 500 feet above ground level. Cosmic and background radiation was subtracted from the readings to obtain the raw data for the maps. Flight lines were spaced 1 mile apart.

Gamma rays penetrate only a relatively thin layer of rock and soil; hence they indicate radioactivity of surface materials only. Gamma ray intensity does not provide information about rocks in the deep subsurface and cannot be used in the same way as gravity, seismic, and magnetic information. On the other hand, gamma ray data com-

monly reveal surface, or near-surface, features, which are not obvious. For mining purposes, gamma ray maps may show valuable mineral deposits (for example, dark areas on the inset map).

The entire state was flown more recently and the final report of that work, published in several oversize volumes, was issued in 1981 under the auspices of the U.S. Department of Energy. However, the aerial radiation data were presented in profile form and have not been reduced to map patterns. The 1981 report provides a much greater variety of classes of information than the earlier work, but has not yet been reduced from many large volumes to a useful summary map.

Explanation

A High average values follow the western highlands where the lithology is clayey sand with gravel and heavy minerals.

B Low average values along the coast associated with quartz sands.

C High average to very high readings most likely due to presence of clay in present and ancient Apalachicola River flood plain.

D Low average values associated with limestone plains veneered with sand.

E High readings in the highlands associated with clayey sand.

F High readings associated with strip mining of Hawthorn formation.

G High readings trending north-south following Trail Ridge may be due to heavy mineral content.

H High average to very high values along a north-south trend.

I Very low values due to quartz sand.

J High average to high readings associated with heavy mineral deposits.

K Very low values associated with St. Johns River and adjacent swamps and organic sands.

L High average to high values trending north-northwest associated with areas of clayey sand deposits containing phosphate.

M High average to high values follow hard rock phosphate deposit.

N Coastal low average values where limestone is close to the surface with a thin quartz sand cover.

O High average values follow Miocene-age clays and phosphate.

Radiation Levels

Very Low	
Low average	High
High average	Very high

The Earth's Magnetic Field

A compass needle points, in general, toward the magnetic north pole, not toward the geographic north pole (true north). The magnetic north pole is not precisely north of any point in Florida (that is, it does not lie along the same longitude). There are local variations in the earth's magnetic field that complicate this picture greatly. As a result of these local variations and of the large distance between the two north poles (about 1800 km), one cannot simply relabel the number system on the compass and get the right result. Instead, a magnetic declination map is produced for each decade showing the correction which must be made to the compass reading at each point on the map. The agonic line connects all the points at which the compass needle points toward geographic north. In 1985, as the map illustrates, the agonic line was located west of Tallahassee and Key West. East of the agonic line, the declination is given in degrees east. A correction toward the east must be made to the compass reading. For example, a compass reading of N30°W, made at the western tip of Lake Okeechobee, would be corrected toward the east by 1°, thus becoming N29°W. West of the agonic line, corrections must be made toward the west. The isoporic lines show the corrections that must be made each year.

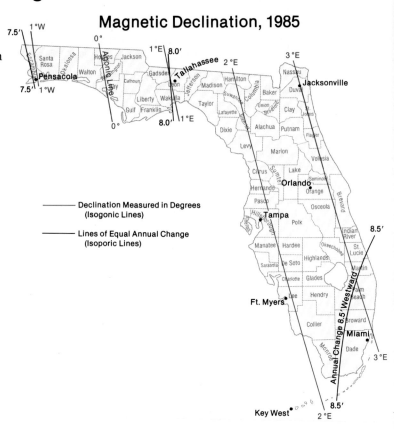

Magnetic Declination, 1985

— Declination Measured in Degrees
   (Isogonic Lines)

— Lines of Equal Annual Change
   (Isoporic Lines)

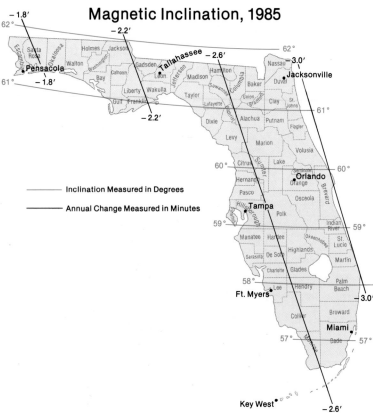

Magnetic Inclination, 1985

— Inclination Measured in Degrees

— Annual Change Measured in Minutes

A compass indicates the direction of the earth's magnetic field in the horizontal plane, but this field also has a vertical component. An instrument designed to indicate vertical direction by swinging freely in a vertical plane is called a dip needle. At the magnetic north pole (90°) the dip needle points straight down while at the magnetic equator (0°) it is horizontal. The angle through which the dip needle is deflected downward in the northern magnetic hemisphere is called the magnetic inclination. The inclination at Jacksonville was 62° in 1985. Although a compass needle is designed to turn in the horizontal plane, its accuracy is slightly affected by magnetic inclination. The steeper the inclination, the less easily the compass needle can turn. A well-made compass has an adjustable, nonmagnetic weight on its needle; this weight can be moved so that, in any given locality, the effects of inclination can be counteracted and the needle can turn freely.

Intensity of the Earth's Magnetic Field

The horizontal magnetic intensity is the strength, in a horizontal direction, of the earth's magnetic field. An ordinary compass needle at any given locality, if turned from its usual position, will swing back so that it again points toward magnetic north. This return to its north-seeking position is the result of the horizontal part of the earth's magnetic field. If the needle is properly mounted, so that it can swing freely in the horizontal plane, the force with which it returns to its north-seeking position is an indication of the intensity, or strength, of the horizontal component.

The strength of the horizontal magnetic field in Florida decreases toward the north. This is because the magnetic field at the magnetic north pole (currently located in northernmost Canada) is entirely vertical, with no horizontal component. At the magnetic equator, the magnetic field is entirely horizontal, with no vertical component. However, the lines on the map are not oriented perfectly east-and-west because of local irregularities in the rocks at depth and because of the geometry of the mechanism, deep in the earth's core, which generates and maintains the magnetic field.

The vertical magnetic intensity is the strength, vertically, of the magnetic field of the earth. A compass needle cannot be used to show vertical magnetic intensity; instead, a special needle, called a dip needle, has been developed. The dip needle is free to swing up and down, rather than horizontally. At the magnetic north pole (in northern Canada, approximately 1800 km from the geographic north pole), a compass needle is useless and a dip needle points straight down. At the magnetic south pole, a dip needle points straight up. At the magnetic equator, a dip needle is horizontal. Florida is north of the magnetic equator; hence the vertical magnetic strength decreases southward and increases northward as shown on the map.

The total magnetic field is a combination of the horizontal and vertical parts of the field. The total field at any given point on the earth's surface can be computed from the horizontal and vertical components. This field applies to the entire earth, but it varies from place to place, being stronger in some locations than elsewhere, and it changes with time, drifting slowly westward (annual changes are given on the maps, and the maps are dated 1985). The field strength also changes in a vertical direction, being zero at the center of the earth and at very great distances from the planet. The other terrestrial planets (Venus, Mars, Mercury) and the moon do not have significant planet-wide magnetic fields.

The earth's magnetic field is generated in the outer part of the core. The generating mechanism has roughly eight main parts, each of which causes some of the variability that we see at the surface of the planet. The features shown on the maps on this page reflect, in good part, the shape of one of these main parts. The fact that these features change shape and position, with time, indicates that the generating mechanism evolves in some manner not now fully understood.

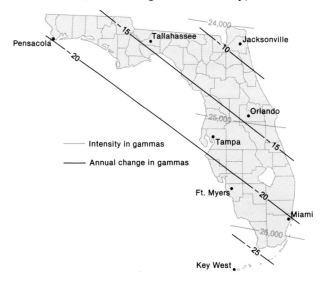

Horizontal Magnetic Intensity, 1985

Intensity in gammas

Annual change in gammas

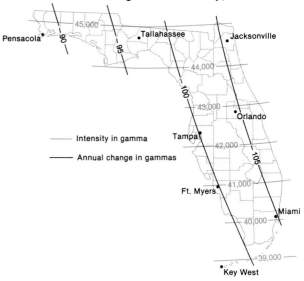

Vertical Magnetic Intensity, 1985

Intensity in gamma

Annual change in gammas

Total Magnetic Intensity, 1985

Intensity in gammas

Annual change in gammas

Tides

Tides are of two kinds: those driven by the wind (particularly during storms) and those driven by the gravitational pull primarily of the sun and the moon. The gravitational, or astronomical, tide is very regular and easy to predict, because it depends on the precise motion of the earth and the moon. The storm tide depends on the shape of the coastline and the strength, direction, and duration of the wind. Storm tides, therefore, are hard to predict. Instead, they are best recorded as historical events. Hurricane tides in bays may reach 6 to 8 meters; the storm waves are even higher.

The bottom map shows, in bar-graph form, observed and extrapolated storm-tide or storm-surge heights for Florida. The first category gives an estimate, at selected points, of the highest storm surge to be expected within any 100 years. The second category shows the estimated surge for the most severe hurricanes. The third and fourth categories show actual observations at selected points.

The hundred-year storm tide map gives the maximum area in which storm-surge flooding can be anticipated. The third map provides data on the astronomical tide. The tidal day at most places is 24 hours 50 minutes long. Tides are, in general, higher in the Atlantic than in the Gulf of Mexico and higher in coastal concavities than along straight or convex shores.

Tides are highly complicated in estuaries, lagoons, and bays, partly because inlets and outlets are not arranged regularly. Tidal effects in an estuary may be complicated because of variations in river flow. During very dry seasons (low river flow) a high astronomical tide may drive seawater along a river bed (under the fresh water) for great distances. Such seawater has been observed on the St. Johns river bed near Palatka, more than 100 km (60 miles) from the river's mouth.

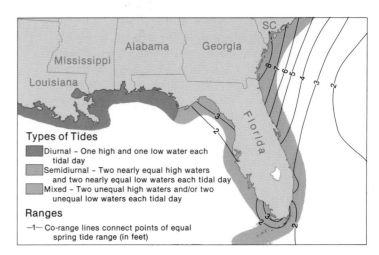

Types of Tides

- Diurnal – One high and one low water each tidal day
- Semidiurnal – Two nearly equal high waters and two nearly equal low waters each tidal day
- Mixed – Two unequal high waters and/or two unequal low waters each tidal day

Ranges

—1— Co-range lines connect points of equal spring tide range (in feet)

Hundred-Year Storm-Tide Zone

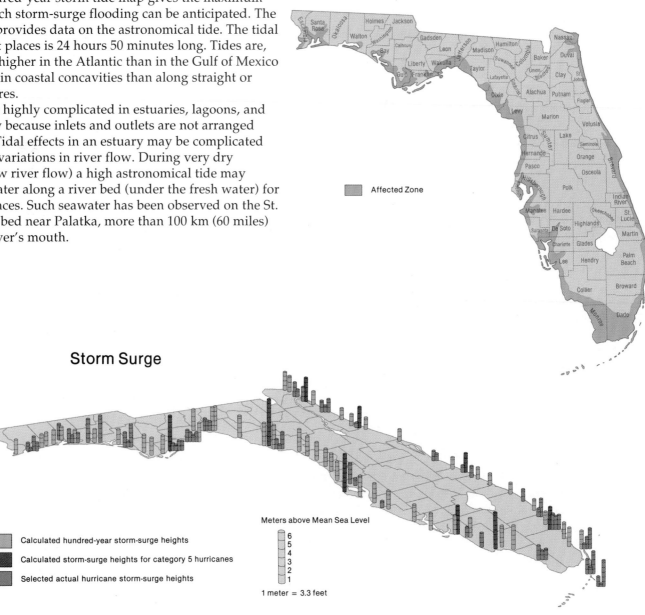

Affected Zone

Storm Surge

Calculated hundred-year storm-surge heights

Calculated storm-surge heights for category 5 hurricanes

Selected actual hurricane storm-surge heights

Meters above Mean Sea Level

6
5
4
3
2
1

1 meter = 3.3 feet

Temperature and Salinity

The Gulf Stream is a current of warm water that flows out of the Gulf of Mexico, eastward past the southern tip of Florida, and northward along the Atlantic coast. The temperature pattern indicates the position of the Gulf Stream in most of these maps of sea-surface temperature. Its day-to-day changes and its meandering path, however, cannot be seen on these maps. The color pattern indicating sea surface temperature shown on the map of maximum winter temperature results from the effect of the Gulf Stream on surrounding water and does not define the width of the Gulf Stream itself, which is relatively narrow.

River and creek water is much less salty than ocean water. In coastal areas along rainy parts of the continent, or next to the mouths of large rivers, the mixture of fresh water—from the continent—with ocean water reduces the salinity. The influence of Mississippi River water is obvious, especially at the western edge of the map of spring salinity. Run-off from the southeastern states is lowest in the fall months, as can be seen by comparing these four maps.

Sea Surface Temperature
in Degrees Fahrenheit

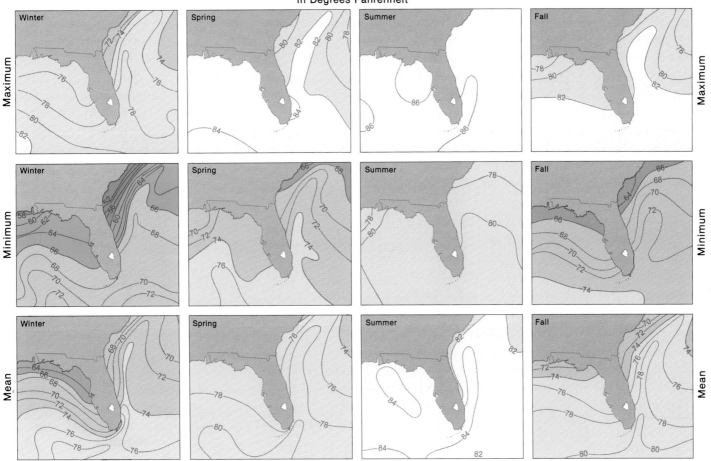

Mean Sea Surface Salinity
in Parts per Thousand

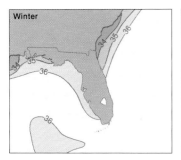
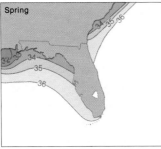
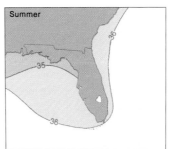
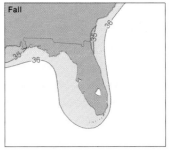

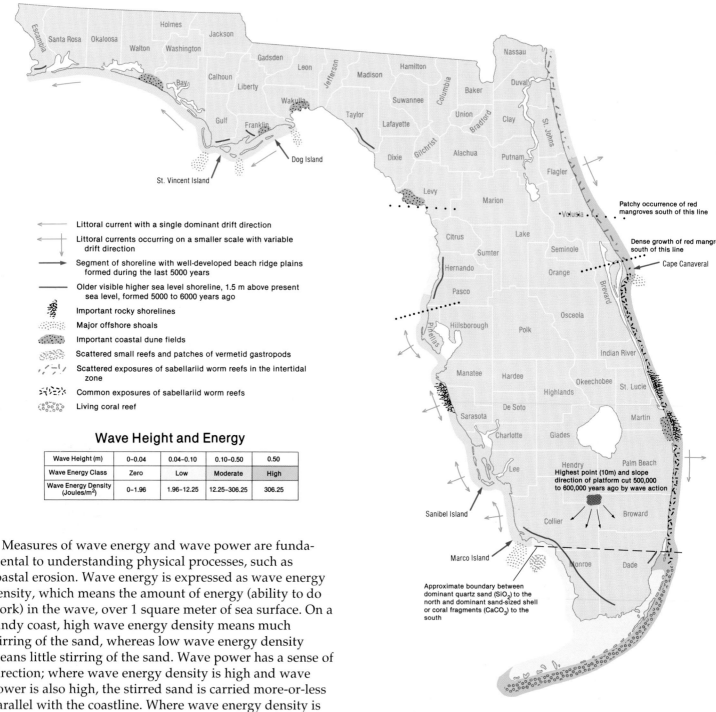

Coastal Features

Legend:

← Littoral current with a single dominant drift direction

Littoral currents occurring on a smaller scale with variable drift direction

→ Segment of shoreline with well-developed beach ridge plains formed during the last 5000 years

— Older visible higher sea level shoreline, 1.5 m above present sea level, formed 5000 to 6000 years ago

Important rocky shorelines

Major offshore shoals

Important coastal dune fields

Scattered small reefs and patches of vermetid gastropods

Scattered exposures of sabellariid worm reefs in the intertidal zone

Common exposures of sabellariid worm reefs

Living coral reef

Patchy occurrence of red mangroves south of this line

Dense growth of red mangroves south of this line

Cape Canaveral

Highest point (10m) and slope direction of platform cut 500,000 to 600,000 years ago by wave action

Approximate boundary between dominant quartz sand (SiO₂) to the north and dominant sand-sized shell or coral fragments (CaCO₃) to the south

Wave Height and Energy

Wave Height (m)	0–0.04	0.04–0.10	0.10–0.50	0.50
Wave Energy Class	Zero	Low	Moderate	High
Wave Energy Density (Joules/m²)	0–1.96	1.96–12.25	12.25–306.25	306.25

Measures of wave energy and wave power are fundamental to understanding physical processes, such as coastal erosion. Wave energy is expressed as wave energy density, which means the amount of energy (ability to do work) in the wave, over 1 square meter of sea surface. On a sandy coast, high wave energy density means much stirring of the sand, whereas low wave energy density means little stirring of the sand. Wave power has a sense of direction; where wave energy density is high and wave power is also high, the stirred sand is carried more-or-less parallel with the coastline. Where wave energy density is high and wave power is low, the stirred sand is commonly moved seaward. Where both are low, little or no sand is moved at all (very little beach erosion occurs).

Along the Atlantic coast waves are very energetic, whereas along some parts of the Gulf of Mexico there is very little wave action. The small blue arrows indicate—in general—the direction of sand transport. On the east coast, for example, this combination of arrows along with high wave energy density means severe beach erosion.

Mangrove swamps, reefs of several types, and other coastal features affecting beach erosion are also shown on the large map. The small map shows the sediment type, red indicating mostly sand. The term *sand* here relates to grain size and not to shell content.

Texture of Bottom Sediments

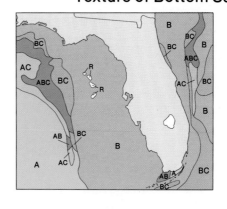

Explanation

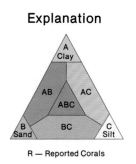

R — Reported Corals

Old Shorelines

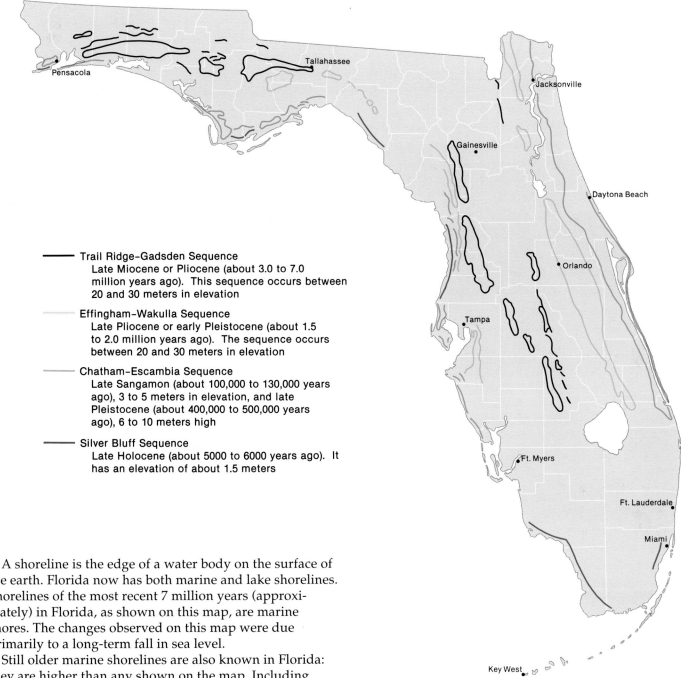

—— Trail Ridge-Gadsden Sequence
Late Miocene or Pliocene (about 3.0 to 7.0
million years ago). This sequence occurs between
20 and 30 meters in elevation

—— Effingham-Wakulla Sequence
Late Pliocene or early Pleistocene (about 1.5
to 2.0 million years ago). The sequence occurs
between 20 and 30 meters in elevation

—— Chatham-Escambia Sequence
Late Sangamon (about 100,000 to 130,000 years
ago), 3 to 5 meters in elevation, and late
Pleistocene (about 400,000 to 500,000 years
ago), 6 to 10 meters high

—— Silver Bluff Sequence
Late Holocene (about 5000 to 6000 years ago). It
has an elevation of about 1.5 meters

A shoreline is the edge of a water body on the surface of the earth. Florida now has both marine and lake shorelines. Shorelines of the most recent 7 million years (approximately) in Florida, as shown on this map, are marine shores. The changes observed on this map were due primarily to a long-term fall in sea level.

Still older marine shorelines are also known in Florida: they are higher than any shown on the map. Including these older shorelines, the general sequence within the state is from older (higher) to younger (lower). The evidence within Florida indicates that, for about 10 or 15 million years, sea level has been dropping. The drop shown on the map is about 30 meters, and the total drop for the shorelines mentioned here is about 70 or 80 meters. This fall in sea level is thought to have been the result of gradual growth of various very large glaciers, such as the one that covers much of Antarctica today.

The history of the ocean level, over the last several million years, is known in more detail; during the most recent 2 or 3 million years, sea level dropped at least four times, to positions perhaps as much as 120 meters below present mean sea level.

Global sea level, roughly 20,000 years ago, was about 140 meters lower than today. By 6,000 years ago, as two of the major ice sheets melted, it had risen to 2 meters higher than its present position; evidence for this "high" stand can be seen in many parts of the state's coast. Since 6,000 years ago, sea level has changed, either up or down, at least four times; each change was in the range of 1 to 3 meters. The last such change is dated at roughly 1,000 years ago. These changes took place at various rates, in some instances perhaps as fast as 1 or 2 meters per century.

In the latest hundred years, sea level has been rising very slowly, probably a total of 15-20 cm. Whether it will rise by 1 or 2 meters, in the next century, or will drop, is a matter of great concern for the state. A rise of a meter or more would increase beach erosion along almost all of the shoreline.

Beach Ridges

St. Vincent Island

Beach ridges are linear sand ridges that were deposited along the beach face in areas characterized by a gentle offshore slope, low wave energy, and an abundant sand supply. Beach ridges form only on accreting beaches. Because they form on the beach face, they indicate the location and orientation of the coastline, as well as the approximate sea level (in areas that have not been tectonically uplifted or depressed) at the time they were formed. Several spectacular beach-ridge plains have formed in Florida. Among the most spectacular were Sanibel Island, Cape Canaveral and St. Vincent Island. Of these St. Vincent is the only one still preserved in pristine condition.

Beach ridges are constructed by the process of wave run-up in the swash zone by waves that fall in the long-term "maximum wave energy" category (Stapor and Tanner, 1972). The internal structure of beach ridges indicates that all or almost all of the ridge is constructed by wave run-up, with very little washover (Tanner and Stapor, 1972). Internal bedding is almost exclusively composed of planar, seaward-dipping cross beds. The ridge grows upward and seaward as material is deposited. In Florida beach ridges typically have heights of 1-3 meters, with spacings of tens of meters.

Stapor (1973) described several basic types of beach-ridge patterns, each of which is indicative of specific depositional environments. Stapor's categories are: 1) ridges convex seaward, occurring at the distal prograding tip of spits; 2) ridges concave seaward, which are being actively eroded perpendicular to their ridge and swale orientation; 3) ridges concave seaward deposited in embayed sections of the coast; and 4) ridges convex seaward, which represent net seaward growth, not lateral extension. Category 3 beach ridges predominate on St. Vincent Island. Beach ridges that are essentially parallel indicate that sediment was transported from offshore without significant longshore transport. Splayed ridges (increasing ridge crest spacing from one end to the other) indicate that longshore drift supplied the sediment for their construction. According to Stapor the direction of decreasing ridge crest spacing indicates the direction of the longshore drift.

Florida has numerous areas where beach ridges have been deposited in the past; however, there are few areas where ridges are being deposited today because of a long-term shortage of sediment for their construction. This is evidenced by the predominance of eroding coastline over stable or accreting coastline in Florida.

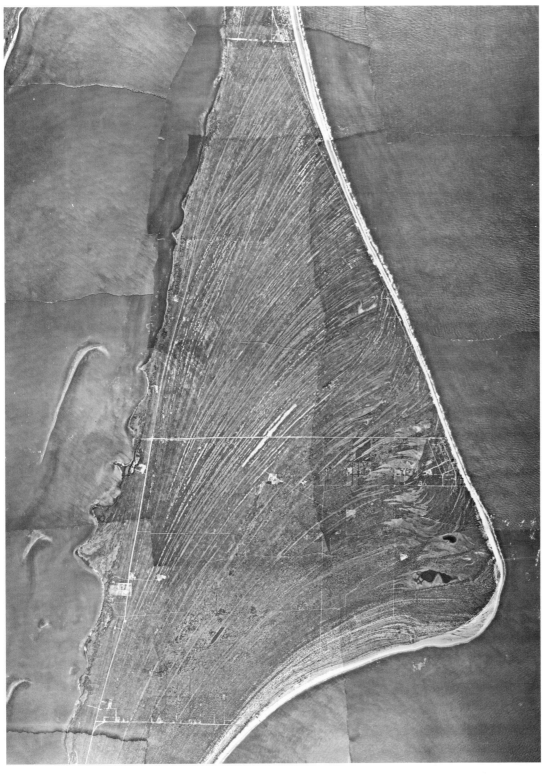

CAPE CANAVERAL

Many beach ridges evident on aerial photographs are difficult or impossible to locate in the field. The topographic expression of ridges and swales is degraded through time by a variety of geomorphic processes. Erosion by wind and rain, and karst dissolution of calcareous sediments within and beneath the ridge reduce ridge slope and height. Development of dunes on the surface of the ridge can further mask the characteristic shape of the ridge. On older ridges the topographic expression may be com-

pletely gone. These ridges show up in aerial photographs due to the different sediments and moisture regimes of the ridges and swales and the differences in vegetation on the ridges versus the swales. Swales collect fine grained sediments, organic material and are wetter compared to the sandy and drier ridges. The sedimentologic and vegetation signature remains even after the topographic expression of ridge and swale has deteriorated.

The Effect of Latitude on Climate

With the exception of Hawaii, no state extends farther into the tropics than Florida. Key West is located 24°30′N of the equator, the same latitude as Tampico, Mexico; Sao Paulo, Brazil; and Hong Kong. The angle of the sun has much to do with the degree of heating (insolation) at the earth's surface: the higher the angle of the sun, the more intense the insolation. The closer a place is to the equator, the higher the average angle of the sun throughout the year. Furthermore, the closer a place is to the equator, the less the difference between the angle of the sun at the time of the winter solstice (December 21), when at noon it is lowest on the horizon than at any other time of the year, and that of the summer solstice (June 21), when at noon it is highest. At Key West, on June 21 the angle of the sun is almost perpendicular to the earth, while on December 21 it is 42°. The sun, consequently, can do a much more effective job of heating here than along latitudes farther north, where the angle is lower.

The lines on the maps on this page are called isotherms and connect places of equal temperature. Latitude is not the only variable to affect the temperature at a specific place. If it were, the isotherms would be parallel to the equator. Altitude and proximity to a large water body are also very important. For example, both the Appalachian Mountains and the Atlantic Ocean influence temperature. In the winter there is a greater difference (35°F) between the average temperatures of, for example, New York and Orlando, than in the summer when the angle of the sun in both cities is sufficiently high to intensely heat the earth's surface.

Seasonal Sun Angles

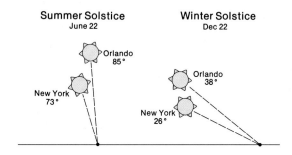

Normal Daily Maximum Temperature
January

Normal Daily Maximum Temperature
July

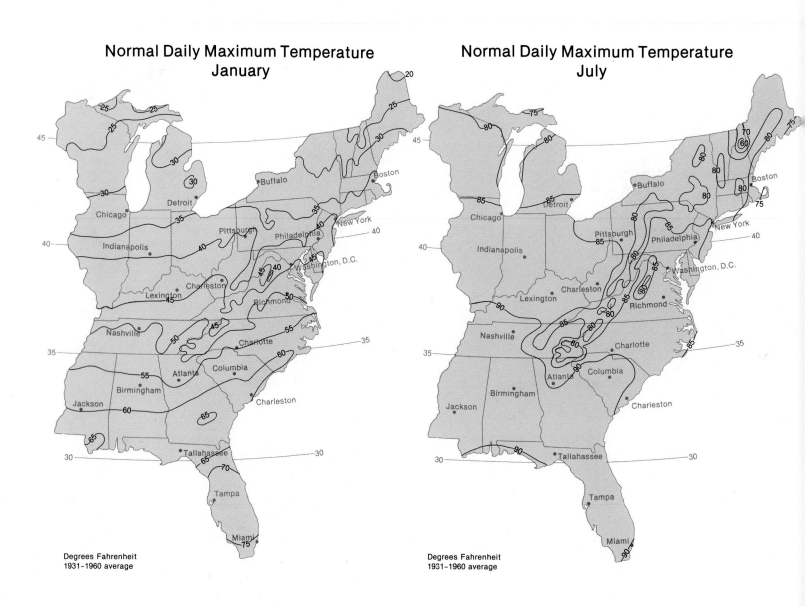

Degrees Fahrenheit
1931–1960 average

Degrees Fahrenheit
1931–1960 average

Seasonal Weather Patterns

The photographs on this page were taken from weather satellites. Land areas and individual states have been outlined in white and black dots, but with little precision. The photo in the lower left was taken February 13, 1978, and shows a weak cold front across the Florida peninsula and the Gulf of Mexico. The front is marked by the strip of white clouds that extends from the Georgia coast southwestward across Florida and into the Gulf of Mexico. Cold, clear air lies to the northwest and warm clear air to the southeast. The high temperature that day was 83°F in Orlando, 75°F in Jacksonville, and 29°F in Chicago and Cincinnati.

The photograph on the lower right was taken February 6, 1979, showing a warm front across northern Florida, extending along the Gulf coast through Texas. Warm, moist air had moved onto the continent from the Gulf and the Atlantic Ocean, and was rising over cooler air over the Southeast. At the same time a cold front was moving into the South, and the next day the two met (occluded) over Alabama, Georgia, and the Carolinas. High temperatures on the Florida peninsula reached 77°F in many places, while the temperature was –7°F in Chicago and –2°F in Cincinnati. In the ascent of the warm over the cold air, stratus clouds formed, blanketing a large portion of the nation. Rain and snow often occur under these conditions.

The upper photograph, taken during the afternoon of June 2, 1990, shows clouds over Florida. Air above the Gulf of Mexico and the Atlantic Ocean, however, is mostly clear. This is a typical Florida condition during the hot summer months. The temperature of the state's land surface rises during the day, causing air near the ground to become lighter and to rise. This air is replaced by moist air from the Gulf of Mexico and the Atlantic Ocean. The air usually reaches sufficient height that water vapor within it con-

denses into clouds. By mid-afternoon dense cumulus clouds form. Precipitation, when it occurs, is usually in the form of torrential thunderstorms. On June 2, 1990, it rained 1.10 inches in Tarpon Springs, 2.25 inches in Dade City (near Tampa), .97 inches in Orlando, and .84 inches in Gainesville. The day's high temperature ranged from 86°F in coastal Miami Beach to 95°F in Tallahassee and Orlando.

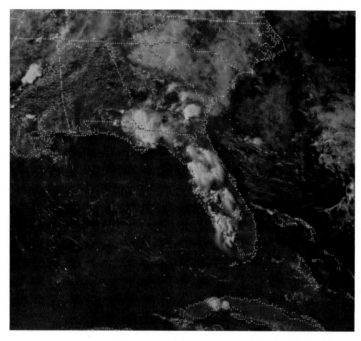

Summer Cloud Pattern, June 2, 1990

Winter Cold Front, February 13, 1978

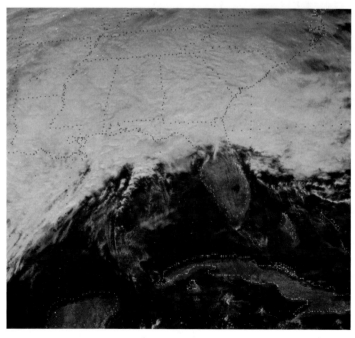

Winter Warm Front, February 6, 1979

The Effect of Land and Water on Climate

The sun is the earth's primary source of energy. For the air to be heated the sun's rays must first heat the surface of the earth. They are then reflected from it, heating the air from the surface upward. When the sun's rays hit land, heat is concentrated in its upper surface, because the density of the earth's material prevents them from penetrating deeply. When the sun's rays strike water, they penetrate a great distance, even hundreds of feet. The ground therefore heats more rapidly than water, but loses its heat more rapidly as well. The same can be said of the air above these surfaces.

No part of Florida is more than 80 miles from a large water body. The surface water temperature of both the Atlantic Ocean and Gulf of Mexico rises to about 84°F in the summer and falls to approximately 70°F in the winter. This temperature range is considerably less than that of the state's land surface. The closer one lives to the sea, the stronger the influence of the water's temperature on that of the air. Average maximum atmospheric temperatures are higher in the interior than along the coast and minimum temperatures are lower, since the ground both gains and loses heat rapidly. There are substantial differences in temperatures between places on the ocean and those a few miles away: for example, between Miami Beach and Miami, 8 miles away. Temperatures over 90°F are very rare on Miami Beach but quite common in Miami.

Surface Temperatures on a Summer Day

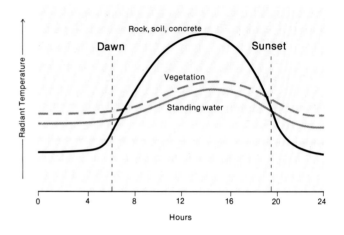

Average Annual Maximum Daily Temperature

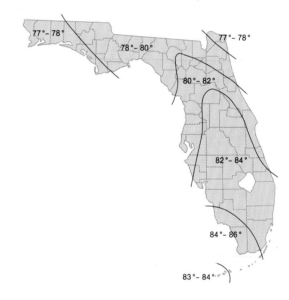

The Effect of Water on Temperature

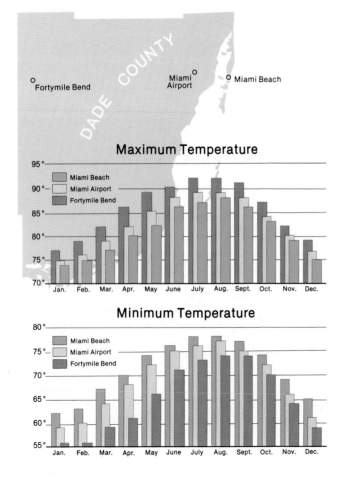

Average Annual Minimum Daily Temperature

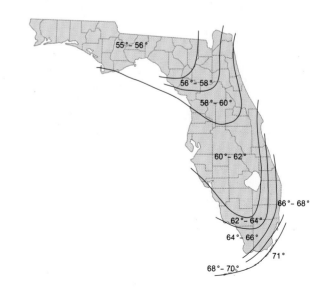

Temperature Extremes

Florida is erroneously thought of as a state with excessively high temperatures. In fact, many states have recorded maximum temperatures higher than Florida. Nearly all have also recorded lower minimum temperatures. The coldest temperature ever recorded in the state was -2°F in Tallahassee in 1899; the highest was 109°F in nearby Monticello in 1931.

High maximum temperatures are far more frequent in the interior than along either coast. The Atlantic Ocean modifies the coastal temperatures far more than does the Gulf of Mexico, since the state's prevailing winds are from the east. From Key West through Jacksonville is a narrow coastal strip where temperatures rarely reach 90°F. High temperatures are most frequent on the southwest side of the peninsula, where the warm season is long, and distance from the Atlantic Ocean is relatively great.

Cold fronts from the north are common during the winter, but they usually lose their strength rapidly before they penetrate very deeply onto the peninsula. Over 40 percent of the days in north Florida have minimum temperatures below 40°F, whereas in central Florida only 20 percent of the days have minimum temperatures that low. Occasionally particularly severe cold fronts do push deeply into the state.

Annual Average Temperature Extremes

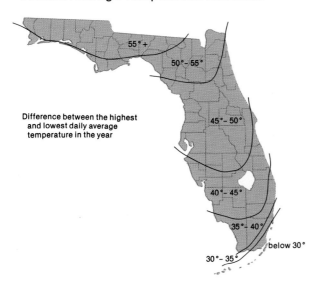

Days per Year with Maximum Temperature 88° F or Higher

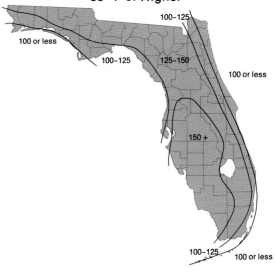

Percentage of Days Dec.–Feb. with a Minimum Temperature below 40° F

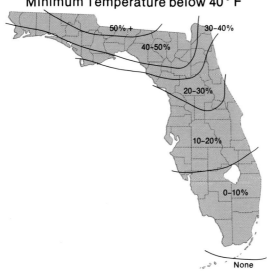

Florida's Most Severe Twentieth-Century Cold Wave, January 21 and 22, 1985

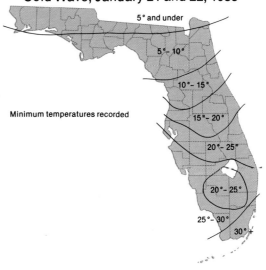

Arrival of the Seasons

Florida has the same progression of seasons as places to the north. The transition from one season to another is less distinct especially in south Florida, where the temperature difference between summer and fall is so small that trees do not display fall colors. Many plants bloom throughout winter and spring, but cease flowering during the summer and fall, when temperatures are too high.

The maps indicate a north-south trend for the arrival of fall, winter, and spring. The arrival of summer is largely determined by proximity to the Atlantic Ocean. Until June, winds off the ocean keep temperatures relatively low on the Atlantic seaboard.

The Beginning of Spring

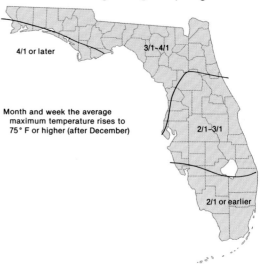

4/1 or later

3/1-4/1

Month and week the average maximum temperature rises to 75° F or higher (after December)

2/1-3/1

2/1 or earlier

The Beginning of Winter

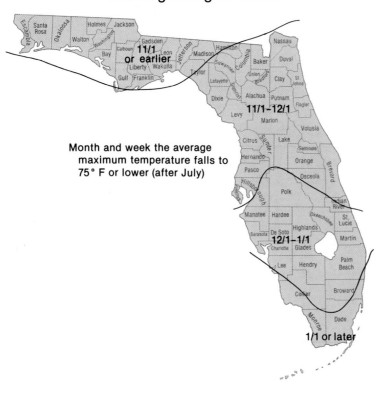

11/1 or earlier

11/1-12/1

Month and week the average maximum temperature falls to 75° F or lower (after July)

12/1-1/1

1/1 or later

The Beginning of Summer

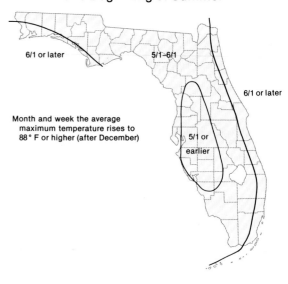

6/1 or later

5/1-6/1

6/1 or later

Month and week the average maximum temperature rises to 88° F or higher (after December)

5/1 or earlier

Winter Days in which Temperature Exceeds 75° F

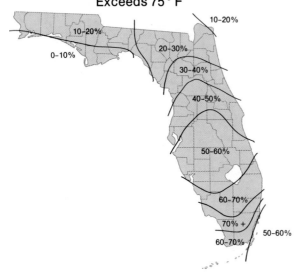

10-20%

10-20%

0-10%

20-30%

30-40%

40-50%

50-60%

60-70%

70% +

60-70%

50-60%

The Beginning of Fall

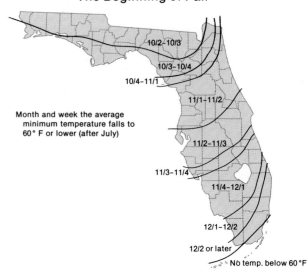

10/2-10/3

10/3-10/4

10/4-11/1

11/1-11/2

Month and week the average minimum temperature falls to 60° F or lower (after July)

11/2-11/3

11/3-11/4

11/4-12/1

12/1-12/2

12/2 or later

No temp. below 60°F

Cold Weather in Florida

First Freeze in Fall

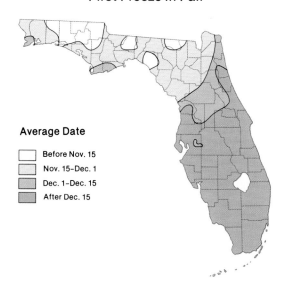

Average Date

- Before Nov. 15
- Nov. 15–Dec. 1
- Dec. 1–Dec. 15
- After Dec. 15

Florida is most famous for its mild winters. The farther south one goes on the peninsula, the milder the winters. Nonetheless, no part of Florida —not even Key West— escapes periodic blasts of cold air from the North.

North Florida winters are distinct from those of the peninsula. In north Florida freezing temperatures arrive earlier, last longer, and are lower than farther south. Meteorologists have defined a line, running roughly between St. Augustine and Cedar Key, to the north of which winters are considered continental; to the south, they are considered peninsular. The frequency of freezes decreases rapidly south of this line. Proximity to the coast, particularly the Atlantic, also has a strong influence on temperature. The last freeze of the winter is normally considerably later in the interior of the peninsula than along the coasts. Measurable amounts of snow fall in Florida about once each decade, usually in the north. Snow, however, has been seen in the air as far south as Miami.

Last Freeze in Spring

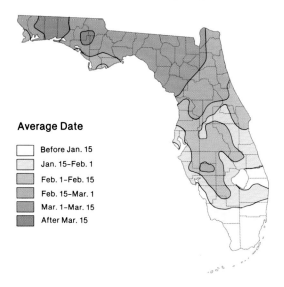

Average Date

- Before Jan. 15
- Jan. 15–Feb. 1
- Feb. 1–Feb. 15
- Feb. 15–Mar. 1
- Mar. 1–Mar. 15
- After Mar. 15

Measurable Snowfall

Average Growing Season

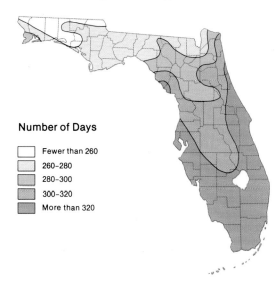

Number of Days

- Fewer than 260
- 260–280
- 280–300
- 300–320
- More than 320

SNOW, Jacksonville, December 1989

Rainfall

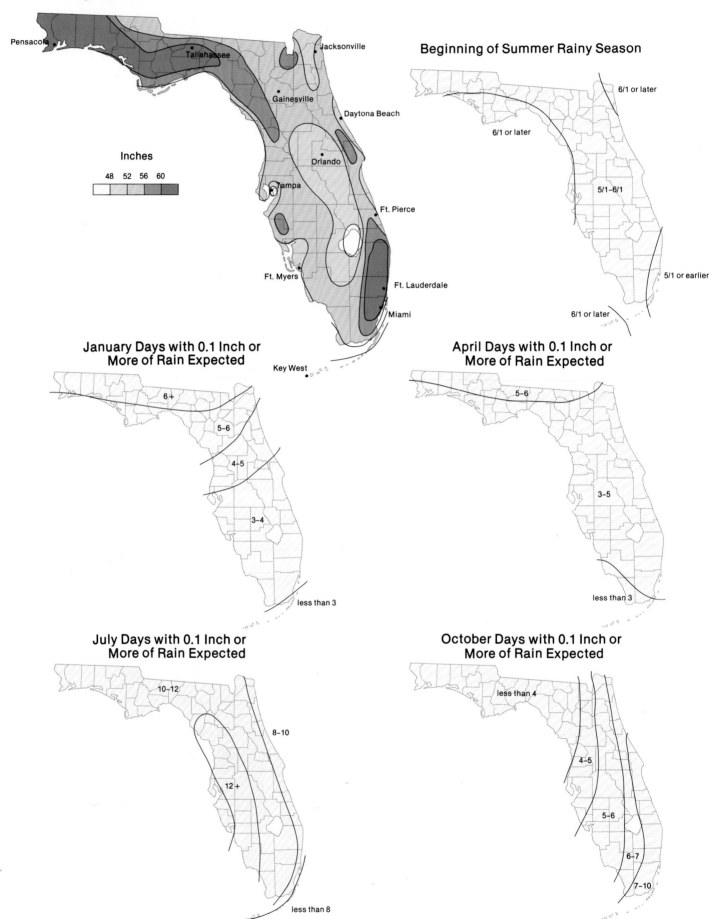

Average Annual Rainfall, 1951–1980

Pensacola
Tallahassee
Jacksonville
Gainesville
Daytona Beach
Orlando
Tampa
Ft. Pierce
Ft. Myers
Ft. Lauderdale
Miami
Key West

Inches

48 52 56 60

Beginning of Summer Rainy Season

6/1 or later
6/1 or later
5/1–6/1
5/1 or earlier
6/1 or later

January Days with 0.1 Inch or More of Rain Expected

6+
5–6
4–5
3–4
less than 3

April Days with 0.1 Inch or More of Rain Expected

5–6
3–5
less than 3

July Days with 0.1 Inch or More of Rain Expected

10–12
8–10
12+
less than 8

October Days with 0.1 Inch or More of Rain Expected

less than 4
4–5
5–6
6–7
7–10

Potential Evaporation

On an average day Florida receives about 150 billion gallons of rainwater, as well as 25 billion gallons of water from rivers leaving Georgia and Alabama. It must be remembered that on an average day over 100 billion gallons of water evaporate from the state's surface or are transpired into the atmosphere by plants, leaving 75 billion gallons to enter the ground or move along its surface. The balance between the water available for use by humans

and what they need is sufficiently delicate to warrant a discussion of potential evapotranspiration.

The term *potential evapotranspiration* refers to the amount of water that would be evapotranspired if there were always enough water in the soil for the use of vegetation. A simple way of measuring potential evapotranspiration is to calculate evaporation from a lake. Florida has an average annual precipitation which varies between 40 inches in Key West and 64 inches in Tallahassee. This would seem sufficient to meet all of the state's needs. The high summer temperatures of Florida, however, cause rapid evaporation. As a result the rainfall surplus is much smaller than total rainfall. It is particularly small on the southwestern side of the peninsula, where the seasonal drought is longest, as is the duration of the hot season. Northwest Florida has the largest rainfall surplus. Here summers are wet, and winters are both cool and wet. Rain during the winter returns to the atmosphere through evaporation much more slowly than during the summer, because of low temperatures.

The relationship of temperature and rainfall is illustrated by the diagrams showing the water budgets of Tallahassee and Miami. Tallahassee has a large surplus of water during the fall and winter, and a small one at the height of the summer, when rainfall is so heavy that even rapid evaporation does not prevent a surplus. Deficits in rainfall occur during the spring and fall, normally dry seasons. Miami has a long period of surplus rainfall, which mainly occurs during the warm and wet season. Like Tallahassee summers, Miami summers have so much rainfall that even high temperatures will not result in enough evaporation to cause a deficit. Miami's rainfall deficit occurs in the winter, when it seldom rains.

Rainfall Surplus over Potential Evaporation

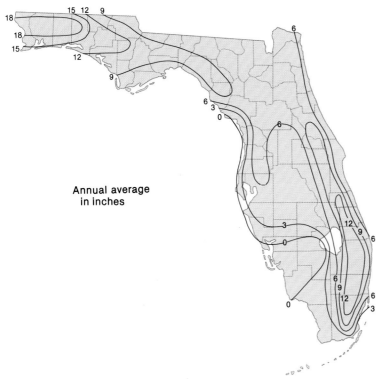

Annual average
in inches

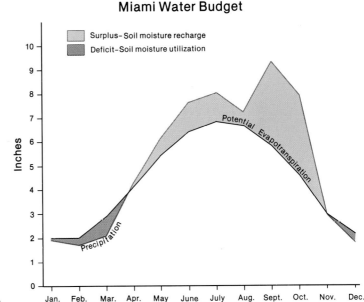

Sunshine

Average Monthly Total Hours of Sunshine

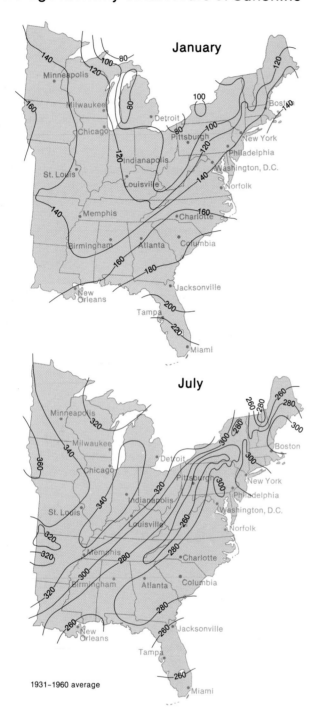

January

July

1931–1960 average

Average Percentage of Total Possible Sunshine

January

July

1931–1960 average

Florida is called the Sunshine State, because it is sunnier than other portions of the eastern United States during the winter. The skies over Florida are obscured far less by clouds than those in more northern latitudes, and the sun is above the horizon longer during the winter in Florida than in the north. During the summer there are fewer hours of sunlight in Florida than farther north, and the percentage of possible sunshine is somewhat lower. Typically by noon throughout Florida during the summer large thunderclouds cover the sky. Many Floridians regard the frequency of cloudy summer afternoons a blessing, since they are considerably cooler than sunny afternoons.

During the winter the sun shines less over north Florida than south Florida. North Florida is affected more by the winter storm systems that cross through the United States. Days may pass without sunshine. Also, during winters in north Florida morning fog is common. This condition results when moist air drifts in from the Gulf of Mexico and the Atlantic Ocean and is chilled to the dewpoint by the cool ground over which it passes. Fog is rare in south Florida, and almost nonexistent in Key West, the sunniest city in the state.

Wind Direction

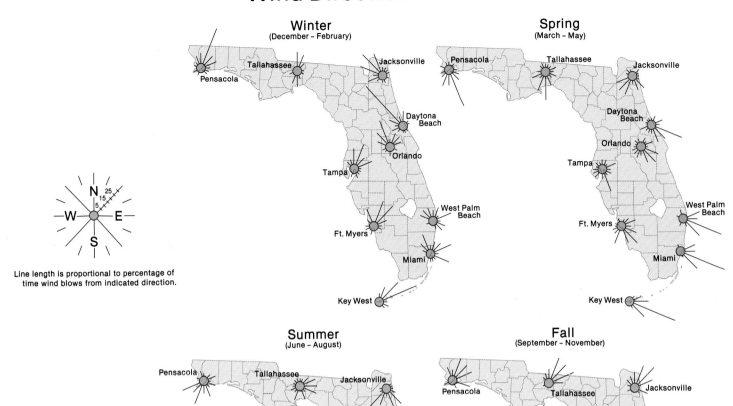

Line length is proportional to percentage of time wind blows from indicated direction.

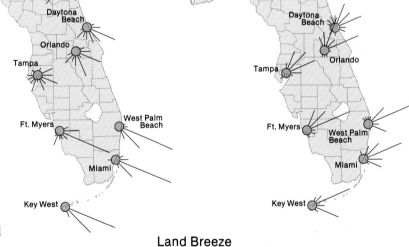
Land Breeze

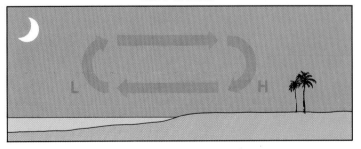
Sea Breeze

Florida's prevailing winds are not typical of those of the rest of the continental United States, which mainly lies within the Westerly Wind Belt. Florida's winds, particularly in the spring, summer, and fall come out of the east. They are sometimes called the Trade Winds and spiral out of the Bermuda High Pressure cell found in the North Atlantic. In the spring and summer they most frequently come from the southeastern quadrant, while in the fall and winter they blow from the southwestern quadrant. These prevailing winds are far more constant in spring and fall than at other times of the year. During winter and spring the northern portion of the state does not have the same prevailing winds as the peninsula because it is heavily influenced by high and low pressure systems that pass through the Westerly Wind Belt to the north.

Temperatures along Florida's coasts are modified by sea and land breezes, which are strongest in the summer. Land-sea breezes are diurnal. During the day the land heats more rapidly than the water, and a convectional circulation system develops. Air rises over the land, and the resulting low pressure pulls air in off the water (sea breeze). During the late evening the reverse takes place, since the water has a higher temperature than the land. Air is pulled from the land (land breeze) into the low pressure area that has developed over the water. The sea breeze can lower temperatures significantly as far as fifteen miles into the interior.

Mixing Heights and Ventilation

The *mixing height* is an important concept in connection with air pollution. It is the thickness of a layer of air, resting on the ground surface, in which vigorous vertical mixing occurs. Smoke, or any other airborne pollutant, spreads easily upward through this layer to the mixing height. Above that height much less vertical mixing takes place. Only the afternoon mixing height is shown on the maps; it is generally higher than the morning mixing height, because heating of the ground during the day promotes vertical mixing. The brown haze layer, which airplanes go through in taking off and landing at major airports, is approximately the same as the mixing layer. The difference is that the brown haze layer is observed by a person at one specific spot, whereas the mixing height is computed from weather station data, perhaps at some other point. The maps show clearly that the mixing layer is thickest during the summer, when ground heating is greatest, and thinnest in the winter, when ground heating is least.

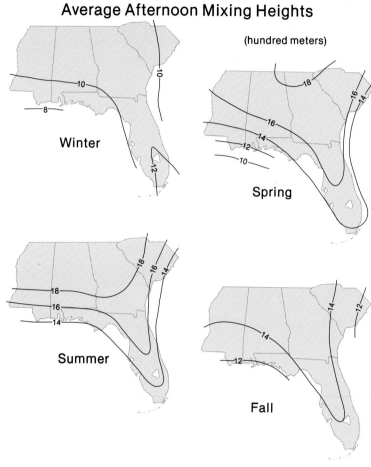

Average Afternoon Mixing Heights

(hundred meters)

Winter

Spring

Summer

Fall

Afternoon Ventilation

Average Wind Speed through the Afternoon Mixing Layer in Meters per Second

Winter

Spring

Summer

Fall

On calm days the mixing layer tends to be thin, and pollutants tend to collect in the air close to the ground. Generally on windy days the mixing layer is thicker, and pollutants are much less concentrated. They are also carried more easily from the source into other areas. Highest spot concentrations, however, often occur under windy conditions when pollutants from elevated sources are mixed downward to the surface. Under these conditions, concentrations are highly variable in time and space. Therefore, wind speed is important in determining the concentration and areal distribution of pollutants. The term ventilation is related to wind speed; it specifies the rate at which air is mixed. Wind speed is not constant from the ground surface upward but increases with height. For these maps, two types of measurements were used: (a) ground surface air speed from noon (Eastern Standard Time) until 4:00 P.M. (EST); and (b) air speed aloft, taken systematically at different heights up to 4,000 or more meters, at 7:00 P.M. (EST). This is the earliest time of measurement aloft after afternoon heating has modified the wind patterns; it produces better results than those obtained about midday before afternoon heating has taken place.

Heating and Air Conditioning

Florida became immensely popular after World War II in part because of the rapid introduction of air conditioning. Today, most Florida residents and tourists can escape the summer heat and humidity. Comfort, however, is achieved through considerable costs in energy. Heating expenses are minimal, except in north Florida, but cooling is expensive.

Heating engineers have devised an index to estimate energy demands for heating and cooling, called heating and cooling degree days. It is assumed that neither heating nor cooling is required when the outside temperature is 65°F. The number of degrees that the mean temperature for the day falls below 65°F are heating days, and the number of degrees that the mean temperature for the day is above 65°F are cooling degree days. If the mean temperature of a station were 60°F on December 3, there would be 5 heating degree days on that date. If the average temperature on July 10 were 90°F, the number of cooling degree days would be 25.

The state's cooling season extends far beyond summer and even in north Florida in January the mean daily temperature sometimes rises above 65°F. The state's southernmost city, Key West, has the most cooling degree days and the least heating degree days. Niceville, near Pensacola, has the most heating degree days, and among the fewest cooling degree days. When heating and cooling degree days are combined, there is remarkably little difference between north and south Florida. The cost of heating and air conditioning depends on the occupants' tolerance for heat and cold and the energy source. Florida homeowners generally pay less to control temperatures in their houses than people in the North. An average Florida community may have 3,000 cooling and 1,000 heating degree days, whereas throughout the Lower Great Lakes area communities have between 6,000 and 7,000 heating and between 750 to 1,200 cooling degree days.

Annual Heating Degree Days

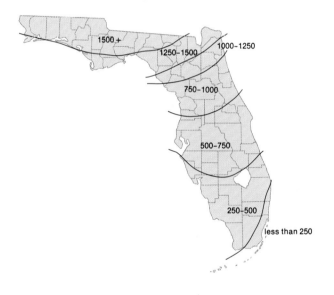

Annual Cooling Degree Days

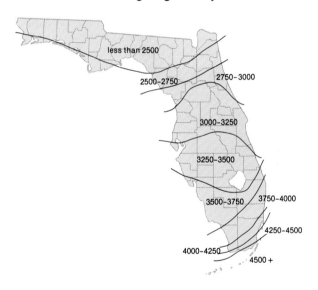

Annual Combined Heating and Cooling Degree Days

Cooling Degree Days as a Percentage of Annual Cooling and Heating Degree Days

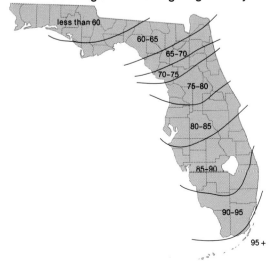

Humidity and Temperature

Florida's most important natural resource is its climate. Tourism is the state's major contribution to the national economy, greatly exceeding the contribution of agriculture, manufacturing, or mining. Tourism is largely dependent on the fact that winter on the Florida peninsula is much milder than places farther north.

A comfort index based on both humidity and temperature has been devised. For most people, high humidity accompanied by high temperatures is uncomfortable because sweat does not evaporate from the skin rapidly under these conditions.

Florida has one of the highest annual rainfalls of any place in the nation, and a large share of that rain falls during the summer. In that season humidity and temperatures are high.

Until this century Florida summers were not only physically unpleasant for most people, but they could also be dangerous to their health. Tropical diseases, most spread by insects, were common during that season. During the twentieth century means to prevent and cure tropical diseases were discovered. In addition, the widespread adoption of air conditioning made life far more pleasant indoors. Most Florida homes are air conditioned, as are automobiles, public buildings, shopping malls, and offices. Clothes today are lighter weight than in the past, and fashions more appropriate to days of excessive heat and humidity. For most Floridians summer is the season to stay inside, and winter is for outside recreation, just the opposite of states in the North.

In January Florida's peninsula is rated by the Comfort Index as comfortable (0) or warm (1). The warm portion is in the southwest, centered on the new, but rapidly growing tourist and retirement city of Naples. North Florida is considered comfortable to cool, except in the Pensacola area, where it is cool to cold. More severe cold fronts descend on Pensacola than other Florida cities on the same latitude. Approximately once each decade snow covers the ground in parts of north Florida.

Comfort Index

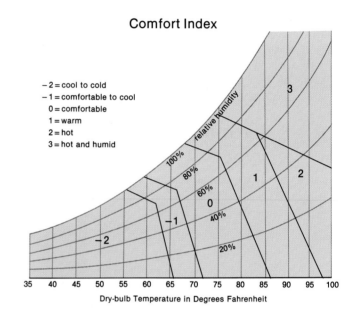

-2 = cool to cold
-1 = comfortable to cool
0 = comfortable
1 = warm
2 = hot
3 = hot and humid

Dry-bulb Temperature in Degrees Fahrenheit

Comfort Zones, January

Comfort Index for Selected Florida Cities

	J	F	M	A	M	J	J	A	S	O	N	D
Daytona Beach	0	0	0	1	2	3	3	3	3	1	1	0
Ft. Myers	0	0	1	1	2	3	3	3	3	2	1	0
Gainesville	0	0	0	1	2	3	3	3	3	1	0	0
Jacksonville	-1	0	0	1	1	3	3	3	3	1	0	-1
Key West	0	0	1	1	3	3	3	3	3	3	1	1
Miami	0	0	1	1	2	3	3	3	3	3	1	1
Orlando	0	0	0	1	2	3	3	3	3	1	0	0
Pensacola	-2	-1	0	0	1	3	3	3	2	1	0	-1
Tallahassee	-1	-1	0	1	1	3	3	3	3	1	0	-1
Tampa	0	0	0	1	2	3	3	3	3	1	0	0
Vero Beach	0	0	1	1	2	3	3	3	3	1	1	0
W. Palm Beach	0	0	1	1	2	3	3	3	3	3	1	0

-2 = cool to cold
-1 = comfortable to cool
0 = comfortable
1 = warm
2 = hot
3 = hot and humid

Thunderstorms

Days with Thunderstorms per Year

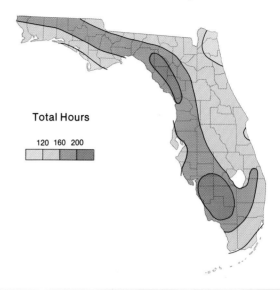

Number of Days

70 80 90

Hours of Thunderstorms per Year

Total Hours

120 160 200

THUNDER CLOUDS DEVELOPING OVER EVERGLADES DURING THE MORNING
Infrared film was used to enhance the contrast.

TWO WATERSPOUTS AND LIGHTNING BOLT EMERGING FROM A SQUALL LINE,
near Key West, 1980

Tornadoes

High Frequency

High Frequency

High Frequency

Florida experiences more thunderstorms than any place
on earth except East Africa. Some places have more than 90
thunderstorms each year, most occurring in the summer
when the interior of the peninsula heats up during the day,
causing the air to rise. When moist air from the Gulf of
Mexico and the Atlantic Ocean is sucked into the center of
the rising air, the resulting turbulence produces thunderstorms.

Hurricanes

Hurricanes are intense tropical low-pressure systems. They develop over tropical oceans during the spring and summer, deriving their energy from the warm water. *Typhoons* of the Pacific, *cyclones* of the Indian Ocean, and *willy-willies* of Australia are different names for the same atmospheric phenomenon. They can develop sustained wind velocities of over 150 miles per hour. Wind speed is, to a great extent, dependent upon the pressure gradient between the outside and inside of the storm. They may be 400 miles in diameter, but normally are much smaller.

Between 1900 and 1989 Florida experienced fifty-six hurricanes. Most have been categorized on the Saffir/ Simpson scale as minimal or moderate. Hurricanes reach Florida with greater frequency in September than any other month. It is at that time that air and ocean conditions are best for their creation and development. Hurricanes evolve from weak low-pressure systems. Evolution usually begins in the Atlantic, but they sometimes are born in the Caribbean and even the Gulf. Water temperatures must be high, and no hurricane has reached Florida before June or after November. June and November storms have been notably weaker than those of September, when water temperature is highest. Few of these weak systems ever pass into the hurricane stage.

These tropical storms tend to drift westward. The path of a hurricane is governed by pressure systems that it encounters as it moves. Very often hurricanes meet high pressure systems over the United States. These deflect them. Their paths then often begin to turn northward. Although this path followed by hurricanes has been less frequent in recent decades than in the past, it is still sufficiently common that the coast between the Florida Keys and Cape Canaveral has become known as hurricane alley. Since 1970 the northwestern panhandle of the state has experienced an unusually high number of hurricanes.

Cross Section of a Hurricane

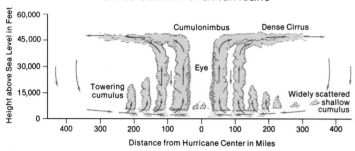

Saffir/Simpson Hurricane Category

Category	Central Pressure (Inches)	Winds (Mph)	Surge (Feet)	Damage
1	≥28.94	74–95	4–5	Minimal
2	28.50–28.91	96–110	6–8	Moderate
3	27.91–28.47	111–130	9–12	Extensive
4	27.17–27.88	131–155	13–18	Extreme
5	< 27.17	>155	>18	Catastrophic

Florida Hurricanes 1900–1989
Number of Landfalls

Category	June	July	Aug	Sept	Oct	Nov	
1	2	1	2	5	6	2	18
2	2	1	2	3	6	2	16
3		1	1	9	5		16
4				5			5
5				1			1
	4	3	5	23	17	4	56

Number of Landfalls

Category	SE	SW	NE	NW	
1	5	5		8	18
2	5	2	3	6	16
3	7	5		4	16
4	3	2			5
5	1				1
	21	14	3	18	56

First Sighting of Storm

	Atlantic	Gulf	Caribbean	
June	1			1
July	3		3	6
Aug	4	1		5
Sept	16	2	5	23
Oct	3		14	17
Nov	2		2	4
	29	3	24	56

Hurricanes have brought tragic loss of life and property to Florida. Early evidence of their ferocity can be found in the many sailing ships—some loaded with treasure—lost by the Spanish along the Atlantic coast. In this century hurricanes have claimed almost 3,000 lives and property loss (in 1989 dollars) has reached nearly 6 billion dollars.

Until the middle of this century the state did little to protect property or to prepare the population for hurricanes. Hurricanes in 1926 and 1928 killed hundreds of people when a levee that held back the waters of Lake Okeechobee broke. The strongest hurricane ever to hit Florida occurred on Labor Day 1935, drowning many on the Florida Keys. These early disasters motivated the state to prepare the population for hurricanes and to adopt stringent building codes. Since 1945 fatalities have been far fewer. Despite greater development regulation, hurricanes continue to damage property primarily from flooding. Most hurricanes are accompanied by huge amounts of rainfall and also, along the coast, by storm surge.

Storm Surge

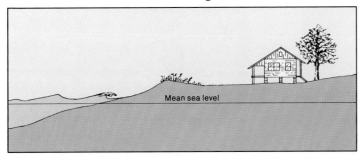

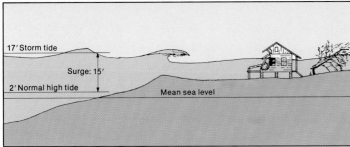

RESCUE TRAIN SWEPT OFF TRACKS BY WIND AND WATER, Labor Day hurricane, 1935, Islamorada

Fatalities and Damages from Selected Hurricanes 1926–1989

Year	Fatalities	Damage (millions)	Description
1926	243	$ 737.9	— Severe damage in Miami area, Lake Okeechobee, and Pensacola.
1928	+ 2,000	167.2	— Many casualties and heavy property damage in Lake Okeechobee area when levees broke.
1929	3	5.6	
1930	0	.7	
1932	1	1.3	
1933	2	3.6	— Heavy property damage on east coast, including widespread citrus loss.
1935	408	92.0	— "Labor Day Hurricane." Record low barometric reading. Huge loss of life and property in Keys.
1936	7	1.6	
1939	1	.4	
1941	6	5.4	
1944	18	366.0	— Extensive damage in Tampa Bay area.
1945	4	330.0	— Damage very heavy in Dade County.
1946	0	41.8	
1947	17	233.6	— Large intense storm. Wind and water damage along southeast coast.
1948	3	78.9	
1949	2	207.5	— Storm center passed over Lake Okeechobee but levees held.
1950	6	144.1	— Two hurricanes, one on west coast, other on east. Extensive damage.
1951	0	8.5	
1953	0	20.6	
1956	7	29.5	
1957	5	.4	
1959	0	6.4	
1960	13	1,131.9	— Severe damage to southeast Florida, including the Keys.
1963	1	.4	
1964	11	1,281.5	— Extensive damage in northeast Florida.
1965	13	484.8	— Extensive flood damage in Miami and the Keys.
1966	9	50.7	
1968	9	21.2	
1972	9	107.8	— Extensive damage to Panama City.
1975	2	204.0	— Storm surge from Ft. Walton Beach to Panama City.
1979	0	8.1	— Two hurricanes, one on east coast, the other on west coast.
1985	4	102.0	— Two hurricanes in the northern Gulf did damage in the panhandle.
1987	0	6.9	— Some damage in the Keys.

Note: Damage estimates are in 1989 dollars.

Florida Hurricanes in the Twentieth Century Through 1989

Year	Date of landfall	Name	Category	Year	Date of landfall	Name	Category
1903	Sep 11	—	2	1941	Oct 5	—	2
1904	Oct 17	—	1	1944	Oct 18	—	3
1906	Jun 16	—	2	1945	Jun 24	—	1
1906	Oct 17	—	2	1945	Sep 15	—	3
1909	Oct 11	—	3	1946	Oct 8	—	1
1910	Oct 17	—	3	1947	Sep 17	—	4
1911	Aug 11	—	1	1947	Oct 11	—	1
1915	Sep 4	—	1	1948	Sep 21	—	3
1916	Oct 18	—	2	1948	Oct 5	—	2
1916	Nov 15	—	1	1949	Aug 26	—	3
1917	Sep 29	—	3	1950	Sep 4	Easy	3
1919	Sep 10	—	4	1950	Oct 17	King	3
1921	Oct 25	—	3	1953	Sep 26	Florence	1
1924	Sep 15	—	1	1956	Sep 24	Flossy	1
1924	Oct 21	—	1	1960	Sep 9	Donna	4
1925	Nov 30	—	1	1964	Aug 27	Cleo	2
1926	Jul 28	—	2	1964	Sep 9	Dora	2
1926	Sep 16	—	4	1964	Oct 14	Isabel	2
1928	Aug 17	—	2	1965	Sep 8	Betsy	3
1928	Sep 16	—	4	1966	Jun 9	Alma	2
1929	Sep 28	—	3	1966	Oct 4	Inez	1
1932	Sep 1	—	1	1968	Oct 18	Gladys	2
1933	Jul 30	—	1	1972	Jun 19	Agnes	1
1933	Sep 3	—	3	1975	Sep 23	Eloise	3
1935	Sep 3	—	5	1979	Sep 3	David	2
1935	Nov 14	—	2	1985	Sep 11	Elena	3
1936	Jul 31	—	3	1985	Nov 21	Kate	2
1939	Aug 11	—	1	1987	Oct 13	Floyd	1

Note: The higher the category, the more powerful the hurricane. Hurricanes were unnamed before 1950.

Surface Water

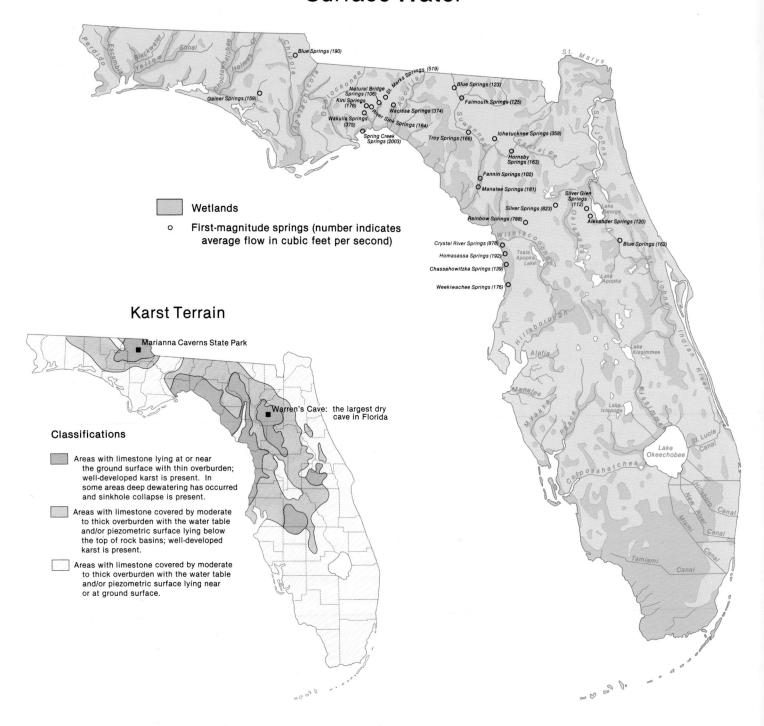

Karst Terrain

Classifications

Areas with limestone lying at or near the ground surface with thin overburden; well-developed karst is present. In some areas deep dewatering has occurred and sinkhole collapse is present.

Areas with limestone covered by moderate to thick overburden with the water table and/or piezometric surface lying below the top of rock basins; well-developed karst is present.

Areas with limestone covered by moderate to thick overburden with the water table and/or piezometric surface lying near or at ground surface.

The surface water features shown on this map include streams (rivers and creeks), canals, springs, lakes, and wetlands. The latter are of two main types: swamps and marshes. Swamps are characterized by a tree cover and marshes by a grass cover. Wetlands are generally in stream valleys, along the coast, or adjacent to lakes. Wide interior wetlands are an exception: they owe their existence to the almost flat, essentially featureless geometry of the landscape and the extremely gentle slope of the ground surface. This gentle slope angle, south of Lake Okeechobee, occurs because this part of the state was sea floor, perhaps around a million years ago. Several drainage canals have been dug across the broad wetlands in the southern part of the state.

The term *karst* refers to a set of surface features in areas of relatively soluble rock types, such as limestone, dolomite, and gypsum. Florida has the first two. Karst regions are characterized by many caves, springs, sinkholes, sinkhole lakes, solution valleys, and solution prairies, as well as a few natural bridges (entirely different from the sandstone bridges of Utah). Karst depends on many factors, such as solubility of the rocks, thickness of soluble materials, physical relief, depth to the water table, and age of the materials. Extreme southern Florida has poor karst development, because it has very low relief, a shallow water table, and relatively young rocks.

Florida has both alluvial and nonalluvial streams. Alluvial streams carry loads of sand, silt, or clay. All streams in the panhandle are alluvial, the largest of which is the Apalachicola River. Many streams within the peninsula are nonalluvial. The St. Johns River is the largest nonalluvial river in the state. The slope of the stream bed is extremely low; therefore, the flow velocity is unusually small, and a very large channel is required to transport a relatively small amount of water. For a good part of its length, the St. Johns is about 3 kilometers wide, which is much wider than the lower Mississippi River and as deep. Streams also may be permanent or intermittent. Florida's main streams are permanent.

Runoff is calculated by subtracting the amount of water that soaks into the ground, the amount retained in the soil and used by plants, and the amount that evaporates from total rainfall.

Average stream water temperature increases from cool, along the northern border, to warm, in the southeast. The variability of water temperature is greatest in the north, where air temperature varies the most.

Annual Runoff

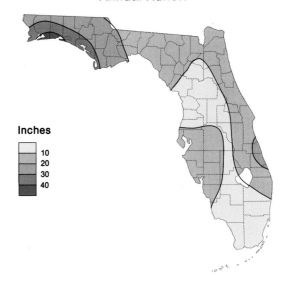

Inches

- 10
- 20
- 30
- 40

Average Stream Temperature

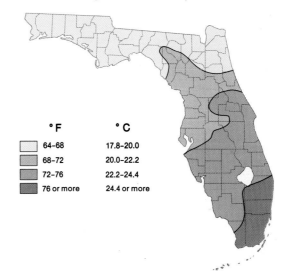

°F	°C
64–68	17.8–20.0
68–72	20.0–22.2
72–76	22.2–24.4
76 or more	24.4 or more

Discharge of Selected Florida Rivers and Major World Rivers

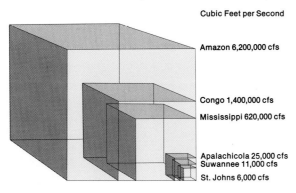

Cubic Feet per Second

Amazon 6,200,000 cfs

Congo 1,400,000 cfs

Mississippi 620,000 cfs

Apalachicola 25,000 cfs
Suwannee 11,000 cfs

St. Johns 6,000 cfs

Discharge of Major Florida Rivers

River	Gauging Site (Nearest town)	Miles Above Mouth	Average Annual Discharge (cfs)	Average Annual Runoff (in.)	Drainage Area Above Site (sq. mi.)
Coastal					
Apalachicola	Blountstown	78	24,768	19.11	17,600
Suwannee	Wilcox	33	10,635	14.98	9,640
St. Johns	DeLand	142	3,158	14.00	3,066
Choctawhatchee	Bruce	21	7,198	22.29	4,384
Escambia	Century	52	6,300	22.43	3,817
Peace	Arcadia	36	1,170	11.61	1,367
Ochlockonee	Bloxham	65	1,796	14.36	1,700
Withlacoochee *	Holder	38	1,105	8.22	1,825
St. Marys	Macclenny	100	683	13.25	700
Yellow	Milligan	40	1,181	25.68	624
Perdido	Barrineau Park	27	754	25.99	394
St. Marks	Newport	14	669	16.96	535
Blackwater	Baker	35	342	22.66	205
Tributary					
Oklawaha	Conner	51	1,186	13.46	1,196
Kissimmee	Okeechobee	8	1,409	8.00	2,300
Withlacoochee *	Pinetta	22	1,672	10.72	2,120
Alapaha	Jennings	21	1,873	15.14	1,680
Santa Fe	Fort White	18	1,625	21.79	1,017
Chipola	Altha	54	1,495	25.98	781
Shoal	Crestview	7	1,104	31.60	474

* Note: There are two separate, unconnected rivers named "Withlacoochee."

Groundwater

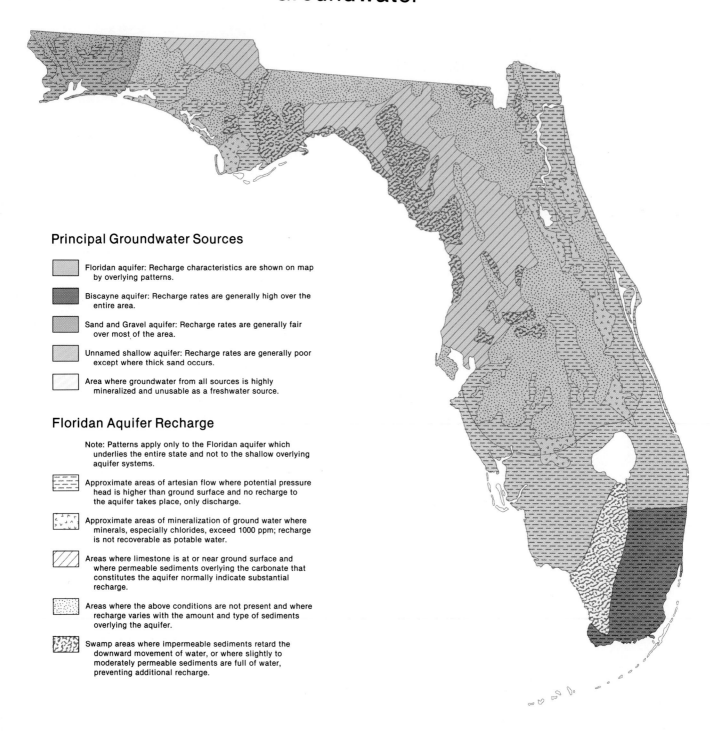

Principal Groundwater Sources

Floridan aquifer: Recharge characteristics are shown on map by overlying patterns.

Biscayne aquifer: Recharge rates are generally high over the entire area.

Sand and Gravel aquifer: Recharge rates are generally fair over most of the area.

Unnamed shallow aquifer: Recharge rates are generally poor except where thick sand occurs.

Area where groundwater from all sources is highly mineralized and unusable as a freshwater source.

Floridan Aquifer Recharge

Note: Patterns apply only to the Floridan aquifer which underlies the entire state and not to the shallow overlying aquifer systems.

Approximate areas of artesian flow where potential pressure head is higher than ground surface and no recharge to the aquifer takes place, only discharge.

Approximate areas of mineralization of ground water where minerals, especially chlorides, exceed 1000 ppm; recharge is not recoverable as potable water.

Areas where limestone is at or near ground surface and where permeable sediments overlying the carbonate that constitutes the aquifer normally indicate substantial recharge.

Areas where the above conditions are not present and where recharge varies with the amount and type of sediments overlying the aquifer.

Swamp areas where impermeable sediments retard the downward movement of water, or where slightly to moderately permeable sediments are full of water, preventing additional recharge.

An aquifer is a body of rock or sediment that is sufficiently permeable to yield important quantities of groundwater from springs or wells. Most potable water is located within 50–200 meters of the surface. Beneath this supply of potable water, rock pores are filled with salt water.

The water supply in the aquifers of the state comes from rain that falls directly on the state or on adjacent states within a short distance of the state line. Rainwater that moves slowly downward past the soil zone and into the uppermost aquifer is said to recharge that aquifer. If water withdrawn through wells and springs exceeds the recharge, the aquifer will be depleted.

In artesian aquifers water rises above the top of the aquifer. This rise shows that the aquifer is being recharged in some adjacent, higher area and that the water is under pressure as a result. Areas of recharge are shown on the map. In areas where artesian aquifers discharge to the surface, there is no recharge.

Along the coast where wells pump large quantities of water, saltwater intrusion may occur. Groundwater may acquire undesirable properties in other ways: where soluble minerals are present in the rocks, they may dissolve into the groundwater.

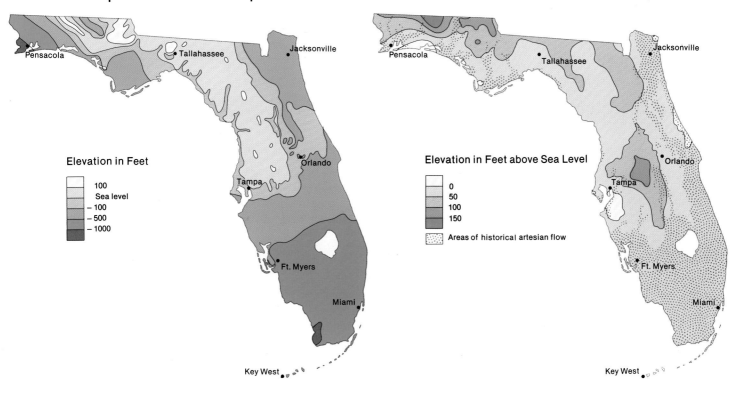

Top of the Floridan Aquifer

Elevation in Feet

- 100
- Sea level
- −100
- −500
- −1000

Floridan Potentiometric Surface, 1985

Elevation in Feet above Sea Level

- 0
- 50
- 100
- 150

Areas of historical artesian flow

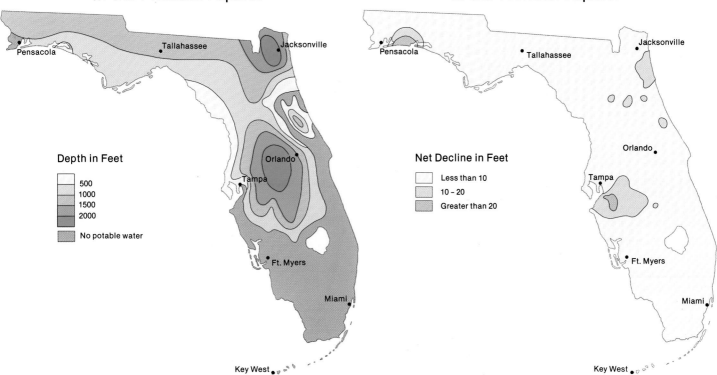

Depth to Base of Potable Water in the Floridan Aquifer

Depth in Feet

- 500
- 1000
- 1500
- 2000

No potable water

Decline in Potentiometric Surface, 1980–1985 in the Floridan Aquifer

Net Decline in Feet

- Less than 10
- 10 – 20
- Greater than 20

The Floridan aquifer system underlies the entire state at varying depths below land surface. However, potable water does not occur everywhere in the Floridan. In these areas, residents obtain water from shallower aquifer systems or through reverse osmosis. The Floridan aquifer system is a confined or artesian aquifer system. The level to which water will rise in a properly constructed well is called the potentiometric surface. Where the potentiometric surface occurs above the land surface, natural artesian flow of water occurs. The thickness of the fresh-water lens in the Floridan varies dramatically from zero to more than 2000 feet. Groundwater levels can be dramatically affected by heavy pumpage of wells. In these areas, the potentiometric surface will show a decline as in Tampa and Pensacola. If the potentiometric surface is drawn down below sea level, salt water may intrude and replace the fresh water.

Freshwater Supply

Freshwater Withdrawals

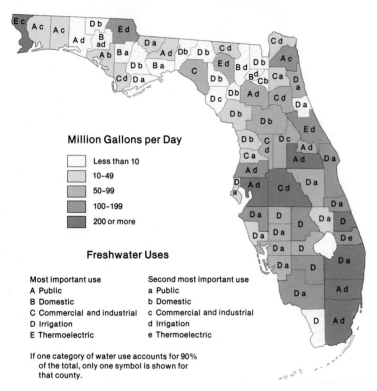

Million Gallons per Day

- Less than 10
- 10–49
- 50–99
- 100–199
- 200 or more

Freshwater Uses

Most important use	Second most important use
A Public	a Public
B Domestic	b Domestic
C Commercial and industrial	c Commercial and industrial
D Irrigation	d Irrigation
E Thermoelectric	e Thermoelectric

If one category of water use accounts for 90%
of the total, only one symbol is shown for
that county.

Freshwater Withdrawals by Source

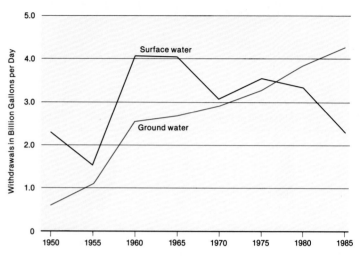

Freshwater Withdrawals by Category

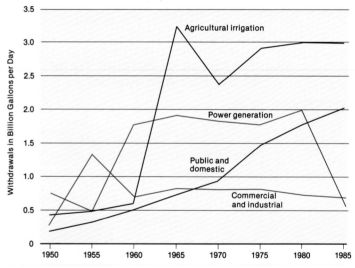

Florida is underlain by sedimentary rock layers. Most sediments were deposited in the ocean and contain seawater trapped in the spaces between grains of sediment. Over the years, this salt water interacted chemically with some of the minerals present, so that pore water is now typically two to six times as salty as seawater. This highly saline water is called connate water. Connate water is encountered, typically, at depths of tens of meters to a few hundred meters.

Rainwater, falling on the ground surface, soaks in, in part, providing a thin layer of fresh water in the upper part of the stack of sedimentary rocks. This thin layer is called meteoric water. It overlies connate water. Water wells are drilled into meteoric water but not into connate water. On beaches and near-shore islands, a very thin layer of meteoric water overlies ocean water, which in turn overlies connate water.

The large map shows the uses of meteoric well water, by counties, as well as the quantities used.

The degree to which water drains from, or through, the soil is shown by the soil drainage map. Drainage depends on slope as well as rock type; if the surface is flat, water cannot run off very well, and if the rock has very few pores, water cannot soak in very well.

Soil Drainage

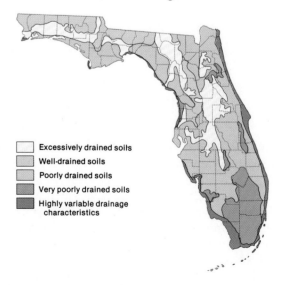

- Excessively drained soils
- Well-drained soils
- Poorly drained soils
- Very poorly drained soils
- Highly variable drainage characteristics

Water Quality

Maximum Orthophosphate Concentrations in Streams

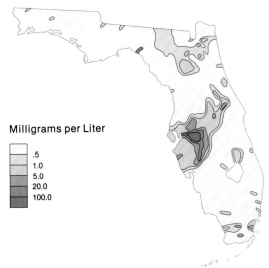

Milligrams per Liter

.5
1.0
5.0
20.0
100.0

Aquifers are recharged primarily by streams and only secondarily by hillside run-off. The chemistry of stream water is controlled by both natural and artificial processes; even in an untouched wilderness, stream water contains chemicals from the weathering of rocks in the uplands. Municipal and industrial effluents, as well as farmland run-off, may add other materials. These chemicals are added to subsurface water through insoak, or infiltration, but infiltration is very slow, and therefore changes in water chemistry in aquifers lag behind changes at the surface. Because aquifers are rock layers, made up of mineral particles, they also contribute to groundwater chemistry. For this reason, the groundwater will never be identical with the contribution from streams. Some groundwater is much saltier than the ocean; much of this salinity is obtained from minerals occurring in the rock. Aquifers are located at different depths; ordinarily, the most shallow aquifer is the least salty (sodium chloride content is least) but is also influenced the most by insoak.

Chloride Concentration in the Upper Floridan Aquifer

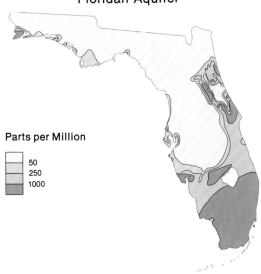

Parts per Million

50
250
1000

Water Hardness of the Upper Floridan Aquifer

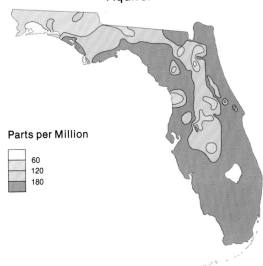

Parts per Million

60
120
180

Chemical Quality of Stream Water

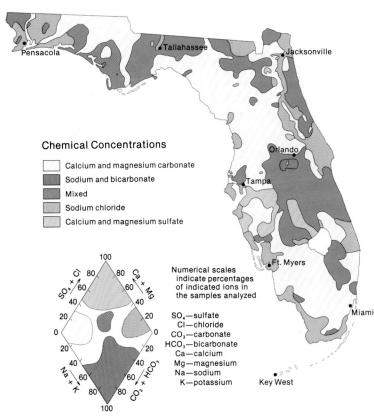

Chemical Concentrations

Calcium and magnesium carbonate
Sodium and bicarbonate
Mixed
Sodium chloride
Calcium and magnesium sulfate

Numerical scales indicate percentages of indicated ions in the samples analyzed

SO₄—sulfate
Cl—chloride
CO₃—carbonate
HCO₃—bicarbonate
Ca—calcium
Mg—magnesium
Na—sodium
K—potassium

Sources Influencing Quality

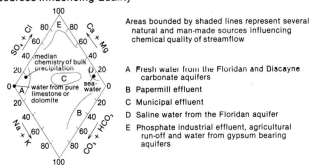

Areas bounded by shaded lines represent several natural and man-made sources influencing chemical quality of streamflow

A Fresh water from the Floridan and Biscayne carbonate aquifers
B Papermill effluent
C Municipal effluent
D Saline water from the Floridan aquifer
E Phosphate industrial effluent, agricultural run-off and water from gypsum bearing aquifers

Soil Types of Florida

Soil is a thin surficial layer of loose material derived by weathering processes from the rock below. Its character depends on the mineralogy of that rock, and on climate and plant cover. Engineers commonly identify a material as a soil regardless of its organic contents; however, many soil scientists insist that soil must contain at least some organic matter.

Soils in Florida vary locally but are generally sandy, excessively well drained, and low in fertility. The more organic soils are found in areas of low elevation where wetlands occur. Florida's most fertile soils are in upland regions of northern Florida, once an area of thriving plantations, and south of Lake Okeechobee, where sugarcane and winter vegetables are grown.

A modern and widely used soil classification, prepared by the United States Department of Agriculture, is followed on these pages. It uses coined words to identify soil types having differences in degree of development and nature of the various horizons. These are the A (or upper) horizon, consisting of organic matter mixed with rock material; the B horizon (underneath A), which has been enriched by humus, calcium carbonate and iron and/or aluminum oxides carried downward by water from A; and the C horizon (bedrock).

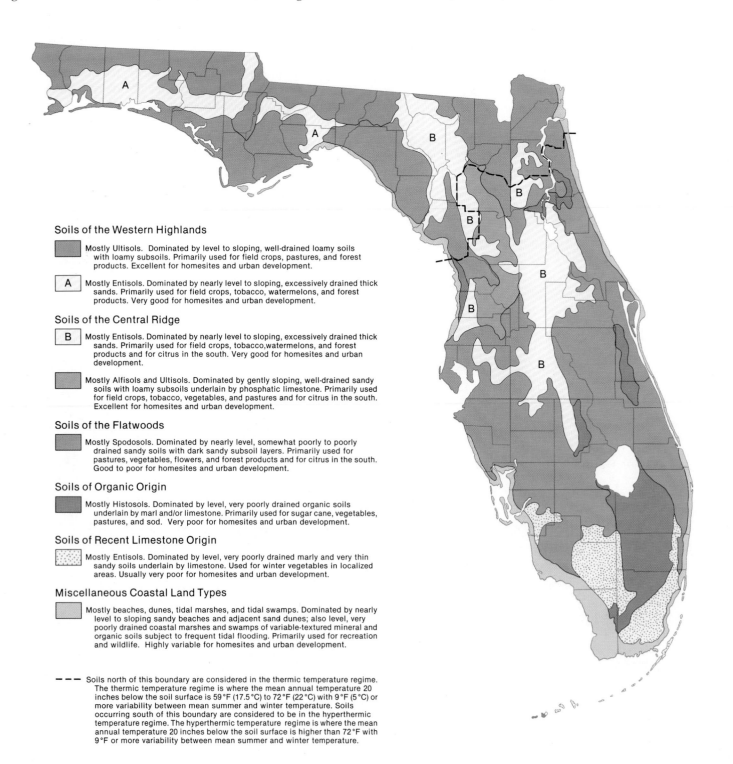

Soils of the Western Highlands

Mostly Ultisols. Dominated by level to sloping, well-drained loamy soils with loamy subsoils. Primarily used for field crops, pastures, and forest products. Excellent for homesites and urban development.

A   Mostly Entisols. Dominated by nearly level to sloping, excessively drained thick sands. Primarily used for field crops, tobacco, watermelons, and forest products. Very good for homesites and urban development.

Soils of the Central Ridge

B   Mostly Entisols. Dominated by nearly level to sloping, excessively drained thick sands. Primarily used for field crops, tobacco,watermelons, and forest products and for citrus in the south. Very good for homesites and urban development.

Mostly Alfisols and Ultisols. Dominated by gently sloping, well-drained sandy soils with loamy subsoils underlain by phosphatic limestone. Primarily used for field crops, tobacco, vegetables, and pastures and for citrus in the south. Excellent for homesites and urban development.

Soils of the Flatwoods

Mostly Spodosols. Dominated by nearly level, somewhat poorly to poorly drained sandy soils with dark sandy subsoil layers. Primarily used for pastures, vegetables, flowers, and forest products and for citrus in the south. Good to poor for homesites and urban development.

Soils of Organic Origin

Mostly Histosols. Dominated by level, very poorly drained organic soils underlain by marl and/or limestone. Primarily used for sugar cane, vegetables, pastures, and sod. Very poor for homesites and urban development.

Soils of Recent Limestone Origin

Mostly Entisols. Dominated by level, very poorly drained marly and very thin sandy soils underlain by limestone. Used for winter vegetables in localized areas. Usually very poor for homesites and urban development.

Miscellaneous Coastal Land Types

Mostly beaches, dunes, tidal marshes, and tidal swamps. Dominated by nearly level to sloping sandy beaches and adjacent sand dunes; also level, very poorly drained coastal marshes and swamps of variable-textured mineral and organic soils subject to frequent tidal flooding. Primarily used for recreation and wildlife. Highly variable for homesites and urban development.

– – –   Soils north of this boundary are considered in the thermic temperature regime. The thermic temperature regime is where the mean annual temperature 20 inches below the soil surface is 59 °F (17.5 °C) to 72 °F (22 °C) with 9 °F (5 °C) or more variability between mean summer and winter temperature. Soils occurring south of this boundary are considered to be in the hyperthermic temperature regime. The hyperthermic temperature regime is where the mean annual temperature 20 inches below the soil surface is higher than 72 °F with 9 °F or more variability between mean summer and winter temperature.

Western Highlands Ultisol

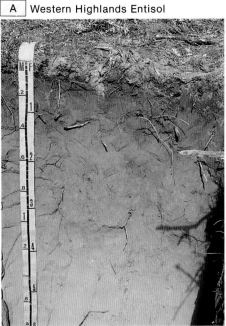

Orangeburg Loamy Fine Sand – uniform red sandy clay loam subsoil.

A Western Highlands Entisol

Lakeland Fine Sand – uniform brownish-yellow sandy subsoil.

B Central Ridge Entisol

Candler Fine Sand – brownish-yellow sandy subsoil.

Central Ridge Alfisol

Zuber Loamy Fine Sand – strong brown sandy clay loam subsoil underlain by gray sandy clay which in turn overlies phosphatic limestone.

Flatwoods Spodosol

Myakka Fine Sand – dark colored sandy horizon that is weakly cemented with organic matter.

Histosol

Pahokee Muck – black well-decomposed organic materials underlain by limestone.

Entisols of Recent Limestone Origin

Perrine Marl – composed primarily of calcium carbonates underlain by limestone.

Florida Ecosystems

An ecosystem consists of a community of coexisting species together with the nonliving parts of their habitat. In a healthy ecosystem these biotic and abiotic components provide a framework through which energy of solar origin is transferred and within which nutrients such as nitrogen and phosphorus circulate. Various kinds of plants, animals, and microorganisms are included in a typical ecosystem such as a particular kind of forest, prairie, swamp, lake, stream, or reef. Florida's natural ecosystems are especially valuable because of the disproportionately large contribution they make globally to biological diversity or "biodiversity." The state was colonized over evolutionary time by a diverse mixture of species from continental areas to the north and tropical Caribbean areas to the south. Semi-isolation by ocean on three sides subsequently contributed to a surprisingly high 8 percent of Florida's vascular plant, fish, amphibian, reptile, bird, and mammal species (and important subspecies) that are found nowhere else in the world, according to the Nature 2000 Task Force (Governor's Office, Tallahassee, 1990). Present-day Florida is considered a global "hot spot" for biodiversity by conservation organizations and by public agencies with strong conservation mandates.

People have been interacting with and modifying Florida's ecosystems for at least 10,000 years. Over most of this time their use of natural resources was sustainable. Their activities did not cause any significant decrease in the ability of the environment to maintain clean air and water, as well as productive, biologically diverse ecosystems. However, the massive human uses of Florida's natural environment in the twentieth century are clearly unsustainable. Deforestation in the north, wetland drainage in the south, agriculture in the center, and creeping urbanization everywhere have caused massive losses of natural ecosystem diversity and productivity. Perhaps the major challenge of the next century is to create an environmentally, as well as economically, sustainable way of living.

The brief summaries that follow describe the major natural ecosystems of Florida and some important ways in which they have been impacted by human activities. The descriptions are based primarily on information obtained from *Ecosystems of Florida* (edited by R.L. Myers and J.J. Ewel, 1990). Other useful descriptions can be found in "Guide to the Natural Communities of Florida" (Florida Natural Areas Inventory and Department of Natural Resources, 1990) and "26 Ecological Communities of Florida" (USDA Soil Conservation Service, 1981). The term *natural* is relative because it may never be possible to know exactly what the major ecosystems of Florida were like at the time of European settlement, before the level of human impacts increased dramatically. The general nature of these ecosystems is, nevertheless, reasonably discernable in the remnants that exist today.

The maps accompanying the descriptions are also taken from Myers and Ewel. Several of these closely follow Davis's 1967 "General Map of Natural Vegetation of Florida." They reconstruct the original location and extent of the major natural terrestrial and wetland ecosystems of the state, even though important portions of most of these ecosystems have been converted to other uses. The maps are a baseline against which to gauge losses due to human impacts over the past several hundred years, as well as a key to where future ecosystem protection and restoration projects might be most profitably located. The best remaining examples of Florida's natural ecosystems are most likely to occur within the boundaries of their original map locations, usually in areas protected and managed at least partly for conservation of their biodiversity.

The collective properties managed by public agencies and private groups, such as national forests, state parks, and private refuges, form a fragmented but extremely important Nature Reserve System of Florida. Enlarging and/or connecting these fragments into a more integrated and comprehensive protected area system is a critically important goal of the next decade but will not by itself suffice to maintain the existing biodiversity of Florida. In addition, human activities in the vicinity of reserves should contribute to protection of biodiversity in the reserves, and Floridians everywhere must live in closer harmony with their natural heritage.

Coastal Ecosystems

TROPICAL CORAL REEFS

SUBSTRATE: Limestone base created by skeletal deposits of dead corals and coralline algae.

TOPOGRAPHY: Bank reefs—three-dimensional, forest-like structures on continental margin seaward of larger islands of the Florida Keys; patch reefs—smaller, roughly circular structures in waters less than 10 meters deep.

VEGETATION/ALGAE: Microscopic algae live symbiotically in outer parts of coral polyps (i.e., coral bodies); calcareous algae also live among the corals and secrete thin layers of limestone; reefs are often closely associated with adjacent sea grass beds.

FAUNA: Over 60 species and subspecies of corals and algae; hundreds of fish and invertebrate species; numerous species of commercial and recreational value, including spiny lobster, grouper, snapper, parrotfish, and butterfly fish. Many reef species have specialized food requirements, narrow niches, and complex life cycles.

PROCESSES/DYNAMICS/ABIOTIC FACTORS: Highly transparent, warm, relatively nutrient-poor waters are favorable; terrestrial vegetation, including mangroves along shoreline, filters sediments, organic debris, and nutrients.

HUMAN IMPACTS: Nutrient pollution is a serious problem, as are impacts from hurricanes, ship groundings, certain fishing practices, and excessive recreational use; as long as nutrient levels remain favorable, communities may have the potential to recover.

Coastal Ecosystems

INSHORE MARINE HABITATS*

SUBSTRATE: Mixtures of sand, silt, clay, and shell fragments.

TOPOGRAPHY: Low-lying, coastal areas, covered by shallow water.

VEGETATION/ALGAE: Submerged sea grass beds are one of the most productive and important habitats of inshore marine systems; these beds are also substrates for epiphytic (attached) algae, an important component of the sea grass food web.

FAUNA: Benthic (bottom) organisms determine to a considerable degree the community that lives in overlying water column; many fish and invertebrate species spend all or part of their life cycle in these habitats; shrimps, blue crabs, and spotted seatrout are examples of especially important recreational and commercial species; oysters are concentrated in inshore areas along the Gulf coast, particularly the Apalachicola estuary.

PROCESSES/DYNAMICS/ABIOTIC FACTORS: Habitats contain sea water diluted by land run off; water temperature, salinity, and dissolved oxygen are important determiners of species diversity and overall ecosystem productivity.

HUMAN IMPACTS: Upland restrictions of freshwater flow; removal of wetlands and grass beds; pollution from industrialization, urbanization, recreation, and agriculture.

*Estuaries, broadly defined

MANGROVES

SUBSTRATE: Waterlogged, anaerobic, brackish sediment deposited by freshwater runoff and tides, and increased by organic matter from mangroves.

TOPOGRAPHY: Low-lying, intertidal zone, with some extensive to irregularly flooded higher fringe areas.

VEGETATION: Three species of true mangroves—red mangrove dominates middle and lower portions of intertidal and upper subtidal zone; black mangrove dominates upper intertidal zone and irregularly flooded higher elevations; white mangrove is found in patches in higher parts of intertidal zone; buttonwood is often on upland fringe; all grow as trees or large shrubs.

FAUNA: Valuable habitat for wide range of invertebrates and vertebrates, including 220 fish and 181 bird species; habitat of endangered American crocodile and Florida manatee.

PROCESSES/DYNAMICS/ABIOTIC FACTORS: Limited by temperature to tropics and subtropics; fluctuations of water level necessary for proper development; salt water excludes potential plant competitors; hurricanes may prevent mangroves from reaching maximum heights.

HUMAN IMPACTS: Thousands of acres have been destroyed and replaced with filled and developed land; can be seriously damaged by oil spills and herbicides; both sport and commercial fisheries decline when mangroves are destroyed.

SALT MARSHES

SUBSTRATE: Brackish, often waterlogged, largely anaerobic, sandy sediment.

TOPOGRAPHY: Relatively flat, intertidal areas on, or sloping up slightly from, permanent water edge.

VEGETATION/ALGAE: Nonwoody, salt-tolerant plants; principal species are smooth cordgrass (on Atlantic side) and black needlerush; above mean high water level are numerous vascular plant species in addition to black needlerush; several hundred species of benthic microalgae and phytoplankton; a few species of large, multicellular seaweeds; occasional mangroves in warmer areas.

FAUNA: Abundant food and cover for resident and transient animals; nursery grounds for many fish and shellfish of commercial and recreational importance; many visiting birds and three exclusive residents—clapper rails, long-billed marsh wrens, and seaside sparrows; endangered Atlantic salt marsh snake.

PROCESSES/DYNAMICS/ABIOTIC FACTORS: Rate of net primary production of organic matter among highest of any global ecosystem; aerial habitat above water dominated by marsh grasses and insect/spider/bird food webs.

HUMAN IMPACTS: Little alteration before 1940s; most extensive impact has been from water impoundment and ditching for mosquito control; dumping of domestic and industrial liquid and solid waste, including dredged materials, is also a serious threat.

DUNES AND MARITIME FORESTS

SUBSTRATE AND TOPOGRAPHY: Sandy, sometimes mixed with calcium carbonate; Linear barrier islands and some other shorelines along coast; sandy capes; typically contain parallel zones of upper beach, undulating foredune, transition or "backdune," and stable dune, sloping upward and away from the water's edge.

VEGETATION: Foredunes contain grasses such as sea oats; a variety of forest vegetation is characteristic of stable dunes: going south from Cape Canaveral on east and from Tampa Bay on west, gradually changes from domination by temperate species to domination by tropical species; at least 22 species of endemic plants are found in dunes and maritime forests.

FAUNA: Beaches are the most important nesting site for loggerhead turtle in Western Hemisphere, as well as for several species of shore birds, including the endangered snowy plover; dunes and forests are wintering grounds for many other bird species and habitat for several special-interest species of small rodents.

PROCESSES/DYNAMICS/ABIOTIC FACTORS: Wind- and wave-driven sand interact with pioneer grasses to build dunes; waves from hurricanes may destroy dunes.

HUMAN IMPACTS: Development of beach front, with greatest impacts near Ft. Walton, Jacksonville, Palm Beach, Ft. Lauderdale, Miami, and Clearwater–St. Petersburg; by 1975 nearly 20% of Florida's barrier islands had been developed; exotic plants such as Australian pine, Brazilian pepper, and sisal are also a serious problem.

Freshwater Wetlands and Aquatic Ecosystems

RIVERS AND SPRINGS

SUBSTRATE: Often sandy but sometimes exposed limestone, silt, or clay.

TOPOGRAPHY/HYDROLOGY: Most rivers and streams slow flowing; some panhandle rivers originate at higher elevations and are faster flowing; most springs are artesian. Of 24 major rivers, 21 flow south or west to the Gulf, 2 flow north and east to the Atlantic, and 1 flows south to Lake Okeechobee.

VEGETATION/ALGAE: At least 130 species of aquatic plants in rivers, streams, and adjacent marshes; numerous planktonic algal species in larger, slow-flowing rivers and various kinds of springs.

FAUNA: Immature stages of many insects and extensive snail and mollusc fauna in rivers; crayfish common in clear, spring-fed rivers; at least 126 native fish species, with greatest number in west; Okaloosa darter, shortnose sturgeon, and West Indian manatee considered endangered.

PROCESSES/DYNAMICS/ABIOTIC FACTORS: Sand-bottom streams are slightly acid and moderately colored; swamp-and-bog streams are very acid and darkly colored; calcareous streams are cool, clear, and alkaline; large rivers carry considerable silt and clay and are always muddy.

HUMAN IMPACTS: Channelization, dredging, diversion, and dam construction; introduction of exotic plant and fish species; removal of groundwater, followed by saltwater intrusion; industrial pollution.

LAKES

SUBSTRATE: Dominantly sandy with beds of clay, phosphatic mudstone, and peat; usually underlain by limestone.

TOPOGRAPHY/HYDROLOGY: Most Florida lakes formed by dissolution of limestone bedrock, subsequent groundwater flow into subterranean caverns, and collapse of surface layers. 7800 lakes greater than 1 acre; most are small, shallow, and in central, sandy ridge part of state; Okeechobee produced by an uplifted sea-floor depression, is by far the largest.

VEGETATION/ALGAE: Density and diversity of microalgal species dependent on trophic level; aquatic plants, macroalgae, mosses, and floating flowering plants particularly important in Florida's numerous shallow lakes.

FAUNA: Molluscs, crustaceans, larval and adult insects common; about 40 species of native fishes.

PROCESSES/DYNAMICS/ABIOTIC FACTORS: Trophic (nutrient) status varies; most lakes are poorly to moderately supplied with nitrogen and phosphorus nutrients and have low to medium densities of microalgae and aquatic plants.

HUMAN IMPACTS: Discharge of nutrients and other pollutants from human activities; siltation from forest clearing; exotic plant species such as water hyacinth and hydrilla clog waterbodies and change their chemical composition; native fish experience competition from 21 established exotic fish species.

SWAMPS

SUBSTRATE: Saturated with water for varying periods each year; amount of organic matter depends on length of saturation, source of water, and fire frequency.

TOPOGRAPHY: Low-lying; along drainages, around lakes, and in small ponds.

VEGETATION: About 100 species of trees, shrubs, and woody vines commonly found; river swamps most diverse and productive; cypress usually dominates in swamps with frequent fires and fluctuating water levels; high frequency of endemic epiphytes in south Florida swamps.

FAUNA: Many invertebrate species; large and diverse fish populations in swamps adjacent to rivers and lakes; many common amphibians and some reptiles depend on swamps for reproduction; considerable diversity of birds and mammals; rare and endangered birds and mammals most likely to occur in cypress swamps and mixed hardwood swamps.

PROCESSES/DYNAMICS/ABIOTIC FACTORS: Annual length of soil saturation, amount of organic matter accumulation in soil, source of water, and fire frequency determine major characteristics of Florida swamps.

HUMAN IMPACTS: Drainage, filling, mining, logging, water pollution, invasion of human-introduced exotic plants such as Melaleuca; in south Florida, alteration of hydroperiod affects swamps rapidly and profoundly.

FRESHWATER MARSHES

SUBSTRATE: Peat in deep-water marshes with long hydroperiods; marl or sandy in marshes with moderate to short hydroperiods and seasonal drying.

TOPOGRAPHY: Low, flat, poorly drained.

VEGETATION: Dominant species are herbaceous plants such as water lily, cattail, maidencane, and pickerelweed; most are of temperate age; the Everglades marsh, which is by far the largest, is dominated by sawgrass.

FAUNA: Abundant animal life but not diverse, except for birds; both temperate and tropical birds abound; habitat for the endangered Cape Sable seaside sparrow, snail kite, and wood stork; the American alligator is an important animal in many Florida marshes; white-tailed deer use freshwater marshes extensively, along with the endangered Florida panther.

PROCESSES/DYNAMICS/ABIOTIC FACTORS: Shallow water at or above the soil surface for much of the year; fire is of crucial importance in limiting invasion of woody vegetation; fire period in deep-water marshes is every 3–5 years; shallow marshes tend to burn on a 1–3 year cycle.

HUMAN IMPACTS: Campaigns to drain wetlands throughout history of Florida following European settlement; between mid-1950s and mid-1970s, 24% of Florida's remaining marshes were drained; many more have been severely altered by unnatural flooding.

Upland Ecosystems

PINE FLATWOODS AND DRY PRAIRIES

SUBSTRATE: Relatively poorly drained, acidic, sandy soils.

TOPOGRAPHY: Low, flat

VEGETATION: Pine flatwoods—overstory of longleaf, slash, or pond pine dominates; shrub understory contains species such as saw palmetto, wax myrtle, gallberry, and wiregrass. Dry prairies—similar to pine flatwoods but lacking pine overstory.

FAUNA: Diverse birds, mammals, reptiles, and amphibians are found in pine flatwoods, e.g., eastern diamondback rattlesnake, threatened red-cockaded woodpecker, white-tailed deer, threatened Florida black bear, endangered Florida panther. Dry prairies are primary habitat of threatened crested caracara and threatened sandhill crane.

PROCESSES/DYNAMICS/ABIOTIC FACTORS: Natural fires tend to maintain relatively stable stands of pine flatwoods and dry prairies.

HUMAN IMPACTS: Flatwoods and dry prairies combine to produce the most extensive type of major terrestrial ecosystem in Florida; they are now being converted to many uses, including agriculture, pasture for livestock, and urbanization; alteration of natural fire regimes can cause major changes in species composition, even when not accompanied by land-use conversions.

SCRUB AND HIGH PINE

SUBSTRATE: Droughty, sandy, low-fertility soils.

TOPOGRAPHY: Hilly uplands.

VEGETATION: Scrub—shrubby evergreen oaks and/or Florida rosemary; may have a sand pine or slash pine overstory; contains 13 federally listed endangered or threatened plant species. High pine—longleaf pine interspersed with deciduous oaks, especially turkey oak, with an herbaceous layer usually dominated by wiregrass.

FAUNA: Scrub—several thousand species of arthropods; threatened Florida scrub jay, Florida scrub lizard, threatened sand and blue-tailed mole skinks, gopher tortoise, threatened Florida black bear, white-tailed deer, bobcat, gray fox, spotted skunk, raccoon. High pine—many broadly distributed vertebrates; endangered red-cockaded woodpecker, bobwhite quail, Sherman's fox squirrel, gopher tortoise.

PROCESSES/DYNAMICS/ABIOTIC FACTORS: Scrub—dependent on infrequent, high-intensity fires. High pine—dependent on frequent, low-intensity fires.

HUMAN IMPACTS: Scrub—ecosystem rare, even prior to European settlement; after earlier losses to agriculture, now threatened primarily by real estate development. High pine—6.5 billion board feet of virgin longleaf pine removed in Florida in late 1800s and early 1900s; does not regenerate well; very few good examples of old growth longleaf pine remain.

TEMPERATE HARDWOOD FORESTS
"HAMMOCKS"

SUBSTRATE: Soils generally contain more organic matter and moisture than adjacent, well-drained sandy soils.

TOPOGRAPHY: On slopes between upland pinelands and lake margins or floodplain forests and marshes; also in some uplands protected from fire.

VEGETATION: In typically narrow bands; varies from warm temperate, mixed deciduous-evergreen flora (e.g., oaks, hickories, beech, magnolia) in north to subtropical evergreen flora in south; many species of trees but few species of herbs, except for diverse ferns in peninsular hammocks; hammocks on the Apalachicola Bluffs contain *Torreya taxifolia*, a tree on the verge of extinction, as well as other endemic plant species.

FAUNA: Diversity of vertebrates, including bobcat, gray fox, white-tailed deer, southern flying squirrel, Mississippi kite, barred owl, pileated woodpecker, eastern diamondback rattlesnake.

PROCESSES/DYNAMICS/ABIOTIC FACTORS: Continually being modified by changing and variable environment; combinations of species in some hardwood forests were not present before European settlement.

HUMAN IMPACTS: Amount of land in hammocks has changed little over past 200 years but composition of plant species has been affected by human disturbance; increasingly threatened by residential/commercial development, e.g., around Gainesville and Tallahassee.

SOUTH FLORIDA ROCKLAND

SUBSTRATE: Shallow soils over outcroppings of limestone; subtropical to tropical hardwood hammock soils are largely organic.

TOPOGRAPHY: Uplands.

VEGETATION: Hammocks—forests of evergreen, broad-leaved trees typical of Bahamas and Greater Antilles; many tropical epiphytes; more than 150 species of trees and shrubs native to hammocks of Dade, Monroe, and Collier counties. Pine forests—dominated by south Florida variety of slash pine; diverse understory of mostly tropical shrubs, as well as many endemic herbs.

FAUNA: Vertebrates, except for birds, of temperate origin and derived largely from southeastern U.S. fauna; West Indian land birds, such as mangrove cuckoos, butterflies, and land snails are widespread in tropical hammocks of Florida Keys; endangered Schaus butterfly and smallest white-tailed deer in U.S.

PROCESSES/DYNAMICS/ABIOTIC FACTORS: Pine forests occur in areas with permanent, fresh groundwater; fire required for maintenance of pine forests; some hammock trees such as gumbo limbo and mahogany also appear to require openings from fire or other disturbances in order to regenerate.

HUMAN IMPACTS: Habitats rapidly shrinking from urban development; many earlier hammocks and pinelands cleared by logging or for agriculture; exotic plants such as Brazilian pepper are major threat; exotic tropical vertebrates increasing rapidly and spreading geographically.

Wildlife Habitats

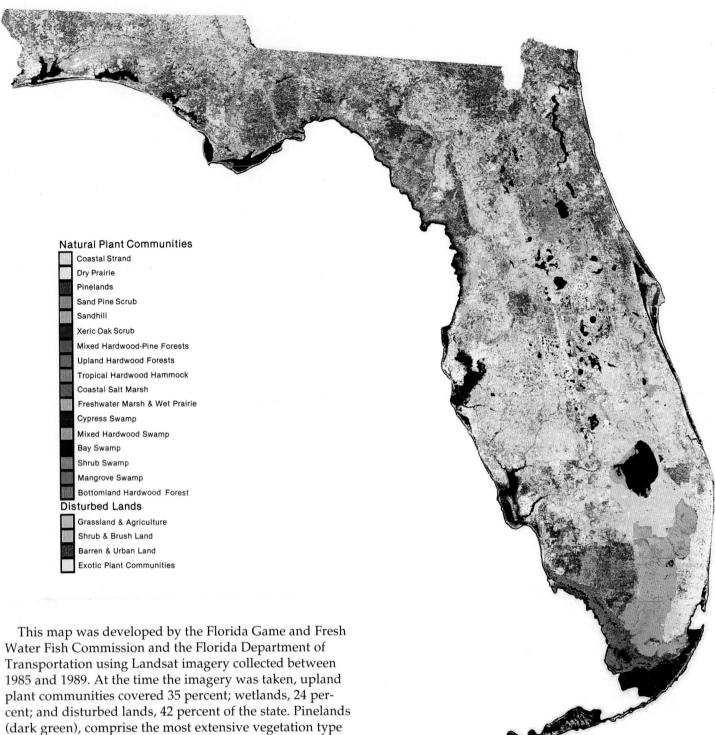

Natural Plant Communities
- Coastal Strand
- Dry Prairie
- Pinelands
- Sand Pine Scrub
- Sandhill
- Xeric Oak Scrub
- Mixed Hardwood-Pine Forests
- Upland Hardwood Forests
- Tropical Hardwood Hammock
- Coastal Salt Marsh
- Freshwater Marsh & Wet Prairie
- Cypress Swamp
- Mixed Hardwood Swamp
- Bay Swamp
- Shrub Swamp
- Mangrove Swamp
- Bottomland Hardwood Forest

Disturbed Lands
- Grassland & Agriculture
- Shrub & Brush Land
- Barren & Urban Land
- Exotic Plant Communities

This map was developed by the Florida Game and Fresh Water Fish Commission and the Florida Department of Transportation using Landsat imagery collected between 1985 and 1989. At the time the imagery was taken, upland plant communities covered 35 percent; wetlands, 24 percent; and disturbed lands, 42 percent of the state. Pinelands (dark green), comprise the most extensive vegetation type accounting for 19 percent of the land area. Grasslands and agriculture (yellow) are the second most abundant cover type accounting for 18 percent of the land area. The least abundant (0.04 percent) cover type is coastal strand (dark pink), dominated by herbaceous plants growing on sand dunes and inhabited by numerous rare plants and animals.

The orange spot in the center of the state represents the sand pine scrub forests in the Ocala National Forest. The extensive patch of blue-green at the tip of the peninsula represents the sawgrass marshes and wet prairies of the Florida Everglades. The dark red areas to the west of the Everglades are the cypress swamps of the Big Cypress National Preserve. The olive green areas along the extreme southwestern coast are the mangrove swamps of the Ten Thousand Islands region. The bright red specks just northwest of Lake Okeechobee are the few remaining patches of Florida's rare scrub communities, home to many endangered plants and animals. The bright pink slivers running north-south in the panhandle are bottomland hardwood forests. Florida's many bays, lagoons, and lakes appear in black. The large patches of white are Florida's urban centers. Very obvious is development along the southeast coast, around Tampa Bay and Charlotte Harbor, and in the vicinities of Orlando, Jacksonville, and Pensacola.

Apalachicola River Valley

Formed by the confluence of the Chattahoochee and Flint rivers at the Florida-Georgia line, the Apalachicola is the largest river in the state in terms of discharge. Although the Apalachicola is only 106 miles long, the Chattahoochee extends 400 miles into the mountains of north Georgia. Each winter, the Apalachicola overflows its banks and deposits silt in a floodplain up to 4.5 miles wide. Over time, the repeated floods have resulted in a rich soil that supports a diverse forest community dominated by bottomland hardwoods, represented by the bright pink strip on the map. In the lower third of the river the bottomland hardwoods give way to mixed hardwood swamps (tan). At the mouth of the river, the mixed hardwood swamps give way to a freshwater marsh community (blue-green).

The Apalachicola River and its tributaries are home to many rare species of plants and animals found nowhere else in Florida. During the Ice Ages when glaciers covered vast areas of the northern U.S., many species moved south along the river corridor to escape the cold. After the climate warmed and the glaciers retreated, some species remained in the steephead ravines and bluffs along the northern end of the river. The river empties into Apalachicola Bay, an estuary formed by St. Vincent, St. George, and Dog islands. The tremendous volume of freshwater and nutrients mixing with the salty waters of the Gulf of Mexico creates ideal conditions for the growth of oysters.

The Everglades

The remaining portions of the Florida Everglades are represented by the large patch of blue-green. Originally an uninterrupted stretch of marshes extended from Lake Okeechobee to Florida Bay. Massive drainage projects in the first half of the 1900s converted 65 percent of the famous "river of grass" to agricultural and urban uses. The remaining portions have been vastly altered by hydrologic changes and water pollution. Within the remaining Everglades, tree islands can be seen as scattered patches of blue. The light brown patches in the northern portions of the Everglades are shrub swamps, indicators of the drier conditions resulting from drainage.

West of the Everglades on slightly higher ground is the Big Cypress Swamp. Clearly visible are the cypress swamps (dark red), wet hardwood forests (blue), and wet prairies (blue-green). Also present are pine forests (scattered green dots). The narrow strip of tan running north-south in the western half of the area is Fakahatchee Strand, a lush subtropical hardwood swamp. A network of roads is visible in the cypress swamps to the west. Here thousands of lots were sold to northerners during the 1940s and 50s. Southwest of the Everglades and Big Cypress Swamp is the most extensive area of mangroves (olive green) in North America. To the east, the heavily urbanized areas (white) of Miami, Ft. Lauderdale, and West Palm Beach are clearly visible. The urbanizing areas of Cape Coral, Ft. Myers, and Naples appear along the west coast.

Amphibians and Reptiles

Florida has nearly 170 species of reptiles and amphibians classified in thirty-one families. This high number of species is the result of great diversity in climate (both temperature and rainfall), complexity and range of habitats, and geologic history of the state including sea level changes and temperature fluctuations.

Among the smallest amphibians found in the state are the oak toad and some tree frogs, which reach a maximum size of one to one and one-fourth inches. With the exception of sea turtles, which breed on Florida beaches, the alligator snapping turtle is the largest reptile, occasionally exceeding 100–150 pounds in weight and three feet in length. Of the six species of dangerously poisonous snakes present in Florida, the pygmy rattlesnake accounts for approximately 20 percent of the 300–400 poisonous snakebites each year in Florida. Luckily, the bites from this and other venomous Florida snakes are seldom fatal, and typically result in no more than one fatality annually.

Oak Toad
Bufo quercicus

Blind Salamander
Haideotriton wallacei

Pig Frog
Rana grylio

Southern Dusky Salamander
Desmognathus auriculatus

Squirrel Tree Frog
Hyla squirella

Spotted Newt
Notophthalmus perstriatus

Little Grass Frog
Limnaoedus ocularis

Dwarf Siren
Pseudobranchus striatus

American Alligator
Alligator mississippiensis

Florida Softshell Turtle
Trionyx ferox

Green Anole
Anolis carolinensis

Coral Snake
Micrurus fulvius

Alligator Snapping Turtle
Macroclemys temmincki

Eastern Indigo Snake
Drymarchon corais

Atlantic Loggerhead Turtle
Caretta caretta

Shaded area shows
nesting range.

Eastern Diamondback Rattlesnake
Crotalus adamanteus

Gopher Tortoise
Gopherus polyphemus

Pygmy Rattlesnake
Sistrurus miliarius

Fishes

In Florida there are well over 200 native species of freshwater fish representing twenty-five families. Over 95 percent of the species are members of six families: Cyprinidae (minnows), Centrarchidae (sunfish and bass), Ictaluridae (catfish), Catostomidae (suckers), Cyprinidontidae (killifish), and Percidae (darters). These species range in size from less than an inch to four or five feet.

Much of the observed species diversity can be attributed to the wide variety of freshwater habitats present in the state. Because of the relatively short time fish have had to colonize the new lakes and streams that remained after the last sea level decline, far fewer species of freshwater fish are found south of the Suwannee River than in the northern and western portions of the state.

Saltwater species have not been included although large numbers of them regularly invade Florida's fresh waters. Florida also has approximately eighteen species of established exotic freshwater fish, which are not depicted either. These fish are becoming an increasingly serious problem, particularly in the southern part of the state, where they are successfully competing with native species.

Flagfish
Jordanella floridae

Spotted Sunfish "Stumpknocker"
Lepomis punctatus

Florida Gar
Lepisosteus platyrhincus

Bluefin Killifish
Lucania goodei

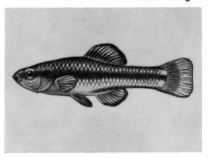

Spotted Bullhead
Ictalurus serracanthus

Brown Darter
Etheostoma edwini

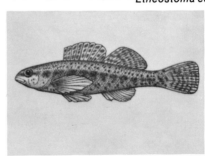

Seminole Killifish
Fundulus seminolis

Sailfin Shiner
Notropis hypselopterus

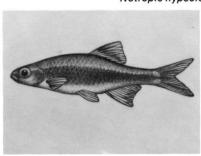

Birds

Florida has a tremendous variety of bird species. Only two other states in the United States, Texas and California, can boast bird populations as heterogeneous as Florida's. Diversity of habitats, from coastal marshes and beaches to dense pine and hardwood forests, combines with the state's location along primary bird migration routes to produce this exceptionally rich variety of avifauna. Over 425 species—approximately half of all bird species in the United States—may be observed in Florida if migratory species that pass through the state to and from wintering grounds are counted. New species such as the cattle egret, first sighted near Lake Okeechobee in 1952, occasionally become established by natural means. In addition, Florida's climate is conducive to the survival of nonnative species that escape or are released from captivity. The official state bird, the mockingbird, is abundant and widely distributed throughout the United States, with the exception of the Pacific Northwest.

Limpkin
Aramus guarauna

Chuck-Wills-Widow
Caprimulgus carolinensis

Brown Pelican
Pelecanus occidentalis

Florida Burrowing Owl
Athene cunicularia floridana

Florida Grackle
Quiscalus quiscula

Louisiana Heron
Egretta tricolor

Black Vulture
Coragypus atratus

Anhinga
Anhinga anhinga

Mammals

The mammals of Florida are represented by approximately eighty native species. Nearly two-thirds of these forms are terrestrial, while the remaining one-third are aquatic. A very wide variability within species is characteristic of many Florida mammals. Some of the reasons for this include the great north-south expanse of the state and the associated range of temperatures, the historic fluctuations in sea level which have alternately isolated and rejoined populations of mammals, the extensive freshwater resources of Florida, and variety of shallow water coastal ecosystems. An example of a mammal showing wide variation is the old-field mouse, which is quite different in coat color and body shape throughout its range from the Panhandle through south central sections of the state. The present range of the armadillo in Florida is the result of both a natural extension eastward of a Louisiana population and northward movement of an escaped population that became established in central Florida in the 1930s.

Southeastern Pocket Gopher
Geomys pinetis

Florida Water Rat
Neofiber alleni

Old-field Mouse
Peromyscus polionotus

River Otter
Lutra canadensis

Florida Weasel
Mustela frenata

Marsh Rabbit
Sylvilagus palustris

Nine-banded Armadillo
Dasypus novemcinctus

Bobcat
Lynx rufus

Endangered Species

Endangered species are organisms in danger of extinction if factors causing the decrease in their populations or distributions continue. These forms are characterized by critically low populations or by their unique presence in habitats that have been or currently are being reduced in size or degraded in quality. The greatest danger in most cases is not that every individual of a species will be killed, but that population density will decline to a level below which reproduction is adversely affected. This condition ensures the eventual disappearance of a species. As in other areas of the United States, rapid development and extensive habitat manipulation in Florida have been largely responsible for the decline of certain species. In some cases, however, minor modifications to development plans can prevent localized extinction.

The animals shown on this page have been selected from the endangered fauna list issued by the Florida Game and Fresh Water Fish Commission. Failure to select a species should not be interpreted as a statement on its relative importance. This list currently contains over 100 species.

Three fish are considered endangered in Florida: the Okaloosa darter, the blackmouth shiner, and the shortnosed sturgeon. Six reptiles are endangered, including the American crocodile, the Atlantic ridley, and the Atlantic green turtle, whose breeding areas have been severely affected by human development. Of the twenty-one endangered mammals in the state, twelve are endemic to Florida. Nine species of birds in Florida are designated as endangered.

Historic Range
Present Range

Wood Stork
Mycteria americana

American Crocodile
Crocodylus acutus

Florida (Scrub) Jay
Aphelocoma coerulescens

Okaloosa Darter
Etheostoma okaloosae

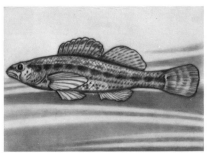

Manatee
Trichechus manatus

Everglade Kite
Rostrhamus sociabilis

Florida Panther
Felis concolor

HISTORY AND CULTURE

When Ponce de León sighted Florida in the early spring of 1513, his presence in what he thought of as a new land had been preceded by thousands of years of Indian occupancy. At least 100,000 Indians were living there. Those in the north were agriculturalists, while most of those in the south lived off the natural bounty of land and sea. The Indians in the north shared many features with other Indians of the Southeast, including settlement in villages, chief-centered political organization, and elaborate burial rituals.

The First Spanish Period, 1513–1763

By 1500 Spain had achieved political unification. The final reconquest of Spain from the Moors occurred in 1492, the very year Columbus reached the West Indies. Its nobles, their military and crusading goals within Spain accomplished, were now seeking new realms to conquer. For Ponce de León and the leaders who followed him to the coasts of Florida—Ayllón, Narváez, de Soto, de Luna, and others—the search for wealth and the fascination of uncharted lands led them and their men to the limits of human endurance. At the beginning of de Soto's march inland from Tampa Bay, when a long procession of

mounted knights, foot soldiers, and servants set forth, major Spanish colonial activity in Florida might have seemed assured, but this was not to be; the fortunes in gold and silver that Cortés and Pizarro encountered in Mexico and Peru were not to be found in *la Florida*.

The failure to find riches dampened Spanish interest in Florida, but French efforts to establish a colony, first under Jean Ribault at Port Royal Sound in present-day South Carolina in 1562, then under René de Laudonnière at the mouth of the St. Johns River in 1564, forced the Spanish emperor Philip II to act. Pedro Menéndez de Avilés, Captain General of the Spanish Treasure Fleets, was dispatched to eliminate the French presence and to found a Spanish settlement. Both charges were quickly accomplished in 1565 and the resulting settlement, San Augustín, was to be the primary Spanish settlement in Florida in the following 200 years.

Missionary activity began with the founding of St. Augustine. The first mission field was extended northward along the coast of present-day Georgia and South Carolina, and in the 1600s a second mission chain was established westward as far as the Apalachee Bay region. By 1710, however, virtually all of these thatch-roofed, wattle-and-daub missions had been destroyed by English-led Indian attacks launched from the new English colony of Carolina.

Spain valued Florida for its location. Spanish Florida together with Cuba commanded the vital sea route from the Gulf of Mexico and helped shelter Mexico from potential rival European colonial expansion. Few Spanish colonists came to Florida. Throughout the two centuries of Spanish rule the colony depended on government subsidy. By 1763, when Florida was yielded to Britain in the treaty ending the Seven Years' War, the population of St. Augustine was only about 3,000, that of Pensacola under 800. War, disease, and forced or voluntary migrations out of Florida had virtually eliminated the original Indian tribes in the colony.

British Rule, 1763–1783

Among the first acts of Florida's new rulers was a proclamation creating the two separate colonies of East and West Florida, each with its own seat of government, at St. Augustine and Pensacola respectively. The western boundary of the new colony of West Florida was fixed at the Mississippi River.

With the Spanish and the Indians gone, the British had essentially an empty territory. To encourage settlement, two types of land grants were made: large allotments not requiring homesteading by the recipient and smaller parcels to heads of families stipulating settlement for confirmation of title. A number of plantations based on slave labor and growing primarily indigo and rice appeared especially along the St. Johns River and adjacent coastal areas in East Florida. Creek Indians from Georgia and present-day Alabama filtered into the vacant interior of northern Florida, and began to be called Seminoles.

The Second Spanish Period, 1784–1821

The defeat of Britain by the combination of American, French, and Spanish forces brought Spain back to East and West Florida by the peace treaty of 1783. In the ensuing thirty-five years, however, continuing decline of Spanish power and increasing numbers of Americans north of Florida progressively eroded the viability of the two colonies. By 1819, the western boundary of Spanish political control in West Florida had retracted eastward to the Perdido River.

During the second Spanish term in Florida, additional land grants were made, mainly in northeastern East Florida and contiguous to Pensacola Bay. Sugarcane plantings began in northeastern Florida. Creek Indians continued to move into Florida. American incursions across the border in search of runaway slaves increased, as did attacks on Indians thought to be sheltering slaves. Recognizing its inability to control increasing turbulence in its colonies, Spain ceded East and West Florida to the United States in 1819 with transfer being finalized in 1821.

Territory and Early Statehood, 1821–1876

Andrew Jackson, nominated by President Monroe and confirmed by the Senate as first governor of the two colonies acquired from Spain, organized a single Territory of Florida with two counties, Escambia and St. Johns. The new legislative council met at Pensacola, the old capital of West Florida, in 1822 and at St. Augustine, the former capital of East Florida, in 1823. These two chief settlements

of the new territory were separated by 400 miles of virtual wilderness, rendering desirable a more central site for a capital. Tallahassee was accordingly founded in 1824 midway between the two older settlements, and the territorial council met there for the first time late in that year.

Settlement in the territorial period occurred primarily in the area between the Suwannee and Apalachicola rivers, in what became known as Middle Florida. A government land survey, which had to precede the sale of public lands to settlers, was initiated at Tallahassee in 1824 with the demarcation there of the east-west baseline and north-south meridian from which the rectangular township and range survey system was then extended. Meanwhile, settlement in East Florida and in the Pensacola area was slowed by unclear land titles associated with grants made by previous regimes. Moreover, much of northern peninsular Florida was occupied by Indians until the end of the Second Seminole War (1835–42).

As cotton production expanded westward from the Atlantic seaboard, it largely bypassed Florida, but some planters with their slaves did move into extreme northern Middle Florida in the territorial and early statehood period and an east-west plantation belt centered in Leon County developed along a zone of comparatively fertile loamy soils. One of the earliest railroads in the United States, from Tallahassee to St. Marks, was built to expedite the export of cotton to the textile mills of England and New England.

With the end of the Second Seminole War the peninsula southward to the Kissimmee valley was opened for settlement. Land title problems in northeast Florida and the Pensacola area were also gradually resolved. Except in the specialized plantation districts, the first wave of frontier settlement generally consisted of woods ranchers who came with their tough, wiry cattle. These cattlemen, gradually displaced over much of northern Florida by small farmers, continued to drift southward into the peninsula. The new small farms, which were forest-girt clearings with patches of corn, sweet potatoes, cotton, and a bit of sugarcane for syrup, became common by 1850. Plantations producing long-staple Sea Island cotton and sugarcane increased in the St. Johns River country, and an isolated sugarcane plantation district emerged along the Manatee River. Apalachicola flourished on the export of Georgia and Alabama cotton. After 1855 railroad construction became significant in northern Florida. Remote from all these changes, a unique amphibious economy involving fishing, turtling, sponging, salt making and shipwreck salvaging developed on the Keys and in the shallow tropical seas enveloping them. Key West, with an 1860 population of over 2,800, was one of the two largest cities in Florida; the other was Pensacola.

In 1850 approximately 50 percent of Florida's population was white, but in plantation areas, the black population outnumbered the white. After the Seminole wars the few remaining Seminoles melted into the hammocks of the Everglades. In the twentieth century their descendents have become politically active and have revitalized traditional Seminole culture.

Florida, along with the rest of the South, emerged from the Civil War with a virtually bankrupt economy. Coastal settlements had been raided and heavily damaged and much railroad and other equipment was inoperative. Railroad companies had defaulted on their bond obligations. Plantation organization, disrupted by emancipation, was replaced with sharecropping.

Sales of cotton and timber gradually alleviated to some extent the state's straitened economic conditions. Cotton again flowed to mills in England and New England. Florida already had a long history of timber cutting, but the scale of operations to supply markets in Europe and the American Northeast now increased dramatically. By the 1870s hundreds of ships cleared Pensacola, Jacksonville, Fernandina, and other ports each year with cargoes of pine, cypress, and oak timber.

New Directions, 1876–1900

As Reconstruction years receded into the past, new currents in the Florida economy became perceptible. In its characteristics and its leadership the new economy was to depart increasingly from that of the antebellum era. Whereas the plantation owners had been the social, political, and economic leaders of an agrarian state, the new leaders were to come into Florida from other areas, chiefly the North, bringing with them capital for transportation, land speculation, tourism, mining, finance and other business enterprises. Although accelerating changes came to Florida in the final decades of the nineteenth century, they did not at first produce wholesale changes in the landscapes of the state. Many attributes of earlier Florida survived beyond 1880, in some cases well into the twentieth century. Not only the old cotton plantation belt of northern Florida but other areas into which cotton production had spread, such as Alachua County, continued to grow the traditional crop until the end of the century and beyond. In 1880, unfenced or open-range grazing of cattle prevailed over a huge area extending from the vicinity of St. Augustine southward and southwestward to the Gulf coast. Florida had all the attributes of open-range ranching in the Old West, including the roundup, branding, corrals, the long drive along cattle trails, and the cow town of Ft. Myers, where cattle changed hands before shipment to Cuba. Frederic Remington, artist of the Old West, came to Florida to capture scenes from this phase of old Florida.

The steamboat, which had appeared on Florida rivers earlier in the century, not only survived into the later nineteenth century, but actually reached its greatest use in these years. Steamboats hauled local passengers and freight, and their river trips to new hotels and scenic springs such as Silver Springs contributed to the initial development of a tourist industry in the state. We can at least glimpse this feature of a now vanished Florida through the lines of Sidney Lanier describing his trip up the Oklawaha River: "As we advanced up the stream our wee craft even seemed to emit her steam in more leisurely whiffs..." As the river narrowed he wrote: "The lucent current lost all semblance of water. It was simply a distillation of many-shaded foliages, smoothly sweeping along beneath us." And as night came: "The stream, which had been all day a baldrick of beauty, sometimes black and sometimes green, now became a black band of mystery. But presently a brilliant flame flares out overhead: they have lighted the pine-knots on top of the pilot house."

After 1880, railroad construction was implemented by the sale of 4 million acres of state-owned land at twenty-five cents per acre to Hamilton Disston, a Philadelphia entrepreneur and speculator, thereby providing the state with funds to clear liens on state-owned land acreages incurred from earlier railroad promotion. The combination of new state land grants to railroad companies to underwrite construction costs and a new group of railroad developers led by rivals Henry Plant and Henry Flagler resulted in rapid, and at times feverish, extension of lines southward on the peninsula. During the first few years of the new railroad building period, new lines connected existing settlements, but soon the rails were pushed southward faster than the pace of settlement. Thereafter, at Tampa, Palm Beach, and Miami, as in much of the western United States, settlement followed the railroads. Completed railroads encouraged the beginning of rapid population growth in southern Florida.

In other ways the face of Florida also began to change. Citrus production increased and advanced southward down the central sandy and hilly axis of the peninsula toward the Orlando area. As the Florida railway system finally became effectively linked with the larger national rail system in the 1880s, winter fruit and vegetable production in the more nearly tropical parts of Florida began. Lumbering spread outward along new railroad lines. Mining of phosphate began. Improvements in Florida port facilities, especially at Tampa, followed the congestion and confusion during the Spanish-American War. Cigar making, which had been introduced earlier at Key West by Cubans, followed Vincente Ybor to Tampa. Sponging developed out of Tarpon Springs.

As the twentieth century began, Jacksonville with a population over 28,000 had become the largest city in Florida. Pensacola and Key West each had somewhat over 17,000 and Tampa had almost 16,000.

The Twentieth Century

In the twentieth century Florida's population and economy have grown rapidly. In the nineteenth century the state's relative rates of population and economic growth had been high, but only because the starting base for measurement had been so small; in absolute growth Florida lagged behind many other parts of the United States. In the present century, however, and particularly since midcentury, Florida's absolute increases in population and in economy have ranked among the highest in the nation.

Although many factors have contributed to the dynamism of Florida's growth in population and economy in the present century, of fundamental significance has been the state's almost tropical peninsula that is politically part of a large, wealthy country of some 250 million people whose territory lies predominantly in middle latitudes where climates tend toward prolonged winter cold. Florida's middle latitude connections underlie in particular three major aspects of its twentieth century economy: retirement, tourism, and much of its agriculture. In the present century, Florida has become the retirement home of millions of Americans. Tourism, from its small beginnings in the latter nineteenth century, has expanded enormously. Although it was Florida beaches, lakes, and landscapes that were at first prized by winter visitors seeking respite from winter cold, the subsequent addition of other tourist-related attractions such as Disney World now brings domestic and foreign visitors year-round. And major segments of Florida's twentieth century agriculture produce subtropical crops for the nation's wealthy middle latitude markets. Citrus plantings, particularly after exceptional freezes in the 1890s decimated groves in the original citrus area in northeast Florida, continued to extend southward on the peninsula. Production of out-of-season fruits and particularly vegetables expanded for the large and wealthy wintertime market in the North. Sugarcane preempted much of the new agricultural area that was developed south of Lake Okeechobee.

Other twentieth century changes in Florida's economy have also effected major alteration in Florida life and landscapes. Cotton production ended because of a complex of factors including the boll weevil and was replaced by a more diversified agriculture of soybeans, corn, and hay crops, and by forest. Some of the old cotton belt plantations were acquired as long-range investments by northern capital and became forested quail plantations. Open-range cattle grazing ended toward midcentury as cattle tick fever and screwworm fly infestations were eradicated and as cattlemen acquired and fenced land, replaced native range with planted pastures, and introduced superior livestock strains. These changes made possible a new form of livestock ranching linked for the first time to an American rather than a Cuban market. New types of manufacturing appeared, including large pulp and paper mills, chemical plants and light aircraft, whereas certain earlier industries such as cigar manufacture declined. Military reservations such as Eglin Air Force Base became significant in the state's economy. Steamboat traffic disappeared. Rail passenger travel earlier increased, then almost disappeared in the face of new highways and air travel, leaving the railroads primarily as freight carriers. The largest-scale phosphate mining in the country appeared in part of Polk and Hillsborough counties, and came to dominate outbound cargoes at the port of Tampa. After midcentury the space complex in Brevard County anchored the eastern end of a belt of higher population density which developed across central Florida.

By the opening years of the twentieth century, the Everglades were regarded as a barrier to further settlement and their drainage was urged. Programs of drainage beginning in 1906 drastically modified the hydrology of inland south Florida, and new agricultural developments on the deep organic soils south of Lake Okeechobee became possible. But as people moved into the interior of south Florida, they encountered an environment quite different from anything they had previously experienced. Costs in life and fortune were high, as in the hurricanes of 1926 and 1928. Engineering works were undertaken to deal with the perceived excess of water in the region, but more recently potential long-run deficiencies in south Florida's water supply have begun to be recognized. Problems of sound land and water management in south Florida remain unsolved.

Florida's population had been concentrated in the northern end of the state, but in the twentieth century the earlier pattern was fundamentally altered as population concentrations shifted to the central and southern parts of the peninsula. Population moving into southern Florida became essentially coastal, being channeled onto the slightly elevated Atlantic coastal ridge and along the Gulf coast and away from the interior wetlands. Urban sprawl developed. The search for jobs in urbanized southern Florida attracted black people as well as whites southward, producing inner city black ghettos with accompanying economic and social problems, particularly in Miami. A persistent theme in Florida's history, the relationship with Cuba, was again manifested in the second half of the twentieth century with the large Cuban refugee influx into the Miami area, heightening the Hispanic character of what has become Florida's largest urban complex. Indeed, viewed in broader perspective, population has been converging on southern Florida from both North America and Latin America.

When President Monroe appointed Jackson to organize the Territory of Florida in 1821, he implied that among other expected improvements, smuggling would henceforth be contained. By the latter twentieth century, however, the scale of smuggling into Florida far surpassed the operations of smugglers in Jackson's day. The location of Florida relative to Latin America, and its long coastline, have encouraged the routing through Florida of much of the drugs smuggled into the United States.

Florida in the twentieth century has had its own population explosion. Residences built for retirees range from spacious homes to sprawling mobile home parks. But among those who migrated to the state were individuals possessing wealth and an interest in the arts; and their museums, theatres, concert halls, libraries, and homes that now grace its cities display an exceptional diversity of architectural styles. In its display of examples of new approaches to architecture and urban design, Florida has become an outstanding part of the United States. Examples, visible in all parts of the state, range from the newly designed Florida panhandle town of Seaside to the curving building in Orlando housing the World Headquarters of the Turbine Division of Westinghouse and to the new Caribbean Marketplace in Miami, which in 1991 received the prestigious American Institute of Architects award.

The in-migration of many younger persons responding to rapidly expanding employment opportunities, particularly in service occupations, created enormous pressures in turn for still more services, including an expansion in the system of public and private universities and colleges. But the very pace and scale of population growth threaten to destroy much of Florida's beauty and to impair irreparably the ecology upon which its well-being depends. Excessive drainage of wetlands, construction of miles of artificial waterfront, hazardous waste discharges, and unplanned urban sprawl are manifestations of population growth outrunning orderly, careful accommodation to the special qualities of the Florida environment. By 1990 thirteen million Floridians had a far less stable relationship with the environment than had the Indians of Ponce de León's time.

Early Maps of Florida

The 1584 Ortelius Map—This map entitled "Florida" first appeared as a page of the 1584 edition of Abraham Ortelius's atlas of the world. Ortelius was a cartographer and publisher who lived in Antwerp. This map, which was actually drawn in Spain by Geronimo de Chaves, is regarded as one of the most important early maps of the southeastern part of North America. It was widely copied until the eighteenth century. The map contains the names of thirty-four capes, bays, and rivers, and twenty-two Indian settlements. Names appearing along the coastline were derived from other Spanish maps published earlier in the century, whereas interior details are similar to those first appearing on a sketch map drawn by a member of the de Soto expedition. The map as well as the Le Moyne map on this page show that in the sixteenth century Florida was conceived to be essentially all of southeastern North America.

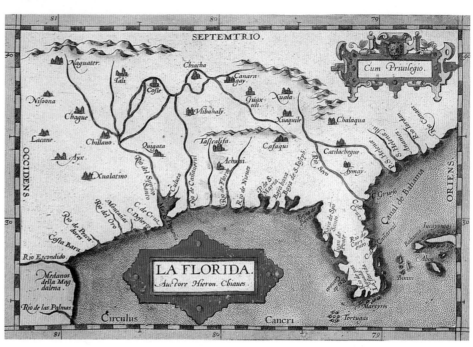

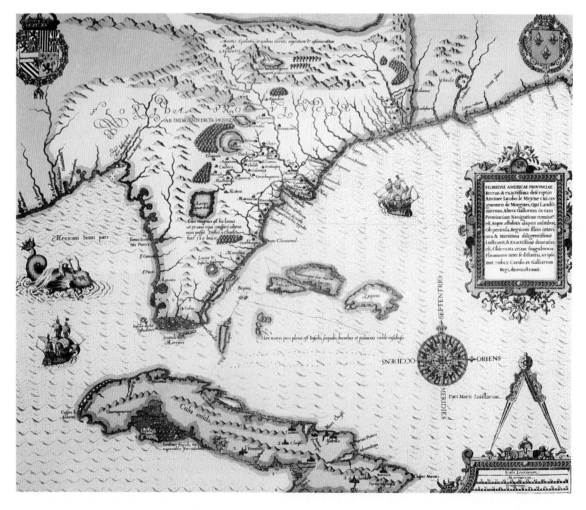

The 1591 Le Moyne Map—Jacques Le Moyne de Morgues was an artist who traveled with René de Laudonnière in his attempt in 1564 to found a French colony at the mouth of the St. Johns River. During the short time that Le Moyne was in Florida he produced striking pictures of Indian life and Florida scenery as well as this map and a narrative. Le Moyne's coastal details in the vicinity of the St. Johns River (called the "May" River on his map) are relatively good, but north of the St. Johns his coastline curves much too far to the east. Le Moyne used Latin coastal names previously given by Ribault on his first voyage to America; an example is "Portus Regalis" for Port Royal. He also used a few coastal names of Spanish origin. Le Moyne's largest lake in the Florida peninsula may refer to Lake George. The waterfall he shows pouring into a lake in the "Montes Apalatci" may depict Indian references to Niagara Falls. Le Moyne's map was eventually published at Frankfurt in 1591 by Theodore de Bry in a volume entitled *Florida*.

The 1764 Bellin Map—Jacques Nicolas Bellin became Royal Hydrographer of France at the height of his career. He produced many maps and published a five-volume work entitled *Petit Atlas Français* in 1763. The following year he published 581 maps in a new edition of his atlas, which he retitled *Petit Atlas Maritime*. This map was also published in that year.

The map is in general fairly accurate for the former French colonial area at the mouth of the Mississippi River, but is highly inaccurate for the Florida peninsula. St. Augustine and St. Marc d'Apalache, the old Spanish fort at St. Marks, are on the map, as is Lake Okeechobee as Lac du St. Esprit. The St. Johns River (Riv. de St. Juan) is shown as extending completely across the Florida peninsula, and Dog Island (I. des Chiens) is shown as including St. George Island. The coast at Boca Raton was inscribed as "Bouche de Ratones."

The 1847 Mitchell Map—Samuel Augustus Mitchell was a geographer, cartographer, and publisher of geographical works in Philadelphia. He produced a series of atlases between 1839 and 1866. This map of Florida is from his *Universal Atlas* of 1847.

The map reflects the generally more accurate knowledge of northern Florida at that time compared with southern Florida. The shape of the peninsula as mapped displays many errors, such as at Tampa Bay. The large counties in the thinly populated sections of the peninsula contrast markedly with the smaller counties of northern Florida. At the time this map was drawn, some of the information incorporated into it was out of date.

Prehistoric Indians

The first Indians to enter the Florida peninsula around 12,000 B.C. were not explorers, adventurers, or settlers, but nomads following the big game animals upon which their survival depended. Sea level was lower and rainfall less plentiful than today. Mastodons, camels, mammoths, bison, and horses roamed vast grasslands in search of food and fresh water. Indians spread throughout the peninsula and into the Keys. Big game animals gradually became extinct, probably as a result of a wetter climate with forests replacing grasslands and overexploitation by human hunters. Food sources shifted to small game and shellfish.

Populations increased and some groups moved inland to areas more suitable for growing corn, beans, squash, and other crops. Different styles of pottery decoration became unique to certain regions. Some groups began burying their dead along with elaborate pottery and other goods in earthen mounds. By A.D. 1000 the Mississippian culture, originating farther north and eventually including much of the Southeast, extended into Florida. Today the only evidence of these first Floridians is contained in those remaining archeological sites that represent dozens of distinctive Indian cultures.

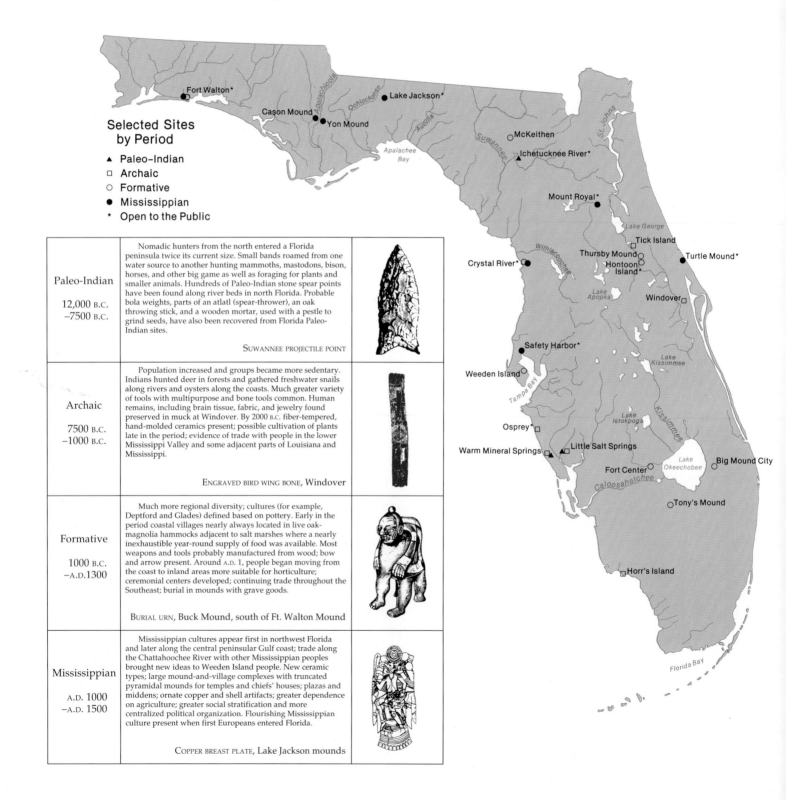

Selected Sites by Period

▲ Paleo-Indian
□ Archaic
○ Formative
● Mississippian
* Open to the Public

Period	Description	Artifact
Paleo-Indian 12,000 B.C. –7500 B.C.	Nomadic hunters from the north entered a Florida peninsula twice its current size. Small bands roamed from one water source to another hunting mammoths, mastodons, bison, horses, and other big game as well as foraging for plants and smaller animals. Hundreds of Paleo-Indian stone spear points have been found along river beds in north Florida. Probable bola weights, parts of an atlatl (spear-thrower), an oak throwing stick, and a wooden mortar, used with a pestle to grind seeds, have also been recovered from Florida Paleo-Indian sites. SUWANNEE PROJECTILE POINT	
Archaic 7500 B.C. –1000 B.C.	Population increased and groups became more sedentary. Indians hunted deer in forests and gathered freshwater snails along rivers and oysters along the coasts. Much greater variety of tools with multipurpose and bone tools common. Human remains, including brain tissue, fabric, and jewelry found preserved in muck at Windover. By 2000 B.C. fiber-tempered, hand-molded ceramics present; possible cultivation of plants late in the period; evidence of trade with people in the lower Mississippi Valley and some adjacent parts of Louisiana and Mississippi. ENGRAVED BIRD WING BONE, Windover	
Formative 1000 B.C. –A.D.1300	Much more regional diversity; cultures (for example, Deptford and Glades) defined based on pottery. Early in the period coastal villages nearly always located in live oak-magnolia hammocks adjacent to salt marshes where a nearly inexhaustible year-round supply of food was available. Most weapons and tools probably manufactured from wood; bow and arrow present. Around A.D. 1, people began moving from the coast to inland areas more suitable for horticulture; ceremonial centers developed; continuing trade throughout the Southeast; burial in mounds with grave goods. BURIAL URN, Buck Mound, south of Ft. Walton Mound	
Mississippian A.D. 1000 –A.D. 1500	Mississippian cultures appear first in northwest Florida and later along the central peninsular Gulf coast; trade along the Chattahoochee River with other Mississippian peoples brought new ideas to Weeden Island people. New ceramic types; large mound-and-village complexes with truncated pyramidal mounds for temples and chiefs' houses; plazas and middens; ornate copper and shell artifacts; greater dependence on agriculture; greater social stratification and more centralized political organization. Flourishing Mississippian culture present when first Europeans entered Florida. COPPER BREAST PLATE, Lake Jackson mounds	

Tribal Areas at Time of European Contact

At the time of European contact most Florida Indians were members of five groups: the Timucua, Apalachee, Ais, Tekesta, and Calusa. Those in the north were agriculturalists—growing corn, beans, and squash—while most of those in the south lived off the natural bounty of the land and the sea. Florida, then as now, was a fisherman's paradise.

Some early Florida environments were better suited to Indian habitation than others. Locations with a source of fresh water, high dry ground, comfortable microclimate, and near reliable food sources were preferred. The coastal strand and pine flatwoods were not as densely settled as areas along rivers, estuaries, lagoons, and hardwood hammocks; but, nearly all environments offered at least some important resources. For agriculturalists, fertile soils were necessary; for hunters and gatherers, fresh and brackish bodies of water supplied steady sources of shellfish, bony fish, small game, and plant foods.

Estimates of Florida's aboriginal population range from 100,000 to 900,000, a population figure not reached again in Florida until 1920. Higher estimates are based on evidence that European diseases began decimating the Florida Indian population shortly after the arrival of Columbus in Hispaniola. Old World pathogens quickly made their way through the Southeast via Native American trade routes. Smallpox, measles, influenza, even the common cold, were all deadly to the Indians.

Florida Indians were victims of Spanish slave raids at least as early as 1520. When Pánfilo de Narváez landed in the Tampa Bay area in 1528, the Indians were found to have "many boxes of merchandise from Castilla." The Spaniards also "found samples of gold," which the Indians told them came from the province of Apalachee to the north. The Indians encountered by Narváez were the Tocobaga, a group of small chiefdoms whose leaders waged frequent war against each other.

From the Tocobaga, Narváez and his expedition moved northward in search of gold through swampy unpopulated flatwoods until they reached the Apalachee in the vicinity of present-day Tallahassee. The Apalachee "loomed big and naked and from a distance looked like giants. They were handsomely proportioned, lean, agile, and strong." Eleven years later one of de Soto's men remarked on the abundance of corn and other food in all the Apalachee villages.

Neighboring the Apalachee to the east were the Timucua, composed of at least fifteen separate tribes sharing a common language. More is known about the Saturiwa—encountered by the French in 1562 and immortalized in the drawings of Le Moyne—than any other Timucuan group. Each village had its own chief who was under the jurisdiction of a head chief who exacted tribute.

Less is known about the Indians in the southern portion of the state. The best known group is the Calusa, whose vast domain was ruled by a single chief. Although lacking agriculture, the Calusa developed elaborate political, social, and trade networks. They were also expert wood carvers, and the many ceremonial items recovered from a Calusa site on Key Marco display great artistic skill. The most complex prehistoric culture in south Florida may not have been along the coast but in the Lake Okeechobee basin. These people not only had a sophisticated political and social organization, but they also grew corn. Striking similarities between their form of maize horticulture and that originating in the savannas of northern South America have led to the suggestion that the southern part of Florida was populated by people migrating from South America through the Antilles.

STORING THEIR CROPS IN THE PUBLIC GRANARY. Engraving by Jacques Le Moyne de Morgues who accompanied René de Laudonnière to Florida in 1564.

Early Spanish Exploration

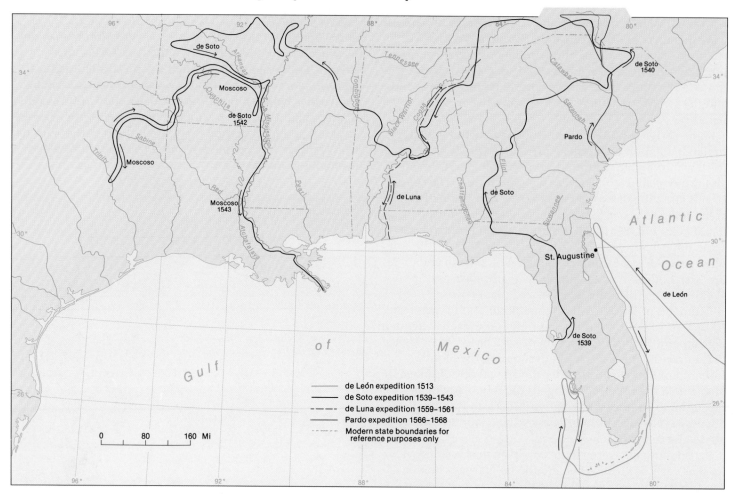

de León expedition 1513
de Soto expedition 1539–1543
de Luna expedition 1559–1561
Pardo expedition 1566–1568
Modern state boundaries for reference purposes only

Routes of Spanish Treasure Fleets

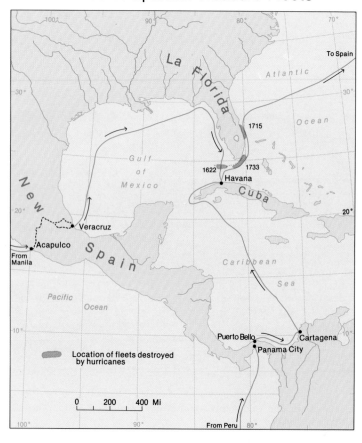

Location of fleets destroyed by hurricanes

Once the Spanish colonial empire had expanded into the West Indies following the voyages of Columbus, an interest arose in what might lie beyond. In response, the Spanish monarchy sponsored a series of expeditions to discover, explore, settle and exploit unknown lands north of Cuba. In 1512 the king of Spain gave Juan Ponce de León a patent to "discover and govern the island of Bimini and its people." On April 2 of the following year Ponce encountered, not Bimini, but the coast of an unknown land and, going ashore during the ensuing week, claimed his discovery for the Spanish crown. As it was the Easter season, *Pascua Florida* in Spanish, he named the land "La Florida." Subsequently he sailed southward around Florida and into the Gulf, but although he had also discovered the Straits of Florida, he did not attempt to found a settlement.

Over the next fifty years the Spanish reached Florida repeatedly, but they were to underestimate grossly the requirements for founding a permanent settlement there. Ponce himself died leading a second expedition to Florida in 1521, this time to colonize the new land. Upon landing he was mortally wounded in an Indian attack and the expedition returned to Cuba. In 1528 Pánfilo de Narváez and a company of 400 landed in Florida to establish a colony; eight years later only four survivors finally reached Mexico on foot.

The largest and most famous of the sixteenth century Spanish expeditions into the mainland of North America north of Cuba was that of Hernando de Soto. Many attempts have been made to plot the long and complex expedition route. The most comprehensive attempt was that of the U.S. de Soto Expedition Commission established by a congressional resolution in 1935. During the half century since the publication of that major effort in 1939, much new information has become available, including that from modern archaeology, allowing Hudson and associates to plot a new version of the de Soto route. This revised route appears on page 86.

De Soto and a force of some 600 disembarked from nine vessels near the mouth of the Little Manatee River on September 25, 1539, and began a march that took them into virtually every present state in the Southeast. They went through relatively densely populated, strong and socially cohesive Indian chiefdoms such as the chiefdom of Coosa in northern Georgia, and through uninhabited "no-man's-land" between chiefdoms. Indian reactions ranged from friendship to hostility. The social impact of the expedition on the Indians was often harsh and even brutal. The expedition brought European diseases to which Indians had no immunity.

Upon the death of de Soto early in 1542 in southeastern Arkansas, Luis de Moscoso took command and a plan was formulated to march overland to Mexico. In the vicinity of the Trinity River, however, this plan was abrogated in the face of apparent declining Indian food supplies toward the southwest and the meeting with fundamentally different Indian languages which the expedition's Indian interpreters could not understand. The expedition returned to the Mississippi River, constructed a fleet of boats during the winter of 1542–43, and eventually reached Mexico by water. Of the original force of six hundred, 311 survived.

Some twenty years after de Soto another abortive attempt at mainland colonization was made, this time by Tristán de Luna through Pensacola Bay and then through the interior of Alabama and Georgia. Two further expeditions were lead by Juan Pardo; the first of these is also shown on the map of explorations.

The failure of the de Luna effort following fifty years of other fruitless colonization ventures appears to have discouraged the Spanish monarchy's colonial ambitions in La Florida, but this flagging interest was jolted abruptly in 1564 by news that the French had erected a fort at the mouth of the St. Johns River. The French move was prompted by colonial ambition and by the potential for attacking Spanish treasure fleets. Spain's response to this unwelcome news was swift and violent. The esteemed military leader Pedro Menéndez de Avilés was dispatched to establish a settlement on Florida's east coast and to eliminate the French presence. Menéndez in 1565 largely wiped out the French (although a few of them, including Jacques Le Moyne, the artist and mapmaker, escaped), and established St. Augustine. Spanish objectives at St. Augustine were primarily political and military. The new settlement served as an outer bastion of the Spanish empire, and it helped to protect Spanish treasure fleets from French and other corsairs.

The meteoric rise in Spanish merchant shipping for transporting silver and other valued cargoes from Mexico and Andean South America back to Spain understandably attracted corsairs, particularly at first the French, whose attacks became progressively more frequent. The Spanish response was the convoy, called *flota* (fleet) in which ten to fifty or more merchant vessels were accompanied by warships.

The lower map on page 86 shows the approximate average routes followed by the two separate *flotas* or treasure fleets as they converged on Havana, one from Puerto Bello in Panama via Cartagena, the other from Veracruz. After 1565 the Veracruz convoy also carried oriental goods which reached Mexico via the trans-Pacific "Manila galleons." Upon leaving Havana the two treasure fleets, now sailing together, headed northward through the Straits of Florida and then northeastward past Bermuda. This route enabled ships to benefit from the westerlies of higher latitudes and from the Gulf Stream, both of which were well known before the middle of the sixteenth century. Moreover, along this route St. Augustine could assist in treasure fleet defense.

THE FIRST CHRISTMAS MASS IN AMERICA, the de Soto expedition, painted by Claribel Jett

The Spanish Mission Period

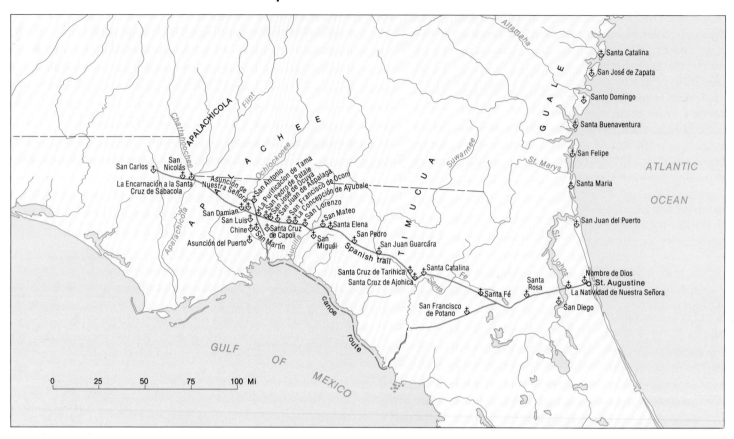

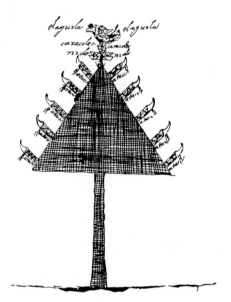

APALACHEE BALL GAME POST AND LEGENDS. The ball game continued after missionization. John Hann records San Luis friar Father Paiva's description of the event as "a barbarous game, that only people lacking the knowledge of God could play. It has to be [played] at midday or at two in the afternoon, and, in the summer. . . . It is to eleven strikes with the ball that they fire at the pole. And it must be with the foot. . . . If it remains on the pole it is worth two. . . . a leading man throws the ball in the midst of all of them. . . . And they fall upon one another at full tilt. And the last to arrive climb up over their bodies, using them as stairs. Others [step on] their faces, heads, or bellies, as they encounter them, taking no notice [of them] and aiming kicks without any concern . . . . while in other places still others pull at arms or legs with no concern as to whether they may be dislocated or not . . . .When this pileup begins to become untangled, they are accustomed to find four or five stretched out like tuna."

Missions in Florida, as in all of Spanish America, had political, economic, and cultural, as well as religious functions. They were a buffer against the English to the north and the French to the west. The relatively fertile fields of the Indians—particularly the Apalachee—yielded food sorely needed by the inhabitants of St. Augustine. The Spaniards, few in number compared with the Indians, used Indian labor for construction of their fortifications in St. Augustine. Friars instructed the Indians in Spanish, crafts, and livestock and farming techniques as well as religion, and attempted to alter those aspects of the Indians' social, sexual, and religious life, such as polygyny and sorcery, contrary to the laws of the Catholic Church. The Spanish recognized—and took advantage of—the Indian political organization of chiefs and subchiefs. Special recognition was accorded in mission communities to chiefs and their families as well as to talented ballgame players and medicine men.

The mission period in Florida did not leave any great architectural monuments characteristic of missions in Spanish America and the southwestern United States. Friars would erect a cross at an existing village with a principal chief and leave instructions for building a church. Mission buildings were wattle and daub. Roofs were thatched with palm or palmetto, making the buildings extremely susceptible to destruction by fire.

The first group to attempt to missionize the Indians were the Jesuits. Their efforts, begun in 1566, ended in complete failure six years later. The Franciscans arrived in 1573. Missions were established among the Eastern Timucua and the Guale Indians along the southern Georgia coast. Despite the deaths of four priests and one lay brother at the hands of the Guale Indians in September 1597, apparently over a friar's attempt to deprive the heir to a major chieftainship of his rights to succession unless he gave up polygyny, the Franciscans remained.

In 1606 the first mission was established among the Western Timucua at Potano. All Timucua towns had been brought under mission control by 1633, and the Spanish began to expand into Apalachee territory. Neither the Timucua nor the Apalachee completely accepted Spanish control. Rebellions occurred in Apalachee territory in 1647 and in both Timucuan and Apalachee territory in 1656, largely over exploitation of the Indians as laborers. The revolts were extinguished with such extreme cruelty that six priests left the area in protest. Epidemics also occurred among the Indians, killing thousands between 1649 and 1659. The Bishop of Santiago de Cuba, Gabriel Díaz Vara Calderón, visited Florida in 1674, traveling to thirty-two

missions and counting 13,152 Christian Indians.

In 1680 the English and their Indian allies began a series of attacks and slave raids on Florida's aboriginal population. With less than 100 English soldiers and 1,500 Indians, Colonel James Moore from Carolina attacked St. Augustine in 1702, leaving all the coastal missions in ruins. In the winter of 1703–04 Moore attacked the province of Apalachee. Dissatisfied with steadily increasing demands on their time, labor, and resources, at least two Apalachee villages surrendered to English-led invaders without a fight. Mission villages, satellite settlements, and several Spanish ranches were reduced to ashes. Florida's mission population dispersed to English Carolina, St. Augustine, and Pensacola and Mobile. By 1763, when the last of Florida's southern Indians went to Cuba with the Spanish, there were virtually no members of Florida's original Indian population left in Florida.

EXCAVATION OF THE CONVENT, SAN LUIS DE TALIMALI. From 1656 until its destruction in 1704, San Luis was the military, religious, and administrative center of the mission system among the Apalachee Indians. Occupying a commanding hill 2 miles west of the present state capitol complex in Tallahassee, San Luis was the home of the deputy governor for Apalachee. San Luis's population was estimated to be 1,400 in 1675. The San Luis complex contained an Apalachee village, a church, a convent for the friars, a cemetery, a council house, a ballfield, and a blockhouse where the deputy governor resided. The council house was among the largest known Indian buildings in the Southeast (118 ft. in diameter) and was capable of accommodating 2,000–3,000

persons. San Luis's elaborate fort was not built until the late 1600s in response to the growing English threat.

In 1983 the site of San Luis was purchased by the State of Florida and opened to the public in 1985. The Secretary of State, Division of Historic Resources, is responsible for developing the 50-acre property as a historic and archaeological site. Excavations have been conducted at the church complex and Spanish village as well as at the council house. In 1991 excavation of the Apalachee village began. San Luis is opened to the public every day of the year except Thanksgiving and Christmas. Each year in October Rediscover San Luis is held during which seventeenth-century colonial lifeways and crafts are recreated.

Historical Boundaries of Florida

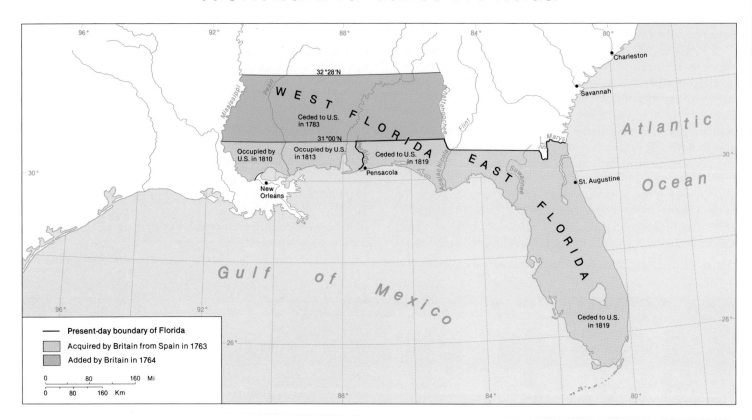

Florida, to Spanish explorers and mapmakers, included most of the southeastern part of the present-day United States (Ortelius map, p. 82). The first agreement to limit Florida came with the Treaty of Paris in 1763 when Britain acquired Florida from Spain. The new owner issued a proclamation creating two Floridas: West Florida, between the Mississippi and Chattahoochee-Apalachicola rivers and south of lat. 31° N excluding the Isle of Orleans; and East Florida, between the Apalachicola River and the Atlantic Ocean and south of a line drawn from the confluence of the Chattahoochee and Flint rivers to the headwaters of the St. Marys River and then continuing along its course to the Atlantic Ocean. By British Royal Charter in 1764, West Florida was expanded northward to lat. 32° 28' N. When

Spain reacquired Florida in 1783, this area was excluded, reestablishing the 1763 boundary. Florida was again reduced in size in 1795 when Spain designated the Perdido River as its western limit.

In 1803 the United States purchased the Louisiana Territory from France. Although no reference was made to East and West Florida, the United States inferred the new territory included the area between the Mississippi and Perdido rivers. Spain ceded all rights to its territories east of the Mississippi River to the United States by treaty in 1819. This legitimized U.S. ownership of the occupied areas and formalized the area of present-day Florida. In 1821 the area east of the Perdido River became the Territory of Florida, which in turn became a state in 1845.

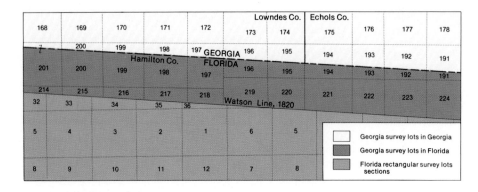

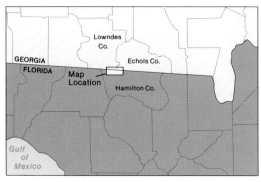

Boundary adjustments between Florida and its neighboring states after 1819 were necessary owing to early surveying errors and omissions. The most significant dispute was over the location of the Georgia-Florida boundary, which had not been fully surveyed. An eventual result of the dispute was that land surveyed as Georgia lots and subse-

quently settled, following earlier independent Georgia surveys of the Florida-Georgia boundary, was transferred to Florida in 1872. In 1970, Florida's seaward boundary with Georgia was formalized by the U.S., extending the border from the mouth of the St. Marys River to the seaward limit of Florida's jurisdiction.

Systems of Land Tenure

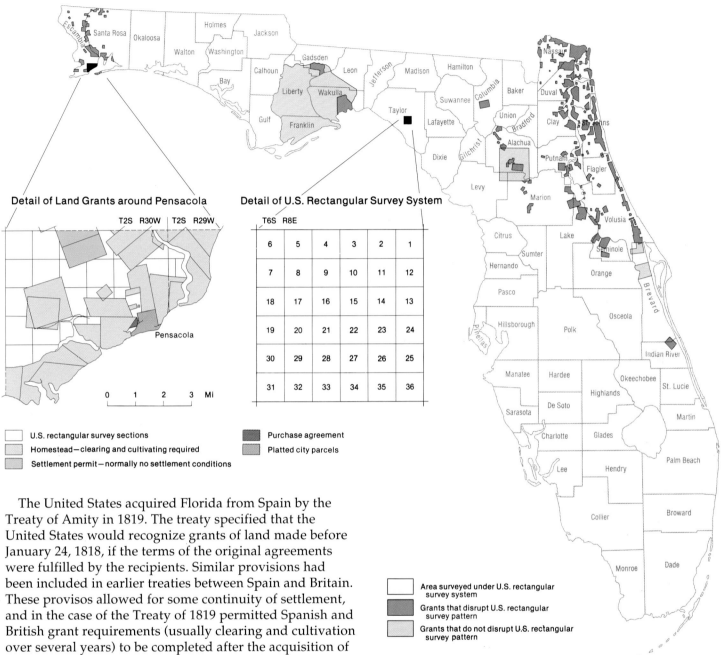

Detail of Land Grants around Pensacola

T2S R30W | T2S R29W

Pensacola

0 1 2 3 Mi

Detail of U.S. Rectangular Survey System

T6S R8E

6	5	4	3	2	1
7	8	9	10	11	12
18	17	16	15	14	13
19	20	21	22	23	24
30	29	28	27	26	25
31	32	33	34	35	36

☐ U.S. rectangular survey sections
☐ Homestead—clearing and cultivating required
☐ Settlement permit—normally no settlement conditions

■ Purchase agreement
☐ Platted city parcels

☐ Area surveyed under U.S. rectangular survey system
■ Grants that disrupt U.S. rectangular survey pattern
☐ Grants that do not disrupt U.S. rectangular survey pattern

The United States acquired Florida from Spain by the Treaty of Amity in 1819. The treaty specified that the United States would recognize grants of land made before January 24, 1818, if the terms of the original agreements were fulfilled by the recipients. Similar provisions had been included in earlier treaties between Spain and Britain. These provisos allowed for some continuity of settlement, and in the case of the Treaty of 1819 permitted Spanish and British grant requirements (usually clearing and cultivation over several years) to be completed after the acquisition of Florida by the United States. The above map shows most of the more significant land grants and purchases confirmed by the United States. Very large tracts were usually outright grants or purchases with no homesteading, whereas ownership of smaller parcels usually required the completion of homestead requirements. The Forbes purchase, the largest single tract (approximately 1,250,000 acres), encompassed much of present-day Franklin, Liberty, Gadsden, Leon, and Wakulla counties. Most of the homestead-type grants to Spanish settlers ranged in size from 50 to 100 hectares (approximately 125 to 250 acres). Much smaller tracts of land were in the form of platted city lots in both Pensacola and St. Augustine; these were usually sold at auctions.

For the most part the land grants in Florida do not conform to the United States rectangular survey system, which was used to divide Florida's vast unsurveyed areas into smaller tracts for sale and settlement. This system,

presently referred to as the Township and Range survey, was a series of six-mile squares divided into thirty-six one-mile-square (640-acre) sections (see inset drawing). These sections were then subdividable into smaller tracts.

The smaller-scale map of Pensacola shows how the grants interrupted the more orderly Township and Range survey system. In many instances the grants themselves overlapped.

Present-day land record maps continue to reflect Spanish and British grant boundaries, and it is not uncommon for a new landowner to find his property being referred to in the deed as part of one of the early land grants.

The Seminole Wars

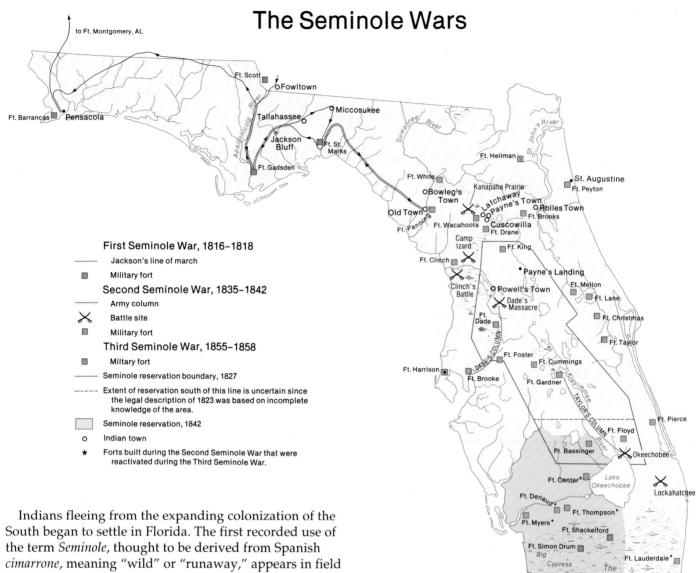

First Seminole War, 1816–1818

————— Jackson's line of march

▪ Military fort

Second Seminole War, 1835–1842

————— Army column

✕ Battle site

▪ Military fort

Third Seminole War, 1855–1858

▪ Miltary fort

————— Seminole reservation boundary, 1827

- - - - - Extent of reservation south of this line is uncertain since the legal description of 1823 was based on incomplete knowledge of the area.

▨ Seminole reservation, 1842

○ Indian town

★ Forts built during the Second Seminole War that were reactivated during the Third Seminole War.

Indians fleeing from the expanding colonization of the South began to settle in Florida. The first recorded use of the term *Seminole*, thought to be derived from Spanish *cimarrone*, meaning "wild" or "runaway," appears in field notes accompanying de Brahm's 1765 map of Florida. By 1800 the Seminoles were prospering, raising cattle and growing crops. Permanent towns had been established from the Apalachicola River to the St. Johns River and from south Georgia to the Caloosahatchee River. In 1814, after their defeat by Andrew Jackson at the Battle of Horseshoe Bend, members of the Red Stick faction of the Upper Creeks joined the Seminoles.

The treaty following the Battle of Horseshoe Bend opened 20 million acres of Creek land for U.S. settlement. Responding to reports of violence between the new white settlers and the Indians, 300 men from Ft. Scott burned the Indian and Black community of Fowltown on November 21, 1817. The Indians retaliated by firing on a barge of soldiers. On December 26, 1817, Andrew Jackson, known to the Indians as the Sharp Knife, invaded Seminole territory, killing Indians and burning their houses. Largely as a result of Jackson's foray, Florida was acquired by the U.S. in 1819.

The Treaty of Payne's Landing signed by a small number of Seminoles in May 1832 required the Indians to give up their Florida lands within three years and move west. When the U.S. Army arrived in 1835 to enforce the treaty, the Indians were ready and the Second Seminole War began. As Major Francis Dade marched from Ft. Brooke toward Ft. King, 180 warriors led by Micanopy, Alligator,

and Jumper attacked. Only one man, Ransome Clarke, of the detachment of 108, survived.

The Second Seminole War was fought guerrilla style in swamps and hammocks and was extremely costly in American lives and wealth. The Indian leader Osceola was captured under a white flag of truce on October 20, 1837. When the war gradually ended in 1842, several hundred Seminoles were shipped to Oklahoma, while others escaped into the Everglades. In 1849 a white man fishing on the Indian River was killed by a group of Indians. Forts were reactivated, and warfare again broke out. Constant military patrols and rewards for the capture of Indians reduced the Seminole population to 100–300 when the Third Seminole War ended in 1858.

Early Settlements

When Spain transferred Florida to Britain by the Treaty of Paris in 1763, the area contained few significant settlements. The mission chain established across northern Florida by the Spanish had been virtually eradicated, along with the associated Indian villages. Most of the remaining Spanish settlements were on the coastline or along the banks of major rivers. The British founded few permanent settlements during their short tenure of ownership. During the Second Spanish Period (1783–1819), Spain was more concerned with maintaining its territory in the New World in the face of challenges by France and Britain than in establishing permanent settlements.

Increased settlement began in northern Florida during the Territorial Period (1821–1845), when farmers from Alabama, Georgia, and the Carolinas, as well as merchants from New England and New York, migrated to Florida. Small commercial towns arose along the Gulf coast as outlets for agricultural products, especially cotton, from the interior of Florida, Georgia, and Alabama. Expansion of settlement into the southern interior of Florida was stimulated by the Seminole Wars and the resultant Armed Occupation Act of 1842, which provided for homesteading of 160-acre tracts on 200,000 acres south of the more heavily settled areas of northern Florida.

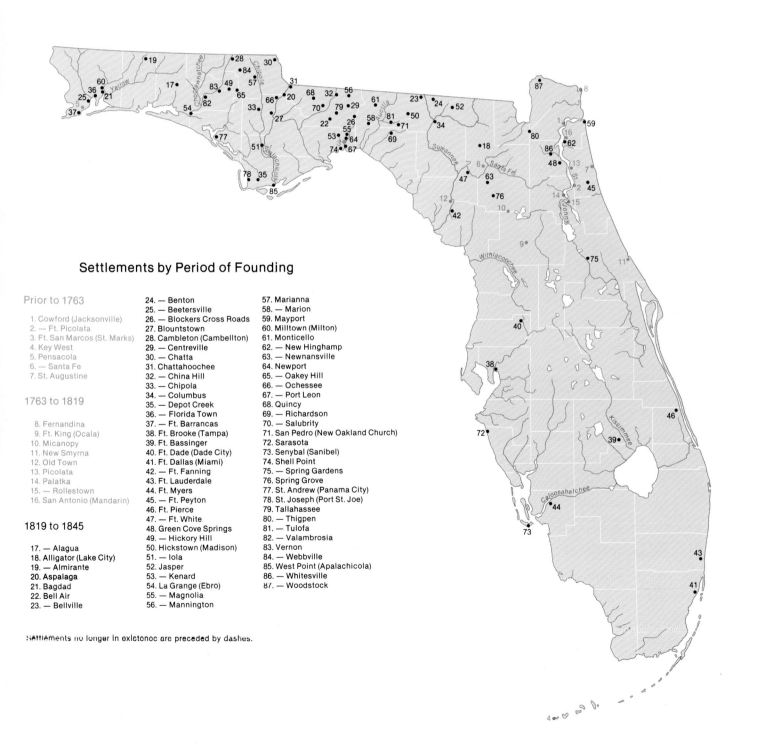

Settlements by Period of Founding

Prior to 1763

1. Cowford (Jacksonville)
2. — Ft. Picolata
3. Ft. San Marcos (St. Marks)
4. Key West
5. Pensacola
6. — Santa Fe
7. St. Augustine

1763 to 1819

8. Fernandina
9. Ft. King (Ocala)
10. Micanopy
11. New Smyrna
12. Old Town
13. Picolata
14. Palatka
15. — Rollestown
16. San Antonio (Mandarin)

1819 to 1845

17. — Alagua
18. Alligator (Lake City)
19. — Almirante
20. Aspalaga
21. Bagdad
22. Bell Air
23. — Bellville

24. — Benton
25. — Beetersville
26. — Blockers Cross Roads
27. Blountstown
28. Cambleton (Cambellton)
29. — Centreville
30. — Chatta
31. Chattahoochee
32. — China Hill
33. — Chipola
34. — Columbus
35. — Depot Creek
36. — Florida Town
37. — Ft. Barrancas
38. Ft. Brooke (Tampa)
39. Ft. Bassinger
40. Ft. Dade (Dade City)
41. Ft. Dallas (Miami)
42. — Ft. Fanning
43. Ft. Lauderdale
44. Ft. Myers
45. — Ft. Peyton
46. Ft. Pierce
47. — Ft. White
48. Green Cove Springs
49. — Hickory Hill
50. Hickstown (Madison)
51. — Iola
52. Jasper
53. — Kenard
54. La Grange (Ebro)
55. — Magnolia
56. — Mannington

57. Marianna
58. — Marion
59. Mayport
60. Milltown (Milton)
61. Monticello
62. — New Hinghamp
63. — Newnansville
64. Newport
65. — Oakey Hill
66. — Ochessee
67. — Port Leon
68. Quincy
69. — Richardson
70. — Salubrity
71. San Pedro (New Oakland Church)
72. Sarasota
73. Senybal (Sanibel)
74. Shell Point
75. — Spring Gardens
76. Spring Grove
77. St. Andrew (Panama City)
78. St. Joseph (Port St. Joe)
79. Tallahassee
80. — Thigpen
81. — Tulofa
82. — Valambrosia
83. Vernon
84. — Webbville
85. West Point (Apalachicola)
86. — Whitesville
87. — Woodstock

Settlements no longer in existence are preceded by dashes.

Plantation Agriculture

Planters from Virginia, the Carolinas, and Georgia, abandoning depleted soils in the older South, began to arrive in northern Florida with their movable capital of slaves early in the territorial period. The Seminoles had been removed, the land was surveyed, and a land office was opened in the new territorial capital of Tallahassee to sell tracts of land for as little as $1.25 per acre. In the quarter century following 1825 a plantation belt emerged, extending along the northern border of Florida through the five counties from Jackson on the west to Madison on the east. The belt was centered mainly on dark sandy loam soils recognized by the newcomers as having relatively high fertility. Development of plantations in areas farther east, some of which also had relatively good soils, was delayed at this time mainly owing to unresolved conflicting land claims originating in the previous British and Spanish periods. In 1850 these five "cotton counties" were producing more than 90 percent of Florida's cotton. Leon County, in the center of the belt, had the largest number of plantations and led all counties in cotton output. Its only

major town, Tallahassee, functioned primarily as a cotton market rather than as state capital.

After 1845, and especially after 1850, plantation agriculture did expand farther east, and especially southeastward into Alachua and Marion counties. By 1860 these two counties had also become cotton counties.

The plantations that were acquired between 1825 and 1860 in northern Florida, generally through piecemeal land purchases based almost invariably on credit, were scattered among larger numbers of smaller farms. Larger plantations typically had between 1,000 and 2,000 acres, divided variously between improved land and timberland, but a few plantations had 3,000 to 5,000 or more acres. The real measure of a plantation owner's wealth was not the number of his acres, however, but rather the number of his slaves. Owners of twenty or more slaves were "planters." Planters having thirty or more slaves commonly employed overseers. Owners of less than twenty slaves usually worked alongside their slaves in the fields. By 1850 some 200 planters had thirty or more slaves each; by 1860 this number had increased to over 400. These planters were the political, economic, and social leaders of society.

Although cotton was almost invariably the principal cash crop on plantations, the plantation owner sought a high degree of self-sufficiency and therefore corn, sweet potatoes, beans and peas, and some sugarcane for molasses were also grown. Livestock included horses, mules, pigs, not infrequently oxen, and even sheep in spite of the humid subtropical climate. Timber and turpentine were other common plantation products.

The planter housed his family and slaves in crude cabins during the earliest years of plantation occupance, but usually within ten years an imposing plantation house had been erected for the family. The new two-story house was often of brick manufactured by slaves from plantation clay deposits; otherwise it was a white-painted frame dwelling. Large windows were deeply recessed into thick walls. Wide verandas with ceilings supported by Greek columns flanked two or more sides of the house. The dwelling, often reached by an oak-lined driveway, was sited on a hilltop offering a commanding view. At some distance from the house were rows of slave cabins, a cotton gin house, a loom house, a blacksmith shop, stables, and a carriage house. Larger plantations also had an overseer's house.

The intense labor required to produce and market cotton began early in the spring and continued into fall with several pickings of the ripening cotton followed by storage, ginning, baling, and haulage into one of the county seats. Cotton traveled from plantation to town in heavy six-mule-team wagons. After weighing in the town, cotton moved on by wagon, water, or the new Tallahassee–St. Marks railroad to coastal points for shipment to New York.

After 1865 cotton production continued but never regained its previous importance, and other types of land uses eventually transformed the cotton fields.

Principal Cotton Producing Areas, 1850

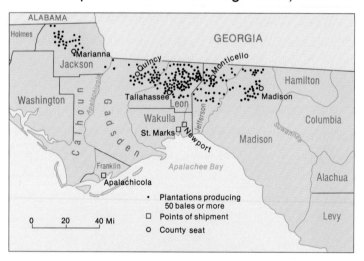

WEIGHING COTTON AT PLANTER'S HOME, end of 1800s

The Civil War in Florida

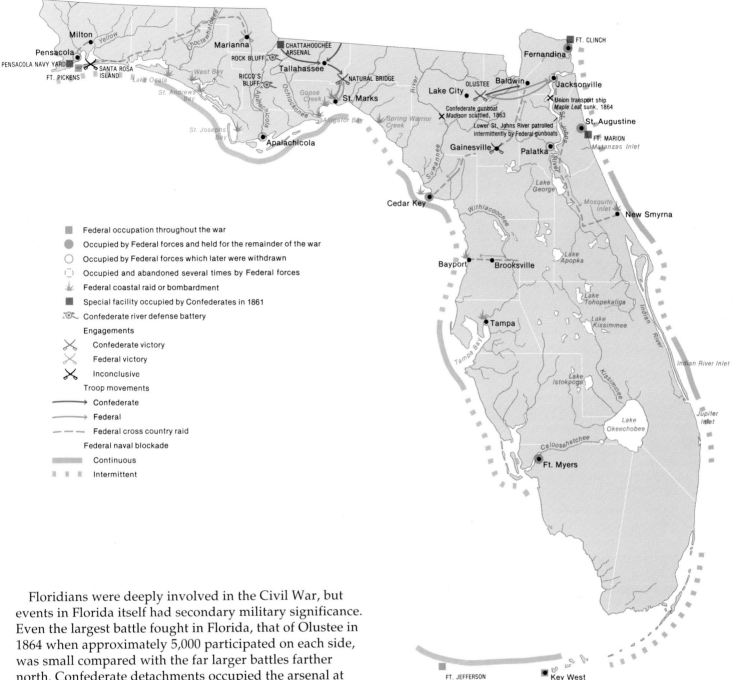

Federal occupation throughout the war
Occupied by Federal forces and held for the remainder of the war
Occupied by Federal forces which later were withdrawn
Occupied and abandoned several times by Federal forces
Federal coastal raid or bombardment
Special facility occupied by Confederates in 1861
Confederate river defense battery

Engagements
Confederate victory
Federal victory
Inconclusive

Troop movements
Confederate
Federal
Federal cross country raid

Federal naval blockade
Continuous
Intermittent

Floridians were deeply involved in the Civil War, but events in Florida itself had secondary military significance. Even the largest battle fought in Florida, that of Olustee in 1864 when approximately 5,000 participated on each side, was small compared with the far larger battles farther north. Confederate detachments occupied the arsenal at Chattahoochee and the Pensacola Navy Yard in 1861, but most Confederate operations were either responses to Federal raiding parties, such as those directed toward Marianna and Gainesville, or moves to check and repulse Federal forces advancing inland, as from Jacksonville in 1864 and toward Tallahassee in 1865. Confederate batteries overlooking the Apalachicola River at Rock Bluff and Ricco's Bluff were manned to prevent Federal gunboats from moving inland toward Columbus, Georgia.

A primary Federal objective was to blockade the coast, and the first blockading ship arrived off Apalachicola in June 1861. On dark nights blockade runners, laden with tobacco, cotton, and turpentine, would attempt to slip out of coastal inlets, or into coastal havens with cargoes of arms and munitions, cloth, tea and coffee, medicines, and a wide range of other goods in short supply in the Confed-

eracy. Federal ships were stationed primarily along stretches of coast such as off St. Andrews Bay and Apalachicola Bay in the west and Mosquito Inlet in the east, where blockade runners could have more effective linkage with the interior. The Indian River inlet was also favored by runners owing to their extensive use of the Bahamas. Federal occupation of coastal points such as Fort Pickens offshore from Pensacola reduced the need for blockading ships. The blockaders captured an estimated 160 vessels during the war. Federal blockading crews also raided coastal saltworks.

Florida had an important role as a larder for the Confederacy, furnishing food crops, livestock, and especially during the earlier war years, salt.

Early Population

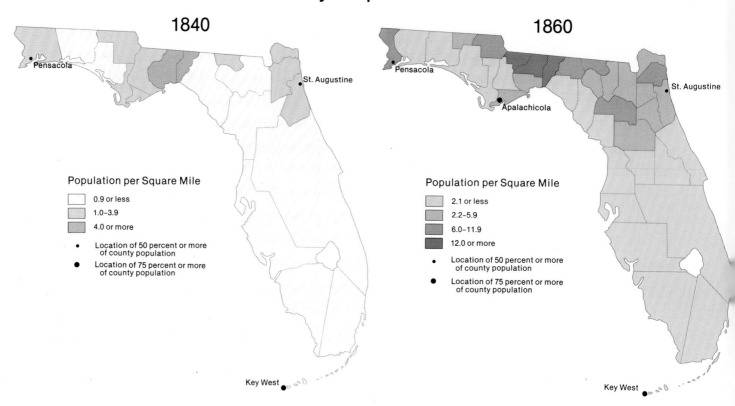

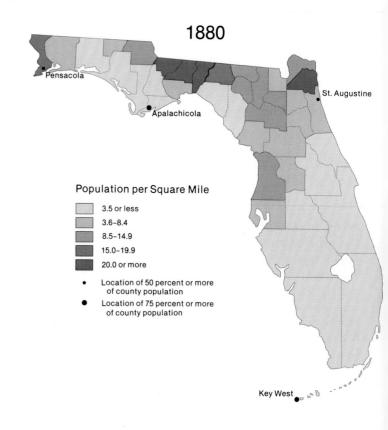

The first census of Florida, taken in 1830, fifteen years before the territory became a state, reported a population of 34,730. St. Augustine, founded in 1565 and the oldest continuously settled town in the U.S., was the only city considered large enough to be separately enumerated in the 1830 census. The only other settlements of any consequence were: Pensacola, first settled in 1559, abandoned two years later and permanently resettled in 1752; Tallahassee, chosen as the territorial capital in 1823 because of its location halfway between St. Augustine and Pensacola; and Key West, long a haven for pirates and adventurers and the site of a U.S. naval base and lighthouse built in the 1820s.

By the 1860 census Florida's population had risen to 140,424, much of which was in the north. Plantation agriculture, primarily of cotton, had developed in north Florida from Madison to Jackson counties. Tallahassee was the hub of the region and the center of the slave trade. Cotton was exported through the bustling port of Apalachicola, where in 1848 Dr. John Gorrie invented an ice-making machine, the forerunner of modern refrigeration and air conditioning. Some of the forts constructed during the Second Seminole War (1835–42), such as Ft. Brooke (Tampa) and Ft. Dallas (Miami), became the locations for later permanent settlements. Cigar manufacturers from Cuba and sponge fishermen contributed to the continuing prosperity of Key West.

By the turn of the century, the state's population exceeded one-half million. Railroads built by Henry Flagler and Henry Plant connected Florida to population centers along the Eastern Seaboard. These men built luxury hotels along their railroads and provided impetus for growth of Tampa, St. Augustine, Ormond Beach, Palm Beach, and Miami. The Spanish-American War further stimulated Florida's growth. The sinking of the U.S. battleship *Maine* in Havana Harbor in 1898 brought troops to Tampa, Key West, and Miami. By 1920 development in Florida was booming—St. Petersburg, Coral Gables, Miami Beach, Sarasota, Palm Beach, and Boca Raton—all experienced

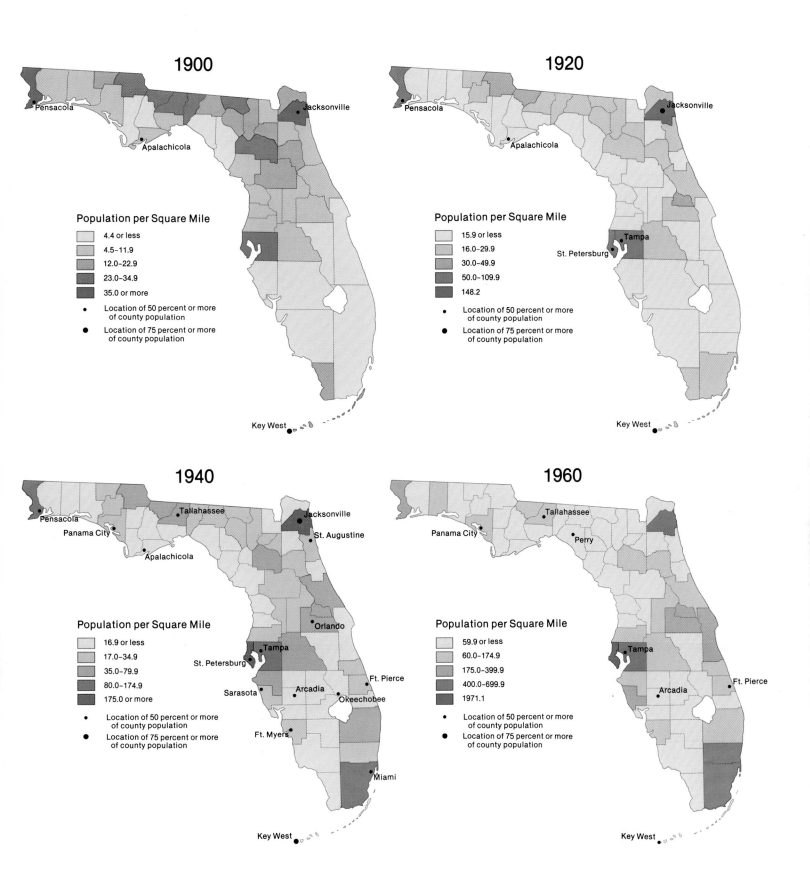

1900

Population per Square Mile

- 4.4 or less
- 4.5–11.9
- 12.0–22.9
- 23.0–34.9
- 35.0 or more

• Location of 50 percent or more of county population

● Location of 75 percent or more of county population

Pensacola
Apalachicola
Jacksonville
Key West

1920

Population per Square Mile

- 15.9 or less
- 16.0–29.9
- 30.0–49.9
- 50.0–109.9
- 148.2

• Location of 50 percent or more of county population

● Location of 75 percent or more of county population

Pensacola
Apalachicola
Jacksonville
Tampa
St. Petersburg
Key West

1940

Population per Square Mile

- 16.9 or less
- 17.0–34.9
- 35.0–79.9
- 80.0–174.9
- 175.0 or more

• Location of 50 percent or more of county population

● Location of 75 percent or more of county population

Pensacola
Panama City
Apalachicola
Tallahassee
Jacksonville
St. Augustine
Orlando
Tampa
St. Petersburg
Sarasota
Arcadia
Ft. Pierce
Okeechobee
Ft. Myers
Miami
Key West

1960

Population per Square Mile

- 59.9 or less
- 60.0–174.9
- 175.0–399.9
- 400.0–699.9
- 1971.1

• Location of 50 percent or more of county population

● Location of 75 percent or more of county population

Panama City
Tallahassee
Perry
Tampa
Arcadia
Ft. Pierce
Key West

phenomenal growth. In Miami Beach in 1925 alone, 481 hotels and apartment houses were built.

Hurricanes and the Depression slowed Florida's growth in the late 1920s and 1930s, but its growth again accelerated in the 1940s, especially in the south. Between 1920 and 1940 the number of urban places in Florida increased from

seven to sixteen. The 1960 census identified increasing suburbanization with a corresponding decrease in the number of urban places. Between 1960 and 1980, Florida's population nearly doubled, increasing from 4,951,567 in 1960 to 9,739,992 in 1980. In 1980, 80 percent of Florida's population was in south and central Florida.

Evolution of Counties

Florida's present sixty-seven counties evolved from the original two counties (St. Johns, all of the territory east of the Suwannee River, and Escambia, from the Suwannee west to the Perdido River) established by Andrew Jackson in 1821. As Florida's population increased, existing counties were partitioned to create new ones, and by 1840 twenty counties had already been established. County boundary maps of the nineteenth century show the prolif-

eration of counties in northern Florida where economic activity and population were concentrated. With twentieth century technological advances, all of Florida, and especially the previously sparsely populated southern peninsula, became available for more intense development.

By 1925, when Gilchrist County was established, all sixty-seven of Florida's present-day counties had been formed. Boundary adjustments, necessitated by political,

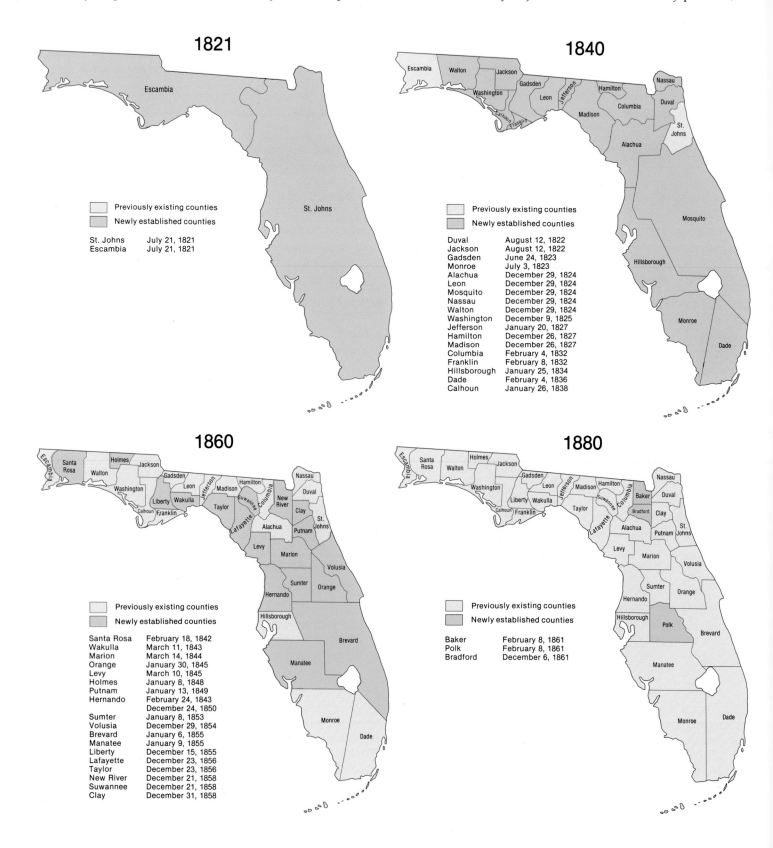

1821

Previously existing counties
Newly established counties

| St. Johns | July 21, 1821 |
| Escambia | July 21, 1821 |

1840

Previously existing counties
Newly established counties

Duval	August 12, 1822
Jackson	August 12, 1822
Gadsden	June 24, 1823
Monroe	July 3, 1823
Alachua	December 29, 1824
Leon	December 29, 1824
Mosquito	December 29, 1824
Nassau	December 29, 1824
Walton	December 29, 1824
Washington	December 9, 1825
Jefferson	January 20, 1827
Hamilton	December 26, 1827
Madison	December 26, 1827
Columbia	February 4, 1832
Franklin	February 8, 1832
Hillsborough	January 25, 1834
Dade	February 4, 1836
Calhoun	January 26, 1838

1860

Previously existing counties
Newly established counties

Santa Rosa	February 18, 1842
Wakulla	March 11, 1843
Marion	March 14, 1844
Orange	January 30, 1845
Levy	March 10, 1845
Holmes	January 8, 1848
Putnam	January 13, 1849
Hernando	February 24, 1843
	December 24, 1850
Sumter	January 8, 1853
Volusia	December 29, 1854
Brevard	January 6, 1855
Manatee	January 9, 1855
Liberty	December 15, 1855
Lafayette	December 23, 1856
Taylor	December 23, 1856
New River	December 21, 1858
Suwannee	December 21, 1858
Clay	December 31, 1858

1880

Previously existing counties
Newly established counties

Baker	February 8, 1861
Polk	February 8, 1861
Bradford	December 6, 1861

economic, and physical land changes, however, have continued. Thirty formal boundary adjustments have been made by the Florida legislature since 1925. For example, construction of a major highway effectively isolated a small rural part of Duval County. The isolated part was legislatively transferred to Clay County through a series of formal boundary changes in 1976, 1978, and 1980. Another more recent boundary adjustment occurred in 1986 when the line between Franklin and Wakulla counties was changed from the eastern shore of the Ochlockonee River to the "thread" (center) of the river. This change officially moved several small islands from Franklin County into Wakulla County.

Not all of the counties established in the nineteenth century are still in existence. Mosquito County, created in 1824, originally included all of Seminole Indian territory within its boundaries. In 1845, through a name change, it became Orange County. Fayette County was created in 1832 and went out of existence in 1834. In 1844 Hernando County, established in 1843 from part of Alachua, was renamed Benton to recognize a U.S. senator who sponsored the Armed Occupation Act of 1842, which made free land available for settlers to homestead in southern Florida. The name was changed back to Hernando in 1850 when Benton fell out of favor with extremists in the Florida legislature. New River County, established in 1858 from part of Columbia, was split to become Baker County and a much smaller New River County early in 1861. Late in 1861 what remained of New River was renamed Bradford County in honor of Captain Richard Bradford, a Florida military officer who was killed in battle barely two months before the name change. St. Lucie County was created as St. Lucia in March of 1844 from part of Mosquito County. In 1855 it was renamed Brevard and its county seat of Ft. Pierce was renamed Susannah. In 1917 St. Lucie County was reestablished and today its county seat is again Ft. Pierce. Efforts were made to establish two other counties (Call, 1828, and Bloxham, 1917) as evidenced in legislative documents, but neither was officially created.

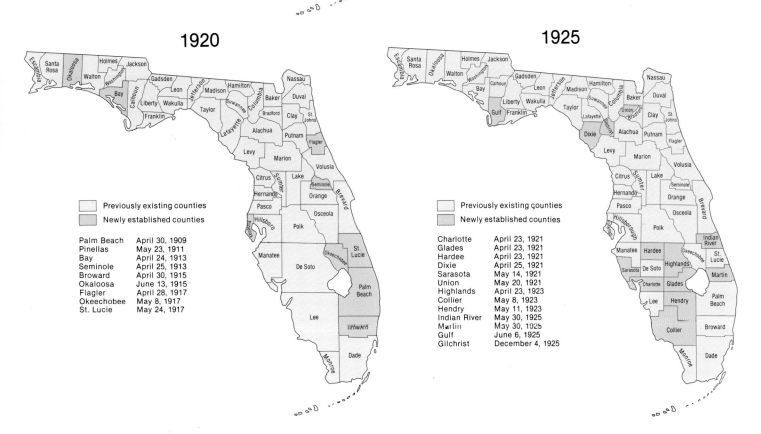

1900

| Previously existing counties | |
| Newly established counties | |

Osceola	May 12, 1887
Lee	May 13, 1887
De Soto	May 19, 1887
Lake	May 27, 1887
Citrus	June 2, 1887
Pasco	June 2, 1887

1920

| Previously existing counties | |
| Newly established counties | |

Palm Beach	April 30, 1909
Pinellas	May 23, 1911
Bay	April 24, 1913
Seminole	April 25, 1913
Broward	April 30, 1915
Okaloosa	June 13, 1915
Flagler	April 28, 1917
Okeechobee	May 8, 1917
St. Lucie	May 24, 1917

1925

| Previously existing counties | |
| Newly established counties | |

Charlotte	April 23, 1921
Glades	April 23, 1921
Hardee	April 23, 1921
Dixie	April 25, 1921
Sarasota	May 14, 1921
Union	May 20, 1921
Highlands	April 23, 1923
Collier	May 8, 1923
Hendry	May 11, 1923
Indian River	May 30, 1925
Martin	May 30, 1925
Gulf	June 6, 1925
Gilchrist	December 4, 1925

Timber

Throughout the nineteenth century and into the twentieth century, demand for Florida forest products, including wood for building and fuel, and for turpentine and rosin known collectively as naval stores, was nearly insatiable. Pines were most abundant, with many virgin or old-growth trees 4 feet or more in diameter and over 100 feet tall. Pines, especially longleaf and slash, accounted for three-fourths of the state's original 25–30 million acres of forests.

In the late 1800s, as tourists and new settlers headed south, ports in north Florida and the panhandle prospered from lumber and naval stores. The completion of the Pensacola and Atlantic Railroad to the east bank of the Apalachicola River early in the 1880s opened the panhandle's forests to large-scale commercial logging. In 1882, 11 sawmills operated in Pensacola alone. The pulp industry of north Florida, established by Alfred I. DuPont and his brother-in-law Ed Ball in the 1930s, continues to dominate many local economies.

North and east of Cedar Key were extensive stands of cedar. By 1896 these first-growth cedar forests had been destroyed for pencils and cigar boxes. South of Cedar Key, loggers removed miles of red mangrove prized by furniture manufacturers. Thousands-of-years-old cypress, first in north and central Florida and later in south Florida, was cut for shingles, shipping crates, boats, and paneling.

Pine forests

Mixed forests — hardwoods, evergreens

Cypress

Mangroves

No forests of commercial value

Citrus

Citrus was first planted in Florida by the Spanish at St. Augustine in the sixteenth century, but it was three centuries later before the first commercial groves were begun. Their development, limited to areas accessible to water transportation, was centered in northeast Florida along the St. Johns River and its tributaries. In the 1830s Douglas Dummett established Florida's first "budded" orange grove on Merritt Island by grafting sweet China orange buds from a grove near Palatka onto wild sour-orange trees. His oranges, whose descendants became known as Indian River oranges, were sought for their sweetness above all others in the New York City market.

Both Henry Plant and Henry Flagler promoted citriculture. In 1880 Plant ran his South Florida Railroad from the docks of Lake Monroe at Sanford to Orlando. Jacksonville and Tampa were linked by rail in 1884. In 1896, following the freeze of 1894–95, which destroyed citrus groves in north central Florida, Flagler completed his railroad to Miami, the only part of the state unaffected by the severe freeze. By 1900 Orange, Lake, and Polk counties had become the principal producers of citrus. The shift in citrus southward has continued into the twentieth century. Perfection by researchers for the Florida Citrus Commission of the process for making frozen orange juice concentrate revolutionized the Florida citrus industry in 1945. The amount of fresh fruit eaten or squeezed by American consumers dropped precipitously and many groves produced oranges solely for concentrate.

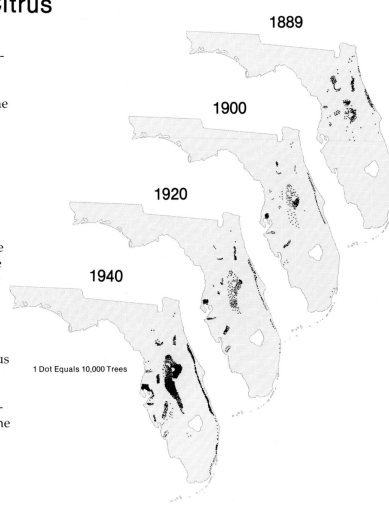

1889

1900

1920

1940

1 Dot Equals 10,000 Trees

Phosphate Mining

Three separate sources of phosphate were actively mined in Florida during the 1890s: hard rock, river pebble, and land pebble. Hard rock mining, such as that shown in the photograph, began after teeth, tusks, and large bones rich in phosphate were discovered at Dunnellon in 1889. Hard rock mining surpassed the other phosphate sources during most years of the 1890s, but after 1906 output declined. River pebble phosphate, occurring particularly in shallow sand bars in the Peace River, was mined until 1908. Boats equipped with steam dredges were employed in mining the bars. Land pebble became the leading phosphate source after 1905 owing to its relatively uniform occurrence in Polk and Hillsborough counties.

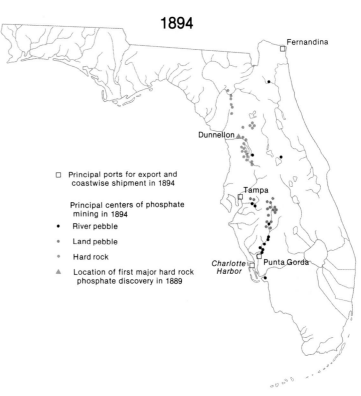

1894

☐ Principal ports for export and coastwise shipment in 1894

Principal centers of phosphate mining in 1894
• River pebble
· Land pebble
◦ Hard rock
▲ Location of first major hard rock phosphate discovery in 1889

HARD ROCK PHOSPHATE MINING, 1890s

Open-Range Ranching

The last large area of open-range ranching in the United States persisted into the twentieth century in peninsular Florida. The range, unowned by the cattlemen, most typically had an understory of wire grass and saw palmetto beneath an open stand of slash and longleaf pine. It was grazed by the Florida cow, a small, bony long-horned descendant of mainly undifferentiated Spanish cattle. Such an animal was able to survive heat, drought, insects, poor forage, and most important of all, cattle tick fever. Cattle were driven overland mainly to Ft. Myers for sale and shipment from nearby Punta Rassa to Cuba.

1880

☐ More productive rangeland
☐ Less productive rangeland
---- Principal cattle trails
◦ Major cattle market
☐ Major coastal points for cattle shipment to Cuba

COWBOYS WRESTLING STEER, by Frederic Remington

Steamboat and Steamship Routes, 1880–1900

No part of the United States was so dependent on sea and river transport as Florida in the latter nineteenth century. The state has an exceptionally long coastline and possesses a number of rivers that needed little or no channel improvement to become navigable. Many settlements remained unserved by railroads until the final years of the century. Florida's leading product, lumber, required low-cost ocean transport to reach markets.

One component of Florida's water transport was scheduled steamship service. A number of steamship routes on both the Atlantic and the Gulf were established by parent railroad companies. A second component was the large fleet of steamboats carrying passengers and freight to hundreds of riverside docks. Some of the smaller steamboats, such as the *Marion* which the accompanying drawing shows steaming on the Oklawaha River, were barely 20 feet broad. In addition to these two components, many hundreds of steamships and sailing vessels arrived at irregular intervals at Florida ports. Their diverse incoming cargoes ranged from machinery to ice. Outbound cargoes included cattle for Cuba, cotton for England, and especially lumber for Europe and the Northeast.

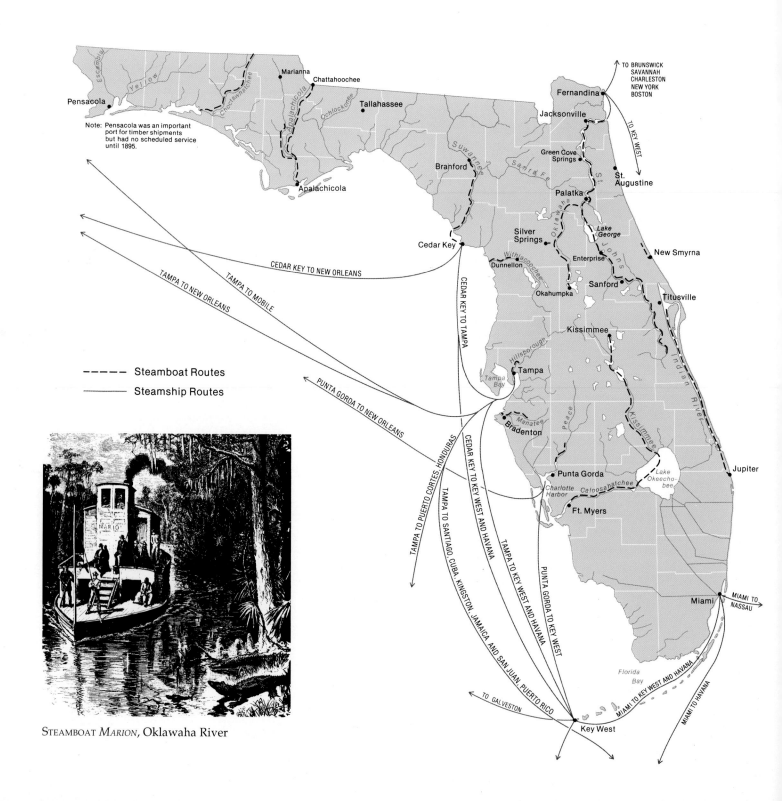

Note: Pensacola was an important port for timber shipments but had no scheduled service until 1895.

- - - - - Steamboat Routes
───── Steamship Routes

STEAMBOAT *MARION*, Oklawaha River

The Growth of Tourism

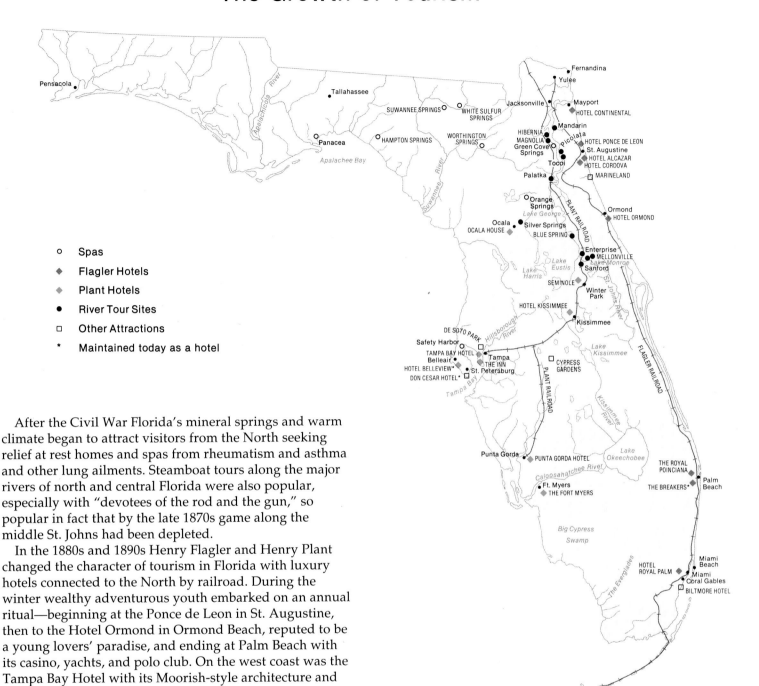

- ○ Spas
- ◆ Flagler Hotels
- ◆ Plant Hotels
- ● River Tour Sites
- □ Other Attractions
- * Maintained today as a hotel

After the Civil War Florida's mineral springs and warm climate began to attract visitors from the North seeking relief at rest homes and spas from rheumatism and asthma and other lung ailments. Steamboat tours along the major rivers of north and central Florida were also popular, especially with "devotees of the rod and the gun," so popular in fact that by the late 1870s game along the middle St. Johns had been depleted.

In the 1880s and 1890s Henry Flagler and Henry Plant changed the character of tourism in Florida with luxury hotels connected to the North by railroad. During the winter wealthy adventurous youth embarked on an annual ritual—beginning at the Ponce de Leon in St. Augustine, then to the Hotel Ormond in Ormond Beach, reputed to be a young lovers' paradise, and ending at Palm Beach with its casino, yachts, and polo club. On the west coast was the Tampa Bay Hotel with its Moorish-style architecture and millions of dollars worth of carpets and art from Europe, and the Hotel Belleview in Belleair, a huge wooden structure with the first hotel golf course.

In 1919, in DeSoto Park in Tampa, less well-to-do tourists traveling to Florida by car formed the first Tin Can Tourist Camp. During the 1920s these camps sprang up around every major city in Florida and along most highways. Miami Beach, incorporated in 1915, was very successfully promoted by Carl Fisher with a pair of elephants—Rosie and Carl, named after himself and his wife—bathing beauties, and $350,000 Roman baths.

BREAKERS HOTEL, in 1901, the year it was built, is Flagler's only remaining working hotel. At the turn of the century, when the average worker earned $1.25 a day, the cost of a five-week Florida vacation including round-trip train fare and accommodations at any Flagler hotel was $350.

Railroads

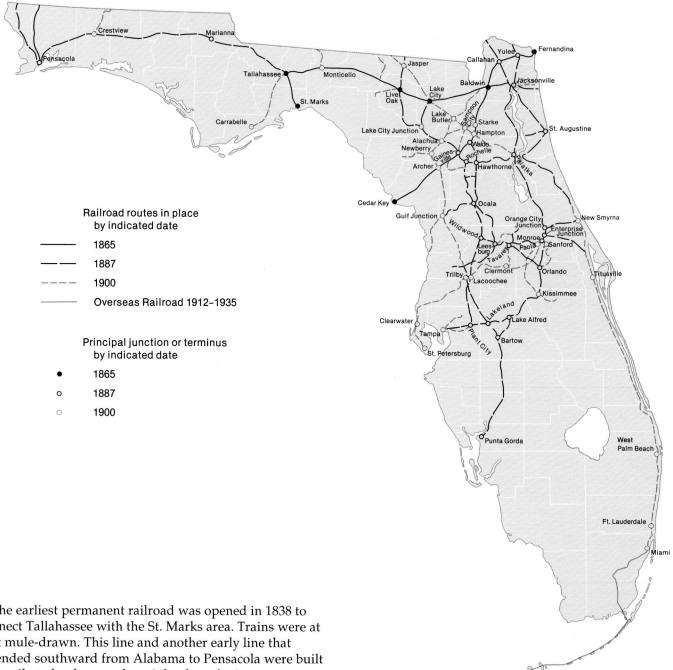

Railroad routes in place
by indicated date

——————— 1865

— — — 1887

- - - - - 1900

——————— Overseas Railroad 1912–1935

Principal junction or terminus
by indicated date

● 1865

○ 1887

○ 1900

The earliest permanent railroad was opened in 1838 to connect Tallahassee with the St. Marks area. Trains were at first mule-drawn. This line and another early line that extended southward from Alabama to Pensacola were built primarily to haul cotton from inland producing areas to ports on the Gulf coast. Two longer rail lines from Tallahassee and Jacksonville and meeting in Lake City were opened in the early Statehood period. Another early line, completed from Fernandina to Cedar Key by 1861, was designed to compete with maritime traffic sailing around the Florida peninsula.

After a twenty-year hiatus, railroad construction was again widespread in the 1880s and 1890s. Pensacola was connected by rail with lines east of the Apalachicola River. Florida's railroads were finally linked effectively with the national railroad network. Primary emphasis shifted to route extensions southward into the more tropical parts of the Florida peninsula in order to tap the possibilities of tourism as well as winter fruit and vegetable transport. As part of this southward thrust, the railhead reached Miami in 1896.

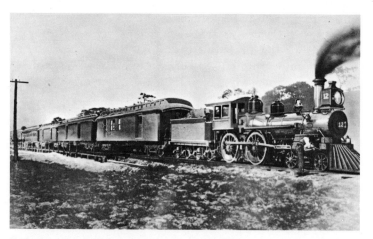

FIRST SCHEDULED TRAIN INTO MIAMI, April 1896

Roads

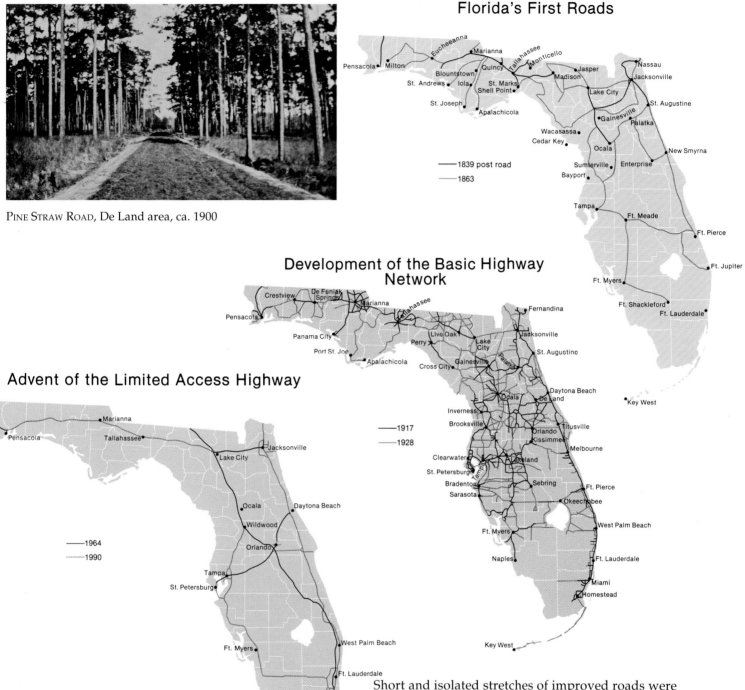

PINE STRAW ROAD, De Land area, ca. 1900

Florida's First Roads

——1839 post road
——1863

Development of the Basic Highway Network

——1917
——1928

Advent of the Limited Access Highway

——1964
——1990

Florida had few roads during the territorial period. Even its best roads, classified in 1839 by David Burr, Geographer to the U.S. House of Representatives, as "four-horse mail post coach roads," were mainly sandy gashes through the forest. Drivers of wheeled vehicles had to avoid stumps and to depend on ferries at all river crossings. Most travel was on foot or horseback.

Roads were improved and new roads constructed very gradually over the following seventy-five years. Construction and maintenance were strictly county responsibilities.

Short and isolated stretches of improved roads were surfaced with brick, shell, limerock, or clay.

Rapid changes in the state's roads began in 1915 with the establishment of a state road department. Federal aid for roads over which mail would move was authorized in 1916. The state road department was directed in 1917 to establish an intercity network of state highways. A massive highway construction program began in the 1920s, and by 1938 state and federal funds had built 9,000 miles of roads. Many tourists and migrants to Florida now began to arrive by automobile.

In the late 1930s the state road department constructed the first "divided two-lane type" pavement outward from Tampa toward Clearwater. Changes accelerated with the 1956 Federal Highway Act providing for high-speed, limited-access interstate highways, and the initiation of construction on the Sunshine State Parkway.

Expansion of the Canal and Levee System

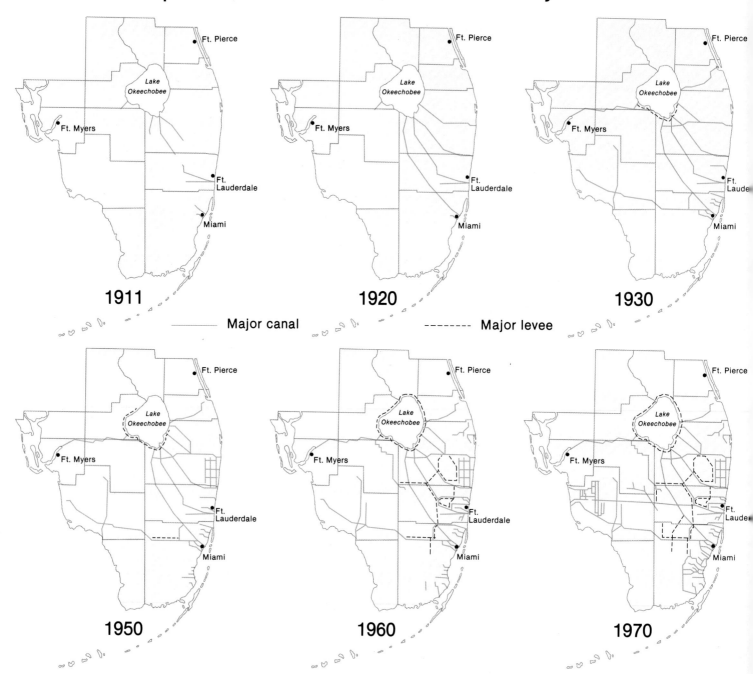

1911

1920

1930

———— Major canal   - - - - - - - Major levee

1950

1960

1970

Many Floridians in the late nineteenth and early twentieth centuries believed that if the standing water in the Everglades were removed, family farms could be established on the rich organic soils south of Lake Okeechobee. The idea of drainage received political support from Napoleon Broward in his campaign for governor in 1904, and two years later, when *The Everglades* moved out from Ft. Lauderdale to commence dredging the North New River Canal, one of the most massive attempts at reclamation in American history had begun. Canals were dug to shunt surplus Lake Okeechobee water directly to the Atlantic. By 1917 four such canals had been completed. Later, particularly after 1950, the earlier emphasis on drainage was succeeded by construction of levees for flood control. Levees were also raised to retain some of the surplus water previously lost to the sea via the drainage canals.

STEAM DREDGE *EVERGLADES*, 1906

Expansion of Agriculture in South Florida

Agriculture in the southern half of Florida, involving primarily winter vegetables, sugarcane and citrus, has developed almost entirely since 1900. To show the expansion of winter vegetable acreage from 1899 through an 85-year period, it has been desirable to compile statistics from an unchanging aggregate area, as the formation of eighteen new counties during this period entailed numerous boundary changes. This aggregate unchanging area is defined by the northern boundaries of Pinellas, Hillsborough, Polk, Osceola, and Brevard counties.

Winter vegetable production began with the inflow of farmer-settlers, the extension of rail lines southward (rails reaching Miami only in 1896), railroad refrigeration, and changes in vegetable processing and national consumption patterns resulting particularly from quick freezing and home refrigeration. Acreage expansion was at times later reversed, as happened with urban expansion onto prime bush and pole bean lands in Palm Beach County. Dade County's tomato acreage declined from 23,700 acres in 1964 to under 11,000 acres in 1982 consequent on urban expansion, with Collier County surpassing Dade County in tomato acreage in the latter year.

Sugarcane acreage grew slowly adjacent to Lake Okeechobee beginning in the late 1920s until its sharp upswing following the embargo imposed on Cuban sugar following the 1959 Cuban Revolution.

Total Acreage of Vegetables and Berries in Central and South Florida

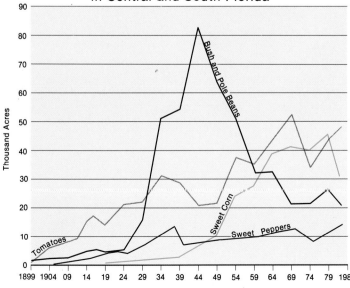

Cultivated Acreage of Major Vegetables in Central and South Florida

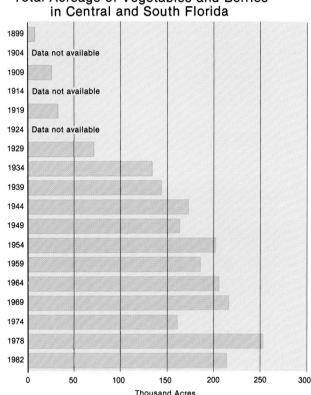

Area of Sugarcane Cultivation

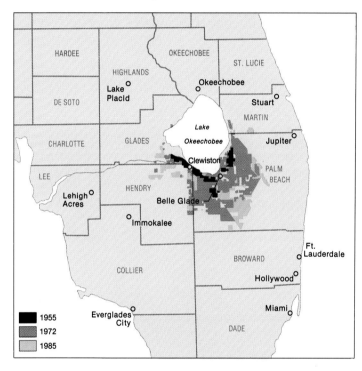

Harvested Sugarcane Acreage for Sugar and Seed

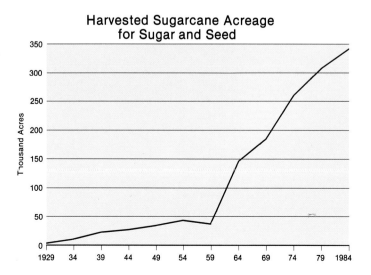

Cigar Manufacturing

Even during Florida's territorial period Key West had achieved the highest mean per capita income of any settlement in Florida, based principally on the thriving market for goods salvaged from the navigationally treacherous Keys area. In 1868 an event occurred that led to a surpassing of even this promising start, for in that year the Ten Years' War for independence from Spain flared in Cuba. The resulting turbulence prompted much of Havana's cigar manufacturing to migrate to nearby Key West. Havana cigar manufacturers who were subsequently to figure in Florida's cigar industry, like Vincente Martinez Ybor, also decided to leave Havana in 1869 for other reasons: tariffs and regulations imposed by the Spanish government; the American tariff on cigars; and *La Liga*, the labor union formed by cigar workers in Havana. By the end of 1869 some 6,000 Cuban cigar makers had already migrated to Key West, and in the following years Key West gradually became the preeminent high-quality cigar manufacturing city in the world. By 1884 Key West, with 80 cigar factories and an annual output of 42 million cigars, had become the largest city in Florida.

A second major geographical shift of the cigar industry, this time from Key West to the new city of Tampa, began in 1886. Although the Havana cigar manufacturers had escaped union activity by their move to Key West, skilled cigar workers began to organize almost immediately. Disputes between labor and factory owners increased, leading to strikes. Then in 1886 a fire destroyed many buildings, including Ybor's factory. Ybor's decision to move was also prompted by inducements offered by Tampa's new Board of Trade. A factory town, becoming known as Ybor City, was erected beyond the northeast margin of Tampa in 1886. As other cigar factories arose in Ybor City and in West Tampa, the city became the world's leading cigar producer, although production also continued in Key West.

The renown of "clear Havana" cigars manufactured in Tampa and Key West (the term *clear* referring to the light color of the tobacco leaf) stemmed both from the tobacco used and the skill of the cigar makers. The best clear Havana cigars were made from tobacco noted for its flavor, smooth burning and easy blending qualities that come exclusively from the Vuelta Abajo district of Cuba. This tobacco was in turn transformed into many combinations of cigar size, shape, color, and style by highly skilled cigar makers using only a wedge-shaped, thin, steel knife and a hard apple-wood platform. So successful economically were the workers that they established large social club-houses containing libraries, auditoriums, theaters and even a hospital. The hand-made cigar industry in Florida began to decline in the 1920s as smoking fashions changed and as machines were introduced.

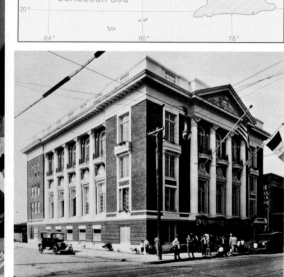

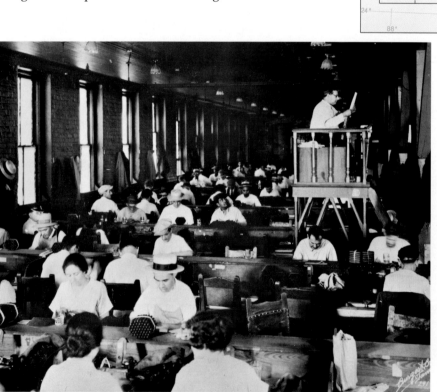

Reader, Cigar Factory, Tampa, 1929

Italian Club, Ybor City, 1919

Sponging

For a century Florida's economy included an important yet unique component having no counterpart elsewhere in the United States—the collection and marketing of sponges. Sponges occur virtually worldwide, but only a very few species have human utility. These are concentrated particularly in two regions, the eastern Mediterranean and under some 9,300 square miles of shallow Gulf waters along parts of the Florida coast. Florida's sponging industry came to be strongly influenced eventually by spongers from the eastern Mediterranean, where sponging had a history stretching back into antiquity.

The Mediterranean linkage did not appear during the first fifty years of Florida's industry, however, when sponging was confined to the Key Grounds centered mainly in Florida Bay. The first sponge market opened at Key West in 1849. The Key Grounds remained the source of sponges for the Key West market for almost twenty-five years, but in 1873 sponges were discovered farther north, in what became known as the Bay Grounds, extending from St. Petersburg to St. Marks. As the abundance and high quality of sponges in the Bay Grounds became better known, spongers began to operate from coastal inlets north of St. Petersburg, particularly from the vicinity of the new settlement of Tarpon Springs. At first Bay Grounds sponges were marketed through Key West, but eventually Tarpon Springs came to dominate marketing.

Until this time sponging in Florida waters had been pursued exclusively by individuals native to Florida, but during 1905–1907 the Florida industry was fundamentally transformed by Greek immigrants and their sponging technology. Sponging in Mediterranean waters had become remarkably concentrated in the hands of generations of Greek spongers living on rocky, dry, virtually treeless Kalimnos and adjacent islands in the Aegean Sea. As they gradually depleted the Aegean sponge grounds toward the end of the nineteenth century, they sailed to more distant grounds, particularly to those in coastal waters of Libya and Egypt. Their sponging expanded not only geographically but technologically; by about 1886 they had begun to employ copper-helmeted diving suits allowing them to sponge in deeper waters. In turn, as thousands of Greek spongers began to migrate in 1905 to the new economic opportunities at Tarpon Springs, they introduced diving suits and diving vessels with air pumps and hoses. They created a major multimillion-dollar industry that only ended toward midcentury with a red tide and then the advent of synthetic sponges.

Mediterranean Origins of Florida's Sponging Culture

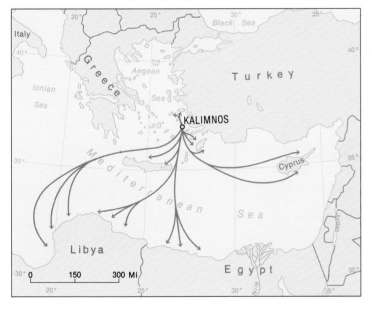

Florida's Sponge Grounds

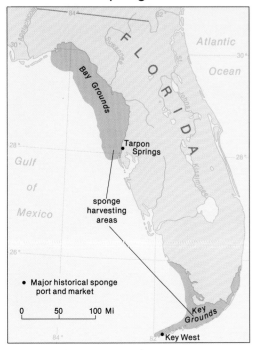

SPONGE MARKET, Tarpon Springs

Presidential Elections

Citizens of Florida first went to the polls to cast their votes for president of the United States in 1848, three years after the territory became a state. A total of 7,905 votes was recorded. One of the new state's twenty-seven counties reported only ten votes, five for each candidate. During Florida's first four presidential elections there were several counties for which no votes were recorded. The missing votes were probably included with the returns from adjacent counties.

The federal election of 1864 took place during the Civil War, and Florida was one of the eleven southern states that did not participate. No county returns are available for the election of 1868, since instead of choosing its electors by the usual method of popular vote, the state chose them through its legislature, giving a thirty-nine to nine majority to Grant. Relative party strength for this election as depicted on the map was derived from 1868 gubernatorial election returns.

The election of 1880 represented a shift of voter support from the Republican to the Democratic side. This shift put Florida on a nearly seventy-year course of Democratic candidate support, which was interrupted only by state support for Hoover in 1928. The almost exclusive Democratic voting pattern was reversed with support for and election of President Eisenhower in 1952. Since then, the majority of Florida's votes have been cast for Republican nominees in five of the seven presidential elections. The number of voters participating in each of Florida's thirty-four presidential elections has increased with population in all but one instance. In 1920, 155,802 votes were cast for president. In 1924 the number dropped to 109,159. This drop was reflected equally in both parties; the 1924 Democratic vote was 68.6 percent and the Republican vote, 68.3 percent of the 1920 totals for each party.

Vote Received by Party Carrying Florida

Year	Party	Percentage of Popular Vote	Year	Party	Percentage of Popular Vote
1848	Whig	57.5	1920	Democrat	58.1
1852	Democrat	60.0	1924	Democrat	56.9
1856	Democrat	56.6	1928	Republican	56.8
1860	Democrat	62.2	1932	Democrat	74.9
1864	None		1936	Democrat	76.1
1868	Republican	64.3	1940	Democrat	74.0
1872	Republican	53.5	1944	Democrat	70.3
1876	Republican	50.0	1948	Democrat	48.8
1880	Democrat	54.1	1952	Republican	55.0
1884	Democrat	53.0	1956	Republican	57.3
1888	Democrat	59.5	1960	Republican	51.5
1892	Democrat	86.1	1964	Democrat	51.1
1896	Democrat	66.0	1968	Republican	40.5
1900	Democrat	71.0	1972	Republican	71.9
1904	Democrat	68.8	1976	Democrat	51.9
1908	Democrat	63.0	1980	Republican	55.5
1912	Democrat	70.1	1984	Republican	65.3
1916	Democrat	69.3	1988	Republican	61.3

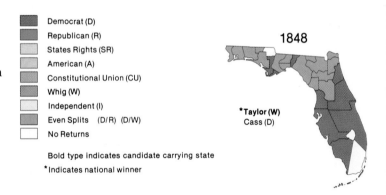

Democrat (D)
Republican (R)
States Rights (SR)
American (A)
Constitutional Union (CU)
Whig (W)
Independent (I)
Even Splits (D/R) (D/W)
No Returns

Bold type indicates candidate carrying state

*Indicates national winner

1848

*Taylor (W)
Cass (D)

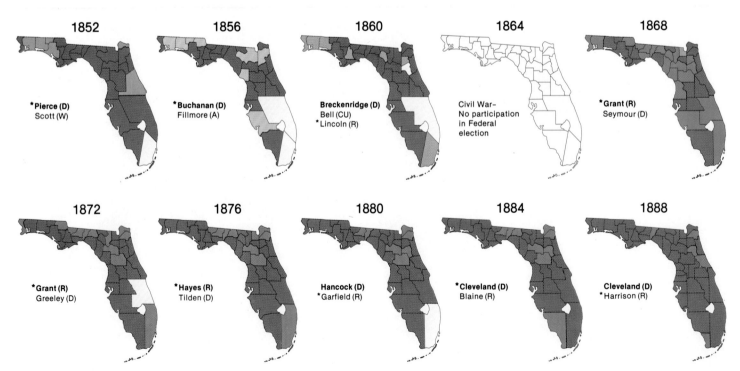

1852
*Pierce (D)
Scott (W)

1856
*Buchanan (D)
Fillmore (A)

1860
Breckenridge (D)
Bell (CU)
*Lincoln (R)

1864
Civil War–
No participation
in Federal
election

1868
*Grant (R)
Seymour (D)

1872
*Grant (R)
Greeley (D)

1876
*Hayes (R)
Tilden (D)

1880
Hancock (D)
*Garfield (R)

1884
*Cleveland (D)
Blaine (R)

1888
Cleveland (D)
*Harrison (R)

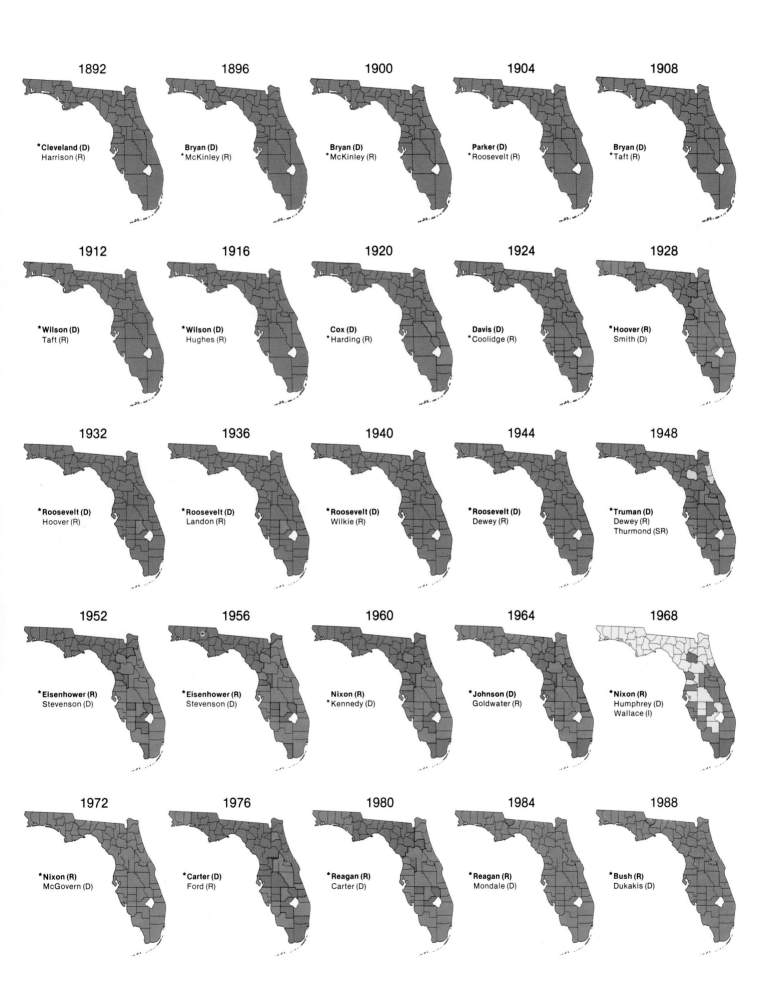

1892
*Cleveland (D)
Harrison (R)

1896
Bryan (D)
*McKinley (R)

1900
Bryan (D)
*McKinley (R)

1904
Parker (D)
*Roosevelt (R)

1908
Bryan (D)
*Taft (R)

1912
*Wilson (D)
Taft (R)

1916
*Wilson (D)
Hughes (R)

1920
Cox (D)
*Harding (R)

1924
Davis (D)
*Coolidge (R)

1928
*Hoover (R)
Smith (D)

1932
*Roosevelt (D)
Hoover (R)

1936
*Roosevelt (D)
Landon (R)

1940
*Roosevelt (D)
Wilkie (R)

1944
*Roosevelt (D)
Dewey (R)

1948
*Truman (D)
Dewey (R)
Thurmond (SR)

1952
*Eisenhower (R)
Stevenson (D)

1956
*Eisenhower (R)
Stevenson (D)

1960
Nixon (R)
*Kennedy (D)

1964
*Johnson (D)
Goldwater (R)

1968
*Nixon (R)
Humphrey (D)
Wallace (I)

1972
*Nixon (R)
McGovern (D)

1976
*Carter (D)
Ford (R)

1980
*Reagan (R)
Carter (D)

1984
*Reagan (R)
Mondale (D)

1988
*Bush (R)
Dukakis (D)

Governors of Florida

Andrew Jackson*
1821

William P. Duval*
1822 - 1834

John H. Eaton*
1834 - 1835

Richard K. Call*
1835 - 1839; 1841 - 1844

Robert R. Reid*
1840 - 1841

John Branch*
1844 - 1845

William D. Moseley
1845 - 1849

Thomas Brown
1849 - 1853

James E. Broome
1853 - 1857

Madison S. Perry
1857 - 1861

John Milton
1861 - 1865

A. K. Allison†
1865

William Marvin‡
1865

David S. Walker
1865 - 1868

Harrison Reed
1868 - 1872

Ossian B. Hart
1873 - 1874

Marcellus L. Stearns
1874 - 1877

George F. Drew
1877 - 1881

William D. Bloxham
1881 - 1885; 1897 -1901

Francis P. Fleming
1889 - 1893

Henry L. Mitchell
1893 - 1897

William S. Jennings
1901 - 1905

Napoleon B. Broward
1905 - 1909

Albert W. Gilchrist
1909 -1913

Park Trammell
1913 - 1917

Edward A. Perry
1885 - 1889

Sidney J. Catts
1917 -1921

Cary A. Hardee
1921 - 1925

John W. Martin
1925 - 1929

Doyle E. Carlton
1929 - 1933

David Sholtz
1933 - 1937

Fred P. Cone
1937 - 1941

Spessard L. Holland
1941 - 1945

Millard F. Caldwell
1945 - 1949

Fuller Warren
1949 -1953

Daniel T. McCarty
1953

Charley E. Johns
1953 -1955

LeRoy Collins
1955 -1961

C. Farris Bryant
1961 - 1965

W. Haydon Burns
1965 - 1967

Claude R. Kirk, Jr.
1967 -1971

Reubin O'D. Askew
1971 - 1979

Bob Graham
1979 - 1987

Wayne Mixson
1987

Bob Martinez
1987 - 1991

Lawton Chiles
1991 -

*   Territorial

†   Not Recognized by
     the Federal Government

‡   Provisional

The State Capitol

1824

1830

1845

1910

1929

1946

PRESENT DAY

Florida's first capitol was three log cabins constructed in 1824 by Gadsden County planters Jonathan Robinson and Sherod McCall near a stream and waterfall, known as the Cascades, which has long since disappeared. These cabins were probably several hundred yards south of the present capitol. Plans for a more permanent capitol were approved in 1825. By 1839 this building had become too small, and the legislative council approved construction of a new building. Completed in 1845, just prior to statehood, the new brick capitol was three-stories high, 151 feet long, 53 feet wide, with front and rear porticos. The capitol remained unchanged until 1891 when a small cupola was added. A major expansion occurred in 1901–02 when north and south wings and a dome were added. In 1921–22 east and west wings were added.

Construction of a new capitol began in 1973 with the decision to restore the old capitol as it existed in 1902 complete with red-and-white awnings depicted on a 1903 postcard. The new 22-story capitol was completed in 1977.

Architecture

CARIBBEAN MARKETPLACE, MIAMI, 1989. Architect: Charles Harrison Pawley. A remodeled warehouse and a symbol for "Little Haiti." American Institute of Architects, Honor Award, 1991; Florida Association/AIA, Award for Excellence in Architecture, 1990.

ATLANTIC BEACH DUNEHOUSES, 1975. Architect: William Morgan. A seaside duplex, with porthole-like openings facing the ocean, set into an existing dune. Energy efficient, the dunehouses are insulated by a 20" thick layer of earth. Florida Association/AIA, Design Award, 1976.

THE ATLANTIS, MIAMI, 1982. Architect: Arquitectonica. A 96-unit, 20-story condominium.   At the 12th floor, a 37-foot cube has been removed to create a sky court. American Institute of Architects, Honor Award, 1983.

FT. JEFFERSON, GARDEN KEY, DRY TORTUGAS ISLANDS, 1846 Ft. Jefferson, the largest of the 19th-century masonry coastal fortifications, was erected by the U.S. government to control the Straits of Florida and was garrisoned during the Civil, Spanish-American and both world wars. Walls are 8 feet thick and 50 feet high. National Monument 1935, National Register 1970.

CA' D'ZAN, THE JOHN AND MABLE RINGLING RESIDENCE, SARASOTA, 1926. Architect: Dwight James Baum. The Ca' d'Zan (Venetian dialect for "House of John") is a 31-room bayfront Venetian Gothic mansion inspired by the Doges' Palace in Venice, Italy, and the tower of the old Madison Square Garden in New York City. National Register 1982.

LA BELLUCIA, PALM BEACH, 1920. Architect: Addison Mizner. The oceanfront home with its red barrel-tile roofs and arched windows is a notable example of Mediterranean Revival architecture. The facade of recessed bays catches tropical breezes and provides ocean views.

FIRE PREVENTION BUREAU, FORT LAUDERDALE, 1987. Architect: Donald Singer. The concrete building sits on the edge of a lake in an east-west orientation. To shade windows facing east and west, concrete sunshades were developed. Florida Association/AIA, Award for Excellence in Architecture, 1987; Florida Concrete and Products Association Award for Concrete Structure of the Year, 1988.

THE GREGORY HOUSE, TORREYA STATE PARK, NEAR BRISTOL, 1849. The Classical Revival plantation house sat on 5-foot-high brick pillars to protect it from floodwaters. In 1935, the house was given to Florida, dismantled, floated across the Apalachicola River, and reassembled with original lumber and wooden pegs. National Register 1972.

MIAMI BEACH ARCHITECTURAL DISTRICT (1920-1940). Contains the largest concentration in the United States of *Moderne* architecture. Characterized by streamlined corners, grouped windows, and applied Art Deco motifs. National Register 1979.

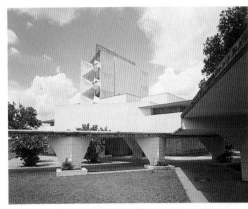

ANNIE PFEIFFER CHAPEL, FLORIDA SOUTHERN COLLEGE, LAKELAND, 1941. Architect: Frank Lloyd Wright. Part of the largest concentration of Frank Lloyd Wright's architecture in the world; designed by Wright during his organic period and built primarily by students between 1937 and 1955. Esplanades connect the cream-colored concrete buildings and provide shelter from the Florida sun and rain. National Register 1975.

RICHARD PEACON/CALVIN KLEIN HOUSE, KEY WEST, CA. 1894. The "Octagon House", an example of "Conch" architecture, a blend of Victorian, Bahamian, New England, and Creole elements. National Register 1971.

WESTINGHOUSE WORLD HEADQUARTERS, STEAM TURBINE-GENERATOR DIVISION, ORLANDO, 1983. Architect: William Morgan. The circular building recalls the radial arrangements of turbine blades and provides panoramic views of Lake Ebby. Florida Association/AIA, Award for Excellence in Architecture, 1985; Florida Concrete and Products Association Award for Outstanding Concrete Structure, 1984.

Cultural Landscapes

BANNERMAN PLACE, Tallahassee, Leon County

SEASIDE, West of Panama City, Walton County

HORSE FARM, Ocala, Marion County

TOBACCO BARNS, Madison County

MOBILE HOME PARK, Brevard County

ST. PETERSBURG BEACH, Don Cesar Hotel, Pinellas County

SUGARCANE, Clewiston, Hendry County

Dairy, Lorida, Highlands County

Carnaval Miami, Calle Ocho, Dade County

De Funiak Springs, Walton County

Popular Regions

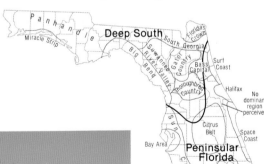

Phosphate Mining, Hamilton County

Citrus, Frostproof, Polk County

Distinctive cultural areas such as New England, the Middle West, and the South are widely recognized. Each region influences the culture of its inhabitants and in turn is molded by them. In a study of the cultural geography of the United States these major regions were in turn divided into nineteen second-order regions, one of which, the "Deep South," was seen to be unsurpassed in the intensity of its inhabitants' regional consciousness. The southern boundary in Florida of this cultural region is depicted by the southward-looping solid line on the map. A different cultural area, "Peninsular Florida," much less "southern" than northern Florida, is south of this boundary. In a separate study, 356 Floridians attending the 1981 Florida Folklife Festival at White Springs answered a questionnaire concerning their perceptions of Florida regions. Their responses are shown by the eighteen popular regions on the map.

Art Museums

THE RED FOULARD, 1924
Pablo Picasso
Norton Gallery of Art

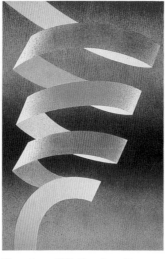

WATER SPOUT 1971, COLD LIGHT SUITE
James Rosenquist
Published by GRAPHICSTUDIO, U.S.F.
USF Art Museum

INTETRA, 1976
Isamu Noguchi
The Society of the Four Arts

AL-BARAQ
Baga (Atlantic); Guinea-Bissau
Appleton Museum of Art
Purchased with funds
provided by A.I. Appleton

DIGNITARY CARRIED ON A COVERED LITTER
Late Pre-Classic, West Mexico
Appleton Museum of Art

THE TRAPPED THIEF, 1650s
Nicholaes van Galen (attr. to)
Lowe Art Museum
University of Miami
Gift of Colonel C. Michael Paul, 1968

BLACK-FIGURE KYLIX (LIP CUP)
Attic, ca. 530 B.C.
Attributed to the Tleson Painter
Tampa Museum of Art: Joseph Veach Noble Collection
Gift of Marvin and Trudy Barkin

THE ADORATION OF THE MAGI, ca. 1340
Master of the Blessed Clare
Lowe Art Museum
University of Miami
Gift of the Samuel H. Kress Foundation, 1961

NATURE MORTE VIVANTE, 1956
Salvador Dali
Salvador Dali Museum

La Creuse en septembre, 1903
Jean-Baptiste Armand Guillaumin
Bass Museum of Art

Landscape, 1944
Milton Avery
Norton Gallery of Art

Red Coat, 1983
Alex Katz
Jacksonville Art Museum

"Summer," Four Seasons Window, 1900
Louis Comfort Tiffany
Charles Hosmer Morse Museum of
American Art

Reading (La Lecture), 1888
Berthe Morisot
Museum of Fine Arts

Hagar and the Angel, ca. 1638
Pietro da Cortona (Berretino)
John and Mable Ringling Museum of Art

Major Fine Art Museums and Centers

Appleton Museum of Art, co-owned by Central Florida Community College Foundation and Florida State University Foundation, Ocala
Art Museum at Florida International University, Miami
Atlantic Center for the Arts, New Smyrna Beach
Bass Museum of Art, Miami Beach
Boca Raton Museum of Art, Boca Raton
Brevard Art Center and Museum, Melbourne
Center for the Fine Arts, Miami
Charles Hosmer Morse Museum of American Art, Winter Park
Cuban Museum of Arts and Culture, Miami
Cummer Gallery of Art, Jacksonville
Florida Gulf Coast Art Center, Belleair
Florida State University Gallery and Museum, Tallahassee
George D. and Harriet W. Cornell Fine Arts Museum, Rollins College, Winter Park
Jacksonville Art Museum, Jacksonville
John and Mable Ringling Museum of Art, Sarasota
Lowe Art Museum, University of Miami, Coral Gables
Morikami Museum and Japanese Gardens, Delray Beach
Museum of African-American Art, Tampa
Museum of Art, Fort Lauderdale
Museum of Arts and Sciences, Daytona Beach
Museum of Fine Arts, St. Petersburg
North Miami Museum and Art Center, North Miami
Norton Gallery of Art, West Palm Beach
Orlando Museum of Art, Orlando
Polk Museum of Art, Lakeland
Salvador Dali Museum, St. Petersburg
Samuel P. Harn Museum of Art, University of Florida, Gainesville
The Society of the Four Arts, Palm Beach
Tampa Museum of Art, Tampa
University of South Florida Art Museum, Tampa
Vizcaya Museum and Gardens, Miami
The Wolfsonian Foundation, Miami Beach

Cape Cod Pier, 1908
William Glackens
Museum of Art, Ft. Lauderdale

Classic Serape, ca. 1860
Navajo
Lowe Art Museum
University of Miami
Gift of Alfred I. Barton, 1956

Public Art Programs

Public art enhances the quality of life and promotes civic pride in communities throughout Florida. In 1973 Dade County set a precedent for cities and counties by establishing Florida's first art in public places program for the commission and purchase of artworks. Art in public places programs are funded mainly by a percentage of construction costs of county and city buildings.

The Art in State Buildings Program was established by the Florida legislature in 1979 and is administered by the Department of State, Division of Cultural Affairs. Funds of one half of one percent of the construction costs for state buildings (not to exceed $100,000) are allotted for acquiring artwork for permanent public display. Through Art in Public Places and Art in State Buildings programs, artists collaborate with architects and designers to integrate artwork with buildings and public spaces.

The communities with Art in Public Places Programs funded by local ordinances or user fees are: Metropolitan Dade County, Brevard County, Broward County, Palm Beach County, City of Orlando, City of Tampa, City of Gainesville, City of Palm Beach Gardens, City of West Palm Beach, City of Royal Palm Beach, and City of Juno.

DAYTONA RENAISSANCE, Robert Fetty, 1989. Daytona Regional Service Center, Daytona Beach. Commissioned by Florida's Art in State Buildings Program. Recalling Stonehenge and other ancient ruins, thirteen columns of white Portland concrete and bent stainless steel are integrated with the building and the site.

MAKING PURPLE, Fernando Garcia, 1987. Okeechobee Metrorail Station, Hialeah. Commissioned by the Metro-Dade Art in Public Places Trust. Neon lighting in skylights throughout the station cycle through eight red-and-blue color combinations that momentarily "make purple" during a fifteen-minute period, submerging commuters in refreshing cool hues.

DROPPED BOWL WITH SCATTERED SLICES AND PEELS, Claes Oldenburg and Coosje van Bruggen, 1990. Metro-Dade Government Center Open Space Park, Miami. Commissioned by the Metro-Dade Art in Public Places Trust. Appears as if a giant bowl of orange sections and peels fell from the sky to the plaza below. Jets of water spurt from pools representing the juice of the splattering orange.

CASABLANCA, FROM THE LITTLE HAVANA SERIES. Mario Algaze, 1990. Florida Department of Law Enforcement Building, Tallahassee. Purchased by Florida's Art in State Buildings Program. Cibachrome photograph, 8"H x 10"W. Part of a series of 40 images taken between 1983–1987 depicting life in Miami's Little Havana.

Folk Arts

Florida is diversely populated with over seventy identifiable ethnic groups, each with distinctive folk arts. Florida folk arts include the performing arts of music, dance, drama, puppetry, and storytelling, as well as visual arts, crafts, rituals, and foodways.

The Bureau of Florida Folklife Programs, Department of State, was created in 1979 to document, present, and encourage folklife and folk arts. Folk Arts Apprenticeships offered by the bureau provide students the opportunity of learning a craft by working intensively with a master. Florida Heritage Awards, another program the bureau coordinates, honors outstanding folk artists and folk cultural advocates.

The Division of Cultural Affairs, Department of State, awards grants to help organizations preserve and encourage public awareness of traditional arts and crafts. The individual artist fellowship program awards grants to traditional folk artists.

Weaving a White Oak Basket, Lucreaty Clark, Florida Folk Heritage Award, 1985. Master of split white oak basketry. Clark learned to make white oak baskets from her parents and grandmother, who worked on cotton plantations in north Florida.

Caning a Chair, Burton Otte, 1978. Otte, of Gainesville, is demonstrating chair caning at the Florida Folk Festival in White Springs.

Playing the Tsabouna, Nikitas Tsimouris, 1991. National Heritage Award, 1991. Florida Folk Heritage Award, 1989. Master of the centuries-old instrument, the tsabouna, a Greek bagpipe made of goat skin. Tsimouris of Tarpon Springs learned to play the tsabouna on Kalimnos Island. In 1968 he emigrated to the United States.

Down By the Old Graveyard, Mario Sanchez, 1976. Florida Folk Heritage Award, 1991. A bas-relief oil painting on wood. Sanchez is a Cuban-American woodcarver-painter of Key West.

Drama, Dance, and Music

Theatre has grown rapidly in Florida since 1956 when the Coconut Grove Playhouse was founded. Now more than thirty professional and a variety of semiprofessional companies are established in Florida. The Asolo Theatre Company, known nationally and internationally, was the first professional theatre company designated by Florida as a state theatre.

The Greater Miami Opera, established in 1941, first brought professional opera to Miami. Opera has grown along with Florida, which now boasts seven professional opera companies, and numerous semiprofessional regional and university and college companies located throughout the state. Professional symphony orchestras are found in most of Florida's metropolitan areas. Regional and univer-

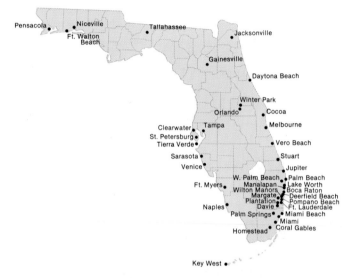

DISNEY–MGM STUDIOS' "NEW YORK" BACKLOT, Lake Buena Vista

©The Walt Disney Company

MAJOR FILM STUDIOS

Disney-MGM Studios, Orlando
Greenwich Studios, Miami
Limelite Studios, Miami
Universal Studios Florida, Orlando

DIE WALKÜRE, Greater Miami Opera, 1989, Miami

PROFESSIONAL OPERA COMPANIES

Fort Lauderdale Opera, Ft. Lauderdale
Gold Coast Opera, Pompano Beach
Greater Miami Opera, Miami
Orlando Opera Company Inc., Orlando
Palm Beach Opera, Inc., Palm Beach
Sarasota Opera Association, Sarasota
Spanish Lyric Theatre, Tampa

PROFESSIONAL THEATRE COMPANIES

Acting Company of Riverside Theatre, Vero Beach
Actors Playhouse, Miami
Alhambra Dinner Theatre, Jacksonville
American Stage, St. Petersburg
Area Stage, Miami Beach
Asolo Theatre Company, Sarasota
Bits'N Pieces Puppet Theatre, Tampa
Brian C. Smith's Off Broadway Theatre on 26th Street, Wilton Manors
Caldwell Theatre Company, Boca Raton
Coconut Grove Playhouse, Miami
The Drama Center, Deerfield
Fantasy Theatre Factory, Miami
Florida Shakespeare Theatre, Coral Gables
Florida Studio Theatre, Sarasota
Golden Apple Dinner Theatre, Sarasota
Golden Apple Dinner Theatre, Venice
Hippodrome Theatre, Gainesville
Jupiter Theatre, Jupiter
The Mark Two Dinner Theatre, Orlando
Naples Dinner Theatre, North Naples
New Playmakers, Tampa
New Theatre, Coral Gables
Orlando Shakespeare Festival, Orlando
Palm Beach Shakespeare Festival, Jupiter
Plantation Dinner Theatre, Orlando
The Public Theatre of Greater Ft. Lauderdale, Ft. Lauderdale
Royal Palm Dinner Theatre, Boca Raton
SAK Theatre & Comedy Lab, Orlando
Seaside Music Theater, Daytona Beach
Showboat Dinner Theatre, Clearwater
Stageworks Theatre, Tampa
Standing-Room-Only Productions, Plantation
The Tampa Players, Tampa
Theatre Club of the Palm Beaches, Manalapan
Tierra Verde Dinner Theatre, Tierra Verde

sity and college symphony orchestras also contribute to the accessibility of symphonic music in Florida.

Professional dance is a relative newcomer to the state, initiated only twenty years ago. Today there are 33 professional dance companies, 74 civic and regional companies, and extensive college and university dance programs.

By 1979 Florida had become one of the leading film production centers in the nation. Universal and Disney/MGM studios opened in 1987 adding to the production facilities already available. Although Florida's film history dates back to 1898, the 1950s Tarzan films starring Johnny Weismuller and featuring Florida's natural springs are well remembered.

The St. Johns River City Band is an official State of Florida band and is one of only two professional brass bands in the U.S. Incorporated in 1984, the St. Johns River City Band is composed of 18 brass instrumentalists and 2 percussionists. Most of the band's concerts have been free and open to the public.

Florida's State Touring Program, initiated by the Florida Department of State, was created in 1979 to bring the state's finest performing arts groups to as many Florida communities as possible at a reduced rate. In addition, many of the performing arts companies conduct educational programs designed specifically for students, teachers, and community members.

A broad range of performing arts from classical to the contemporary are offered in Florida. Music, dance, and drama abound in the state, reflecting the diverse culture and artistic achievements of Floridians.

CAPRICCIO FOR PIANO AND ORCHESTRA ("RUBIES"), Miami City Ballet, Miami Beach

ST. JOHNS RIVER CITY BAND, Jacksonville

PROFESSIONAL BRASS BAND

St. Johns River City Band, Jacksonville

PROFESSIONAL SYMPHONY ORCHESTRAS

Brevard Symphony Orchestra, Inc., Melbourne
The Florida Orchestra, Inc. Tampa
Florida Philharmonic Orchestra, Ft. Lauderdale
Florida Space Coast Philharmonic, Inc., Cocoa
Florida Symphonic Pops, Boca Raton
Florida Symphony Orchestra, Orlando
Florida West Coast Symphony Orchestra, Sarasota
Greater Palm Beach Symphony, Palm Beach
Greater Pensacola Symphony Orchestra, Pensacola
Jacksonville Symphony Orchestra, Jacksonville
Naples Philharmonic, Naples
New World Symphony, Miami Beach
Northwest Florida Symphony Orchestra of Okaloosa, Walton Community College, Niceville
Okaloosa Symphony Orchestra, Ft. Walton
Southwest Florida Symphony Orchestra and Chorus Association, Inc., Ft. Myers
Tallahassee Symphony Orchestra, Tallahassee

PROFESSIONAL DANCE COMPANIES

Bad Dog Dance, Miami
Ballet Concerto Company, Miami
Ballet Flamenco La Rosa, Miami Beach
Ballet Florida, West Palm Beach
Ballet Theatre of Miami, Inc., Coral Gables
Body and Soul Dance Theatre, Davie
Carrington Contemporary Dance, Miami
Case and Company, Stuart
Dance Alive, Gainesville
Dance Arts Foundation, Homestead
Dance Theatre of Florida, St. Petersburg
Demetrius A. Klein and Dancers, Lake Worth
First City Dance Theatre, Pensacola
Florida Ballet at Jacksonville, Jacksonville
Freddick Bratcher and Company, Miami
Gisela Sotomayor Spanish Dance Company, Tampa
Karen Peterson and Dancers, Miami
Key West Dance Theatre, Key West
Kuumba Dancers and Drummers, Tampa
Mary Luft and Company, Miami
Mary Street Dance Theatre, Miami
Miami City Ballet, Miami Beach
Miami Movement Dance Company, Miami
Miami Repertory Ballet Company, Miami
Momentum Dance Company, Miami
New Moves Productions, Inc., Gainesville
Northwest Florida Ballet, Ft. Walton Beach
Oudanoqueciade, Margate
Randy Warshaw Dance Company, Miami
Sarasota Ballet of Florida, Sarasota
Southern Ballet Theatre, Winter Park
Tampa Ballet, Tampa
Troupe El Hiyat, Palm Springs

Religion

The source for the maps and graph on this page is *Churches and Church Membership in the United States*, *1980*, published by Glenmary Research Center. The Glenmary updating will not appear until after publication of this atlas, but basic patterns displayed are not expected to change markedly. Glenmary was able to obtain information on most but not all denominations. For example, data on Greek Orthodox membership were unobtainable. Percentages are therefore slightly higher than if all denominations were included. Information on thirty-seven denominations in Florida was published; the seventeen largest are shown on the graph. Data for certain denominations, e.g., Baptists, are the total membership of two or more organizations

Protestant denominations predominate in northern Florida and in some rural, interior, peninsular counties; many Catholic retirees from the North and Hispanics create higher Catholic percentages in coastal peninsular counties, particularly in southern Florida. Jewish population in southeastern Florida is far larger than implied by membership in Reform Judaism and Conservative Judaism synagogues.

Members of Religious Denominations, 1980

Percentage of County Population

- Less than 30
- 30–39
- 40–49
- 50–59
- 60 or over

Members of Catholic Churches, 1980

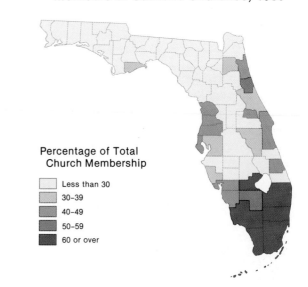

Percentage of Total Church Membership

- Less than 30
- 30–39
- 40–49
- 50–59
- 60 or over

Denominational Membership, 1980

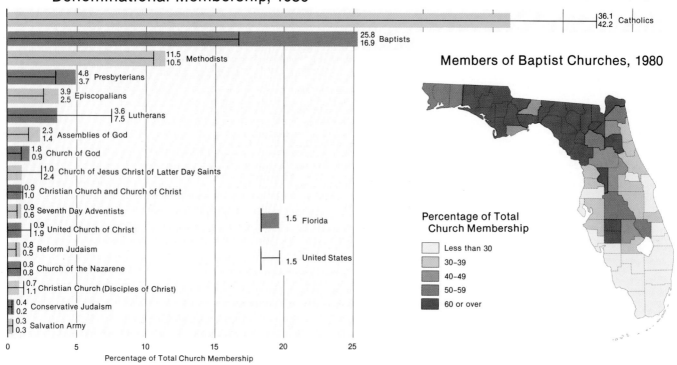

	Florida	United States
Catholics	36.1	42.2
Baptists	25.8	16.9
Methodists	11.5	10.5
Presbyterians	4.8	3.7
Episcopalians	3.9	2.5
Lutherans	3.6	7.5
Assemblies of God	2.3	1.4
Church of God	1.8	0.9
Church of Jesus Christ of Latter Day Saints	1.0	2.4
Christian Church and Church of Christ	0.9	1.0
Seventh Day Adventists	0.9	0.6
United Church of Christ	0.9	1.9
Reform Judaism	0.8	0.5
Church of the Nazarene	0.8	0.8
Christian Church (Disciples of Christ)	0.7	1.1
Conservative Judaism	0.4	0.2
Salvation Army	0.3	0.3

Florida 1.5
United States 1.5

Percentage of Total Church Membership

Members of Baptist Churches, 1980

Percentage of Total Church Membership

- Less than 30
- 30–39
- 40–49
- 50–59
- 60 or over

Language

Dialect Regions

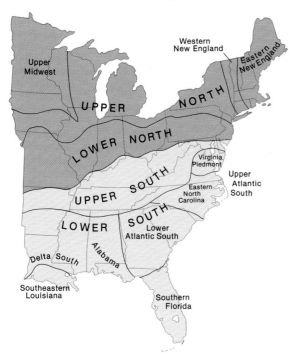

Florida has been populated by many people from other parts of the U.S. as well as from foreign nations. Northern Florida was largely settled, after removal of the Indians, by planters and their slaves from the Carolinas and the Virginia Piedmont. The people of western Florida were similar in culture and dialect to those of adjacent Alabama. Since World War II hundreds of thousands of retirees have settled in Florida. Traditionally those from the Northeast have settled along the Gold Coast and those from the Midwest along the Sun Coast.

Waves of Spanish-speaking people began coming to south Florida in the early 1960s following the Cuban revolution. In 1980 more than 125,000 additional Cuban refugees entered the state. Tens of thousands of Puerto Ricans, Haitians, Mexicans, and Central and South Americans have also immigrated to Florida. In 1980 Hispanics accounted for 8.8 percent of the population; in 1990, for 12.2 percent.

Languages Spoken at Home, 1980

	Persons 5–17	Urban	Rural	Persons 18 & over	Urban	Rural
Chinese	1,592	1,505	87	7,164	6,798	139
French	8,884	8,125	759	63,002	57,620	5,382
German	6,106	5,215	891	61,819	55,271	6,548
Greek	2,068	1,969	99	13,247	12,709	538
Italian	3,112	2,832	280	56,215	52,534	3,681
Philippine Lang.	784	688	96	7,609	7,131	478
Polish	580	488	69	19,752	17,866	1,886
Spanish	164,293	154,360	9,933	621,951	595,059	26,892
Other Specified	13,906	12,903	1,003	137,772	129,701	8,071
Unspecified	4,267	3,349	918	15,541	13,942	1,599

Persons Who Spoke a Language other than English at Home, 1980

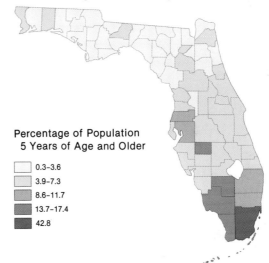

Percentage of Population
5 Years of Age and Older

- 0.3–3.6
- 3.9–7.3
- 8.6–11.7
- 13.7–17.4
- 42.8

Persons Who Spoke English Not Well or Not at All, 1980

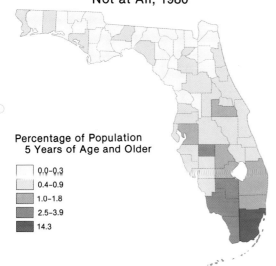

Percentage of Population
5 Years of Age and Older

- 0.0–0.3
- 0.4–0.9
- 1.0–1.8
- 2.5–3.9
- 14.3

Persons Who Spoke Spanish at Home, 1980

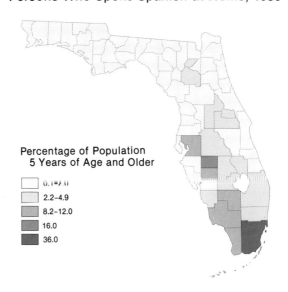

Percentage of Population
5 Years of Age and Older

- 0.1–2.0
- 2.2–4.9
- 8.2–12.0
- 16.0
- 36.0

POPULATION

Florida is geographically part of the South, although its population differs radically from that of other southern states. Florida's demographic history, however, did not begin to diverge markedly from that of its regional neighbors until the middle of the twentieth century. Until then it was basically an agricultural state, populated by whites and blacks, most descended from people who had migrated from other southern states since 1821, the year Florida became a territory of the United States.

The character of Florida began to change rapidly after World War II when the relatively modest but steady flow of mainly southerners into the state was augmented by a flood of white northerners, whose numbers have mounted into the millions over the last forty years. Many of these northerners have been retirees. A little more than a decade after the migration of northerners began, a movement of people from Caribbean nations commenced. At first they were primarily political refugees from Castro's successful revolution in Cuba, but later economic refugees from many other Caribbean nations settled in Florida. Over the past thirty years approximately three-quarters of a million people from the Caribbean have come to live in the state.

Migration to Florida during the last fifty years has made its social geography far more complex today than in the past. The maps on the pages that follow portray the social geographical heterogeneity of this state, while the narrative attempts to explain it.

Population Growth

Since Florida became a territory its rate of population growth has always been high. In most decades since 1830, the year of the first census, the ten-year growth rate has been between 40 and 60 percent. In all census periods the rates of population growth in Florida have been higher than those of the United States as a whole. The nation's population growth rate was highest during the decades of the nineteenth century. In Florida growth rates have been at least triple those of the nation since the 1920s.

In 1830, 34,730 people were enumerated in Florida. Most lived in its north, near the Georgia border. When Florida became a United States territory in 1821, the Midwest and the lower Mississippi valley were being populated by people from the settled portion of the nation or from Europe. In 1817 Andrew Jackson had removed many of the Indians from north Florida in what later became known as the First Seminole War. Florida was now considered a frontier, ready for occupation. Typically the pattern of population growth in frontier America began with a rapid immigration that lasted several decades, followed by a steep decline in the flow once the land had been occupied. Florida's growth rates were high during the first few decades, but were not as high as in territories in the Midwest or the lower Mississippi valley. In fact, most who came to Florida settled in the north, and few moved onto the peninsula, where the true frontier began, and where a second war to remove the Indians was fought from 1835–42. Migration would have increased if it were not for the formidable environmental obstacles that had to be overcome to live and work in subtropical Florida. Elsewhere in the nation were far more attractive frontiers. People did, however, continue to come in relatively large numbers during the nineteenth century. Florida's population during the 1850s reached 100,000, by the 1870s it had risen to 250,000, and by the late 1890s it surpassed 500,000.

It was during the twentieth century that people began to flow into the state in large numbers. By 1923 its population had reached 1 million, double the 1898 figure. The 2 million mark was reached in about 17 more years (1940), 3 million in eleven more years (1951), 4 million in approximately 1955, 5 and 6 million during the 1960s, 7, 8, and 9 million in the 1970s, and 10, 11, and 12 and million during the 1980s. In 1990 the state's population approached 13 million. Florida overtook both Pennsylvania and Ohio in the 1980s, and in 1990 had the fourth largest population in the nation, behind California, New York, and Texas. The rates of growth of Alaska, Arizona, and Nevada were higher than Florida's during the 1980s, but only California exceeded Florida in absolute growth. Florida's delegation to the U.S. Congress grew from 6 in 1950 to 23 in 1992.

National prosperity following World War II explains the huge growth in population of Florida during the past four decades. Soon after the war most families were able to purchase automobiles, and many had the time and money to travel. Many chose Florida for their vacations. Social Security and other retirement benefits available after the war to millions of workers made it possible for many to move to Florida. Employment opportunities mushroomed with the growing numbers of tourists and retirees. The construction industry boomed, as homes, schools, hotels, stores, and offices as well as roads had to be built to meet the needs of new residents and tourists. Visitors and new residents also required a myriad of services, further increasing employment opportunities. Those who came to work and their families created more demand and more jobs. In short, jobs in Florida have been fueled by migration.

Settlement of the State

At the time Florida became a territory of the United States in 1821 there were just two urban settlements, St. Augustine and Pensacola, separated by 275 miles. Each held about 2,000 inhabitants. Neither was chosen as the territorial capital. Instead, land was cleared for the capital from the forest halfway between the two older settlements. A small Indian population was in the area at the time, but no Europeans. The town was given the name Tallahassee, a corruption of a Seminole Indian word for the area. Fortu-

itous for Tallahassee's growth it was located in the best area for cotton cultivation in the territory. For years it was the market town for a prosperous agricultural region and for a brief time was the territory's largest city. Throughout the nineteenth century three-quarters of the state's inhabitants lived in north Florida between the Suwannee and Apalachicola rivers, initially in the part called Middle Florida, which included Tallahassee. Following the Civil War, northeastern Florida, which includes Jacksonville, overtook Middle Florida in population. West Florida barely maintained an 18 percent share of the state's population in the nineteenth century, and most who lived there chose to settle in or around Pensacola. Relatively few people moved down the peninsula during the nineteenth century. In 1860 it contained only 6 percent of the state's population, but by 1900 its share had risen to 28 percent. For decades the most densely populated part of the peninsula was around Orlando where the economy was based on citrus and a handful of other crops that the newly built railroads could ship to the northern United States.

Urban centers in Florida were small throughout the nineteenth century. From 1850 until sometime during the 1890s Key West was the state's largest town. Its importance rested on its strategic location at the entrance to the Gulf of Mexico. The federal government located a naval base there, and several stone forts were built, making the town the "Gibraltar of the Gulf of Mexico." Aside from naval personnel, many of its inhabitants were Cubans and Bahamians. Although visited frequently by winter tourists, it actually had little economic connection with the rest of the state. During the 1890s its population was overtaken in size by both Jacksonville and Pensacola. Jacksonville in 1900 had a population of 28,429 and was thriving as the gateway to the peninsula. Pensacola (17,747 inhabitants) was growing rapidly as a lumber port. Key West in 1900 held 17,114 people, almost 1,000 less than in 1890. Tampa, with a population of 15,839, was the only other city in the state with a population greater than 5,000.

Most population growth during the twentieth century has been on the peninsula. At the beginning of the century north Florida held two-thirds of the state's population, but ninety years later it contained only 20 percent. During the same period the share of the state's population in the northern half of the peninsula (central Florida) rose from 23 percent to 42 percent and the southern half from 5 percent to 38 percent. When Florida became a popular tourist and retirement state after World War II, south Florida became the most rapidly growing part of the state. Since 1970 both south and central Florida have been growing at about the same rate. In-migration to central Florida was greatly stimulated by both the space program, located in Brevard County, and tourism. Tourism was given a big boost with the opening of Disney World in 1971, which was soon followed by many more tourist attractions. After 1970 many retirees began to choose central Florida over the Gold Coast, in part because of fear generated from the growth of drug-related crime and violence in Miami. That city, during the 1980s, had among the highest murder rates of any in the nation.

During the twentieth century the coastal margins of the peninsula have received the vast majority of newcomers.

Retirees and vacationers prefer the beaches of the Atlantic Ocean and the Gulf of Mexico to the rolling hills and numerous small lakes of the interior, and these two groups have been the principal generators of jobs for those who arrived in search of economic opportunity. A string of coastal towns and cities have grown steadily in size during this century. Many have now merged, creating two long and narrow urbanized areas. One extends from Daytona Beach south beyond Miami, another from Ft. Myers to at least 40 miles north of St. Petersburg–Tampa.

Today 92 percent of Floridians live in the state's Metropolitan Statistical Areas (MSAs). Only six states have higher percentages of urban population. In 1960, the U.S. Census only identified six MSAs in Florida. By 1990 their number had risen to twenty. Florida MSAs are among the fastest growing in the nation. For example, the area that now comprises the Naples MSA held only 16,000 people in 1960, but in 1990 was the home of 152,000. Of Florida's five most populous MSAs, Miami-Hialeah, Ft. Lauderdale–Hollywood, Tampa–St. Petersburg, and Jacksonville grew slower than the state average between 1980 and 1990, whereas only Orlando grew faster. New residents are now more frequently choosing to live in smaller MSAs, the larger ones being perceived as congested, and even dangerous. Population growth in Florida outside MSAs is generally slower. Nonmetropolitan north Florida and the interior of the peninsula simply lack the amenities to appeal to many retirees, and few businesses find the economic environment sufficiently attractive to move there.

A gigantic metropolitan area comprising several MSAs, with a total population of 4.3 million people, has emerged on the southeastern coast of Florida between Miami and West Palm Beach. Known as the Gold Coast, one-third of the state's population lives there, including 72 percent of its Hispanics, 40 percent of its blacks, and 37 percent of its non-Hispanic white aged. Its share of the state's Hispanics has remained approximately the same since data became available in 1970. Since 1940 its share of the state's blacks has risen. Throughout the twentieth century, until 1980, the Gold Coast continually increased its share of the state's non-Hispanic aged. During the 1980s the region's share of that group fell 2 percentage points, largely because Miami has lost its attraction as a retirement destination. When this huge urban area began to emerge, Greater Miami had the majority of its population. Its share has been steadily falling, and the counties to its north have begun to grow far faster.

Components of Population Change

Populations grow or decline as a result of the balance of births, deaths, and net migration. Florida's fertility patterns have changed over time much like those of the nation. The birth rate dipped during the economic depression of the late 1920s and early 1930s, moved upward with the baby boom of the 1940s and early 1950s, and dropped progressively during the past two decades. Every birth adds to the state's population, but Florida's exceptional growth is due only in small part to birth rates. Like all Americans, Floridians live longer today than in the past. On the negative side, death rates in Florida are high, since the state has attracted so many retirees. By 1990 deaths in Florida almost equalled births, and in several counties more people die each year than are born. As the percentage of aged in the state's population increases, growth through births is more frequently being canceled by deaths. Population growth by natural increase presently accounts for only 12 percent of the state's growth.

Without question, migration to Florida has been the principal factor in its population increase, contributing 88 percent of the state's increase in population during the 1980s. Within the United States, net migration to Florida has been greatest from the northeastern states, followed by the north central states. Many people come to Florida from other southern states, but almost as many Floridians now leave for these states, making for a small net migration. The majority of those who come from the northeastern and north central states are retirees, although Florida now attracts many in the productive age groups and their dependents. People who come to Florida from southern states generally come with their families to work.

Since 1960 hundreds of thousands of Latin Americans have entered the state, principally from the Caribbean, many without official documents. Initially Cuban exiles from the 1959 Castro-led revolution made up the majority of Latins, but now they come from many Latin American nations, escaping poverty and political upheaval. Canadians, mainly people 65 years of age and older, have for years been a major contributor to the immigrant stream. The newest source of foreign immigrants is Asia, and during the 1980s tens of thousands of Asians arrived. The majority were from China, but many people also immigrated from the Indian subcontinent.

Population Composition

The composition of Florida's population is unusual in two significant respects—its disproportionately high percentage of elderly people and its high percentage of Hispanics. In 1990, 18 percent of all Floridians were 65 years of age or older, compared with 12 percent for the nation. Six counties had percentages in 1990 above 30 percent. Five of these counties are peninsular and face the Gulf of Mexico: Charlotte, Citrus, Hernando, Pasco, and Sarasota. The sixth is Highlands County, northwest of Lake Okeechobee. In these counties, and many others throughout the state, are communities overwhelmingly populated by the aged. The numbers of women, because of their longer life expectancy, exceed the numbers of men at these older ages, and thus women are considerably overrepresented in counties with large shares of the aged.

From the territorial period until the middle of the twentieth century the vast majority of Floridians were either descended from people born in the British Isles or were black. A number of counties near the Georgia border, where cotton and tobacco were important crops, had a black majority for over a century, but today only one remains (Gadsden).

Throughout this century the share of blacks within the state's population has fallen. Their share of the state's population has decreased as a result of the huge number of white in-migrants who have arrived, especially since 1950. Also, during several decades more blacks left the state than arrived. Throughout the last century the share of blacks in the state was over three times the national average, but by

1990 it was approximately the same as the national average. The distribution of blacks in the state has also changed. No longer are most living in small towns or on farms in northern Florida. Today most live in the central cities of the state's largest metropolitan areas. Approximately 40 percent live in the gigantic urbanized area that extends from Miami to West Palm Beach. Many of these blacks live in the city of Miami.

Like other states of the South, Florida attracted few immigrants from Europe during the nineteenth century. However, several thousand Spaniards from Cuba and people of Spanish descent but born on the island left during that island's long civil war to live in Key West, where they established a cigar industry. Following a destructive hurricane they left Key West to relocate in Tampa. Early in this century a handful of Greeks sponge fishermen settled in Tarpon Springs. Small communities of Danes, Czechs, Japanese, and several other nationalities were also established in various places throughout the state at the end of the nineteenth and beginning of the twentieth century, but they were usually short lived.

Ethnicity became a major factor in urban Florida following World War II, when thousands of aged Jews began to arrive in southeastern Florida from the large metropolitan areas in the northern United States. Until then Ybor City, an Hispanic area of Tampa, and "Little Havana" in Miami were the only urban ethnic neighborhoods of any consequence in the state. Miami Beach was particularly attractive to Jewish retirees, and that community quickly became closely identified with this group. Although other ethnic American retirees arrived from the North at the same time as the Jews, they rarely concentrated in the same communities. The most notable exception was the Finns. Many Finns came from the North to retiree in and around Lake Worth in Palm Beach County.

Florida today has one of the largest Jewish populations in the nation. Most are retirees who spent their productive lives in northern states. Initially they settled primarily in the Miami area, but with the arrival of the Hispanics to that city the Jewish population began to decline. Coincident to that decline, the Jewish population has grown rapidly in counties to the north, and increasingly elsewhere in the state.

No ethnic group has had a greater impact on the state's society than the Hispanics. Hundreds of thousands of Cubans went into exile in Florida following the Cuban Revolution of 1959, and a large percentage chose to live in Dade County. Poverty and civil unrest has driven hundreds of thousands more from Caribbean countries and Mexico to Florida. Today Florida has the fourth largest Hispanic population in the United States. Approximately 72 percent live on the Gold Coast, and most of these reside in the central cities of Hialeah and Miami. Hialeah in 1990 had the highest percentage of Hispanics in its population of any large city in the United States (74 percent) and Miami had the third (56 percent), just behind El Paso, Texas. The Hispanic population of Florida is commonly believed to be overwhelmingly Cuban, but actually it is also comprised of people from many other Latin American nations. Whereas Cubans have concentrated heavily in Dade County, other Latin Americans are more widely distributed throughout the state.

It would be comforting, but not accurate, to say that Florida is a twentieth-century melting pot of diverse racial, ethnic, and age groups. As elsewhere in the United States, a lumpy stew of racial and ethnic groups is a more appropriate metaphor. Nowhere is this better illustrated than in Dade County (Miami), a metropolitan area that has attracted many blacks, aged Jews, young non-Hispanic whites, and Hispanics. Instead of a harmonious integration of these groups over time they have contested for the most attractive parts of the city, and those with the most economic power have won. Today the aged Jews no longer have a large presence; the neighborhoods that they lived in have become Hispanic. Hispanics have also become dominant in middle and upper middle class central city neighborhoods formerly occupied by young non-Hispanic white families. The latter now have either moved to the suburbs or out of the county. Most blacks remain in inner city ghettoes, although many of the more affluent have moved to the suburbs. Though the groups may be different, the same contest for space goes on in the state's other metropolitan areas.

Looking to the Future

Predicting Florida's population in the year 2000 is difficult. A consensus is emerging that growth will not be as great as in the 1980s. This is based on the fact that the nation's age cohort reaching 65 years of age during the decade will not grow substantially. Also, those who will reach retirement age during the 1990s will have a wider choice of retirement places throughout the nation to select from, and fewer will choose Florida. If national economic growth is as slow during the entire decade as it was in the first years, fewer retirees will have sufficient savings to move to Florida. Fewer older migrants to the state will mean fewer new jobs to attract younger people.

Despite a possible reduction in the number of migrants to the state during the 1990s, by the end of the decade there still will be millions more Floridians than when the decade began. The absorption of these new residents will continue to put enormous strain on the state's existing infrastructure. More schools, hospitals, stores, and homes will have to be built, and the transportation system improved. The decision of what and where to build will put a heavy burden on state and local planning agencies.

Population Growth

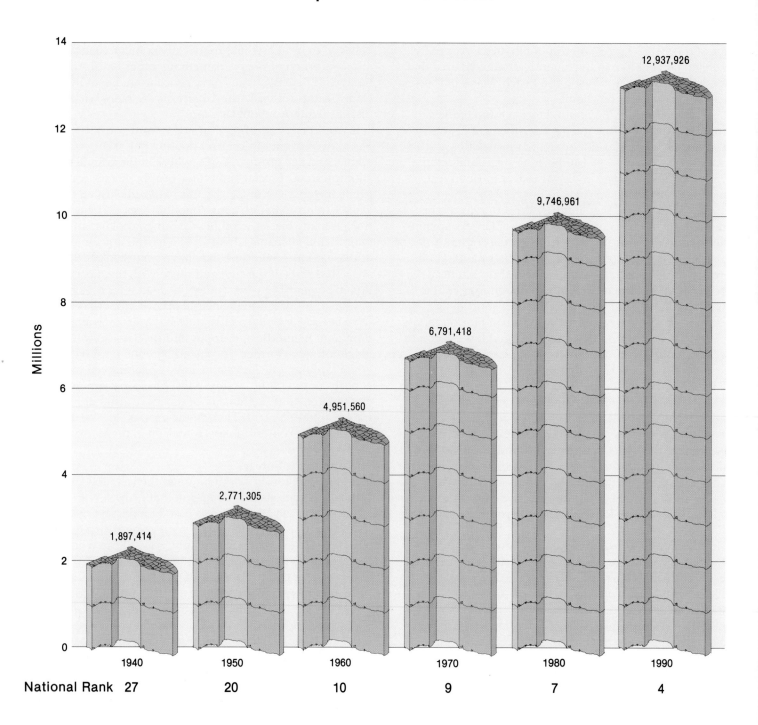

During the nineteenth century, Florida's hot and humid climate and extensive wetlands made it less attractive to settlers than areas elsewhere in the nation. Florida's population, which by 1991 exceeded 13 million, only reached 1 million during the 1930s. Since 1940 Florida's population growth has been phenomenal. During each ten-year interval since that date the growth rate has been well above the national average. During the 1950s the state's population growth rate was especially high.

Following World War II, pension benefits, especially Social Security, induced a growing number of retirees to settle in the state. Housing and service needs of these retirees created a large labor demand. The postwar period also brought increasing affluence to Americans, and the

number of tourists attracted to the state grew rapidly, requiring workers for additional construction and more services. In the 1960s hundreds of thousands of Latin Americans, principally from the Caribbean, began to arrive, further augmenting the population.

The importance of the aged to population growth cannot be minimized nor can the importance of jobs created to meet their needs. During the 1990s the number of people reaching 65 is not expected to increase over the number who reached 65 in the 1980s. Because other Sun Belt states now have attractive areas for retirement, the number of retirees coming to Florida will probably be lower during this decade.

Night Views

Population distribution in the southeastern United States is shown through satellite imagery shot on clear nights in 1974, 1979, and 1989 from the U.S. Air Force's Defense Meteorological Satellite. Florida's rapid population growth is clearly visible. In both 1974 and 1979 the southeastern Florida urban concentration between West Palm Beach and Miami remained distinct from coastal towns farther north. By 1989 urban lighting was almost continuous to Melbourne. In 1974 Bradenton-Sarasota and Ft. Myers–Cape Coral were visible along the southwestern coast. By 1989 urban development was almost continuous between Tampa–St. Petersburg and Ft. Myers. The intense urbanization of the corridor between Tampa and Orlando is also evident. The areas of darkness in northwest Florida and in the interior of peninsular Florida outside the Tampa-Orlando corridor changed little between 1974 and 1989. Growth has largely been along peninsular coasts and in the peninsular interior between Lakeland and Orlando.

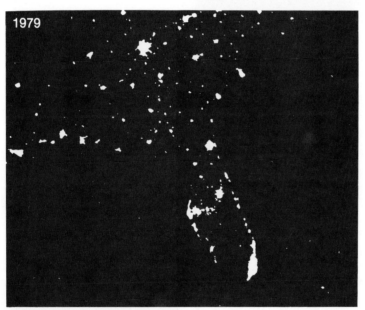

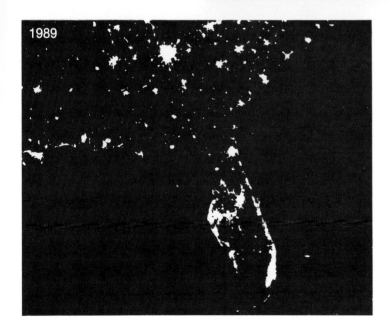

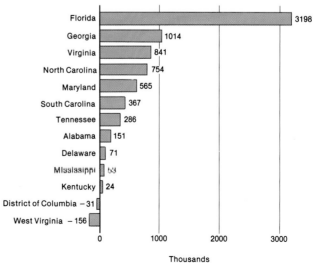

Population Change 1980–1990

State	Thousands
Florida	3198
Georgia	1014
Virginia	841
North Carolina	754
Maryland	565
South Carolina	367
Tennessee	286
Alabama	151
Delaware	71
Mississippi	53
Kentucky	24
District of Columbia	−31
West Virginia	−156

Population Distribution

The 1990 population distribution map was based on the population of county subdivisions defined by the Bureau of the Census. Each dot represents 1,000 persons. Many county subdivisions have populations less than 1,000 and are thus not represented on the map. For this reason, the dots should not be regarded as representing all of the state's inhabitants. The map does, however, show clearly that vast areas of the state are thinly populated.

Florida's population has become increasingly concentrated during this century, as the state evolved from more rural than the nation as a whole to more urban. This process was most rapid after 1940. The first wave of growth after World War II came from retirees. Largely

Population Density, 1990

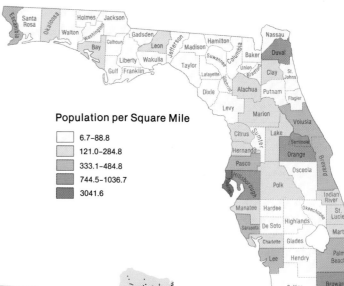

Population per Square Mile

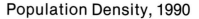

One dot equals 1000 persons
1990 data

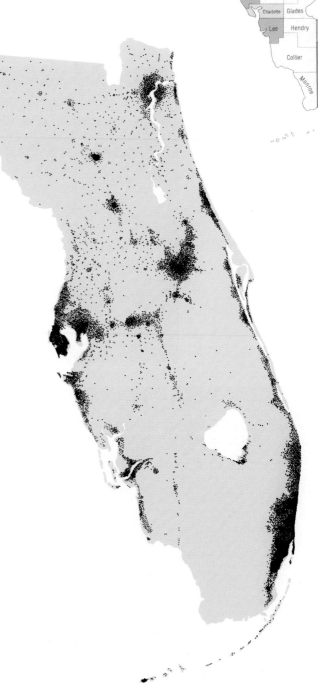

bypassing small retirement communities that had developed throughout the state before World War II, particularly in the central part of the peninsula, and the older sizable retirement community of St. Petersburg, retirees began to settle on the Gold Coast in the southeastern portion of the state. Along with retirees came construction workers and service providers. Today a string of dense settlement extends up almost the entire east coast. Newer large communities, mainly inhabited by retirees, have developed on the Sun Coast of southwestern Florida, and today settlement is almost continuous from Tampa–St. Petersburg to Naples. A population corridor has emerged from the older metropolitan area of Tampa–St. Petersburg through smaller Polk County cities to Greater Orlando, which today is merging with Greater Daytona Beach. Growth here is based on a number of different activities, including agriculture, mining, manufacturing, and tourism. The population of the northern part of the state continues to grow less than that of the peninsula.

The intensity of urban settlement within Florida today is so great that the image of the state both in the eyes of most of its residents, as well as people from elsewhere, is an urban landscape. Nonetheless, much of the state is lightly populated, some places with densities as low as in rural areas of Montana or Wyoming. Some of this area, such as the Everglades and Big Cypress Swamp, is environmentally unsuitable for dense human occupancy. In north Florida the marginally colder winters and distance from beaches and urban centers have contributed to low population density.

Population Change

Population Growth 1960–1970

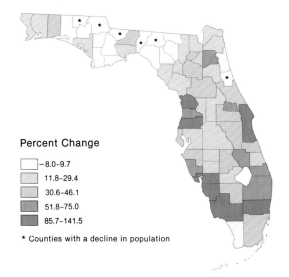

Percent Change

- [ ] −8.0–9.7
- [ ] 11.8–29.4
- [ ] 30.6–46.1
- [ ] 51.8–75.0
- [ ] 85.7–141.5

* Counties with a decline in population

Population Growth 1970–1980

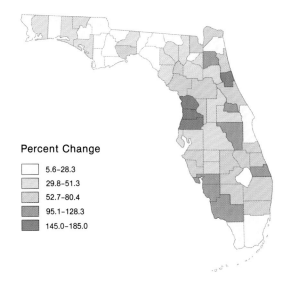

Percent Change

- [ ] 5.6–28.3
- [ ] 29.8–51.3
- [ ] 52.7–80.4
- [ ] 95.1–128.3
- [ ] 145.0–185.0

Population Growth 1980–1990

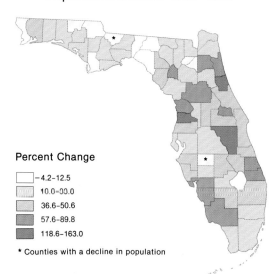

Percent Change

- [ ] −4.2–12.5
- [ ] 10.0–00.0
- [ ] 36.6–50.6
- [ ] 57.6–89.8
- [ ] 118.6–163.0

* Counties with a decline in population

Florida's rapid rate of population growth has been primarily a result of in-migration and immigration. Until 1930, Florida's rate of natural increase was at least as high as that of the nation, but in the last sixty years, with the influx of retirees, Florida's rate of natural increase has been markedly lower than the average for the nation. Today several counties on the Gulf coast have higher death than birth rates.

National prosperity after World War II meant more people were able to retire in Florida, creating jobs in construction and services for younger people. The destination of the majority of new residents has always been the peninsula. Population growth was also stimulated by tourism. Following World War II American families had more discretionary income, and many sought recreational opportunities within Florida, generating jobs. Manufacturing also grew in importance, particularly after 1970.

In the 1950s the highest rates of increase were along the east coast, from Brevard County south, and on the Sun Coast, where retirees made up a large share of the in-migrants. Growth rates in counties within the western panhandle were high, primarily because of the arrival of Navy and Air Force personnel and their dependents. Many north Florida counties lost population during the decade.

During the 1960s growth in Brevard County was particularly rapid, resulting from the opening of the nation's Space Center. The three counties north of St. Petersburg and the southwestern coastal counties also attracted many people, mostly retirees. In the 1970s intense growth continued in the three counties to the north of St. Petersburg, in the southwestern coastal counties, and around, but not in, Orlando. The latter area's growth was largely due to the opening of Disney World. During the 1980s population growth slowed markedly in the southeastern counties of Dade and Broward. Between 1980 and 1990 rates of growth were slowest in Dade, but increased steadily northward to Martin and Indian River counties.

Population Growth
Florida Compared with the United States

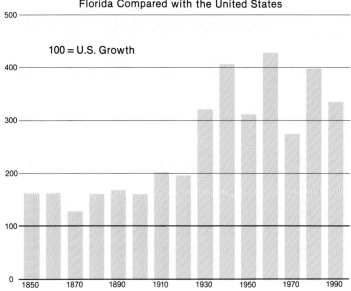

100 = U.S. Growth

Population Change in Nonurban Places

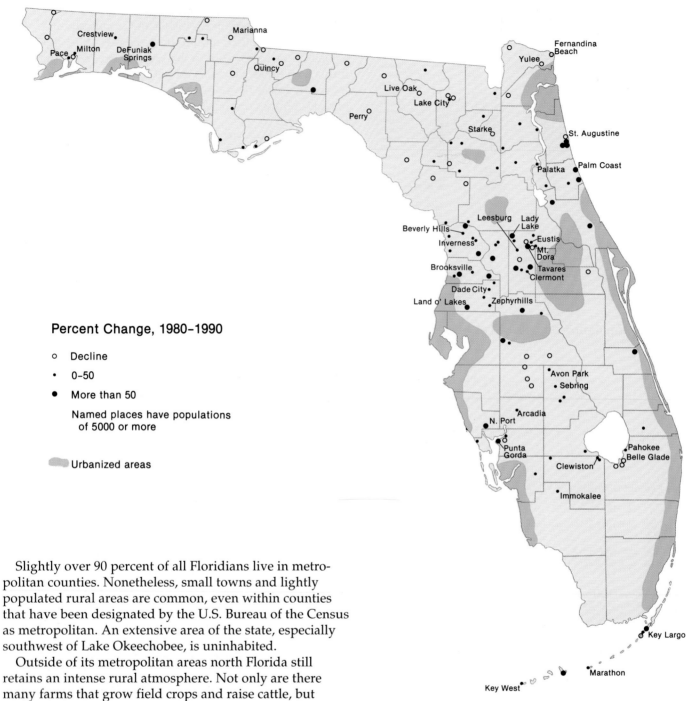

Percent Change, 1980–1990

○ Decline

• 0–50

● More than 50

Named places have populations of 5000 or more

Urbanized areas

Slightly over 90 percent of all Floridians live in metropolitan counties. Nonetheless, small towns and lightly populated rural areas are common, even within counties that have been designated by the U.S. Bureau of the Census as metropolitan. An extensive area of the state, especially southwest of Lake Okeechobee, is uninhabited.

Outside of its metropolitan areas north Florida still retains an intense rural atmosphere. Not only are there many farms that grow field crops and raise cattle, but almost 7 million acres are in tree farms, and several million more are in state or national forests. This part of the state is one of the least attractive to in-migrants. Slow economic growth, and in some places actual economic decline, has meant that many towns far from the region's larger cities are losing population.

During the 1980s central Florida was one of the fastest growing areas of the state. Although its metropolitan areas were the principal beneficiaries of the growth, areas near large metropolitan areas also have grown rapidly. This is particularly true of two places: to the west of Orlando and to the north of Tampa–St. Petersburg. Small market towns serving the surrounding citrus and farming areas are changing their character rapidly. If current population growth continues, by the year 2000 much of what is today nonurban central Florida will be part of a large metropolitan area.

The interior of the southern one-third of the peninsula is primarily in agriculture and cattle ranches. Most towns and villages within it attract few tourists or retirees. Arcadia has a reputation of being a "cow town" since ranching is an important activity in the surrounding area. The towns around Lake Okeechobee, including Immokalee, are filled with agricultural workers engaged in producing the area's vegetables, sugar, and, more recently, citrus.

Metropolitan Statistical Areas

The federal census has identified metropolitan areas since 1960. The names given to these areas, as well as their boundaries, may change from census to census. In 1983 they became known as Metropolitan Statistical Areas (MSAs), replacing the earlier Standard Metropolitan Statistical Area (SMSA) designation. Within a MSA is at least one city with a minimum population of 50,000, or an urbanized area with at least that population. The total MSA must encompass a minimum of 100,000 inhabitants.

At the time of the 1990 census Florida had twenty MSAs, compared to eighteen in 1980. In 1970, however, there were only nine SMSAs, and in 1960 there were seven. The boundaries of two MSAs, Tallahassee and Tampa–St. Petersburg–Clearwater, were redefined between 1980 and 1990.

The central cities of most Florida MSAs contain less than half of the total population of the MSA. The city limits of most of these central cities have not changed since they were defined early in this century, and as a result population growth has been mainly in the suburbs. The Tallahassee MSA is a notable exception, since during the 1980s Tallahassee annexed a large area.

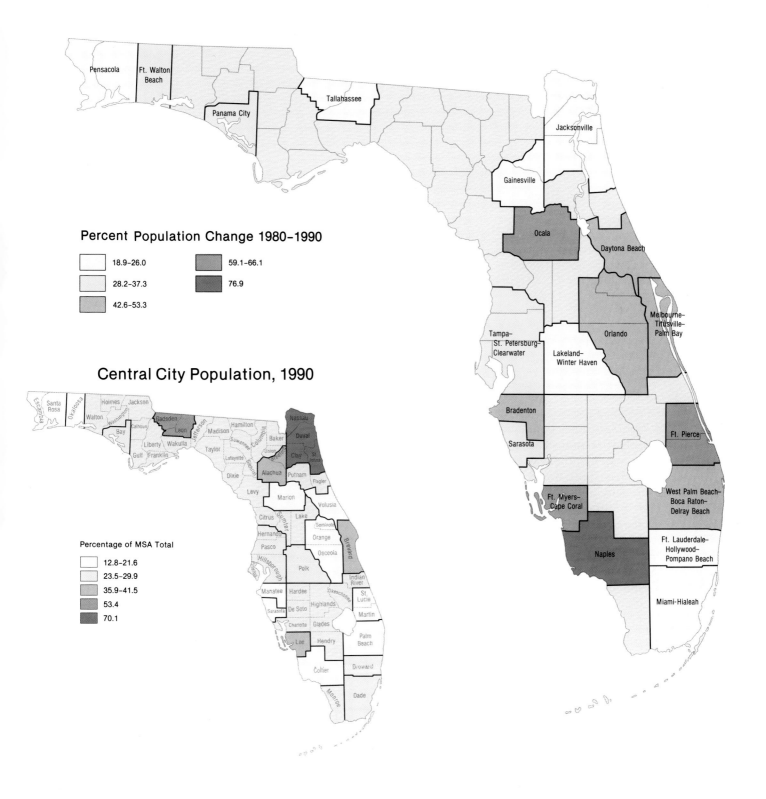

Percent Population Change 1980–1990

18.9–26.0
28.2–37.3
42.6–53.3
59.1–66.1
76.9

Central City Population, 1990

Percentage of MSA Total

12.8–21.6
23.5–29.9
35.9–41.5
53.4
70.1

City Population

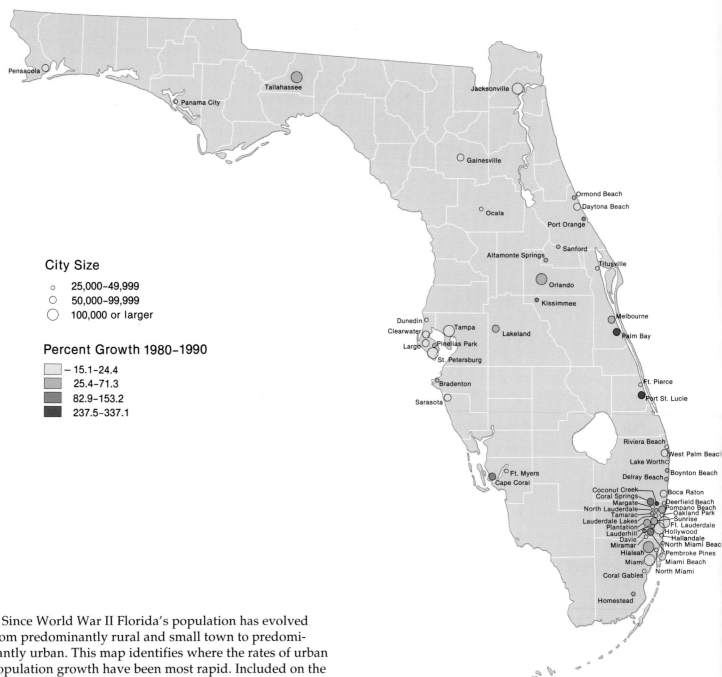

City Size

○ 25,000–49,999
○ 50,000–99,999
○ 100,000 or larger

Percent Growth 1980–1990

– 15.1–24.4
25.4–71.3
82.9–153.2
237.5–337.1

Pensacola
Panama City
Tallahassee
Jacksonville
Gainesville
Ormond Beach
Daytona Beach
Port Orange
Ocala
Sanford
Altamonte Springs
Titusville
Orlando
Kissimmee
Melbourne
Palm Bay
Dunedin
Clearwater
Tampa
Largo
Lakeland
Pinellas Park
St. Petersburg
Bradenton
Ft. Pierce
Port St. Lucie
Sarasota
Riviera Beach
West Palm Beac
Lake Worth
Boynton Beach
Delray Beach
Ft. Myers
Cape Coral
Coconut Creek
Boca Raton
Coral Springs
Margate
Deerfield Beach
North Lauderdale
Pompano Beach
Tamarac
Oakland Park
Lauderdale Lakes
Sunrise
Plantation
Ft. Lauderdale
Lauderhill
Hollywood
Davie
Hallandale
Miramar
North Miami Beac
Hialeah
Pembroke Pines
Miami
Miami Beach
North Miami
Coral Gables
Homestead

Since World War II Florida's population has evolved from predominantly rural and small town to predominantly urban. This map identifies where the rates of urban population growth have been most rapid. Included on the map, however, are only incorporated cities of 25,000 or more inhabitants. A large percentage of Florida's urban residents live in the unincorporated portions of urban counties, many in communities less than 25,000. Older and larger cities do not have the potential for population growth of younger and smaller ones unless they expand through annexation of new land or become more densely populated through construction of multifamily housing.

The populations of many of the oldest large cities in Florida, including Miami, Hollywood, Ft. Lauderdale, Jacksonville, Pensacola, St. Petersburg, and Tampa, experienced little growth between 1980 and 1990. Incorporated cities with particularly high rates of population growth are newer, with large empty areas in which they can expand. Excellent examples are Cape Coral, a planned urban development near Ft. Myers, and Port St. Lucie, north of West Palm Beach.

Cities of High Growth

The cities with high rates of population growth between 1980 and 1990 identified on the map are incorporated places with 1990 populations of 10,000 inhabitants or more. Many towns with smaller populations have grown even faster. Some of these did not even exist in 1980. Florida's influx of population is so great that towns may grow from vacant land to significant size within ten years.

The largest concentration of rapidly growing incorporated places is on the Gold Coast north of Dade County. Dade County's population growth rate has declined, whereas Broward and Palm Beach counties to the north continue to attract retirees, as well as many younger non-Hispanic and Hispanic whites.

The second concentration of rapidly growing incorporated towns is in the Orlando area. All are suburbs of Orlando or are communities meeting the demands of tourists visiting Disney World and other nearby theme parks. Tallahassee is the largest of the fast growing cities on the map. It owes its growth primarily to annexation of suburban areas in the last decade.

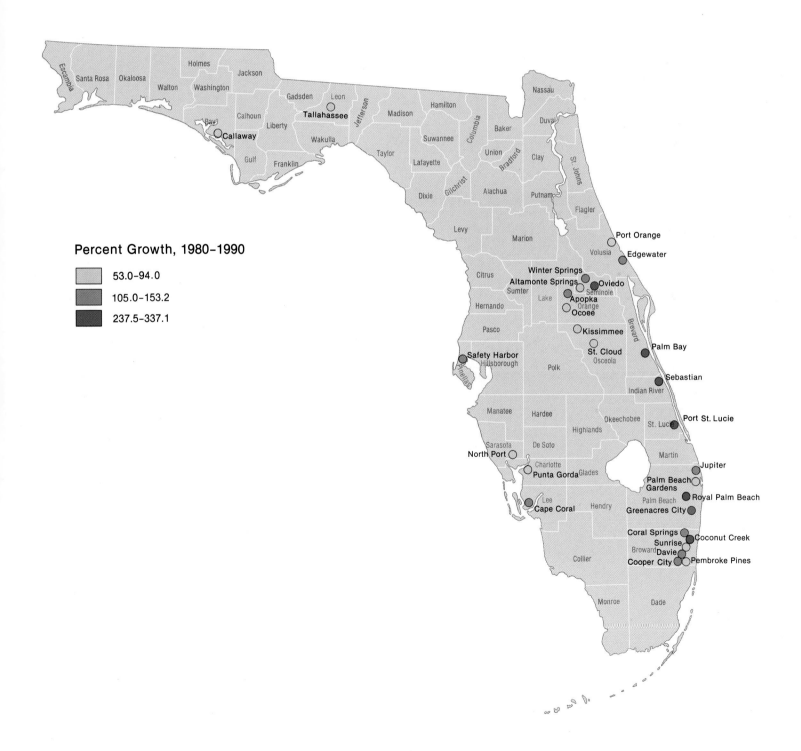

Percent Growth, 1980–1990

53.0–94.0

105.0–153.2

237.5–337.1

Development Along the Gold Coast

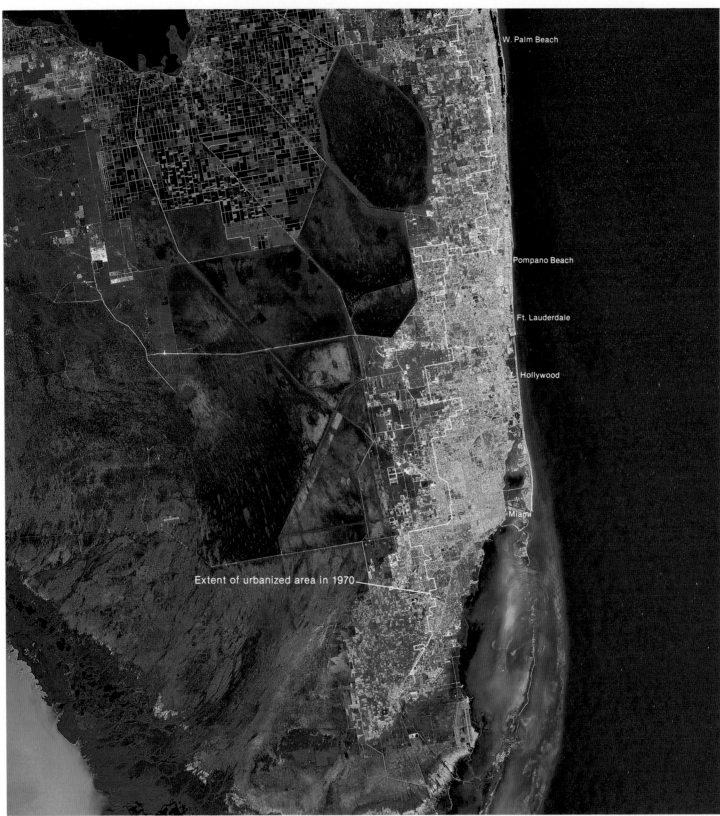

W. Palm Beach

Pompano Beach

Ft. Lauderdale

Hollywood

Miami

Extent of urbanized area in 1970

Since 1950 no part of Florida has absorbed as many people as the three southeastern counties of Dade, Broward, and Palm Beach. Between 1950 and 1990, the combined three-county population increased from 693,705 to 4,056,100. In 1950 a series of communities hugged the coast, one isolated from the other by empty land. Only three of these—Miami, Ft. Lauderdale, and West Palm Beach—had more than 25,000 residents. In 1990 a dense urban settlement extended from southern Dade County northward far beyond West Palm Beach. In all three counties development has also occurred westward, with the greatest westward movement in Dade County.

Birth Rate

Florida's population has grown principally from immigration and immigration. Natural increase (the excess of births over deaths), however, does account for approximately 12 percent of Florida's growth. Birth rates are highest among blacks and second highest among Hispanics, although birth rates vary considerably within the Hispanic population. Birth rates are higher than the state Hispanic average among Mexican and Puerto Rican women, but lower among Cuban women. The average young Cuban family is approximately the same size as the average young non-Hispanic white family. The highest fertility rates in the state occur in rural counties.

Florida Birth Rate

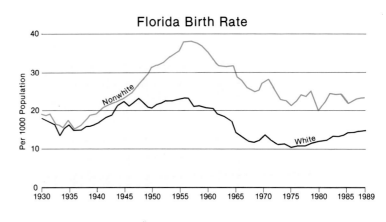

White Birth Rate

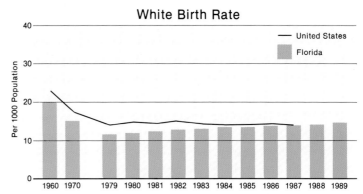

Nonwhite Birth Rate

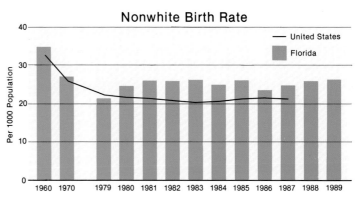

Total Fertility Rate, 1989

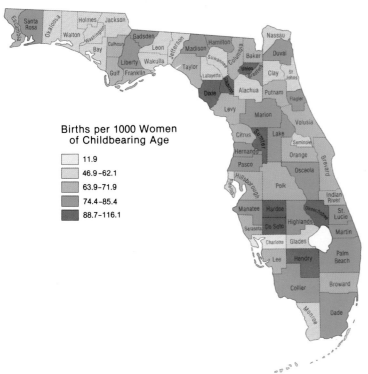

Births per 1000 Women
of Childbearing Age

- 11.9
- 46.9–62.1
- 63.9–71.9
- 74.4–85.4
- 88.7–116.1

White Birth Rate, 1989

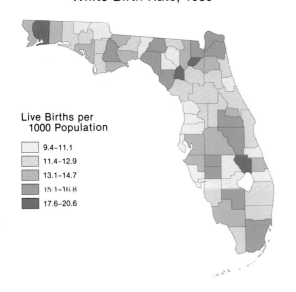

Live Births per
1000 Population

- 9.4–11.1
- 11.4–12.9
- 13.1–14.7
- 15.1–16.8
- 17.6–20.6

Nonwhite Birth Rate, 1989

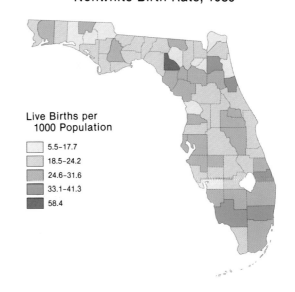

Live Births per
1000 Population

- 5.5–17.7
- 18.5–24.2
- 24.6–31.6
- 33.1–41.3
- 58.4

Death Rate

White, 1987–1989 Average

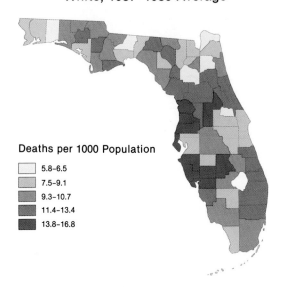

Deaths per 1000 Population

- 5.8–6.5
- 7.5–9.1
- 9.3–10.7
- 11.4–13.4
- 13.8–16.8

In 1989, 132,037 people died in Florida, a death rate of 10.3 people per 1000 inhabitants. The crude death rate among nonwhites in Florida was lower than that for the whites because of the large number of aged whites in the population. The highest white death rates occur in counties where retirees are numerous. Counties where death rates are high among the nonwhite population are in rural north Florida. The infant mortality rate is usually higher in rural than urban areas and is much higher among nonwhites than whites. When death rates are adjusted for age, whites in all age groups have lower death rates than nonwhites. Throughout the 1980s the age-adjusted death rates for whites have continued to fall, but for nonwhites have remained stationary.

Florida's white death rate declined between 1936 and 1956. In 1956 the rate began to rise because of the larger number of retirees settling in the state. The greatest decrease in the nonwhite death rate occurred between 1926 and 1962, when it fell from 20.0 to 9.9 per 1000.

Nonwhite, 1987–1989 Average

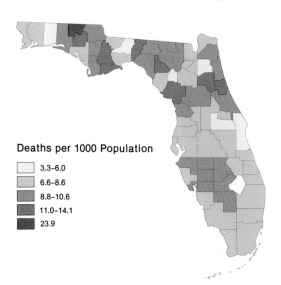

Deaths per 1000 Population

- 3.3–6.0
- 6.6–8.6
- 8.8–10.6
- 11.0–14.1
- 23.9

Death Rate 1920–1989

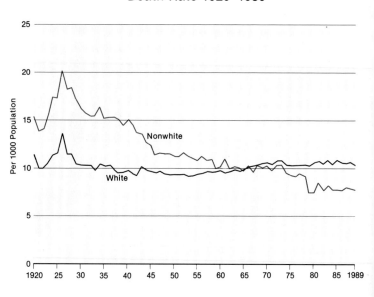

Infant Mortality for Whites, 1987–1989 Average

Deaths per 1000 Live Births

- 0.0–4.2
- 5.7–8.0
- 8.1–10.1
- 10.5–12.7
- 17.2

Infant Mortality for Nonwhites, 1987–1989 Average

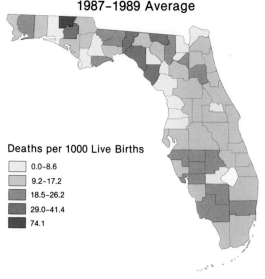

Deaths per 1000 Live Births

- 0.0–8.6
- 9.2–17.2
- 18.5–26.2
- 29.0–41.4
- 74.1

Causes of Death

The leading causes of death in Florida reflect the age distribution of its population. The share of aged in the state's population in 1990 was 18.2 percent, compared with 12.6 percent for the nation. Deaths from diseases of the aged are therefore more common in Florida. High death rates for both heart diseases and cancer occur in counties with high percentages of the aged.

Accidents are the leading cause of death between the ages of 1 and 24. Rates are highest in rural counties. Many of these accidents are auto related, but agriculture and forestry also contribute to the high rural accidental death rates. Acquired Immunodeficiency Syndrome (AIDS) became a significant cause of death within Florida during the 1980s. Deaths from this disease are now among the leading causes in the 25–44 age group. In mid-1990 an estimated 120,000 Floridians tested Human Immunodeficiency Virus (HIV) positive, indicating that AIDS will continue as a leading cause of death throughout the 1990s.

Heart Disease, 1988

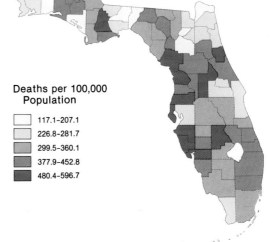

Deaths per 100,000 Population

- 117.1–207.1
- 226.8–281.7
- 299.5–360.1
- 377.9–452.8
- 480.4–596.7

Accidents, 1988

Deaths per 100,000 Population

- 27.7–47.2
- 48.1–67.0
- 73.1–85.1
- 95.7–106.0
- 119.1–136.6

Cancer, 1988

Deaths per 100,000 Population

- 127.3–177.5
- 180.9–228.4
- 235.4–292.3
- 302.7–357.9
- 376.1–453.8

Leading Causes of Death, 1989

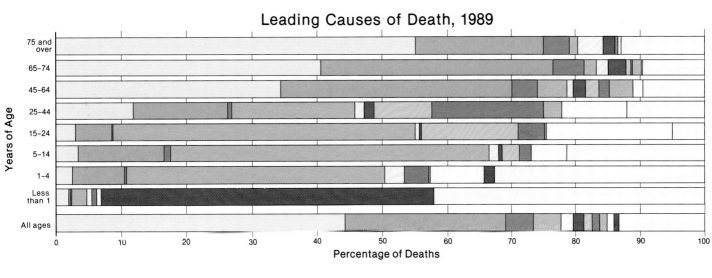

Years of Age

- 75 and over
- 65–74
- 45–64
- 25–44
- 15–24
- 5–14
- 1–4
- Less than 1
- All ages

Percentage of Deaths

- Cardiovascular Diseases
- Cancer
- Chronic Obstructive Lung Disease
- Accidental Injury and Poisoning
- Pneumonia and Influenza
- Diabetes
- Suicide
- AIDS
- Chronic Liver Disease and Cirrhosis
- Homicide
- Perinatal Conditions
- All other causes

Migration

Natural Increase, 1980–1990

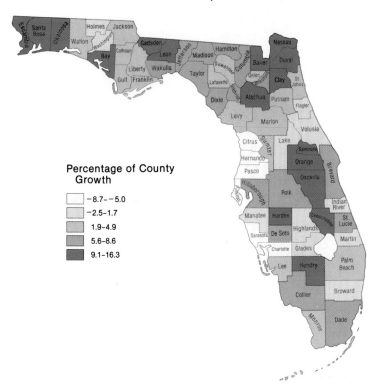

Percentage of County
Growth

☐	-8.7--5.0
☐	-2.5-1.7
☐	1.9-4.9
☐	5.6-8.6
☐	9.1-16.3

Migration Rate, 1960–1970

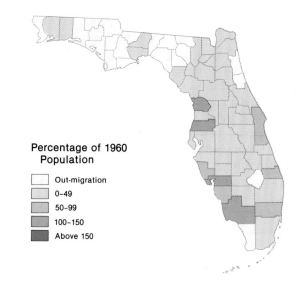

Percentage of 1960
Population

☐	Out-migration
☐	0-49
☐	50-99
☐	100-150
☐	Above 150

Migration Rate, 1970–1980

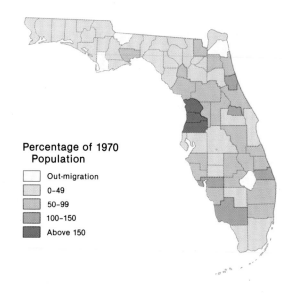

Percentage of 1970
Population

☐	Out-migration
☐	0-49
☐	50-99
☐	100-150
☐	Above 150

Migration Rate, 1980–1990

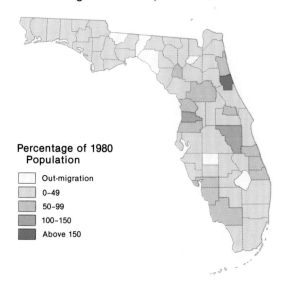

Percentage of 1980
Population

☐	Out-migration
☐	0-49
☐	50-99
☐	100-150
☐	Above 150

Net migration and natural increase are the two components of population growth. Net migration is the excess of people moving into an area over people moving out of an area, and natural increase is the number of births over deaths. Net migration accounts for 88 percent of Florida's population growth. The map indicating natural increase between 1980 and 1990 shows several counties with high percentages of the aged, such as Pinellas, Sarasota, and Charlotte, as well as three counties north of Pinellas County, where more people die each year than are born. Counties with high natural increases have small shares of aged in their populations, including Dade County (Miami), previously noted for its large number of retirees, but now a youthful county.

The pattern of migration into Florida since 1960 shows clearly the growing attraction of the Gulf coast and the more northerly Gold Coast counties for in-migrants. Following the Cuban Revolution of 1959 Dade County became the destination of many Cuban exiles. Later other Hispanics from throughout the Caribbean arrived in south Florida. Dade County began to attract fewer in-migrants from elsewhere in the United States, and some non-Hispanic residents moved to other Florida counties. The counties around Orange (Orlando) have also attracted in-migrants, largely because of the opening of Disney World and other theme parks in the area. Although north Florida no longer experiences the degree of out-migration it did in previous decades, it is still among the slowest growing parts of the state.

Florida is largely populated by people who have come from other places in the United States, particularly the Northeast. People, of course, also leave Florida. About equal numbers of people from Florida move to the West and elsewhere in the South as come from these regions to Florida. Far more people from the North Central and Northeast regions come to Florida than move to these regions from Florida. This is especially true of the Northeast. These two regions are Florida's principal source of retirees.

Migration to Florida from other regions or from elsewhere within the South is to a degree regionalized. Southerners figure prominently among the in-migrants to all parts of Florida, but in North Florida, the Peninsular Interior, and the Space Coast they are especially well represented. People from the Northeast prefer the Gold Coast, where they are the largest group from elsewhere in the U.S. Northeasterners, however, are settling in large numbers throughout the peninsula. People from the North Central states are better represented on the Sun Coast than those from other U.S. regions. Foreigners figure prominently among migrants only on the Gold Coast. These people generally come from Caribbean countries or elsewhere in Latin America.

Place of Birth of Florida Residents, 1980

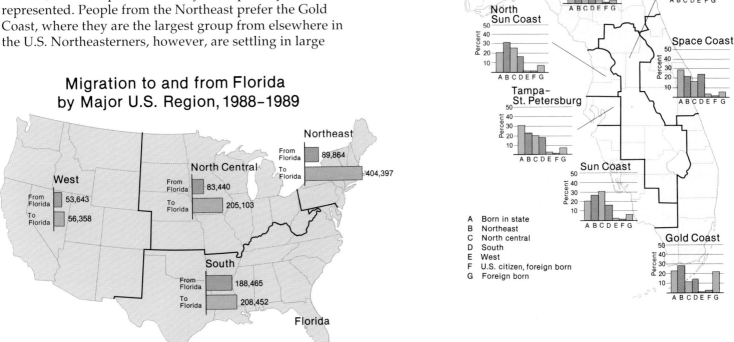

A Born in state
B Northeast
C North central
D South
E West
F U.S. citizen, foreign born
G Foreign born

Migration to and from Florida by Major U.S. Region, 1988–1989

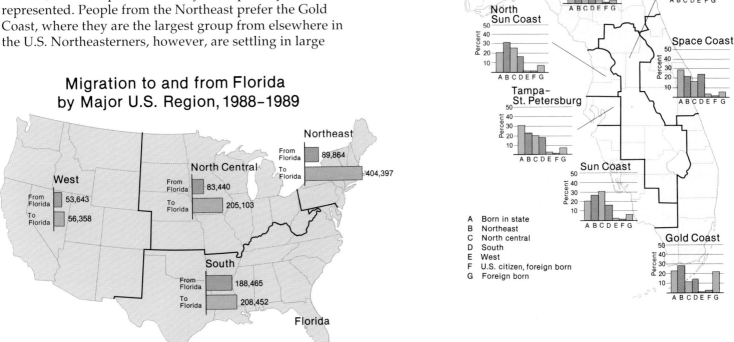

Origin and Number of Immigrants to Florida, 1986–1989

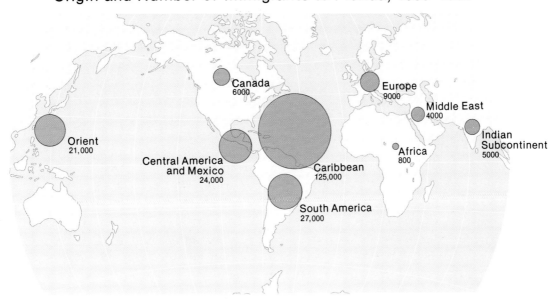

Europeans and Canadians

Many people born in Europe immigrated to other parts of the nation decades before they came to Florida to retire. A higher percentage of the Canadian-born have come to work, but many also choose Florida as a place of retirement. Most who were born in Poland and the USSR are Jews, who lived out their productive lives in the North and moved to the Gold Coast. Italian-born also choose the Gold Coast more frequently than other Florida regions. People from the British Isles and Canada favor the two sides of the peninsula about equally.

Canadians, 1980

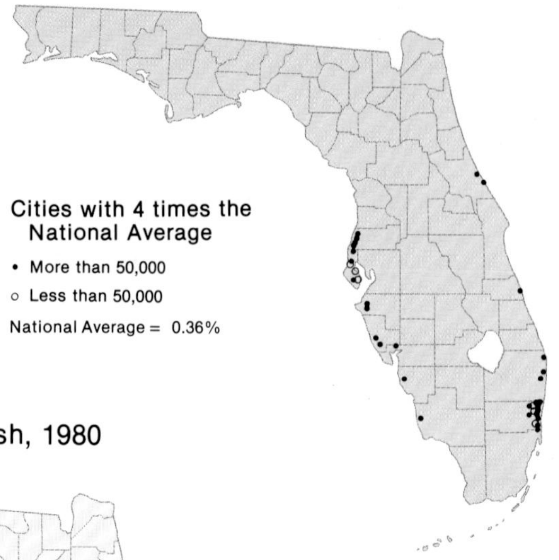

Cities with 4 times the National Average
• More than 50,000
○ Less than 50,000
National Average = 0.36%

British and Irish, 1980

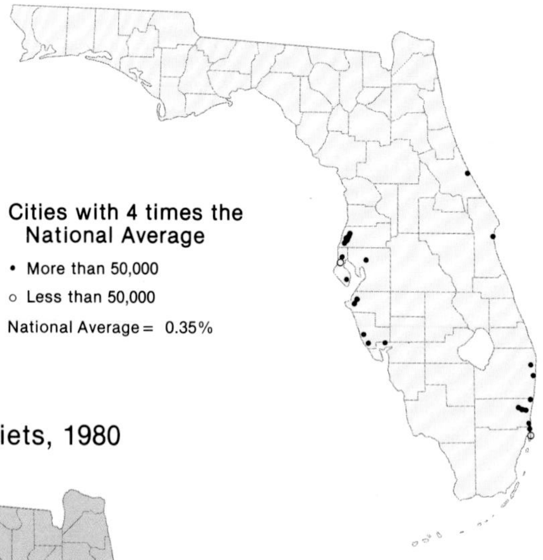

Cities with 4 times the National Average
• More than 50,000
○ Less than 50,000
National Average = 0.35%

Poles and Soviets, 1980

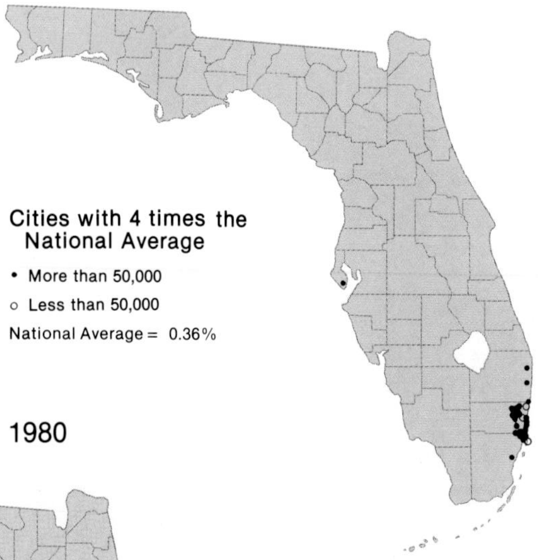

Cities with 4 times the National Average
• More than 50,000
○ Less than 50,000
National Average = 0.36%

Italians, 1980

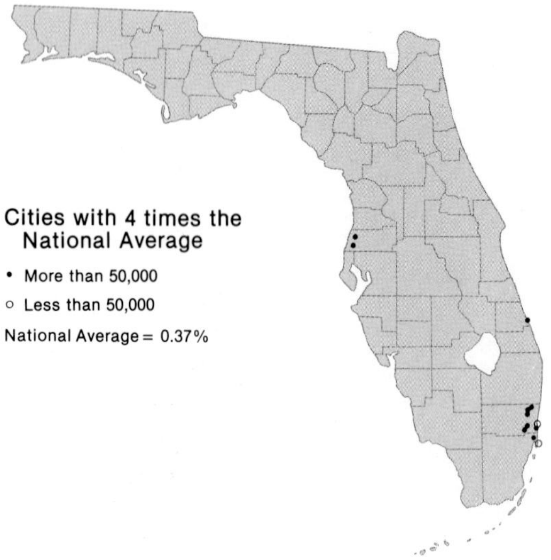

Cities with 4 times the National Average
• More than 50,000
○ Less than 50,000
National Average = 0.37%

Immigration before 1960

Percentage of 1980 Immigrant Group Population
0
10
20
30
40
50
60
70
80
90
Florida
U.S.
Scandinavia
United Kingdom and Ireland
Italy
Poland and the U.S.S.R.
Germany
Canada

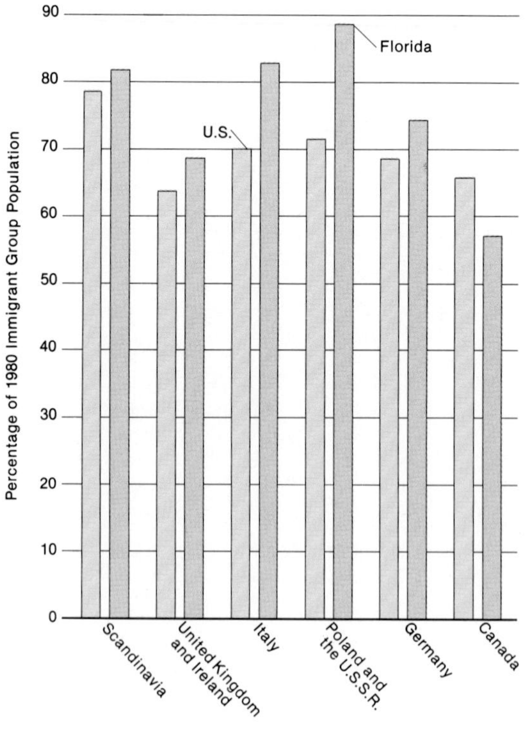

Racial and Ethnic Groups

White, 1990

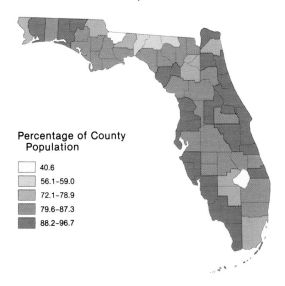

Percentage of County Population

- 40.6
- 56.1–59.0
- 72.1–78.9
- 79.6–87.3
- 88.2–96.7

Black, 1990

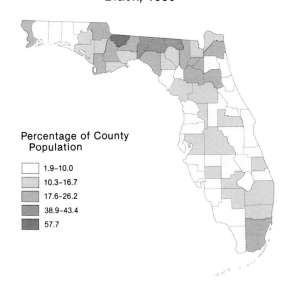

Percentage of County Population

- 1.9–10.0
- 10.3–16.7
- 17.6–26.2
- 38.9–43.4
- 57.7

The ethnic composition of Florida has changed over the last 100 years. The percentage of blacks in Florida's total population has declined steadily throughout the twentieth century, to 14 percent in 1990. The decline during the past decade, however, was less than 1 percent. The precipitous drop earlier in the century in the percentage of blacks in the state's population was because fewer blacks than whites or Hispanics moved to Florida and because many blacks left the state. Today black in-migration is greater than out-migration. In addition, natural increase among blacks exceeds that of both non-Hispanic whites and Hispanics. As a consequence, the group today is growing nearly as fast as the other two groups. Many blacks have settled in Florida's larger cities, especially Miami, Jacksonville, Ft. Lauderdale, St. Petersburg, Orlando, and Tampa. In 1990 the percentage of blacks was also relatively high in the north Florida counties where cotton was grown. During the nineteenth century many of these counties contained more blacks than whites. Today only Gadsden County has so high a share of blacks.

Since 1959 hundreds of thousands of Latin Americans have immigrated to Florida. In 1990, 12.2 percent of the state's population was Hispanic, up from 8.8 percent in 1980 and 6.6 percent in 1970. Hispanics are heavily concentrated in Dade County, where they accounted for 49.2 percent of the county's population in 1990. Recently the number of Hispanics, most working as farm laborers, has significantly increased in many rural counties on the peninsula.

The "other" category includes, among others, American Indians, Chinese, Japanese, Koreans, Filipinos, and Asian Indians. The state's Chinese population grew from 3,133 in 1970 to 30,737 in 1990. Several other groups have almost equaled the Chinese in population growth. Asians of all types have mainly settled in large urban areas. The largest percentages of American Indians are found in counties south of Lake Okeechobee.

Hispanic, 1990

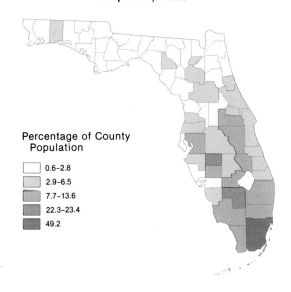

Percentage of County Population

- 0.6–2.8
- 2.9–6.5
- 7.7–13.6
- 22.3–23.4
- 49.2

Other, 1990*

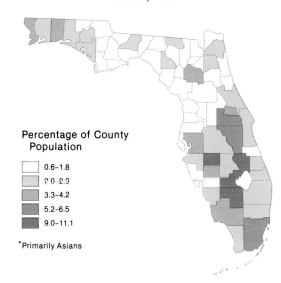

Percentage of County Population

- 0.6–1.8
- 2.0–2.9
- 3.3–4.2
- 5.2–6.5
- 9.0–11.1

*Primarily Asians

Asians and Hispanics

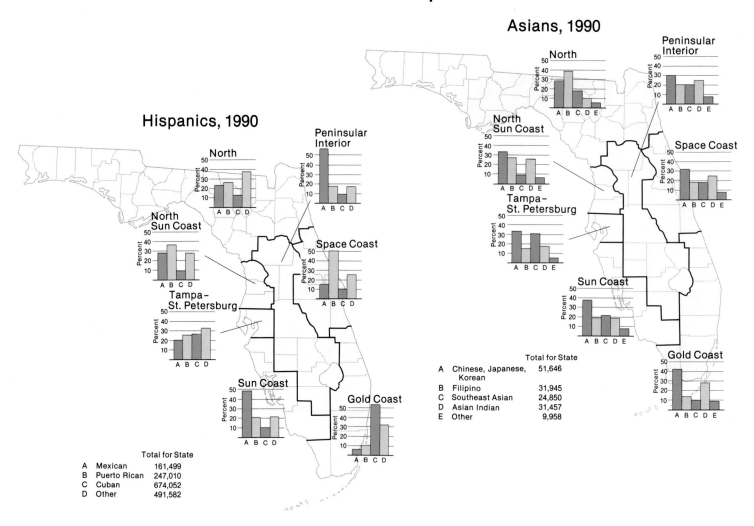

Asians, 1990

North
Peninsular Interior
North Sun Coast
Space Coast
Tampa-St. Petersburg
Sun Coast
Gold Coast

	Total for State
A	Chinese, Japanese, Korean — 51,646
B	Filipino — 31,945
C	Southeast Asian — 24,850
D	Asian Indian — 31,457
E	Other — 9,958

Hispanics, 1990

North
Peninsular Interior
North Sun Coast
Space Coast
Tampa-St. Petersburg
Sun Coast
Gold Coast

	Total for State
A	Mexican — 161,499
B	Puerto Rican — 247,010
C	Cuban — 674,052
D	Other — 491,582

Dispersion of Hispanics

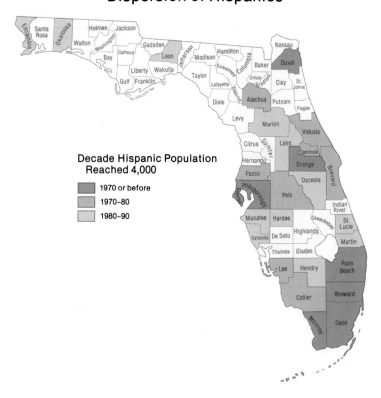

Decade Hispanic Population Reached 4,000

- 1970 or before
- 1970–80
- 1980–90

Since 1959 Hispanics have arrived in Florida in large numbers. They have diffused from the southeast northward, first settling in the larger cities. During the 1980s communities of Hispanics grew even in panhandle cities like Tallahassee, Pensacola, and Ft. Walton Beach. Nonetheless, in 1990, 72 percent of Florida Hispanics lived on the Gold Coast.

On the Gold Coast, Cubans constitute over half of all Hispanics. In the Peninsular Interior and on the Sun Coast, Mexicans form about half the Hispanic group. Whereas Cubans generally have settled in large cities, Mexicans and Mexican-Americans are more commonly found in rural areas, where they often work in agriculture. Puerto Ricans compose half the Hispanics who live on the Space Coast. Many Puerto Ricans are employed in that region's important tourist industry.

Asian migration to the state during the 1980s was especially heavy. Asians, however, are far less concentrated on the Gold Coast than Hispanics. Chinese, Japanese, and Koreans make up over 40 percent of the Asians on the Gold Coast, while Filipinos almost reach that percentage in North Florida. Filipino sailors and Filipino dependents of U.S. naval personnel stationed at the large bases in Jacksonville and Pensacola in part account for this high percentage.

Black Population

The share of blacks in the total Florida population was far higher in the past century than today. Blacks were brought in as slave labor for north Florida cotton plantations while Florida was still a territory. Until the end of the last century the populations of a number of counties in the northern part of the state were over half black. Even today

one, Gadsden County, has a black majority. In this century the proportion of blacks in the state's population began to fall, mainly because of the in-migration of large numbers of whites and the out-migration of large numbers of blacks.

Since 1970 the rate of growth of the black population has nearly equalled the total state growth rate. In the past few decades more blacks from outside the state have moved to metropolitan south Florida. Although more blacks come to Florida today than leave, growth of their numbers continues to be heavily dependent on natural increase (births over deaths).

In this century much of Florida's black population moved from rural to urban areas, particularly Miami, Jacksonville, and Tampa, and nearby communities. A number of suburbs, some quite old, around Miami are predominantly black, including Opa-Locka, Carol City, Brownsville, and Richmond Heights. A number of smaller cities also have proportionately high black populations, for example, Haines City, Belle Glade, Ft. Pierce, and Palatka. The most dramatic twentieth century trend in the distribution of the black population is its shift from the rural north to the urban peninsula, particularly the Gold Coast.

Change in Black Population

Cities of High Black Population, 1990 *

Black Population, 1950–1990

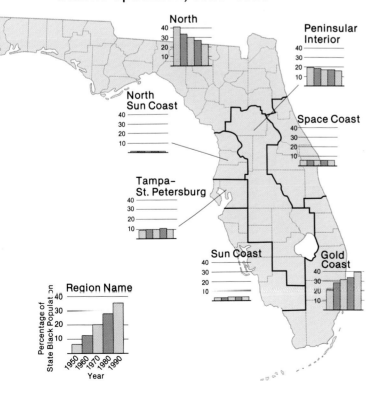

Black and Hispanic Populations

Until the nation implemented the civil rights legislation in the 1960s, blacks could be segregated from whites by law. As a result, ghettoes where blacks were highly concentrated emerged. Most ghettoes were near central business districts of large cities, where employment was available for semiskilled and unskilled workers. Since the 1960s the distribution of blacks in Florida cities has changed. Many middle class blacks have moved to the suburbs, some choosing to live in older black communities and others living in racially integrated neighborhoods. Miami, for example, has a number of black suburbs, some old, some more recently established, including Opa-Locka, Carol City, Richmond Heights, and Brownsville. Florida's central cities, however, continue to be the home of most blacks who live within metropolitan areas. Urban renewal has improved the quality of housing, and population densities generally are lower than what they were in the 1960s or earlier. Nonetheless, these inner city ghettoes have all the problems of their counterparts elsewhere.

White flight from Florida's central cities began in earnest in the 1960s. Today areas within the central cities where non-Hispanic whites predominate are considerably smaller than in 1960. The city of Miami is the only central city of Florida's metropolitan statistical areas that does not have blacks as its dominant ethnic group. Huge numbers of Hispanics have arrived in Miami since 1960. White Hispanic immigrants, however, seldom settled in the black areas of the city, although many black Hispanics did. Instead they moved into non-Hispanic white neighborhoods, some of which blacks might have entered had Hispanics not come to Miami in such numbers. Most non-Hispanic whites have now left Miami's inner city, which

today is 27 percent black, and 53 percent white Hispanic. Miami Beach, once a famous enclave of aged Jews, no longer is dominated by this group. Today Hispanic whites far exceed them in total numbers. Actually, in only one small part of Greater Miami—a small section in the extreme northeast—do non-Hispanic white aged constitute a large share of the total population.

Jacksonville

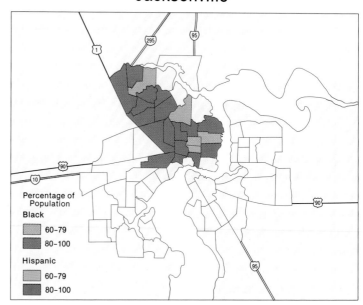

Miami

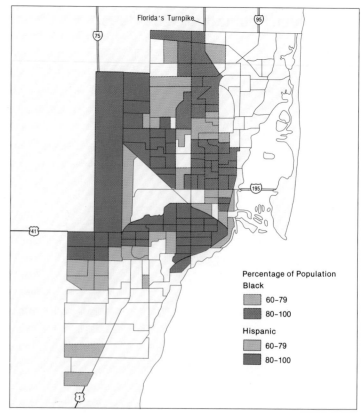

Tampa

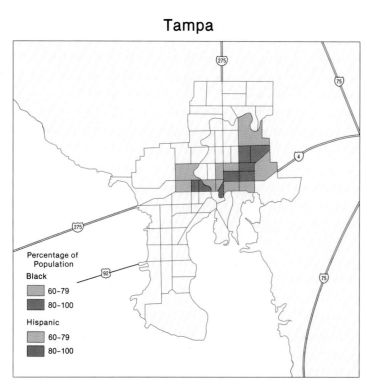

Population Concentrations along the Gold Coast

The Gold Coast of Florida (Dade, Broward, Palm Beach, and Martin counties) has evolved since 1920 into the most culturally heterogeneous region of the state. Prior to 1920 it was lightly populated, by both whites and blacks. Perceived by real estate developers, and later by tourists and immigrants, as the most physically desirable part of the state, the region began to grow rapidly, even before World War II. Initially both whites and blacks poured in to build the tourist infrastructure and provide the services. Later retirees came to take up permanent residency. Many were Jews who concentrated in certain areas, particularly Miami Beach. By the middle of the twentieth century there were discrete areas in which blacks lived, others with high concentrations of aged Jews, and still others where Christian retirees concentrated. Christian retirees often chose to live in smaller towns in Broward and Palm Beach counties. Interspersed among these groups were younger whites, most living as families. Until the 1980s Martin County was largely unaffected by this mass in-migration.

The spatial distribution of groups along the Gold Coast began to change in 1960, following the Cuban Revolution and the mass exodus of people from that nation. The minuscule Hispanic community of the Gold Coast, centered in "Little Havana" to the west of downtown Miami, grew by hundreds of thousands, including many from other Hispanic nations. Hispanic culture quickly became pervasive throughout Miami, as well as other nearby places, particularly Hialeah. In turn, this started a movement of non-Hispanics from Dade County. Many who may have come to Dade County chose to settle farther north on the Gold Coast. Today few aged retire to Miami. Instead they settle farther to the north in Broward, Palm Beach, and even Martin County. Some Hispanics are also beginning to move north, especially into Broward County. Blacks remain highly concentrated in Dade County.

City Population *

○ 5,000–10,000

○ 10,000–50,000

○ Greater than 50,000

Populations 33% or More

Hispanic
Black
Non-Hispanic 65 years or older
No group over 33%

* Named places have populations greater than 20,000

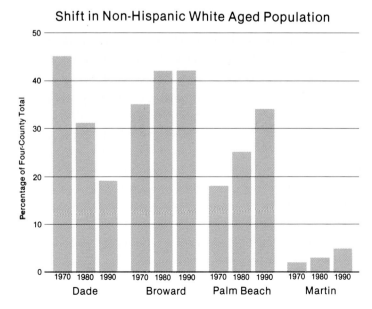

Shift in Non-Hispanic White Aged Population

American Indians

Florida's American Indian population has increased by nearly 30,000 since 1970. The 1990 census figure of 36,335 American Indian, Eskimo, and Aleut people in Florida may be distorted because of the tendency in recent years for non-Indians to claim American Indian ancestry. This increase also reflects the migration to Florida of American Indians from tribes in other parts of the United States and Canada.

In south Florida are a number of large Miccosukee and Seminole state reservations and trust lands. In Tampa are small pieces of Seminole trust land, one of which contains a bingo facility. Northwest Florida is home to Creek Indians and some of their descendents, including members of the Poarch Band of Creek Indians, a federally recognized tribe centered near Atmore, Alabama, and members of the Florida Tribe of Eastern Creeks, an organization of Creek Indian descendents with members concentrated in Calhoun and Walton counties.

Indian Population of Florida*

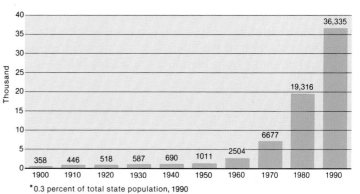

*0.3 percent of total state population, 1990

Indian Population, 1990

Reservations and Trust Lands

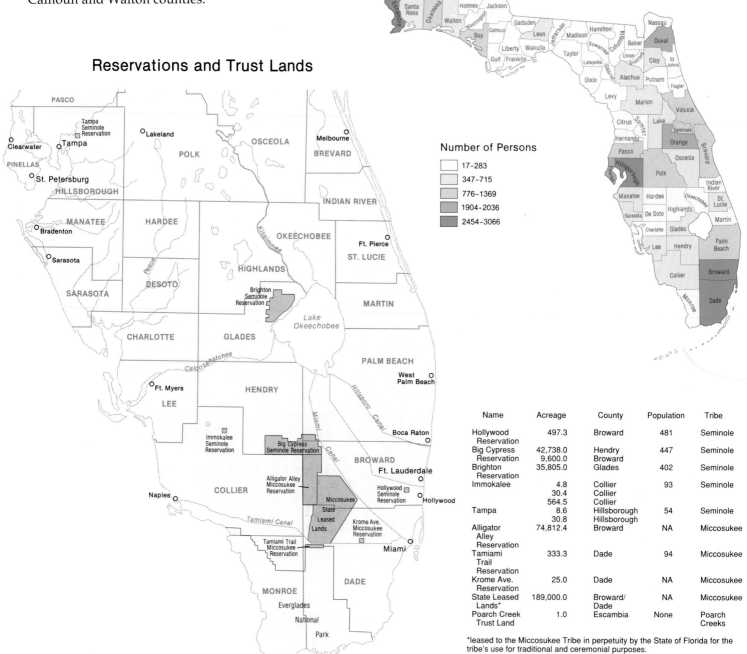

Number of Persons

	17–283
	347–715
	776–1369
	1904–2036
	2454–3066

Name	Acreage	County	Population	Tribe
Hollywood Reservation	497.3	Broward	481	Seminole
Big Cypress Reservation	42,738.0	Hendry	447	Seminole
	9,600.0	Broward		
Brighton Reservation	35,805.0	Glades	402	Seminole
Immokalee	4.8	Collier	93	Seminole
	30.4	Collier		
	564.5	Collier		
Tampa	8.6	Hillsborough	54	Seminole
	30.8	Hillsborough		
Alligator Alley Reservation	74,812.4	Broward	NA	Miccosukee
Tamiami Trail Reservation	333.3	Dade	94	Miccosukee
Krome Ave. Reservation	25.0	Dade	NA	Miccosukee
State Leased Lands*	189,000.0	Broward/ Dade	NA	Miccosukee
Poarch Creek Trust Land	1.0	Escambia	None	Poarch Creeks

*leased to the Miccosukee Tribe in perpetuity by the State of Florida for the tribe's use for traditional and ceremonial purposes.

Marriage and Divorce

Marriage and divorce statistics have been collected in Florida since 1927. Both marriage and divorce rates rose during World War II. By 1950 marriage rates had declined precipitously, and divorce rates declined a few years later. The marriage rate declined gradually until the 1960s, and the divorce rate also declined between 1950 and 1960. Marriage rates have been stable since 1968. The divorce rate remained fairly stable throughout the 1960s, rose during the 1970s, and stabilized in the 1980s.

During the 1950s Florida's liberal divorce laws and short residency requirement attracted many from other states for a quick divorce, contributing to an exceptionally high rate of divorce. More liberal grounds for divorce were legislated in other states during the 1950s and 1960s, reducing the difference between Florida's divorce rate and that for the nation. Nevertheless, today only Arizona, Nevada, and Oklahoma have consistently higher divorce rates than Florida.

Divorce rates show no sharp geographical pattern. They do, however, appear to be lower in the counties where the aged constitute a large share of the population. In counties with small populations an increase of just a few divorces from one year to the next might result in a noticeable increase in the divorce rate. Jefferson County, in north Florida, is a curious anomaly because of a local lawyer who handles divorce cases economically for many people from the nearby city of Tallahassee, located in a contiguous county.

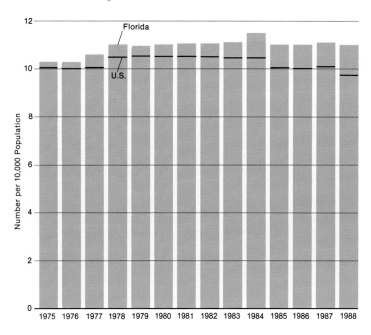

Marriage Rate for Florida and the U.S.

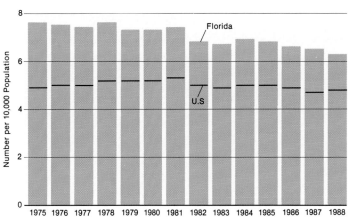

Divorce Rate for Florida and the U.S.

Divorce Rate, 1988

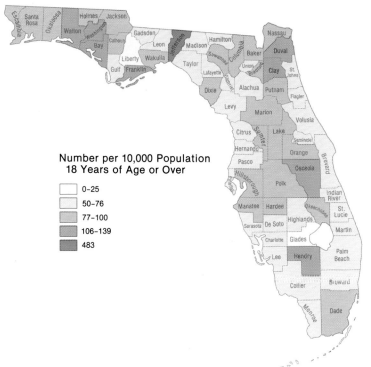

Number per 10,000 Population
18 Years of Age or Over

- 0–25
- 50–76
- 77–100
- 106–139
- 483

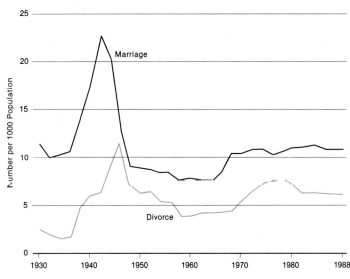

Trends in Florida's Marriage and Divorce Rates

Age and Sex, 1990

Florida's population may be divided into three distinct groups: non-Hispanic white, black, and Hispanic. The age distribution, as well as the sex ratio, of each differs. The share of aged within the non-Hispanic white group is far higher than in the other two. Non-Hispanic white retirees have been coming to Florida in great numbers for decades, augmenting the aged who have spent at least part of their earlier lives here. Few blacks and Hispanics have chosen to retire to Florida, and as a consequence the black and Hispanic populations are more youthful. The black population is especially young, and the large base of the black age-sex pyramid is the result of the group having the highest birth rate of the three as well as the shortest life span. Women outlive men, a fact clearly shown on the graph portraying sex ratios. Among Florida blacks there are far more women than men even in the younger age groups.

The counties whose populations were selected to be portrayed by pyramids are each demographically distinct. Leon County (Tallahassee) with two universities and a community college has many inhabitants between 18 and 24 years of age. Orange County (Orlando) is the home of several large theme parks and has a high proportion of young adults who work in services. Dade County (Miami) has a more mature population than that of Orange County, and Lee County (Ft. Myers) has the most aged of the four. Ft. Myers is now a famous destination of retirees.

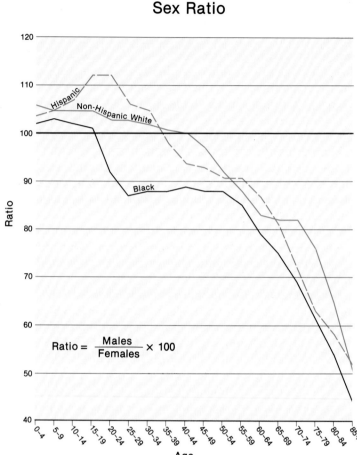

Sex Ratio

$$\text{Ratio} = \frac{\text{Males}}{\text{Females}} \times 100$$

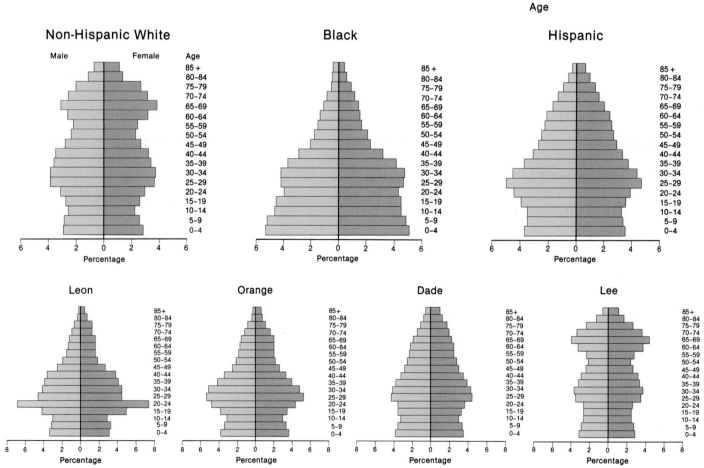

The Aged

In the 1940s large numbers of retirees began to move to Florida. Before 1940 Florida had a smaller percentage of people 65 years and older in its population than the nation as a whole. Until 1940 older males outnumbered older females in the state as a result of the nineteenth-century migration to Florida of more young males than females. After World War II most newcomers 65 years of age and older arrived as couples, and because women generally outlive men, aged women now far outnumber aged men in Florida.

In 1940 most of the aged lived in three regions—the Gold Coast, North Florida, and Tampa–St. Petersburg. Most of North Florida's aged, unlike those elsewhere in Florida, were born within the region. Between 1940 and 1980 the share of the state's aged living in North Florida and in the Peninsular Interior declined, whereas it increased dramatically on the Gold Coast. The Tampa–St. Petersburg region and the Peninsular Interior have had declining shares of the state's aged since at least 1960. The share of the state's aged living on the Gold Coast has declined since 1980, while it has increased on the Space and Sun coasts. The aged today constitute almost one-third of the populations of several counties along the Gulf of Mexico.

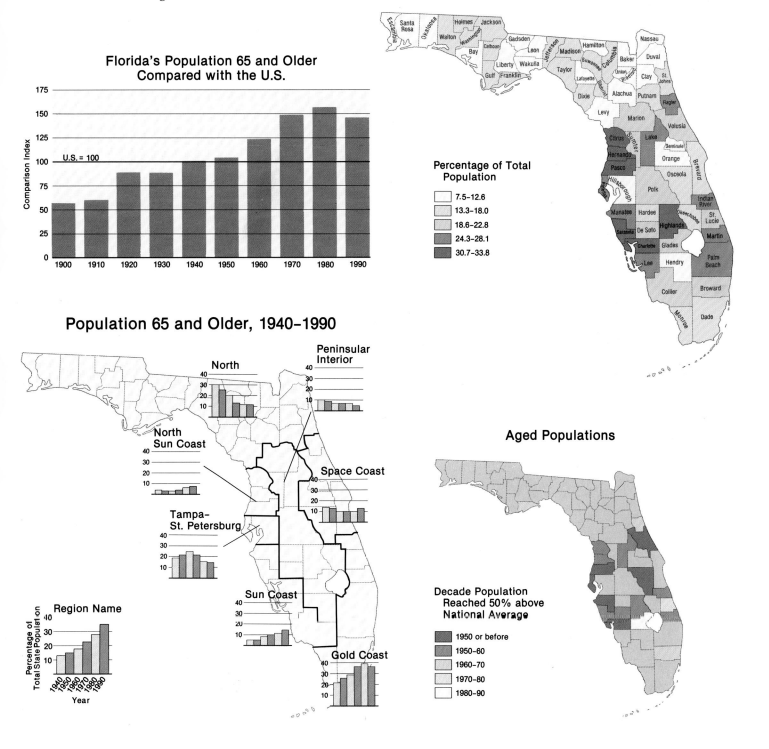

Florida's Population 65 and Older Compared with the U.S.

Population 65 Years and Older, 1990

Percentage of Total Population

Population 65 and Older, 1940–1990

Aged Populations

Decade Population Reached 50% above National Average

The Aged

Retirement communities began to emerge in Florida in the 1930s. Today they may be found in most parts of the state. Many were developed specifically for the aged and provide a wide variety of services, including special protection against crime.

Health planners have become concerned about meeting the needs of the "very" old (those 85 and above), an age group that is growing more rapidly than most others. Today persons 85 and older constitute an especially high share of the aged in Dade and Pinellas counties, where younger retirees no longer settle in as large numbers as they did in previous decades.

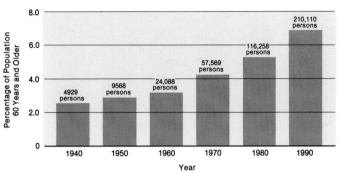

Population 85 Years and Older

Retirement Communities, 1990

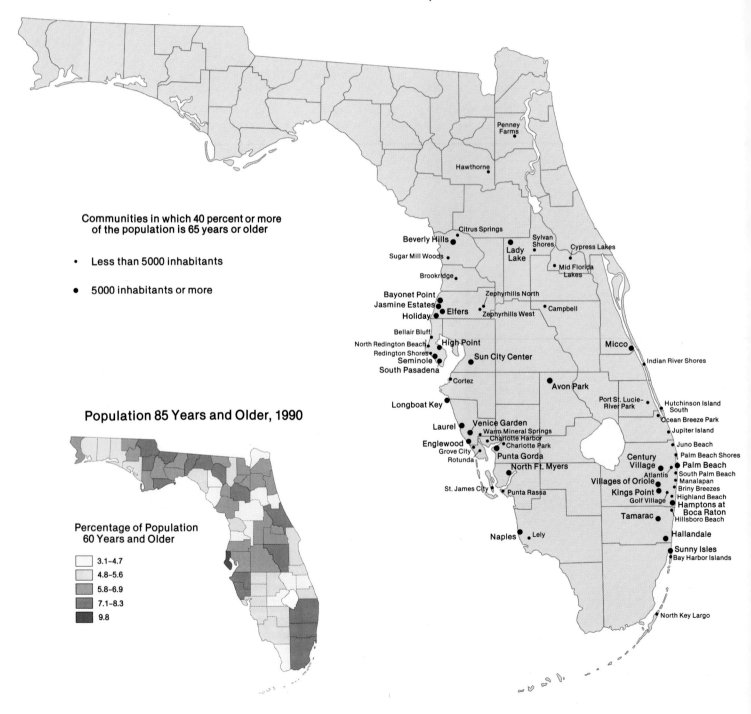

Communities in which 40 percent or more
of the population is 65 years or older

• Less than 5000 inhabitants

● 5000 inhabitants or more

Population 85 Years and Older, 1990

Percentage of Population
60 Years and Older

	3.1–4.7
	4.8–5.6
	5.8–6.9
	7.1–8.3
	9.8

Households

Single-Person Households, 1990

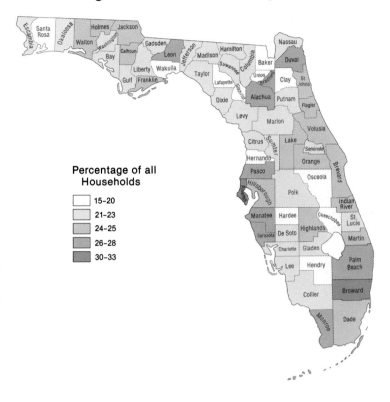

Percentage of all
Households

- 15–20
- 21–23
- 24–25
- 26–28
- 30–33

Single-Parent Non-Hispanic White Households, 1990

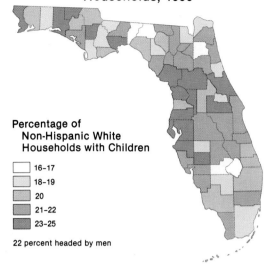

Percentage of
Non-Hispanic White
Households with Children

- 16–17
- 18–19
- 20
- 21–22
- 23–25

22 percent headed by men

Single-Parent Black Households, 1990

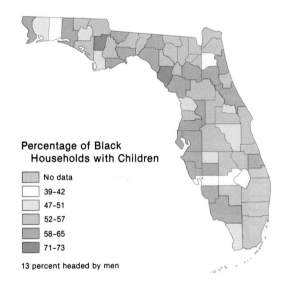

Percentage of Black
Households with Children

- No data
- 39–42
- 47–51
- 52–57
- 58–65
- 71–73

13 percent headed by men

Household Types, 1990

	Non-Hispanic White (%)	Black (%)	Hispanic (%)
Married Couple with related children	20	22	31
Married Couple with no related children	38	13	26
Male householder, no wife present and related children	1	4	3
Male householder, no wife present and no related children	1	3	3
Female householder, no husband present and related children	4	24	9
Female householder, no husband present and no related children	3	6	5
Householder living alone	27	22	17
Householder not living alone, but not in marital situation	6	6	6

Single-Parent Hispanic Households, 1990

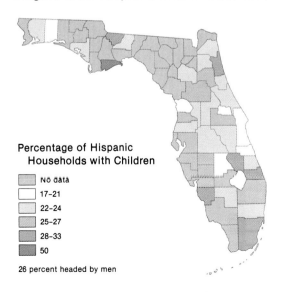

Percentage of Hispanic
Households with Children

- No data
- 17–21
- 22–24
- 25–27
- 28–33
- 50

26 percent headed by men

Since 1970 single-parent households have increased among non-Hispanic whites, Hispanics, and blacks. In 1970, 12 percent of all non-Hispanic white families were headed by a single parent, but by 1990 the percentage had risen to 22. For Hispanics the change was from 10 to 27 percent, and for blacks it rose from 33 percent to 56 percent. Most single-parent families continue to be headed by females. Nonetheless, since 1970 among non-Hispanic whites the share of single-parent families headed by males rose from 17 percent to 22 percent and for Hispanics from 14 to 26. There was no significant change for blacks, the share rising from 12 to 13 percent.

Counties with high percentages of single-person households usually also have high percentages of aged or high percentages of students or military personnel.

Housing

Compared with the nation as a whole, Florida is a state of home owners. The share of Florida's non-Hispanic whites who are home owners is 10 percentage points higher than that for the nation. Although the difference is not as great for Hispanic and black Floridians, their shares also are higher. Home ownership is generally highest among all three groups in north Florida and the northern portion of the peninsula. Alachua County (Gainesville) and Leon County (Tallahassee) have low percentages of home ownership since both have huge college student populations.

Mobile homes are prevalent in many rural counties, both in north Florida and on the peninsula. They have even become very popular in several urban counties, notably Manatee County (Bradenton), where over 20 percent of the housing units are mobile homes. Zoning regulations in some parts of extreme southern Florida, an area vulnerable to hurricanes, restrict the use of mobile homes.

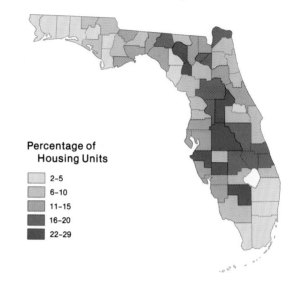

Mobile Homes, 1990

Percentage of
Housing Units

- 2–5
- 6–10
- 11–15
- 16–20
- 22–29

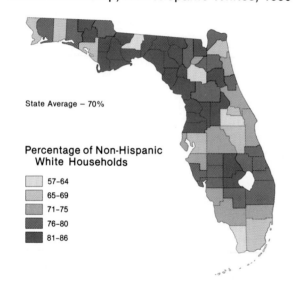

Home Ownership, Non-Hispanic Whites, 1990

State Average – 70%

Percentage of Non-Hispanic
White Households

- 57–64
- 65–69
- 71–75
- 76–80
- 81–86

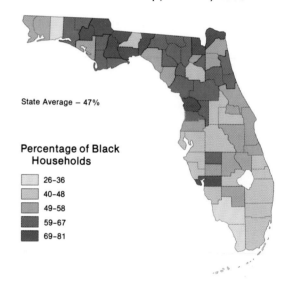

Home Ownership, Blacks, 1990

State Average – 47%

Percentage of Black
Households

- 26–36
- 40–48
- 49–58
- 59–67
- 69–81

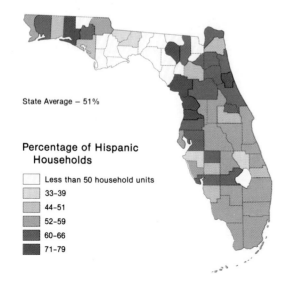

Home Ownership, Hispanics, 1990

State Average – 51%

Percentage of Hispanic
Households

- Less than 50 household units
- 33–39
- 44–51
- 52–59
- 60–66
- 71–79

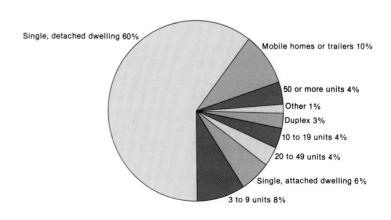

Occupancy by Housing Type, 1990
Percentage of Population

Single, detached dwelling 60%
Mobile homes or trailers 10%
50 or more units 4%
Other 1%
Duplex 3%
10 to 19 units 4%
20 to 49 units 4%
Single, attached dwelling 6%
3 to 9 units 8%

Social Services

Florida's Department of Health and Rehabilitative Services (HRS) is the state's principal provider of social services. The federal government contributes approximately half of the costs of Medicaid and Aid to Families with Dependent Children (AFDC), which are administered by HRS. Food stamps are also provided by the federal government to the state, but their distribution is the responsibility of HRS.

In absolute numbers most of the state's poor live in large metropolitan areas; however, higher percentages of households receive aid in lightly populated rural counties, particularly in north Florida. Dade County (Miami), where the share of households receiving aid is as high as many rural counties, is an exception.

Old Age Assistance, 1989

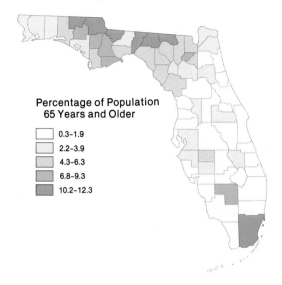

Percentage of Population
65 Years and Older

- 0.3–1.9
- 2.2–3.9
- 4.3–6.3
- 6.8–9.3
- 10.2–12.3

Florida Department of Health and Rehabilitative Services Allocations, 1991

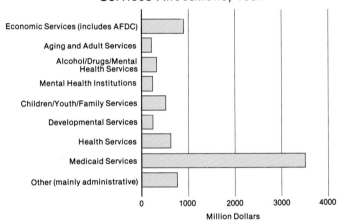

Households Receiving Aid to the Disabled, 1989

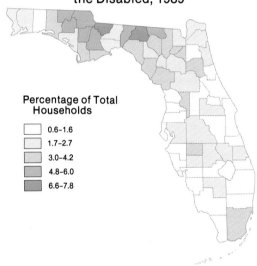

Percentage of Total
Households

- 0.6–1.6
- 1.7–2.7
- 3.0–4.2
- 4.8–6.0
- 6.6–7.8

Food Stamps, 1989

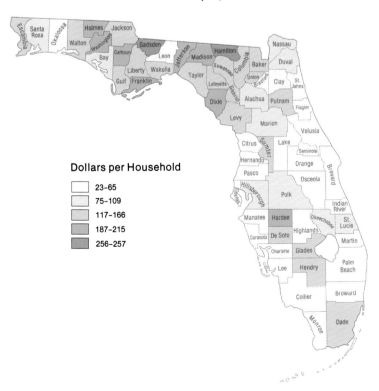

Dollars per Household

- 23–65
- 75–109
- 117–166
- 187–215
- 256–257

Households Receiving Aid to Families with Dependent Children, 1989

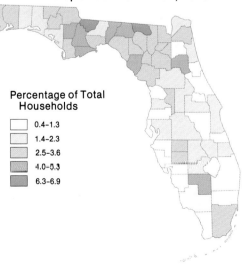

Percentage of Total
Households

- 0.4–1.3
- 1.4–2.3
- 2.5–3.6
- 4.0–5.3
- 6.3–6.9

Health Facilities

Hospital Beds, 1991

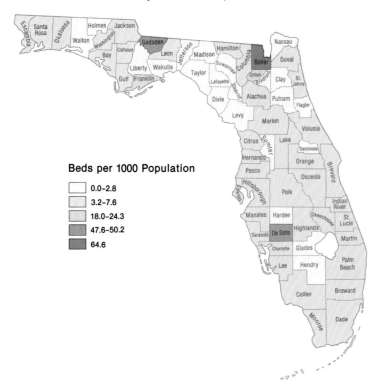

Beds per 1000 Population

- 0.0–2.8
- 3.2–7.6
- 18.0–24.3
- 47.6–50.2
- 64.6

Nursing Home Beds, 1991

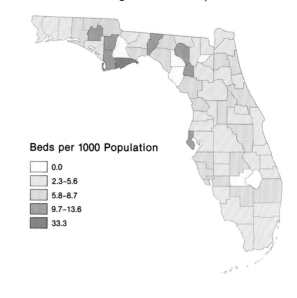

Beds per 1000 Population

- 0.0
- 2.3–5.6
- 5.8–8.7
- 9.7–13.6
- 33.3

Substance Abuse Facilities, 1991

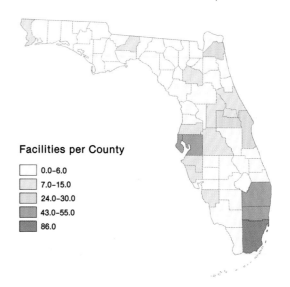

Facilities per County

- 0.0–6.0
- 7.0–15.0
- 24.0–30.0
- 43.0–55.0
- 86.0

The share of the aged in Florida's population is 45 percent higher than the aged's share in the population of the nation. Health care for the aged is a major issue in Florida. The state has over 5,000 health facilities and health service agencies, ranging from small adult foster homes with fewer than 3 beds to large referral hospitals with over 1,000 beds. In 1991 within the state were 317 licensed community hospitals (with a bed capacity of 61,553), 6 state psychiatric hospitals, 1 state correctional hospital, and 1 state tubercular hospital. The federal government operates veterans' hospitals, as well as hospitals on military bases.

Florida today is well provided with hospitals, following a building boom that peaked in the early 1980s. Access to hospital beds is reasonably uniform throughout the state, although a number of rural counties, particularly in the Big Bend area, have relatively few beds per 1,000 inhabitants. Economies of scale make it difficult to operate a modern, well-equipped hospital in an area with a small population. A case in point is that of Gadsden County, whose hospital had to discontinue obstetric services in mid-1991.

Counties with many nursing home beds for each 1,000 inhabitants frequently have populations with large shares of the aged, or else have relatively low populations. The greatest number of substance abuse facilities are in large cities where the largest number of drug users are found.

Hospices, 1991

County	Hospices	Beds	County	Hospices	Beds
Dade	2	30	Brevard	2	10
Broward	3	29	Lee	1	9
Palm Beach	2	28	Lake	1	5
Duval	2	21	Leon	1	4
Pinellas	1	21	Charlotte	1	4
Orange	1	20	Collier	1	4
Sarasota	1	18	Monroe	1	4
Hillsborough	1	15	St. Lucie	1	4
Escambia	1	11	Citrus	1	4
Alachua	1	11	Indian River	1	3
Polk	1	11	Martin	1	2
Volusia	1	11	Okeechobee	1	1

Health Professionals

In 1991 Florida had 32,327 resident physicians with active licenses: 27,000 medical doctors, 1,740 osteopathic physicians, 2,810 chiropractic physicians, and 777 podiatrists. The number of medical doctors per 1,000 persons is highest in the Gold Coast counties and in other large metropolitan areas. Tallahassee and Gainesville are relatively small metropolitan areas, but have high ratios of medical doctors to population. Tallahassee has a regional medical center serving a vast lightly populated area of the state, as well as southwestern Georgia. Gainesville is the home of the University of Florida Medical School and its large teaching hospital, a veterans' hospital, and several community hospitals. The distribution of dentists conforms more closely to population than the distribution of physicians, but specialists generally practice in larger cities. The highest ratios of nurses to population are found in coastal counties from Duval (Jacksonville) around southern Florida to Tampa–St. Petersburg. Dade County, however, has only a moderate number of nurses for every 1,000 residents.

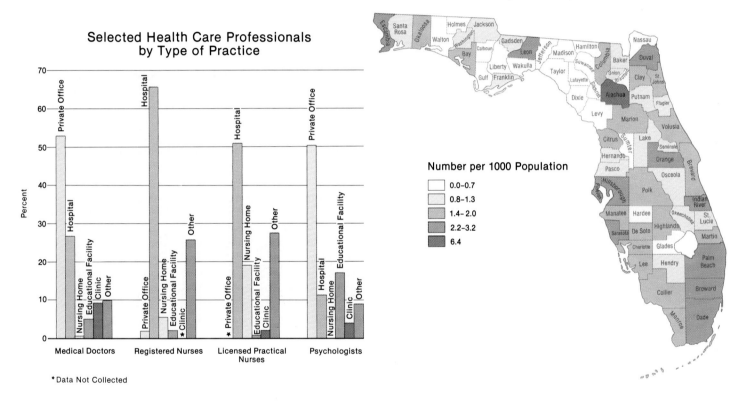

Selected Health Care Professionals by Type of Practice

*Data Not Collected

Physicians, 1991

Number per 1000 Population
- 0.0–0.7
- 0.8–1.3
- 1.4–2.0
- 2.2–3.2
- 6.4

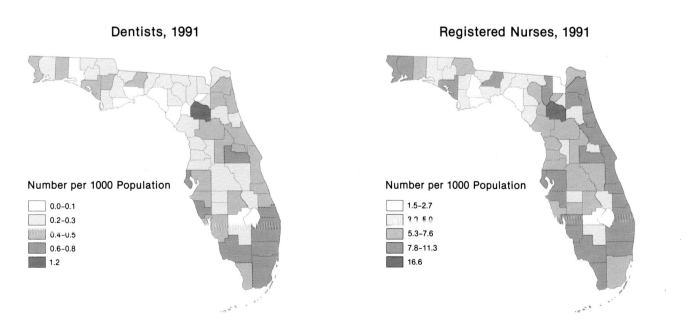

Dentists, 1991

Number per 1000 Population
- 0.0–0.1
- 0.2–0.3
- 0.4–0.5
- 0.6–0.8
- 1.2

Registered Nurses, 1991

Number per 1000 Population
- 1.5–2.7
- 3.2–5.0
- 5.3–7.6
- 7.8–11.3
- 16.6

Hospitals

Admissions to Florida Hospitals, 1949–1989

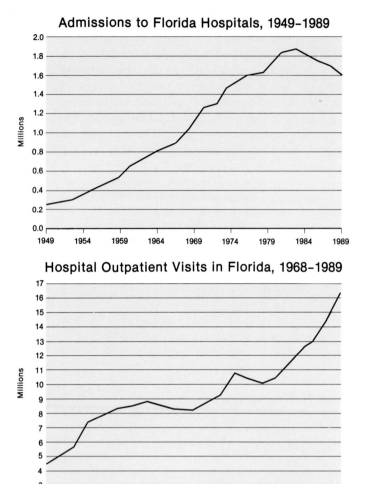

Florida has the fourth highest number of hospital beds in the nation, as well as the fourth largest population. There are general acute care hospitals in all but eight Florida counties (Dixie, Gilchrist, Glades, Jefferson, Lafayette, Liberty, Sumter, and Wakulla). Psychiatric beds are available in 37 counties, substance abuse beds in 28 counties, and rehabilitation hospital beds in 18 counties. Although the number of acute care beds has remained relatively stable, the numbers of psychiatric, substance abuse, and comprehensive medical rehabilitation beds have increased significantly in the last few years. Most Floridians live within easy driving distance to hospitals with highly specialized medical facilities. Helicopter emergency medical services have greatly reduced the time it takes for those needing hospital care to reach a facility.

Since the early 1980s, despite the arrival of millions of migrants to the state, many of whom are of retirement age, admissions to hospitals have declined. Florida's bed utilization has dropped significantly since 1984 as a result of the implementation of the Medicare Diagnostic-Related Group (DRG) reimbursement system and other factors such as modification in medical practices, increased utilization controls, increased competition, and managed care contracting. While hospital admissions have declined in recent years, outpatient visits have grown at approximately the rate of population growth. Growth in outpatient visits is indicative of the recent drop in hospitalization for many routine procedures. Despite a decline in hospital admissions since 1983 and an increase in outpatient visits, the rate of outpatient visits per million in Florida is below the national average.

Hospital Outpatient Visits in Florida, 1968–1989

Trauma Centers with Helicopter Emergency Medical Services, 1990

Circle represents distance of 50 miles from trauma center

Selected Special Services

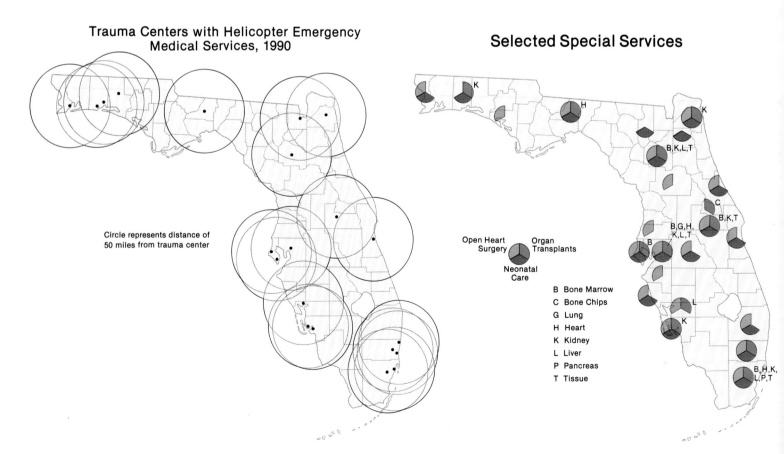

Open Heart Surgery   Organ Transplants

Neonatal Care

B Bone Marrow
C Bone Chips
G Lung
H Heart
K Kidney
L Liver
P Pancreas
T Tissue

Health Care Costs

In 1990 Florida had 5.2 percent of the nation's population, but received 7.2 percent of the money budgeted for Medicare, a federal health program for the aged. The disproportionately higher share of federal Medicare payments to Florida is the result of the large number of people 65 years of age and older in its population. The state only receives 3.5 percent of federal Medicaid funds, which are for basic health services to certain categories of poor people. In 1988, cost per day in a Florida hospital was 10 percent higher than the national average and cost per stay was 7 percent higher, but the average daily room charges were 12 percent lower.

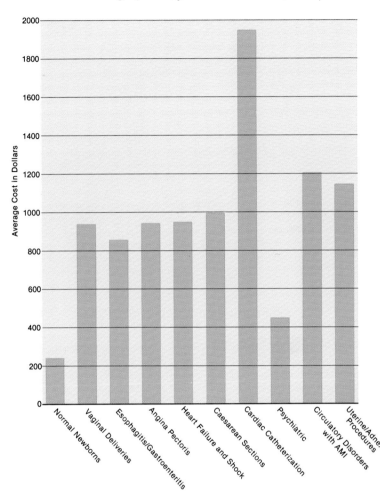

Patient Charge per Day for Florida Hospitals, 1988

Source of Payment for Hospital Charges, 1988

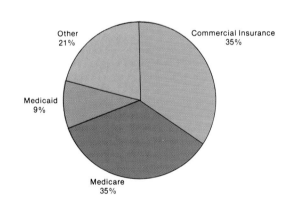

Average Length of Hospital Stay for Discharged Patients, 1988

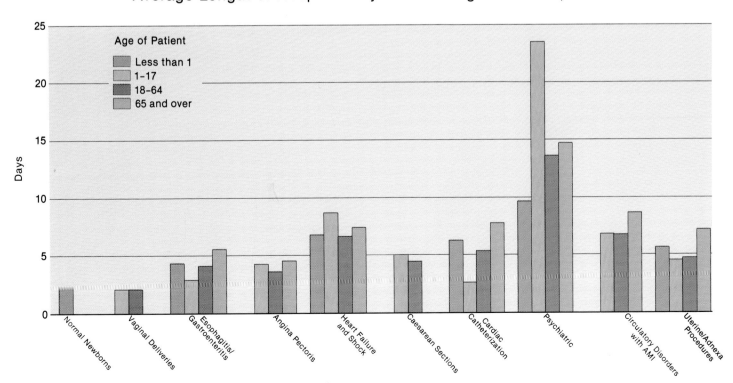

Primary and Secondary Education

High School Dropouts, 1988-1989

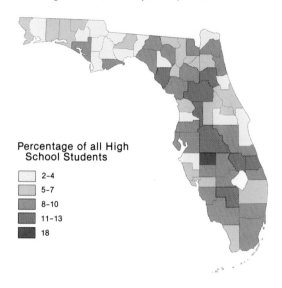

Percentage of all High
School Students

- 2-4
- 5-7
- 8-10
- 11-13
- 18

Expenditures per Pupil, 1989-1990

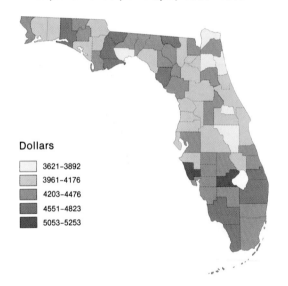

Dollars

- 3621-3892
- 3961-4176
- 4203-4476
- 4551-4823
- 5053-5253

K-12 Students in Private Schools, 1988-1989

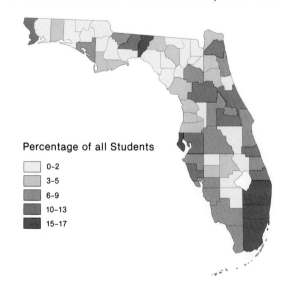

Percentage of all Students

- 0-2
- 3-5
- 6-9
- 10-13
- 15-17

Florida is divided into sixty-seven school districts, one for each county. Property taxes are collected in each school district for public primary and secondary education. Florida, however, was one of the first states to adopt a plan for state support of education in order to balance the quality of instruction from county to county. For example, in Collier County, where per capita income is high, local sources finance 75 percent of the school district's operating budget; whereas in Liberty County, where per capita income is low, 75 percent of the school budget comes from the state. Despite efforts to equalize funds available for schools, expenditures per pupil vary considerably by county, although some poor counties as well as wealthy ones have high expenditures.

High school dropout rates are highest in the more rural counties. The high dropout rate in some of these counties, especially those on the peninsula, may be attributed to the presence of a large number of migrant laborers and their families. A small percentage of Florida students attends private school. Catholic school attendance figures heavily on the Gold Coast. In north Florida private school attendance increased following desegregation of the public schools. A higher share of graduating seniors on the Gold Coast enter college than in any other region.

Graduating Seniors Entering College, 1989

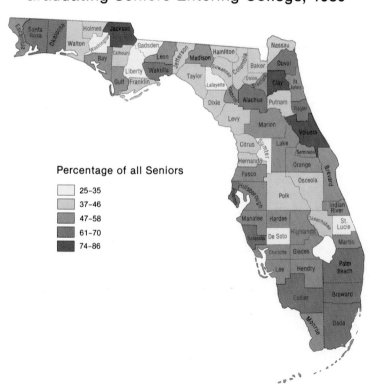

Percentage of all Seniors

- 25-35
- 37-46
- 47-58
- 61-70
- 74-86

Average Annual Teachers' Salaries *

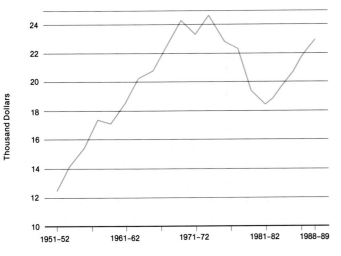

* Based on 1982–84 constant dollars

Annual Expenses per Student *

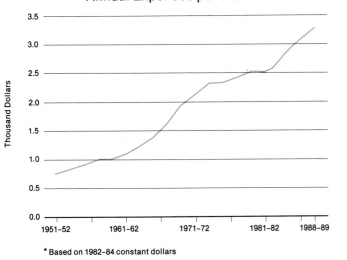

* Based on 1982–84 constant dollars

Students per Classroom Teacher, 1988–1989

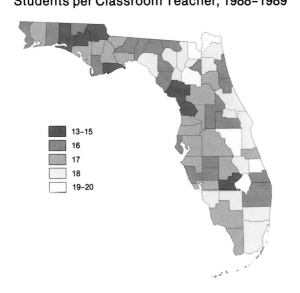

Entry-Level Teachers' Salaries, 1989–1990

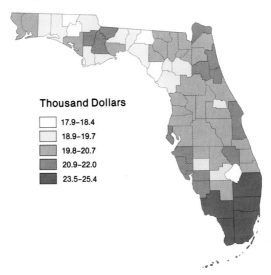

Thousand Dollars

17.9–18.4
18.9–19.7
19.8–20.7
20.9–22.0
23.5–25.4

Average Salaries for Teachers with Master's Degree, 1989–1990

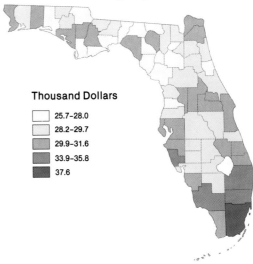

Thousand Dollars

25.7–28.0
28.2–29.7
29.9–31.6
33.9–35.8
37.6

Teachers per Administrator, 1988–1989

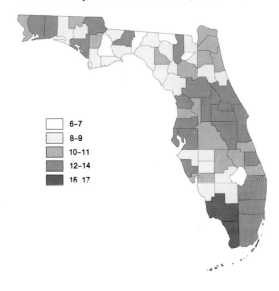

6–7
8–9
10–11
12–14
16–17

Higher Education

Florida offers its residents a wide variety of postsecondary educational opportunities. It has a well-diversified State University System, an accessible Community College System, vocational-technical centers, and

numerous private institutions of learning. The State University System was formed in 1905. As Florida's population grew, the demand for higher education increased, particularly in urban areas. Today the State University System consists of nine universities located strategically throughout the state. Several have branch campuses. The Florida legislature authorized construction of a tenth university in southwestern Florida to be opened in the late 1990s. Of the numerous private colleges and universities throughout the state the University of Miami is the largest.

The Community College System of Florida as well as its system of vocational-technical centers are among the most well developed in the nation. Both systems were designed so that every resident of Florida would be within commuting distance of either a college or a center. Community colleges offer the equivalent of the first two years of liberal arts education found in the State University System. Any graduate receiving the associate of arts degree from these institutions may enter a state university as a junior. Area vocational-technical centers and many community colleges offer training leading to specific careers and help workers to upgrade their skills. They often collaborate with area employers in developing their programs. Almost a million students enroll annually in vocational education programs.

Institutions Offering Bachelor Degrees or Higher

Public Community Colleges

Vocational-Technical Schools

Universities

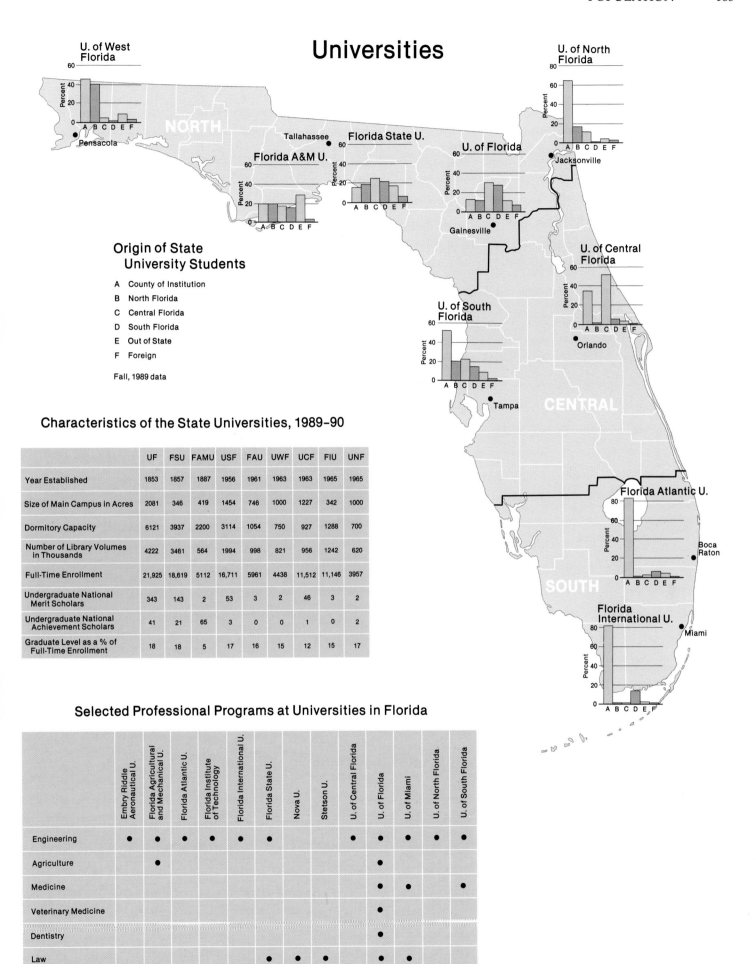

U. of West Florida

U. of North Florida

Tallahassee

Florida State U.

Florida A&M U.

U. of Florida

Gainesville

U. of Central Florida

Orlando

U. of South Florida

Tampa

Florida Atlantic U.

Boca Raton

Florida International U.

Miami

Pensacola

Jacksonville

NORTH

CENTRAL

SOUTH

Origin of State University Students

A   County of Institution
B   North Florida
C   Central Florida
D   South Florida
E   Out of State
F   Foreign

Fall, 1989 data

Characteristics of the State Universities, 1989–90

	UF	FSU	FAMU	USF	FAU	UWF	UCF	FIU	UNF
Year Established	1853	1857	1887	1956	1961	1963	1963	1965	1965
Size of Main Campus in Acres	2081	346	419	1454	746	1000	1227	342	1000
Dormitory Capacity	6121	3937	2200	3114	1054	750	927	1288	700
Number of Library Volumes in Thousands	4222	3461	564	1994	998	821	956	1242	620
Full-Time Enrollment	21,925	18,619	5112	16,711	5961	4438	11,512	11,146	3957
Undergraduate National Merit Scholars	343	143	2	53	3	2	46	3	2
Undergraduate National Achievement Scholars	41	21	65	3	0	0	1	0	2
Graduate Level as a % of Full-Time Enrollment	18	18	5	17	16	15	12	15	17

Selected Professional Programs at Universities in Florida

	Embry Riddle Aeronautical U.	Florida Agricultural and Mechanical U.	Florida Atlantic U.	Florida Institute of Technology	Florida International U.	Florida State U.	Nova U.	Stetson U.	U. of Central Florida	U. of Florida	U. of Miami	U. of North Florida	U. of South Florida
Engineering	●	●	●	●	●	●			●	●	●	●	●
Agriculture		●								●			
Medicine										●	●		●
Veterinary Medicine										●			
Dentistry										●			
Law						●	●	●		●	●		
Pharmacy		●								●	●		●
Architecture		●								●	●		●

Crime

Florida's crime rate in nearly all categories has always been higher than the national average. Data for the seven categories of crime identified by the Federal Bureau of Investigation are reported on this page. Florida usually ranks among the top five states in all the FBI crime categories except motor vehicle theft. In some years Florida has led the nation in rates of burglary, larceny, robbery, and aggravated assault.

Although the table of crime rates on this page indicates a decline in several categories, it should be remembered that the table compares Florida crime rates with those of the nation. If national crime rates are rising, and they are in several categories, it only shows that Florida's are rising less than those of the nation, but they still remain well above the national averages.

Five Florida metropolitan areas have exceptionally high rates of both violent and nonviolent crime: Greater Miami, Tampa, Jacksonville, Gainesville, and Tallahassee. These communities are quite different from each other: Greater Miami has a large Hispanic population; Gainesville and Tallahassee have many young university students; and Jacksonville has large employment in manufacturing as well as the military. Nonviolent crime is unusually high, but violent crime rates are at or below the state average in the Metropolitan Statistical Areas of Ft. Lauderdale, West Palm Beach, Lakeland, Ocala, and Pensacola. The panhandle generally has much lower crime rates than peninsular counties.

Annual fluctuations in frequently committed crimes, such as burglary, are consistent throughout Florida despite differences in population density and in racial and ethnic composition. For example, when the burglary rate of Greater Miami rises or falls, rates change in the same direction in Jacksonville and Gainesville.

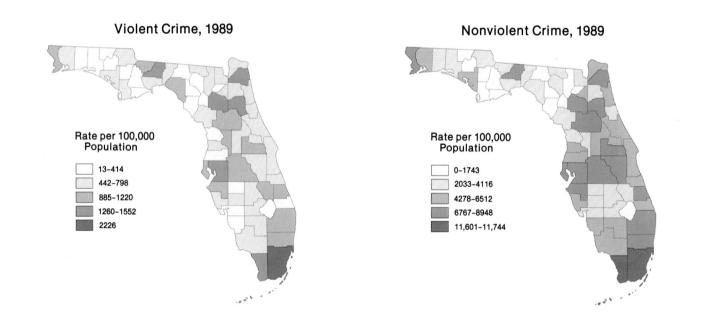

Violent Crime, 1989

Rate per 100,000 Population

- 13–414
- 442–798
- 885–1220
- 1260–1552
- 2226

Nonviolent Crime, 1989

Rate per 100,000 Population

- 0–1743
- 2033–4116
- 4278–6512
- 6767–8948
- 11,601–11,744

Florida's Crime Rates in Relation to U.S. Rates

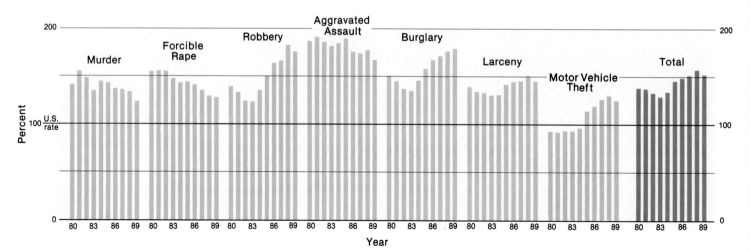

Florida has become one of the nation's leading ports of entry for marijuana and cocaine. Cocaine is sometimes made into crack within the state, and drug money is also laundered within the state. Thus, Florida law enforcement officers have a far more demanding task than their counterparts in most other states. Florida's drug problems throughout the 1980s were given national attention, not only in the news media, but through movies and television, most notably *Miami Vice*. For a state heavily dependent on tourism such notoriety has been particularly damaging.

Florida became a major port of entry for drugs because it is close to the Caribbean basin and because it has a long stretch of lightly inhabited coastline facilitating illegal entry by sea. Light planes are also used to transport drugs to isolated places in the interior, sometimes landing on the roads of planned developments that were never populated. Large quantities of drugs have also been brought in on freighters and by airplane passengers or in airplane freight. Despite sophisticated surveillance, the volume of drug traffic continues to reflect national demand.

Throughout the 1980s state law enforcement offices have devoted an increasing amount of people, time, and money to control the distribution and sale of drugs. Increasingly the most widely used drug in Florida is cocaine, commonly in the form of "crack." This drug first became popular in the black ghettoes of the state's major cities, but quickly diffused throughout the state, even to rural areas. Drug arrests have risen sharply, and the state government has had to spend large amounts of money to increase prison facilities to accommodate the growing number of people convicted of drug crimes.

Arrests for Drug Sales and Possession

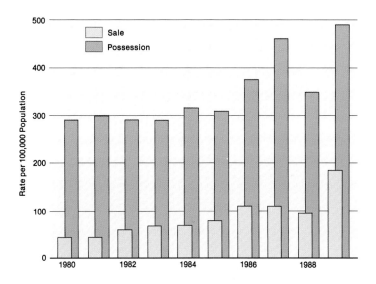

Cocaine and Marijuana Arrests

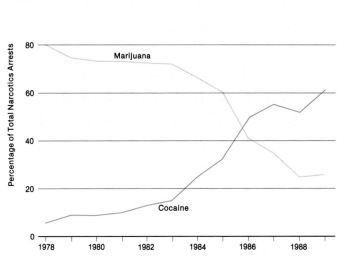

Arrests for Drug Sales and Possession, 1989

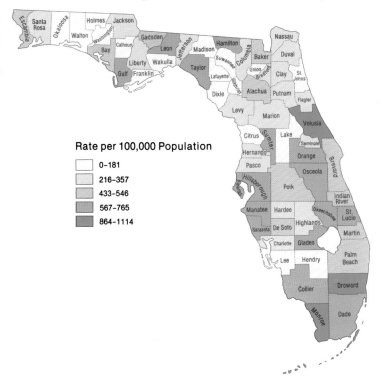

Rate per 100,000 Population

- 0–181
- 216–357
- 433–546
- 567–765
- 864–1114

State Prison Population

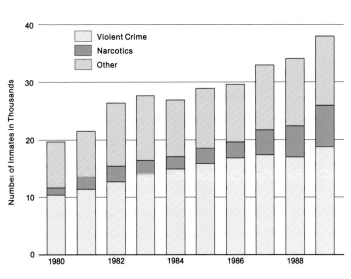

ECONOMY

Florida's economy had been characterized by growth since World War II. The dramatic increase in the state's population, from slightly less than 3 million in 1950 to almost 13 million in 1990, has been largely responsible for this growth. For years, however, Florida's geographical position—a peninsula on the southeastern edge of the continental United States, removed from population centers—contributed to an image of the state as part of the national frontier. At the beginning of the twentieth century, Florida's economy was still relatively weak and its population small. The economy was primarily based on agriculture and forestry. The completion of an efficient railroad link between the state and the rest of the nation in the 1890s began to stimulate many sectors of the economy, including tourism, citrus and vegetable production, forestry, and mining.

During the twentieth century many social and technological changes occurred in the United States. Several of these changes contributed to the population and economic growth of Florida. The most significant change was a new national prosperity. Increased income enabled many Americans to buy agricultural products, such as citrus fruits and winter vegetables, grown in Florida; to visit the state during vacations; and to choose it as a place for retirement. The United States also developed a transportation system capable of delivering both people and goods long distances easily and economically. This system further reduced Florida's isolation from the rest of the nation. In addition, widespread use of air conditioning had an enormous impact upon Florida's economy, making its long summers more bearable.

Florida's leading economic activities, in order of earned income, are services, government, retail trade, manufacturing, construction, finance, and transportation. Nonwage sources of income are also vital to the state's economy. Florida citizens, since so many are retired, receive a higher proportion of their personal income from transfer payments (for example, social security), dividends, interest, and rent than citizens of any other state.

Agriculture

Florida normally leads the southeastern states in value of farm sales and is in the top ten in the nation. The state's climate is hot and humid and its soils are generally low in fertility. As a result, Florida's agriculture is energy intensive, requiring applications of large amounts of herbicides, pesticides, and fertilizers. Although the state usually receives abundant rainfall, rain does not always arrive at the right time of year for crops. Many farms, particularly in southern Florida, have elaborate irrigation systems. Its agriculture produces far higher sales per acre than most states, since much land is devoted to vegetables, citrus, and nursery plants.

Citrus accounts for almost one-quarter of all agricultural sales. Of all the varieties of citrus, oranges account for the majority of total sales (79 percent), with grapefruit a distant second with 17 percent of total sales. Florida's oranges are particularly well suited for orange juice concentrate, and much of the nation's orange juice concentrate is processed in the state. Freezes during the 1980s wiped out production on hundreds of thousands of acres of groves in central Florida, necessitating expansion of the citrus region into the poorly drained area west of Lake Okeechobee, as well as importation of orange juice concentrate from Brazil. Yields in the southern part of the peninsula are often lower than in the central peninsula, but killing freezes are less likely.

Florida's total acreage, production and value of fresh market vegetables is exceeded only by California. Florida ranked high among the states in production of a number of vegetables, including fresh snap beans, cabbage, sweet corn, cucumbers, eggplant, sweet peppers, and celery. The state's special advantage is its ability to produce fresh vegetables for northern markets during the winter and spring. Since the 1970s, however, Florida's winter vegetable industry has faced stiff foreign competition, notably from Mexico. In the summer high temperatures preclude the production of many vegetables. Sugarcane became a major crop in Florida only after the United States severed trade relations with Cuba in 1961. By 1980 sugarcane had become the leading product in dollar value of farm sales among the state's field crops. Almost half of all sugarcane produced in the United States is raised in Florida, almost all on organic soils along the south shore of Lake Okeechobee.

Florida has one of the fastest growing ornamental horticulture industries in the country. The demand within the state from new residents partially accounts for this growth. A national market for its nursery plants developed because Florida's climate permits many tender ornamentals to be grown outside year-round, whereas farther north expensive greenhouses must be used.

Florida's beef cattle industry has grown to national importance, and among southeastern states it is only exceeded by Kentucky. The industry began to grow rapidly only after World War II, when higher beef prices made ranchers more enthusiastic about applying advances in cattle parasite control, animal breeding and pasture improvement. The state has specialized in the sale of yearly stock to feeder lots, mainly on the Great Plains. The dairy cattle industry also contributes to the state's economy, and through most of the year meets the milk demands of the state. Although in recent years the number of dairy cows has decreased, overall production has been maintained because of increased productivity per cow as a result of improved breeding and management.

Forestry

Florida's forests provided one of its first products to reach the national market. Even before the Civil War, steam-powered circular saws were cutting softwood lumber, primarily in northern Florida. In addition, pine was tapped for turpentine and rosin (naval stores). In time, lumber and naval stores production declined in relative importance, but during the twentieth century the development of a process to turn pine into pulp for both cellulose and paper gave the forests a new significance. Because pine matures far more quickly in the South than the North and because land on the southern coastal plain was relatively cheap, pulp and paper companies built mills and bought large areas of land in the South during the 1920s and 1930s. In 1990 Florida had more land in corporate tree farms than any other state except Georgia.

Mineral Production

Florida has a known reserve of phosphate rock, which is primarily used for fertilizer, that is greater in value than that of any other mineral. In terms of sales, Florida produces most of the nation's phosphate, much of which is exported. Although phosphate sales are important to the state's economy, phosphate mining has also resulted in a number of environmental problems, which the industry and state and local governments are working together to solve. These include land reclamation, heavy water usage, ponding of slurry, and the possibility of radiation problems in mined-out sites. Increasingly the industry must also meet foreign competition.

By 1990 the value of petroleum produced in the state had fallen far below that of phosphate, although in 1980 the two were almost equal. There are two areas of petroleum production in the state: one in the southwest, the other in the northwest. The Jay Field in northwest Florida is the most important. Discovered in 1970, its reserves have almost been depleted. Oil companies have engaged in intensive exploration for petroleum off Florida's Gulf coast since the early 1970s. Exploration continues although no discoveries have been made.

Fishing

Florida has a well-developed commercial fishing industry. Its future, however, is threatened by the overfishing of the relatively few commercial species and by foreign competition. Shrimp is the most valuable species caught, accounting for over 40 percent of total sales, followed by lobster, crab, and snapper. Most shrimp are now caught off the Tortugas (west of Key West) and off the Gulf coast. Florida's national importance in both value and weight of the shellfish catch has declined. In part this decline results from overharvesting. Some foreign nations now prevent Florida fishermen from entering their territories. Recently the nation has imported large quantities of shrimp from Ecuador and China, where they are raised in confined areas cheaply. Recognizing the benefits of a stable source of shrimp, Florida investors have spent considerable amounts of time and money attempting to grow them under artificial conditions, but have not had the success of either Ecuador or China.

Manufacturing

Manufacturing has traditionally played a smaller role in the Florida economy than in the economy of the average state. In part this has resulted from the state's remoteness from the major population centers of the nation. The relative importance of industry to Florida has also been inhibited by the state's growing popularity as a tourist and retirement center. Unlike other southern states, the state government of Florida until recently did little to attract manufacturing and even enacted legislation to discourage it. In recent years, however, the state has become more aggressive in pursuit of industry.

By earned income in 1990 the electronics industry was the most important type of manufacturing, followed by transportation equipment (except motor vehicles). Industry is highly concentrated in the state's larger cities, especially those on the southeastern coast, and Tampa Bay. A number of counties with small populations, many of which are in northern Florida, are far more economically dependent on manufacturing than are counties with large cities.

Older manufacturing firms in the state are mainly based on processing the state's raw materials (phosphate, citrus, timber) or are market oriented (printing and publishing, baking, bottling). Market-oriented industries are among the state's most dynamic. For example, the tourist and retirement population has had much to do with the elevation of Florida to among the nation's leaders in the construction of pleasure boats. Printing and publishing, particularly of newspapers, grows along with the population. The electronics industry is relatively new to the state. The beginning of the state's high-technology industry dates from the start of the national space program in 1957 when Cape Canaveral was chosen as the site of the United States launch center. Since then some of the nation's largest technologically oriented corporations have opened facilities in the state, several employing thousands of workers each. Florida's importance in the electronics industry, including computers, is now nationally recognized.

Construction

The construction industry, Florida's fifth most important in terms of earned income, has been unstable. Rapid population and economic growth has resulted not only in an active market to meet the needs of new residents, but it has also spawned considerable speculation in the housing market. Construction fluctuates as much by the cost and ease of obtaining loans as by demand. This has led to periods when there is a glut of homes and commercial buildings for sale, as well as periods of scarcity. As in the rest of the nation, housing costs in Florida have risen rapidly. The share of Florida's employed who work in construction is higher than that of the nation. The state's economy is more sensitive than that of most other states to fluctuations in construction.

Wholesale and Retail Trade

In terms of earned income, retail trade is the third most important component of the state's economy. Florida's retail establishments serve tourists, increasing numbers of whom are Latin Americans and Europeans, as well as residents. Florida's recent population growth has brought about an enormous expansion in retail establishments. There are few places in the nation which have experienced a greater growth in the number of large regional malls. In Florida a greater share of total retail sales are made in department stores than in most other states.

In contrast to the state's per capita retail trade, Florida's per capita wholesale trade is below that of the nation. For years, Jacksonville was the state's major wholesale center. Lately Miami, which serves Latin America as well as Florida, has overtaken it, and Tampa and Orlando are increasing in importance as wholesale centers.

In 1979 the state began to authorize "free trade zones," which provide tariff protection for importers, exporters, and manufacturers. The Miami Free Trade Zone, which is especially important in Latin American trade, is by far the largest free trade zone.

Transportation and Foreign Trade

Florida's economic growth, to a great extent, has depended upon the quality of its connection with other places. Trucks move the vast majority of Florida's agricultural and industrial products. Airlines bring a greater percentage of tourists to Florida than to any other state except Hawaii. In large measure the growth of the Miami tourist industry after World War II was the result of combined advertising efforts of airlines, hotels, and car rental agencies. Maintenance facilities for several major airlines, with employment in the thousands, are located in Miami.

Florida's seaports have grown to national dominance in handling cruise ship passengers, and have considerable significance in value of international trade. Latin America and Japan are Florida's principal trade partners. By value of trade, Latin America is the primary destination of Florida exports, and Japan is the major source of the state's imports. Jacksonville is the largest port of entry for Japanese automobiles on the East Coast.

Finance, Real Estate, and Government

Jacksonville, Orlando, Tampa, and Miami are the state's financial centers. Jacksonville long held primacy within the state in banking, but Miami's growing population and its close connection with Latin America now give it far greater national and international importance. Recently, as a result of the state's new branch banking regulations many Florida-based banks have merged with others whose headquarters are in other states. Jacksonville, however, has retained its importance as an insurance center and is the home office of several national insurance companies.

The one category of financial employment that ranks far higher in relative importance in Florida than in the nation is real estate. The state's rapid population growth has given rise to over twice as many real estate employees per thousand people in Florida than in the nation. Counties with exceptionally high ratios of real estate employees are those that attract the most new residents. Although a large share of Florida's population is dependent (retirees and children under fifteen), the percentage of local and state civil servants in the total work force is no higher than that of the nation. Civil servants, however, account for a large share of the work force in Tallahassee and Gainesville. The federal payroll makes an important contribution to the local economy in counties with large military installations.

Tourism

Tourism is Florida's most widely known economic activity. In 1990 slightly over 39 million tourists visited the state, contributing many billions of dollars to the economy. For retail sales considerations, the state's tourists contribute the equivalent of well over 1.5 million residents to the economy, but they require far fewer government services than residents.

National affluence after World War II, broader based than in the earlier part of the century, made it possible for an ever-growing number of people to vacation in Florida. Before World War II, most tourists came by train and in the winter. After the war, whole families began to come, most by car, and commonly in the summer. These tourists were primarily attracted to the beaches along the Atlantic coast. In the 1970s, theme parks were built in the center of the state, the most famous being Walt Disney World. Theme parks have had much to do with an increase in the length of Florida's tourist season to twelve months a year.

The maintenance of a successful tourist industry has not been without difficulties. Florida now must compete with many places throughout the nation and the world for visitors. To date Florida has been successful in the competition for United States tourists, as well as attracting a growing number of tourists from abroad, particularly Europe. A note of concern for the future, however, has arisen if the real cost of gasoline should rise. If fuel should become so expensive as to elevate the cost of transportation to Florida prohibitively, the state's tourist industry would be severely hurt.

Florida Regions

Throughout this century, Florida's Peninsular Coast has experienced dramatic population, and accompanying economic, growth. The population has grown gradually along the coast from traditional retirement centers such as Miami Beach, Ft. Myers, and St. Petersburg. There has also been an influx of younger people into the region who have found jobs primarily in construction and service industries. Dade, Broward, Brevard, and Hillsborough counties are among the state's manufacturing centers, whereas Charlotte, Collier, Lee, and Sarasota counties cater mostly to tourists and retirees. Agriculture once played a more significant role in the Peninsular Coast economy, but urbanization has removed much land from crop and livestock production.

The arrival of so many people to the Peninsular Coast in so short a period has not occurred without problems. With growth have come potential problems of water availability, air quality, and road congestion, as well as social problems. Miami continues to attract many people including increasing numbers from abroad. Few, however, are retirees, who now more frequently choose other coastal counties.

The Peninsular Interior has played a significant role in Florida's economy since the nineteenth century. After the Civil War the citrus industry spread gradually southward from along the St. Johns River and its tributaries to the central highlands. Vegetable farming, cattle raising, and phosphate mining also increased during this period. Today the Peninsular Interior is more economically diverse than any other region in the state, with agriculture, manufacturing, and tourism sharing importance. The majority of Florida's citrus, beef cattle, dairy products, sugarcane, and vegetables are produced in this region. Citrus, sugar cane, and phosphate are processed as well as produced within the region. In addition, Orlando, the region's largest city, has a diversified industrial base, including a growing electronics industry.

Tourism has grown dramatically along the route of Interstate 4 between Tampa and Orlando. Near Orlando is Walt Disney World, the state's most popular tourist attraction, which draws approximately one-quarter of all visitors to Florida, as well as Sea World and Universal Studios. Busch Gardens, another popular tourist attraction, is in Tampa. The Peninsular Interior is popular with retirees as well as with tourists. There are many small planned retirement communities extending as far north as Marion County.

The North is distinct both physically and culturally from the two peninsular regions. It shares many of the physical and cultural characteristics of the two states immediately to its north, Georgia and Alabama. Cotton and timber became the bases of the region's economy before the Civil War, just as they did in southern Alabama and Georgia.

Agriculture and forestry are still major components of North Florida's economy. Farming in the north is more mixed than in the other regions of the state and less energy intensive. Field crops such as peanuts, soybeans, corn, cotton, and tobacco are raised. Beef cattle and, to a lesser extent, hogs are raised on many farms. Around Madison there is a thriving broiler chicken industry, and in Clay County there are large dairy herds. In the 1920s, the large paper mills began to buy poor, cutover lumber company land in the region cheaply. These areas are now operated as huge scientifically managed tree farms, supplying the raw materials for pulp and paper mills, which are scattered from Pensacola to Jacksonville.

The North has a rapidly declining oil field at Jay, northeast of Pensacola. Phosphate is also mined and processed approximately 100 miles west of Jacksonville. Fishing is locally important along the coast, and the shoreline, especially from Panama City to Pensacola, attracts many summer tourists. Naval and Air Force bases are located in the western panhandle and in Duval County, and are major civilian as well as military employers. Tallahassee, the state capital, not only has a major governmental function, but is also the home of two state universities.

Conclusions

In large part, the strength of Florida's economy has been its diversity. Tourism, retirement income, agriculture, manufacturing, and construction are all important to the state's economy, and to a degree insulate it against national cycles in the economy. The state, however, has to resolve two critical problems. First, its tax base is too small to build an infrastructure to accommodate its rapidly growing population. Second, it has to make a greater effort to work out a better relationship between its population and the state's physical environment. The resolution of these problems will greatly improve the state's already attractive national image.

Sectors of the Economy

The location quotient compares an economic sector's share of earned income in Florida with that sector's share of earned income in the nation:

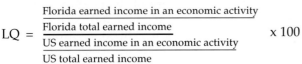

$$LQ = \cfrac{\cfrac{\text{Florida earned income in an economic activity}}{\text{Florida total earned income}}}{\cfrac{\text{US earned income in an economic activity}}{\text{US total earned income}}} \times 100$$

The graphs, which plot location quotients between 1980 and 1989, show that the proportions of agriculture, construction, retail trade, and finance, insurance and real estate earned income within Florida's total earned income are very similar to those of the U.S. as a whole, whereas the service subcategory of amusement, recreation, and hotels is much higher. Because of its large elderly population, Florida might be expected to have a high location quotient for health services, but it does not. This sector's share of earned income is very close to the national average.

Earned Income by Economic Sector
1989

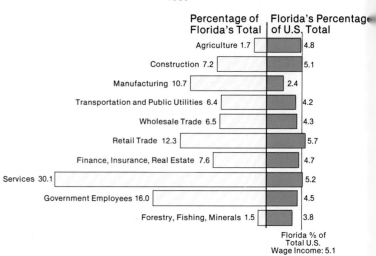

	Percentage of Florida's Total	Florida's Percentage of U.S. Total
Agriculture 1.7		4.8
Construction 7.2		5.1
Manufacturing 10.7		2.4
Transportation and Public Utilities 6.4		4.2
Wholesale Trade 6.5		4.3
Retail Trade 12.3		5.7
Finance, Insurance, Real Estate 7.6		4.7
Services 30.1		5.2
Government Employees 16.0		4.5
Forestry, Fishing, Minerals 1.5		3.8

Florida % of
Total U.S.
Wage Income: 5.1

Comparison of Relative Importance of Florida's Economic Sectors with those of the United States

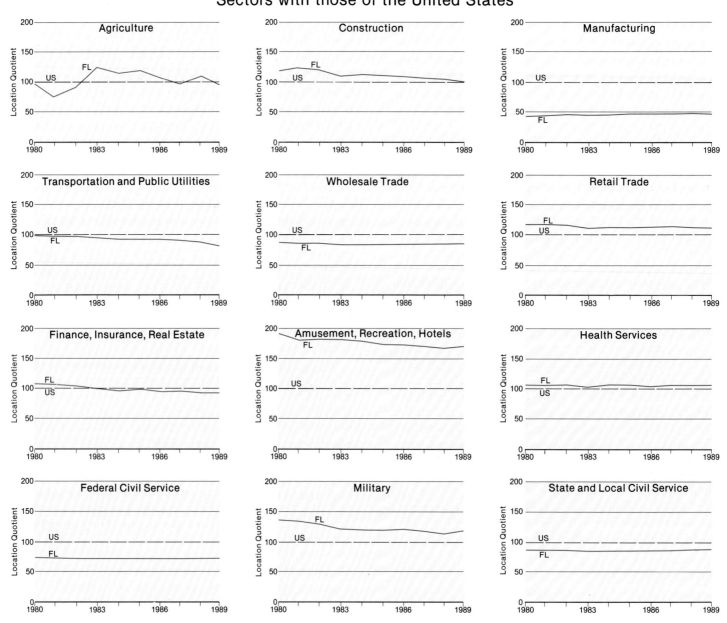

Local Importance of Economic Activities

The location quotient is a measure of regional economic specialization. For example, in a number of counties around Lake Okeechobee, where vegetables and sugarcane are grown, employment in agriculture is at least 50 percent higher than the percentage of agricultural employment for the nation. To the north, particularly in the Big Bend, there are many rural counties where the share of total employment in agriculture greatly exceeds that for the nation.

Mining, almost entirely of phosphates, is of great importance in Polk County as well as several counties in northeast Florida. Employment in construction is of unusually great importance in counties with high in-migration. Manufacturing exceeds the national average in rural north Florida counties, usually where there are only one or two manufacturing plants. Services account for the largest share of total employment, both in Florida and in the nation. In Florida, counties that cater to tourists have the highest percentages of service employment. State, local, and federal employment contributes enormously to total employment in many north Florida counties. The military is a large employer around Jacksonville and in west Florida. State government employs many people in Tallahassee, the state capital and the home of two state universities, as well as in Gainesville, the location of the University of Florida.

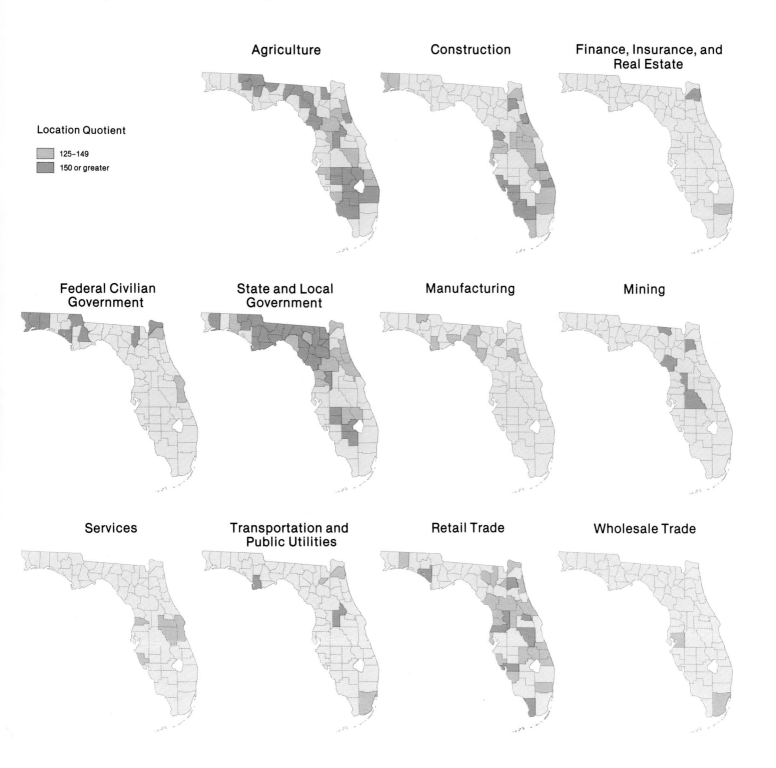

Location Quotient

- 125–149
- 150 or greater

Agriculture

Construction

Finance, Insurance, and Real Estate

Federal Civilian Government

State and Local Government

Manufacturing

Mining

Services

Transportation and Public Utilities

Retail Trade

Wholesale Trade

Nonwage Income

The importance to the Florida economy of transfer payments, as well as interest, dividends, and rent, is enormous. Transfer payments in Florida are primarily in the form of Social Security and federal pensions, but also include unemployment compensation and welfare benefits. Many retirees who settle in Florida supplement their pensions through interest, dividends, and rent. The contributions of transfer payments and interest, dividends, and rent to total personal income of Floridians remain well ahead of these percentages for the nation. The difference between the state and the nation for transfer payments has been decreasing, but the difference between the state and nation for interest, dividends, and rent has risen over the last decade. People who retire in Florida are generally more affluent than those who remain close to where they worked. Many retirees arrive in Florida with a portfolio of stocks and bonds, as well as savings that draw interest and property that yields rent.

The geographical distribution of counties where transfer payments are most significant is different from the distribution of counties where interest, dividends, and rent figure most prominently. Transfer payments contribute more to personal income in rural counties, particularly those of north Florida and near Lake Okeechobee. In some of these counties retirees with modest incomes are numerous; in others the transfer payments mainly support the poor. Interest, dividends, and rent contribute significantly to personal income in counties with large urban populations and in counties where wealthier retirees have settled, such as Sarasota, Collier, Palm Beach, Broward, and Martin. Income from interest, dividends, and rent is of much smaller importance in the personal income of residents in north Florida counties, where there are fewer retirees. Those who do retire in north Florida counties have lower per capita incomes than retirees in the southern coastal counties.

Comparison of Relative Importance of Florida's Nonwage Income with that of the United States

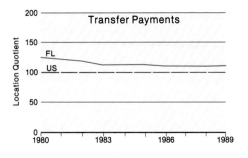
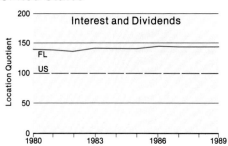

Florida Nonwage Income, 1988

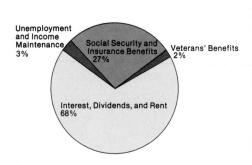

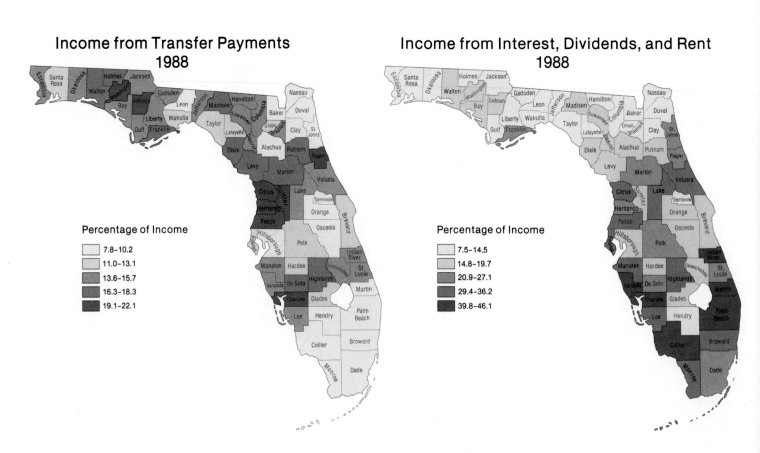

Distribution and Change of Income

Since 1977 Florida's per capita income has become increasingly similar to that of the nation. This is largely because of increase in per capita income in counties outside of the Metropolitan Statistical Areas (MSAs). In 1990 Florida's non-MSA counties had an average per capita income higher than the national average for non-MSA counties, whereas in the 1970s Florida's non-MSA per capita income was well below the national average. A number of Florida's non-MSA counties are attracting wealthy retirees. Per capita income in Florida's MSA counties has not improved compared with MSA counties for the nation as a whole.

Florida's wealthiest cities are mainly found along the lower east coast, historically famous for affluent communities such as Palm Beach. More recently Naples on the southwest coast has emerged as a city with many wealthy inhabitants. Florida's poorest cities are mainly found on the peninsula. The economies of a number of these communities are based on agriculture.

Household Income Extremes, 1989

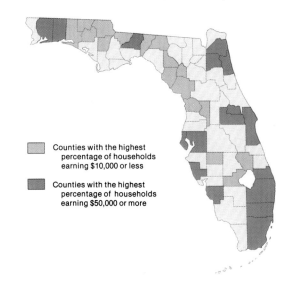

Counties with the highest percentage of households earning $10,000 or less

Counties with the highest percentage of households earning $50,000 or more

Per Capita Income, 1988

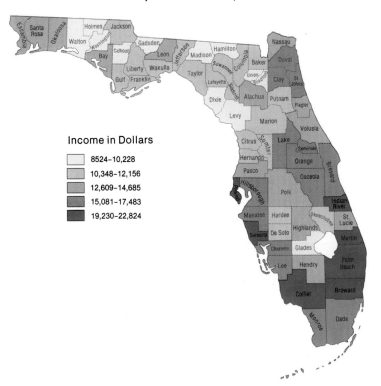

Income in Dollars

- 8524–10,228
- 10,348–12,156
- 12,609–14,685
- 15,081–17,483
- 19,230–22,824

Cities with Highest Per Capita Income, 1988

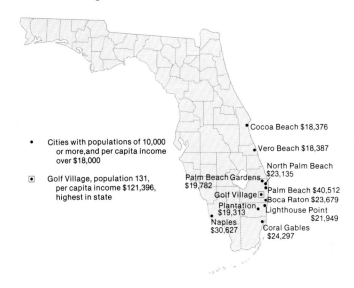

- Cities with populations of 10,000 or more, and per capita income over $18,000
- Golf Village, population 131, per capita income $121,396, highest in state

Cocoa Beach $18,376
Vero Beach $18,387
North Palm Beach $23,135
Palm Beach Gardens $19,782
Palm Beach $40,512
Golf Village
Boca Raton $23,679
Plantation $19,313
Lighthouse Point $21,949
Naples $30,627
Coral Gables $24,297

Florida Per Capita Income as a Percentage of National Average

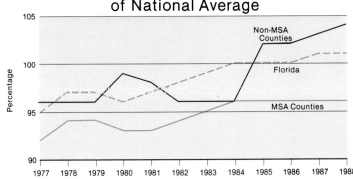

Non-MSA Counties
Florida
MSA Counties

Cities with Lowest Per Capita Income, 1988

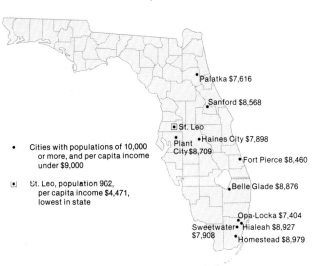

- Cities with populations of 10,000 or more, and per capita income under $9,000
- St. Leo, population 902, per capita income $4,471, lowest in state

Palatka $7,616
Sanford $8,568
St. Leo
Haines City $7,898
Plant City $8,709
Fort Pierce $8,460
Belle Glade $8,876
Opa-Locka $7,404
Sweetwater $7,908
Hialeah $8,927
Homestead $8,979

Variations in Employment

In Florida there is great regional variation in economic activities. Agriculture is especially significant to the Big Bend area and the Peninsular Interior. Construction is important to West Florida and the Sun Coast; manufacturing, to the Big Bend, Peninsular Interior, and Space Coast; wholesale and retail trade, to the Big Bend, Peninsular Interior, and Sun Coast; finance, insurance, and real estate, to Northeast Florida and the Gold Coast; and services, to the Space Coast. Tourism provides many service jobs in the Peninsular Interior and on the Space Coast, since these regions have the state's most popular tourist attractions. It also has a very important high-technology manufacturing base that has grown up around the Kennedy Space Center.

The economies of Northeast Florida and the Gold Coast are similar. The Jacksonville area urbanized much earlier than the Gold Coast, but today has a far smaller population. It is still a major maritime transportation center as well as the headquarters of several major insurance corporations and large banks. The Gold Coast's more recently acquired transportation function is mainly based on movement of goods by air. Miami has become important in finance, in part due to its connections with Latin America.

Difference from State Average by Region

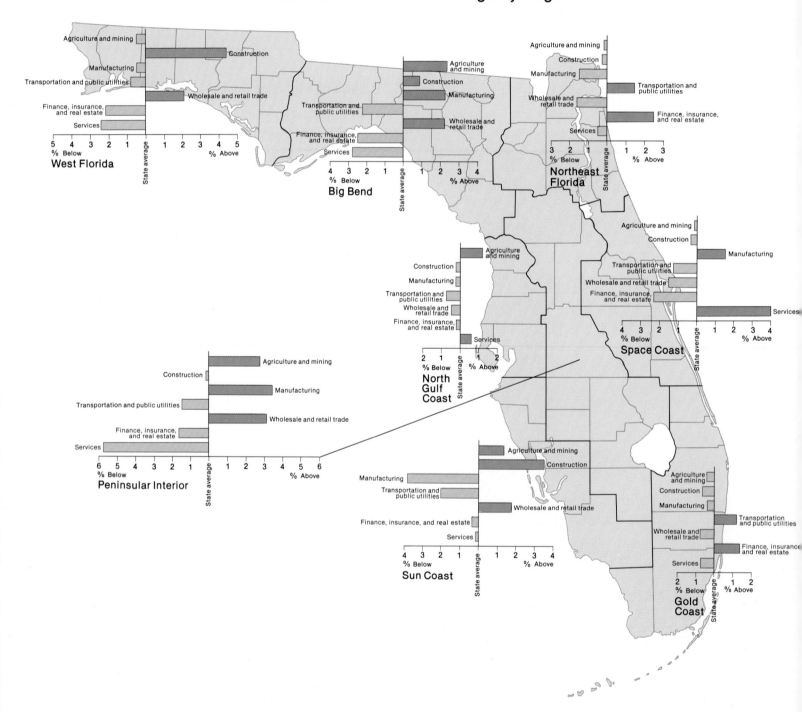

Employment

Florida's nonagricultural employment depends heavily upon tourism, services to retirees, and construction. Consequently it is sensitive to changes in the national economy that affect disposable and retirement income. Since the 1960s, Florida has usually experienced a lower unemployment rate than the nation. Beginning in 1989, however, Florida's unemployment rate began to rise higher than the nation's. This change is largely the result of a more rapid in-migration of people in search of work than growth in jobs. In 1990 an estimated 800 job seekers entered Florida each day. The severe freezes during 1989 and 1990 brought declines in employment related to food production. In 1990 the construction industry began to lay

off workers, the result of a surplus in both new commercial buildings and residences. Manufacturing has been a slow generator of jobs since the middle of the 1980s. Services and retail trade have been the two stable areas of employment, but in 1991 retail sales began to decline, and there were indications of a decrease in tourism.

Seasonality of employment in Florida is much less pronounced than in the past. In the southeast and west, seasonal variation is small. It is largest in the panhandle and central Florida. The panhandle's coast draws many visitors in the summer, but few in the winter. Central Florida's Walt Disney World and other nearby theme parks also have peak attendance in the summer.

Unemployment by Month, 1980–1990

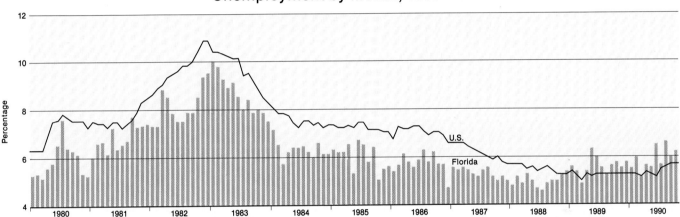

Unemployment, 1989

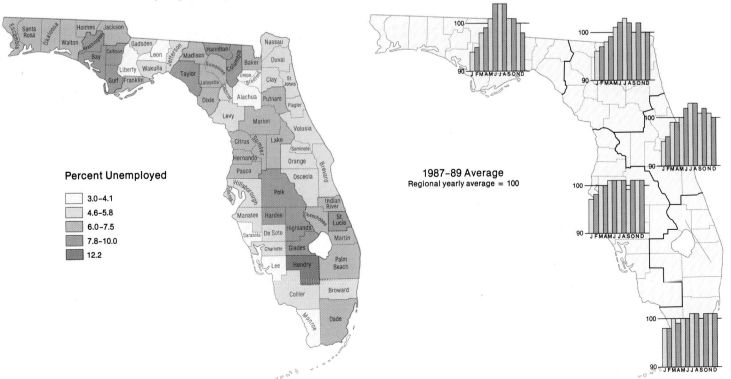

Percent Unemployed

- 3.0–4.1
- 4.6–5.8
- 6.0–7.5
- 7.8–10.0
- 12.2

Monthly Fluctuation in Employment

1987–89 Average
Regional yearly average = 100

A View from Space

This photo of the Florida peninsula was taken by a crew member of the space shuttle *Discovery* from 190 miles above the Caribbean Sea on January 26, 1985, a clear, cool winter day. The photo shows parallel cloud banks off Florida's east coast, associated with a mid-latitude cyclone that had crossed the nation earlier in the week. The West Palm Beach–Ft. Lauderdale–Miami megalopolis is clearly visible, as is the large agricultural area south of Lake Okeechobee. This low area, known as the Mucklands, has rich organic soils that were drained for cultivation early in this century. The elaborate drainage system of canals and water impoundment areas used for controlling water within the Everglades can also be seen. Although almost one-third of the state's inhabitants live south of Lake

Okeechobee, much of the southern peninsula remains unoccupied, the majority of which is under federal and state control.

The state's large bays, estuaries, capes, islands, and beaches stand out conspicuously. The white sand beaches of Miami Beach and Cape Canaveral are readily visible. The dark band which separates the cape from the peninsula is actually a lagoon, although called the Indian River. Though less distinct, urban areas such as Tampa, St. Petersburg, Orlando, Daytona Beach, and Jacksonville may

be identified. The parallel lines that begin just to the west of Lake Istokpoga and extend northward are not man-made. They are ancient beach ridges that are separated from each other by low marshy areas with denser vegetation. Between the St. Johns River and Ocala is a large, lightly populated area covered by scrub pines. Much of this area lies within the Ocala National Forest. Other forests farther to the north also appear as dark areas on the photo. The lighter areas are more open and are often used for grazing, citrus production, and field crops.

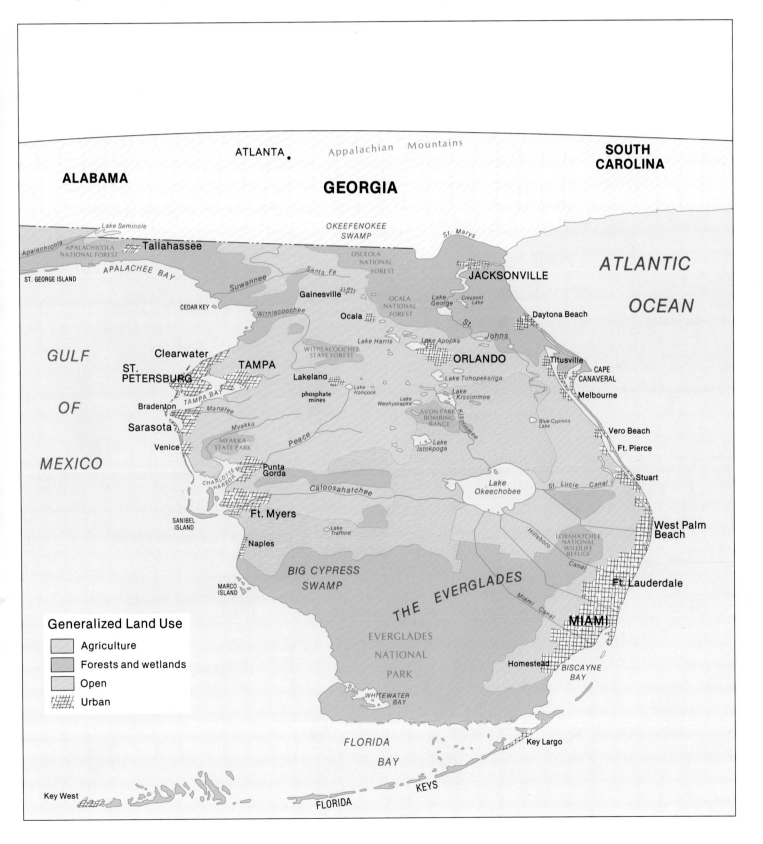

Characteristics of Farms

In 1986, when the most recent agricultural census was conducted, Florida had the eighth highest farm sales of any state in the nation, only surpassed by California and several states in the nation's agricultural heartland.

Farms are largest in counties surrounding Lake Okeechobee where corporate farming of vegetables, sugarcane, citrus, and raising of cattle is most highly developed. In Collier County the Collier family owns approximately 900,000 acres, some of which it farms and some of which it leases. There are three farms in Palm Beach County with acreage of 75,000 or more. North and central Florida have smaller farms. Small-scale farmers came to these two areas in the last century, and many of their descendants continue as owner operators of their family farms.

Farm Size, 1987

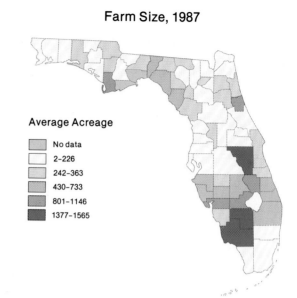

Average Acreage
- No data
- 2–226
- 242–363
- 430–733
- 801–1146
- 1377–1565

Farm Sales
1984–88 Average

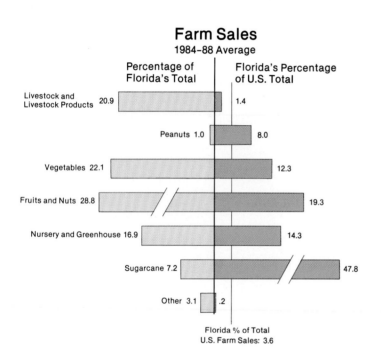

Percentage of Florida's Total | Florida's Percentage of U.S. Total

Livestock and Livestock Products 20.9 — 1.4
Peanuts 1.0 — 8.0
Vegetables 22.1 — 12.3
Fruits and Nuts 28.8 — 19.3
Nursery and Greenhouse 16.9 — 14.3
Sugarcane 7.2 — 47.8
Other 3.1 — .2

Florida % of Total U.S. Farm Sales: 3.6

Value of Farm Land and Buildings, 1987

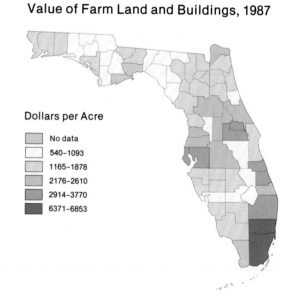

Dollars per Acre
- No data
- 540–1093
- 1165–1878
- 2176–2610
- 2914–3770
- 6371–6853

Full-Owner Farm Operators, 1987

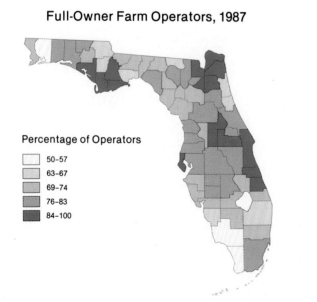

Percentage of Operators
- 50–57
- 63–67
- 69–74
- 76–83
- 84–100

Operators Working off Farms
100 Days or More, 1987

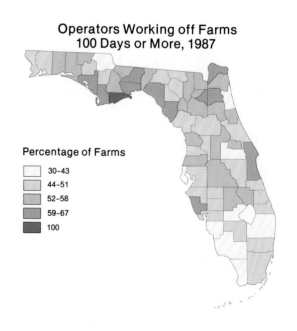

Percentage of Farms
- 30–43
- 44–51
- 52–58
- 59–67
- 100

Farm Economics

Product Sales per Farm, 1987

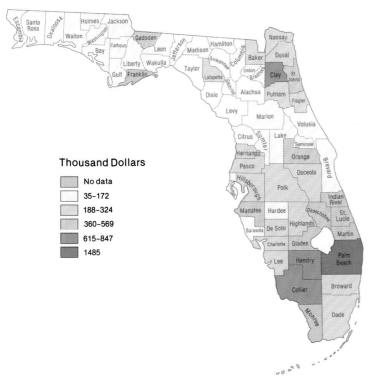

Thousand Dollars

- No data
- 35–172
- 188–324
- 360–569
- 615–847
- 1485

The counties around Lake Okeechobee have the highest product sales per farm. Many of these farms produce vegetables and nursery plants that are high in value compared to the acreage needed to grow them. Sugar produces far less in sales per acre, but the farms on which it is grown are enormous. Vegetables, particularly tomatoes, as well as nursery plants, account for high sales per farm in Gadsden County.

The soil in Florida is generally low in fertility, and the climate conducive to plant diseases and insects. In peninsular Florida as much as one ton of fertilizer is needed annually for each acre. Large quantities of herbicides and pesticides are also applied. Labor costs are higher than in many other parts of the nation, because many Florida crops cannot be mechanically harvested. Contract laborers, usually migrants from the Caribbean basin, harvest vegetables, fruit, and sugarcane as well as care for nursery plants. Elsewhere sugarcane is mainly harvested by machines, but Florida's sugarcane is grown on soft, organic soils on which the machines operate poorly. Irrigation is as important to Florida farmers, particularly in the southern part of the state, as it is to those of California and Arizona.

Irrigated Farmland, 1987

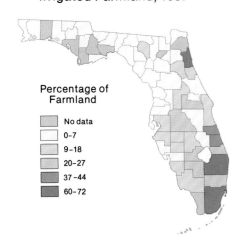

Percentage of Farmland

- No data
- 0–7
- 9–18
- 20–27
- 37–44
- 60–72

Farm Production Costs
1984–88 Average

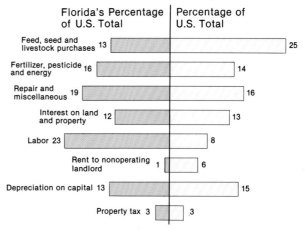

	Florida's Percentage of U.S. Total	Percentage of U.S. Total
Feed, seed and livestock purchases	13	25
Fertilizer, pesticide and energy	16	14
Repair and miscellaneous	19	16
Interest on land and property	12	13
Labor	23	8
Rent to nonoperating landlord	1	6
Depreciation on capital	13	15
Property tax	3	3

Fertilizer and Chemical Costs per Acre, 1987

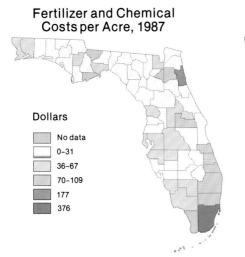

Dollars

- No data
- 0–31
- 36–67
- 70–109
- 177
- 376

Energy Costs per Acre of Farmland, 1987

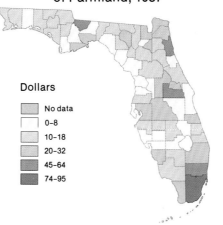

Dollars

- No data
- 0–8
- 10–18
- 20–32
- 45–64
- 74–95

Expenses for Hired and Contract Labor, 1987

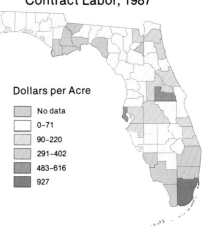

Dollars per Acre

- No data
- 0–71
- 90–220
- 291–402
- 483–616
- 927

Cultivation of Citrus

Florida produces more citrus fruit than any other state. In 1947 Florida overtook California and since then its production has usually been more than double that of California. Florida's largest citrus crop is the orange, grown primarily for its juice. Grapefruit is mainly sold fresh, principally from the Indian River valley on the east coast. Limes and tangelos are produced commercially only in Florida.

During the 1980s Florida's citrus groves were devastated by severe freezes. Hundreds of thousands of acres on the northern edge of the citrus belt have been abandoned. Citrus cultivation has rapidly moved toward the south, principally west and south of Lake Okeechobee. Large corporations have been planting groves on poorly drained land previously regarded as inferior for citrus production. Grove owners in the center of the state have been replanting their groves with varieties of oranges that mature early, and thus stand a better chance of escaping the freezes.

Changes in Citrus Acreage
January 1, 1976–January 1, 1988

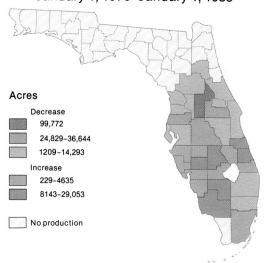

Acres

Decrease
99,772
24,829–36,644
1209–14,293

Increase
229–4635
8143–29,053

No production

Citrus Production, 1988–89 Season

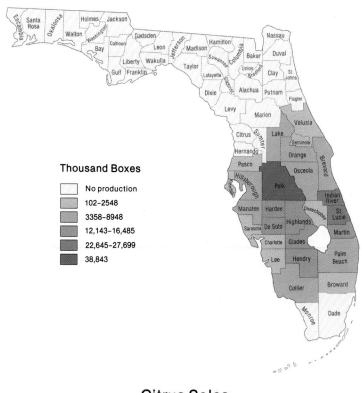

Thousand Boxes

No production
102–2548
3358–8948
12,143–16,485
22,645–27,699
38,843

Relative Acreage Change
January 1, 1976–January 1, 1988

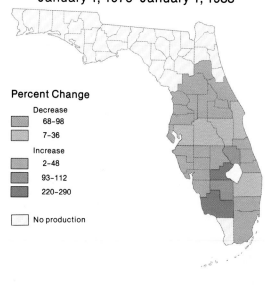

Percent Change

Decrease
68–98
7–36

Increase
2–48
93–112
220–290

No production

Citrus Sales
1988–89 Season

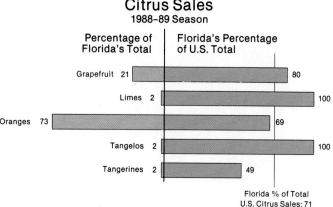

	Percentage of Florida's Total	Florida's Percentage of U.S. Total
Grapefruit	21	80
Limes	2	100
Oranges	73	69
Tangelos	2	100
Tangerines	2	49

Florida % of Total
U.S. Citrus Sales: 71

Regional Citrus Production, 1988–1989

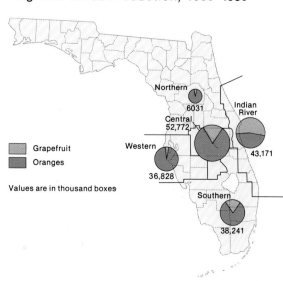

Northern 6031
Central 52,772
Indian River 43,171
Western 36,828
Southern 38,241

Grapefruit
Oranges

Values are in thousand boxes

Citrus Sales

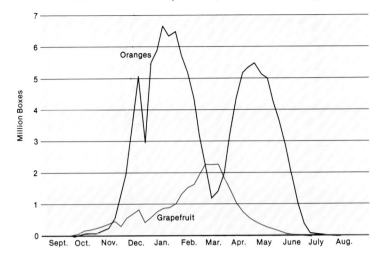

Fruit Processed by Week, 1985–89 Average

Million Boxes

Oranges

Grapefruit

Sept. Oct. Nov. Dec. Jan. Feb. Mar. Apr. May June July Aug.

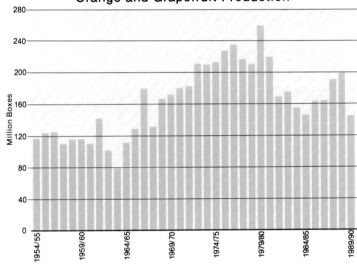

Orange and Grapefruit Production

Million Boxes

1954/55 1959/60 1964/65 1969/70 1974/75 1979/80 1984/85 1989/90

Florida is the nation's leading producer of citrus fruit, principally oranges and grapefruit as well as limes and tangelos. Lemons were grown in Florida before all the groves were destroyed by the freeze of 1895. Today most lemons are grown in California and Arizona.

Florida overtook California in citrus sales shortly after World War II as a result of the rapid growth in sales of frozen orange juice concentrate. The process to make frozen orange juice was developed during World War II and the first plant was opened in Florida after the war. Florida continues to produce most of the nation's frozen orange juice concentrate.

Orange production increased rapidly after 1965, in part as a consequence of massive advertising campaigns mounted by the grove owners association. Production peaked in the 1979–80 season but turned downward as a result of destructive freezes in 1983, 1985, and 1989. The freeze of 1985 was the worst in 86 years. Many groves in the northern part of the citrus belt have had to be abandoned. Growth in grove acreage farther south has partially compensated for the loss, although in 1990 Florida was still buying orange juice concentrate from Brazil to use in its packaging plants.

There are two distinct peaks in the orange harvest, one in January and the other in May. The grapefruit harvest peaks in March, then quickly declines. Oranges and grapefruit are harvested by hand by migrant workers mainly from Mexico and Central America. Because present labor costs are still so low, grove owners have shown little interest in replacing workers with machines.

Most Florida grapefruit is sold fresh to markets east of the Mississippi River. The state dominates the nation's grapefruit sales from September until June, when California and to a smaller extent Arizona briefly become dominant.

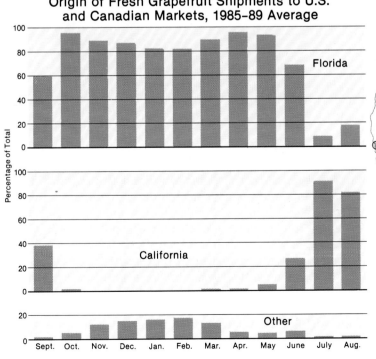

Origin of Fresh Grapefruit Shipments to U.S. and Canadian Markets, 1985–89 Average

Percentage of Total

Florida

California

Other

Sept. Oct. Nov. Dec. Jan. Feb. Mar. Apr. May June July Aug.

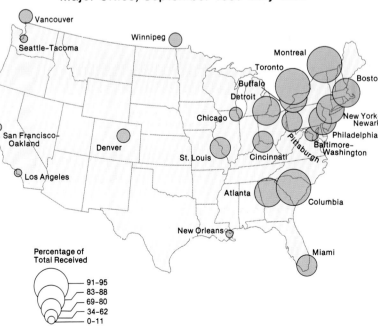

Fresh Grapefruit Shipments from Florida to Major Cities, September 1988–July 1989

Vancouver
Winnipeg
Seattle-Tacoma
Montreal
Toronto
Buffalo
Detroit
Boston
Chicago
San Francisco-Oakland
Denver
St. Louis
Cincinnati
Pittsburgh
New York-Newark
Philadelphia
Baltimore-Washington
Los Angeles
Atlanta
Columbia
New Orleans
Miami

Percentage of Total Received
91–95
83–88
69–80
34–62
0–11

Vegetable Production

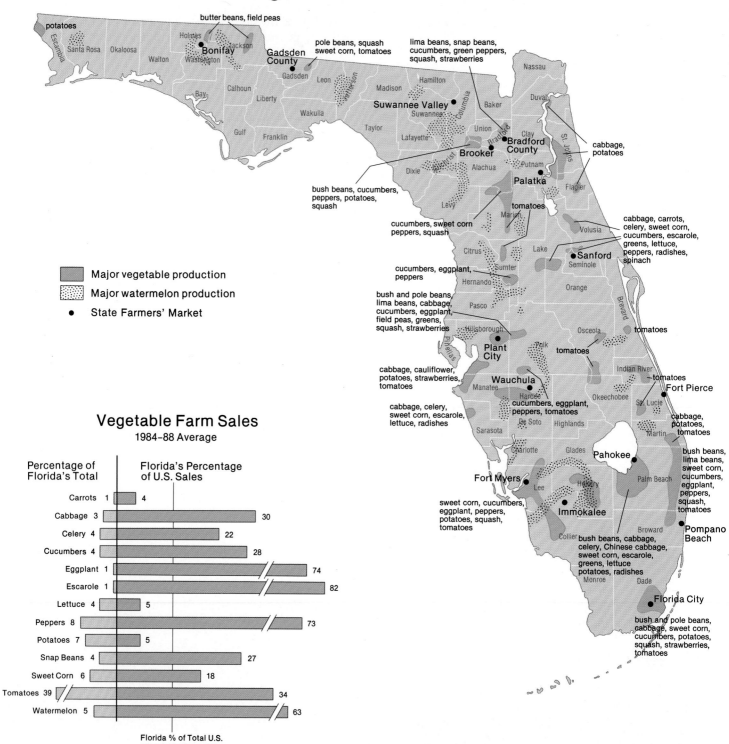

potatoes

butter beans, field peas

pole beans, squash
sweet corn, tomatoes

lima beans, snap beans,
cucumbers, green peppers,
squash, strawberries

Holmes
Santa Rosa   Okaloosa   Jackson
Escambia   Walton   Washington   Bonifay
Gadsden County
Gadsden   Leon   Jefferson
Bay   Calhoun   Liberty   Madison   Hamilton
Gulf   Wakulla   Taylor   Suwannee Valley   Suwannee   Columbia   Baker   Nassau
Franklin   Lafayette   Union   Bradford County   Clay   Duval
Brooker   Dixie   Alachua   Putnam   St. Johns   cabbage, potatoes
bush beans, cucumbers,   Gilchrist   Palatka   Flagler
peppers, potatoes,   Levy   tomatoes
squash   Marion   Volusia   cabbage, carrots,
cucumbers, sweet corn   celery, sweet corn,
peppers, squash   Citrus   Lake   cucumbers, escarole,
greens, lettuce,
cucumbers, eggplant,   Sumter   Sanford   peppers, radishes,
peppers   Hernando   Seminole   spinach
Orange
bush and pole beans,   Pasco
lima beans, cabbage,
cucumbers, eggplant,   Hillsborough   Osceola   tomatoes
field peas, greens,   Plant City   Polk   tomatoes
squash, strawberries   Pinellas   Brevard
Indian River   tomatoes
cabbage, cauliflower,   Wauchula   tomatoes
potatoes, strawberries,   Manatee   Hardee   Okeechobee   Fort Pierce
tomatoes   cucumbers, eggplant,   St. Lucie   cabbage,
cabbage, celery,   peppers, tomatoes   potatoes,
sweet corn, escarole,   De Soto   Highlands   Martin   tomatoes
lettuce, radishes   Sarasota   bush beans,
Charlotte   Glades   Pahokee   lima beans,
sweet corn,
Fort Myers   Palm Beach   cucumbers,
Lee   Hendry   eggplant,
sweet corn, cucumbers,   peppers,
eggplant, peppers,   Immokalee   squash,
potatoes, squash,   Broward   tomatoes
tomatoes   Collier   bush beans, cabbage,   Pompano Beach
celery, Chinese cabbage,
sweet corn, escarole,
greens, lettuce
potatoes, radishes
Monroe   Dade   Florida City
bush and pole beans,
cabbage, sweet corn,
cucumbers, potatoes,
squash, strawberries,
tomatoes

Legend:
▨ Major vegetable production
⋯ Major watermelon production
● State Farmers' Market

Vegetable Farm Sales
1984–88 Average

	Percentage of Florida's Total	Florida's Percentage of U.S. Sales
Carrots	1	4
Cabbage	3	30
Celery	4	22
Cucumbers	4	28
Eggplant	1	74
Escarole	1	82
Lettuce	4	5
Peppers	8	73
Potatoes	7	5
Snap Beans	4	27
Sweet Corn	6	18
Tomatoes	39	34
Watermelon	5	63

Florida % of Total U.S.
Vegetable Sales: 12

Florida is far from the nation's population centers, and its soils are generally low in fertility. Its only physical advantage is a relatively freeze-free winter. Winter and spring vegetables produced in Florida are marketed primarily in states east of the Mississippi River. Florida's share of the nation's production of several vegetables exceeds 70 percent. Heat and competition from northern vegetable areas preclude a summer vegetable season.

The major areas of vegetable production are in south Florida, where freezes are least frequent, but where veg-etable production competes with nursery plant and sugar-cane production, as well as urban development. The largest vegetable region is the Mucklands, an area of rich organic soils south of Lake Okeechobee. To its east is the Atlantic beach ridge, where vegetables continue to be grown despite urban encroachment. The oldest south Florida growing area is in southern Dade County where in some places soil was created by pulverizing exposed bedrock. The newest large south Florida vegetable growing area is around Immokalee. In central Florida vegetables are grown in early spring around Wauchula, Plant City, and Sanford. Significant late spring vegetable production occurs farther north, particularly in Gadsden County.

Marketing of Tomatoes

The tomato was the first vegetable produced in Florida to be marketed nationally. At the beginning of this century, when railroads finally connected south Florida with the rest of the nation, Florida tomatoes began to be sold fresh in northern cities during the winter. Early growers had to overcome problems of plant diseases, insect infestations, and deficiencies of trace elements in the soil. Gradually the Florida winter tomato became an expensive, but readily available item in northern markets. Florida's tomato harvest begins in October and is over by June. When night temperatures remain over 70°F, the plants no longer set fruit. New higher-temperature-tolerant varieties which might extend the season are being developed at the University of Florida.

Florida must compete with Mexico for the United States winter tomato market. Mexico is able to compete well with Florida, despite the greater distance from the large Northeastern markets, because its soils are better and because labor costs are only 10 percent of the labor costs in Florida. Imports from Mexico are controlled by various regulations. The most generous quotas are between January and March, when Florida's share in the national market plummets. The best way for Florida tomato growers to compete with Mexican growers is to lower production costs, particularly labor costs. To lower labor costs, instead of having workers selectively pick a field many times, Florida growers harvest "mature green" tomatoes, which they ripen with ethylene gas. Many "immature green" tomatoes are picked with the "mature green" tomatoes. An immature green tomato that turns red under gas has no flavor.

The majority of Florida's winter tomatoes are produced in southern Dade County and Collier County. Early spring tomatoes are harvested in the Ruskin area, near Tampa. A new, late spring tomato growing area has developed in northern Florida, near Tallahassee.

Tomato Production, 1982–88 Average

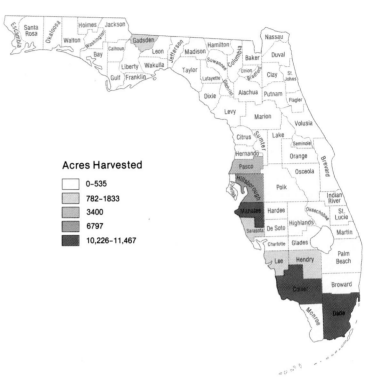

Acres Harvested

- 0–535
- 782–1833
- 3400
- 6797
- 10,226–11,467

Tomatoes Shipped from Florida by Week 1981–87 Average

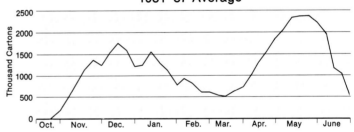

Origin of Fresh Tomato Shipments to U.S. Markets by Week, 1984–88 Average

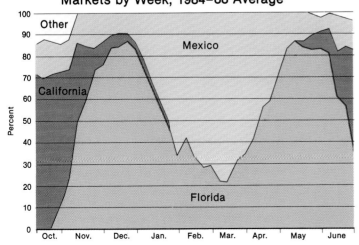

Fresh Tomato Shipments from Florida, 1983–88 Average

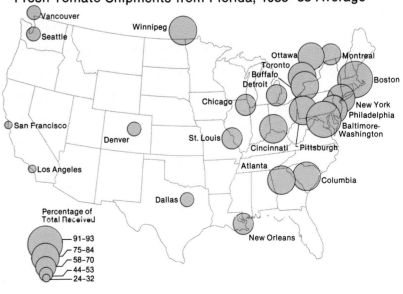

Percentage of Total Received

- 91–93
- 75–84
- 58–70
- 44–53
- 24–32

Location of Field Crops

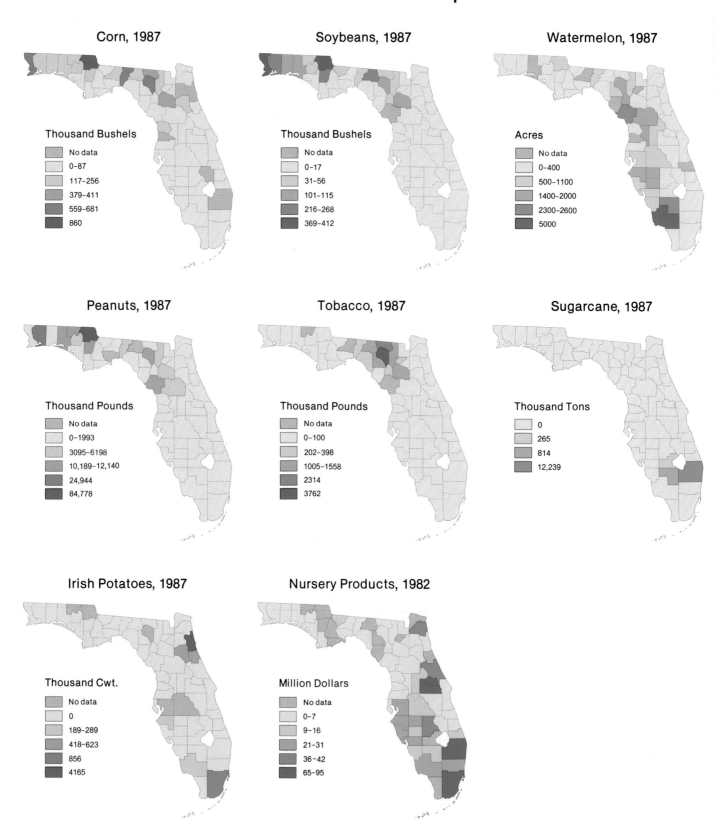

Corn, 1987

Thousand Bushels
- No data
- 0–87
- 117–256
- 379–411
- 559–681
- 860

Soybeans, 1987

Thousand Bushels
- No data
- 0–17
- 31–56
- 101–115
- 216–268
- 369–412

Watermelon, 1987

Acres
- No data
- 0–400
- 500–1100
- 1400–2000
- 2300–2600
- 5000

Peanuts, 1987

Thousand Pounds
- No data
- 0–1993
- 3095–6198
- 10,189–12,140
- 24,944
- 84,778

Tobacco, 1987

Thousand Pounds
- No data
- 0–100
- 202–398
- 1005–1558
- 2314
- 3762

Sugarcane, 1987

Thousand Tons
- 0
- 265
- 814
- 12,239

Irish Potatoes, 1987

Thousand Cwt.
- No data
- 0
- 189–289
- 418–623
- 856
- 4165

Nursery Products, 1982

Million Dollars
- No data
- 0–7
- 9–16
- 21–31
- 36–42
- 65–95

Florida is the leading state in sugarcane production and sales. Nursery products are also economically important. Many plants sold in discount stores and florist shops throughout the nation are raised in Florida. The area around St. Augustine and southern Dade County produce the nation's largest winter harvest of Irish potatoes, much of which is purchased by potato chip companies. The nation's winter and spring demand for watermelons is largely met by Florida. Harvesting begins in Collier County in the southern part of the state and then moves up the state during the spring. Field crops such as corn, soybeans, peanuts, and tobacco are concentrated in the northern part of the state, and although locally economically important, none figures significantly in national sales.

The Effects of Freeze

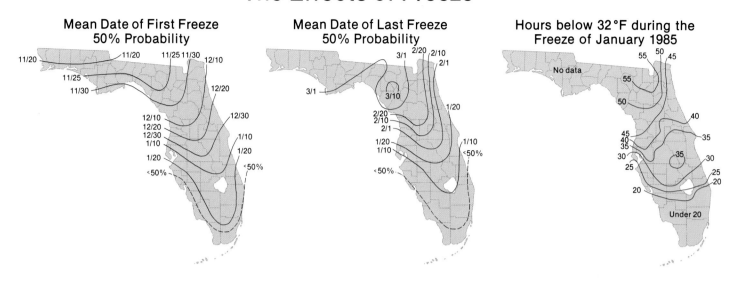

**Mean Date of First Freeze
50% Probability**

**Mean Date of Last Freeze
50% Probability**

**Hours below 32 °F during the
Freeze of January 1985**

Florida Orange Production, 1975/76–1989/90

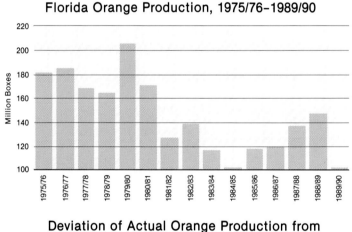

Deviation of Actual Orange Production from Preseason Estimate

Deviation of Fresh Tomato Shipments in 1985 from 1981/82–1986/87 Average

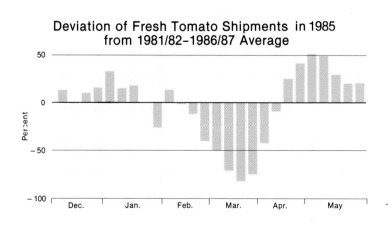

Peninsular Florida's southern latitude does not provide complete protection from freezes, which occur every year in all but the extreme southern counties. Freezes can cause severe damage to fruits and vegetables. Freezes were particularly severe in December 1983, in January 1985, when the state experienced the worst freeze since 1899, and in 1989, when records were set for the length of time temperatures were below freezing.

Vegetable growers can do little to protect their crops against freezes. Tender plants such as tomatoes may be severely damaged, whereas other plants, for example greens and cabbages, can more easily survive. A shortage followed by oversupply may result from freezes. Farmers normally stagger their plantings during the fall to create an extended picking season. After a freeze they are forced to replant all their fields immediately, resulting in a production glut and falling prices.

Citrus growers, who regard their trees as long-term investments, take extreme measures to protect them. Planting is avoided in low, freeze-susceptible areas. When freezes do occur, fires are burned, large fans are used to circulate the air, and trunks of young trees are sometimes insulated against the cold.

Effects of January 21, 1985 Freeze on Vegetable Production, March 1985

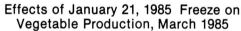

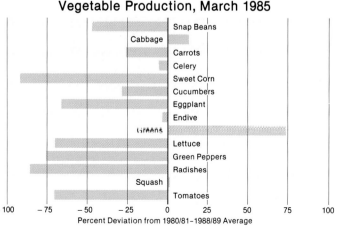

Percent Deviation from 1980/81–1988/89 Average

Livestock Production and Dairying

Cattle and Calves, 1987

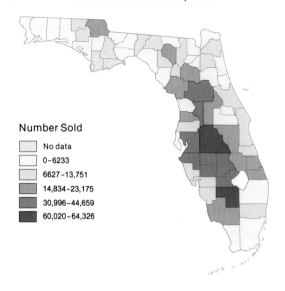

Number Sold

	No data
	0–6233
	6627–13,751
	14,834–23,175
	30,996–44,659
	60,020–64,326

During the nineteenth century the production of livestock was much more important to the Florida economy than it is today. Cattle of low quality were grazed throughout the peninsula and sold to Cuba or driven to other southern states for sale.

Since World War II modern technology has been applied to the cattle industry, which is still concentrated in the watershed of the Kissimmee River and to the west of Lake Okeechobee. Here, once the cattle tick was eliminated and pastures greatly improved, modern breeds of beef cattle were introduced, replacing the small, slow-to-mature descendants of Spanish cattle. Few Florida cattle are slaughtered within the state. Many young cattle are trucked to be fattened in feeder lots in Texas, Oklahoma, and even as far away as California. Fresh milk is produced for Florida markets near the northern shore of Lake Okeechobee, and in Hillsborough and Clay counties. Poultry is a major source of farm income in north Florida, around Madison, where broiler chickens are raised. In the Tampa area chickens are raised for their eggs. Hogs and pigs no longer play the significant role they once did in Florida's economy. The last large Florida sausage factory closed in the early 1980s.

Hogs and Pigs, 1987

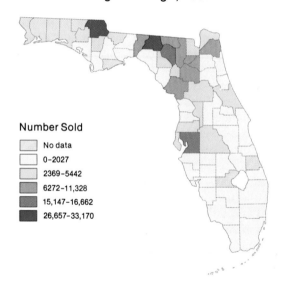

Number Sold

	No data
	0–2027
	2369–5442
	6272–11,328
	15,147–16,662
	26,657–33,170

Livestock and Livestock Products Farm Sales
1984–88 Average

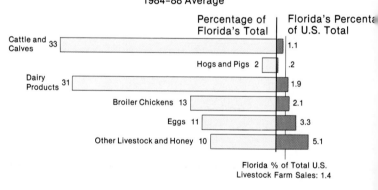

	Percentage of Florida's Total	Florida's Percenta of U.S. Total
Cattle and Calves 33		1.1
Hogs and Pigs 2		.2
Dairy Products 31		1.9
Broiler Chickens 13		2.1
Eggs 11		3.3
Other Livestock and Honey 10		5.1

Florida % of Total U.S.
Livestock Farm Sales: 1.4

Poultry and Poultry Products Sold, 1987

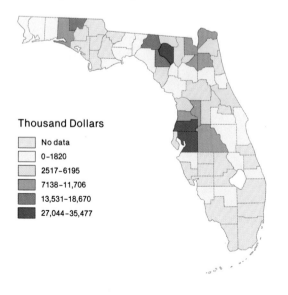

Thousand Dollars

	No data
	0–1820
	2517–6195
	7138–11,706
	13,531–18,670
	27,044–35,477

Dairy Products Sold, 1987

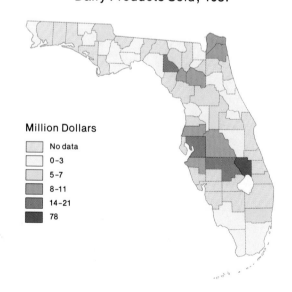

Million Dollars

	No data
	0–3
	5–7
	8–11
	14–21
	78

Location and Production of Minerals

Florida ranks first in the nation in the mining of phosphate for fertilizer and is among the most important in mining peat, also used in agriculture. Limestone, for agricultural lime and cement, as well as titanium, zircon, staurolite, thorium, and monazite are also mined in Florida.

Phosphate production began in the last century in the Peace River valley, east of Tampa, where large deposits of pebble phosphates were found. Throughout the twentieth century this area has continued to be the state's major source of phosphate. During the 1960s smaller pebble phosphate deposits were found in north Florida, near Jacksonville. In recent years Florida phosphate producers have faced fierce competition from producers in North Carolina, as well as Morocco and several Pacific islands. Pebble phosphate reserves in Florida are predicted to last several more decades. The much larger deposits of hard and soft rock phosphates are currently uneconomical to mine.

During the late 1970s and early 1980s the Jay Field, near Pensacola, was producing well over 25 million barrels of

oil annually, as well as large quantities of natural gas. Since 1943 a small amount of oil and gas has come from the Everglades. Despite investment of billions of dollars on offshore oil exploration in the Gulf of Mexico, no well has ever yielded commercial quantities. Drilling in the Gulf has also been strongly opposed by environmental groups.

Mineral Deposits

Major Deposits

- Phosphate
  - Producing
  - Nonproducing
- Monazite and thorium
- Peat

Value of Mineral Production

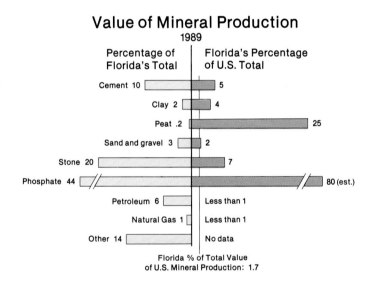

1989

	Percentage of Florida's Total	Florida's Percentage of U.S. Total
Cement	10	5
Clay	2	4
Peat	.2	25
Sand and gravel	3	2
Stone	20	7
Phosphate	44	80 (est.)
Petroleum	6	Less than 1
Natural Gas	1	Less than 1
Other	14	No data

Florida % of Total Value of U.S. Mineral Production: 1.7

Oil and Natural Gas Production, 1989

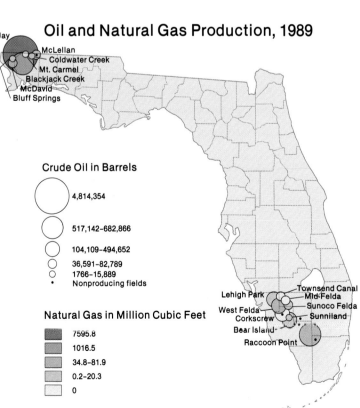

Jay
McLellan
Coldwater Creek
Mt. Carmel
Blackjack Creek
McDavid
Bluff Springs

Crude Oil in Barrels

- 4,814,354
- 517,142–682,866
- 104,109–494,652
- 36,591–82,789
- 1766–15,889
- • Nonproducing fields

Lehigh Park
West Felda
Corkscrew
Bear Island
Raccoon Point
Townsend Canal
Mid-Felda
Sunoco Felda
Sunniland

Natural Gas in Million Cubic Feet

- 7595.8
- 1016.5
- 34.8–81.9
- 0.2–20.3
- 0

Florida Crude Oil Production

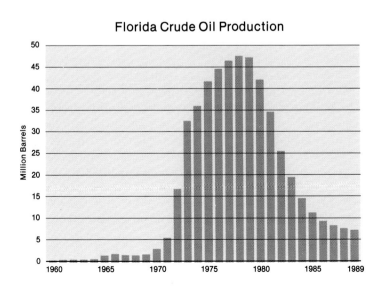

Commercial Fishing

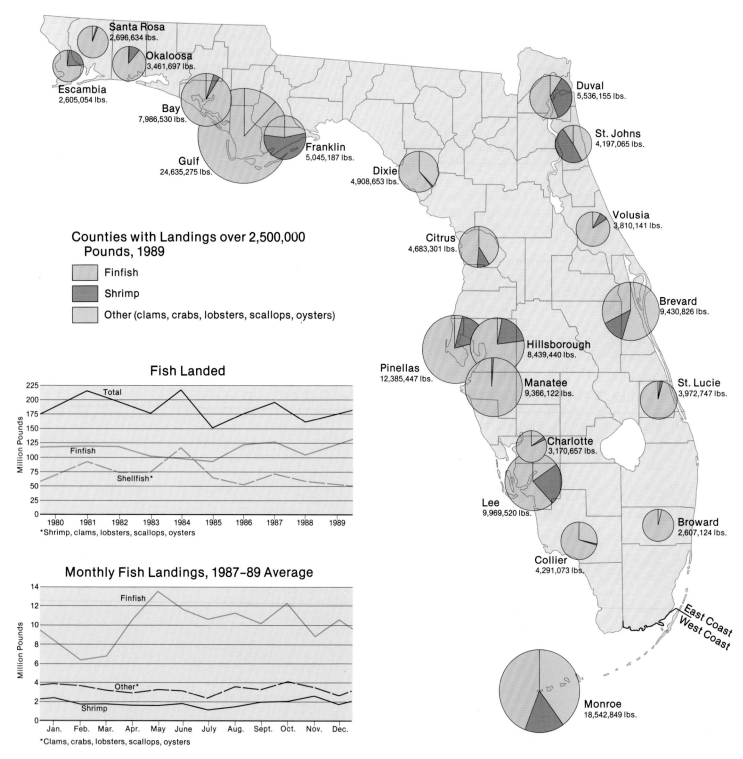

Counties with Landings over 2,500,000 Pounds, 1989

- Finfish
- Shrimp
- Other (clams, crabs, lobsters, scallops, oysters)

Santa Rosa
2,696,634 lbs.

Okaloosa
3,461,697 lbs.

Escambia
2,605,054 lbs.

Bay
7,986,530 lbs.

Gulf
24,635,275 lbs.

Franklin
5,045,187 lbs.

Dixie
4,908,653 lbs.

Duval
5,536,155 lbs.

St. Johns
4,197,065 lbs.

Volusia
3,810,141 lbs.

Citrus
4,683,301 lbs.

Brevard
9,430,826 lbs.

Pinellas
12,385,447 lbs.

Hillsborough
8,439,440 lbs.

Manatee
9,366,122 lbs.

St. Lucie
3,972,747 lbs.

Charlotte
3,170,657 lbs.

Lee
9,969,520 lbs.

Broward
2,607,124 lbs.

Collier
4,291,073 lbs.

East Coast
West Coast

Monroe
18,542,849 lbs.

Fish Landed

Total

Finfish

Shelifish*

*Shrimp, clams, lobsters, scallops, oysters

(Y-axis: Million Pounds, 0–225; X-axis: 1980–1989)

Monthly Fish Landings, 1987–89 Average

Finfish

Other*

Shrimp

*Clams, crabs, lobsters, scallops, oysters

(Y-axis: Million Pounds, 0–14; X-axis: Jan.–Dec.)

Fish Landed by Coast, 1987–89 Average

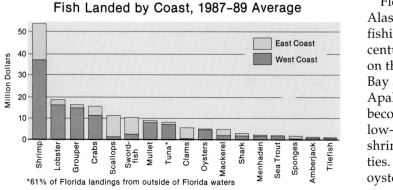

- East Coast
- West Coast

(Y-axis: Million Dollars, 0–50; X-axis categories: Shrimp, Lobster, Grouper, Crabs, Scallops, Sword-fish, Mullet, Tuna*, Clams, Oysters, Mackerel, Shark, Menhaden, Sea Trout, Sponges, Amberjack, Tilefish)

*61% of Florida landings from outside of Florida waters

Florida has the longest coastline of any state except Alaska. Due to transportation and refrigeration problems, fishing was only of local importance until well into this century. Fishing has gradually become more concentrated on the west than on the east coast, especially in the Tampa Bay area and along the coast between Panama City and Apalachicola. By weight of fish landed, Port St. Joe has become the largest fishing port, receiving and processing low-value finfish into fish meal. The largest numbers of shrimping boats are found in Monroe and Brevard counties. Apalachicola Bay is the source of most of the state's oysters. Rock lobster are trapped mainly in the Keys.

Lumber and Pulp Production

Much of Florida, particularly in the north, has an excellent physical environment for the growth of trees of commercial value. During the late nineteenth century millions of acres of longleaf (yellow) pine were cut by lumber companies and sold throughout the eastern United States. In the 1930s much of this acreage was purchased by large paper companies and managed as tree farms, several exceeding 500,000 acres. The federal government also acquired large areas for national forests. Acreage is leased in these forests for commercial cutting. The land has been largely replanted in fast-growing slash pine, which today provides most of the wood for a string of pulp and paper mills between Pensacola and Jacksonville. These mills produce a variety of products. Among the most important is kraft paper used in packaging. One of the nation's largest producers of toilet paper is located in Palatka.

Lumber is also produced in Florida. The majority of this lumber comes from softwoods, primarily longleaf pine and cypress. Florida hardwoods, mainly gum and oak, are far less important than softwoods. Income derived from forest products is especially high in Jacksonville, Ocala, Lakeland, and Miami, where factories that use wood as raw materials are concentrated.

Total Income from Forest Products, 1988

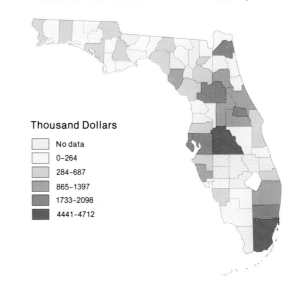

Thousand Dollars

- No data
- 0–264
- 284–687
- 865–1397
- 1733–2098
- 4441–4712

Pulpwood Removal, 1988

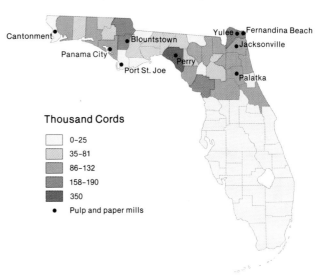

Thousand Cords

- 0–25
- 35–81
- 86–132
- 158–190
- 350
- Pulp and paper mills

Trends in Pine Acreage

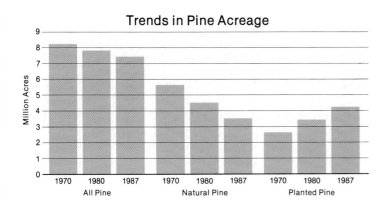

Size of Forest Inventory, 1987

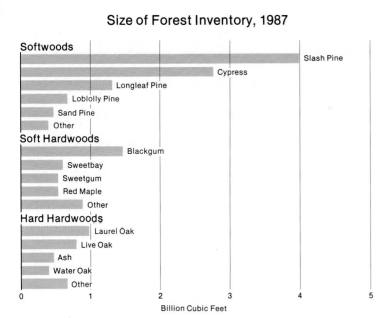

Billion Cubic Feet

Saw and Veneer Log Removal, 1988

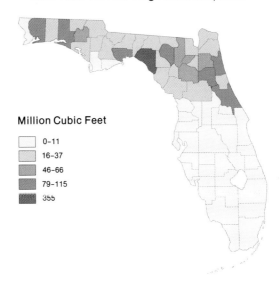

Million Cubic Feet

- 0–11
- 16–37
- 46–66
- 79–115
- 355

Manufacturing

Florida has relatively few raw materials and its location on the nation's periphery has hampered the development of manufacturing. Modern transportation and the state's large increase in population have reduced the liability of distance from market, and in recent years manufacturing in Florida has begun to grow faster than the national average.

Manufacturing is centered in the state's largest cities. In Miami many industries have been attracted by a large pool of inexpensive Latin American labor. High-technology industries have also located in Miami and neighboring counties, as well as around the Kennedy Space Center and in Greater St. Petersburg. In central and north Florida,

agriculture, mining, and forestry provide raw materials for manufacturing. Counties in which manufacturing accounts for a large share of total employment are almost all in north Florida, where populations are low and one or two factories dominate employment.

Earned Income from Manufacturing
1989

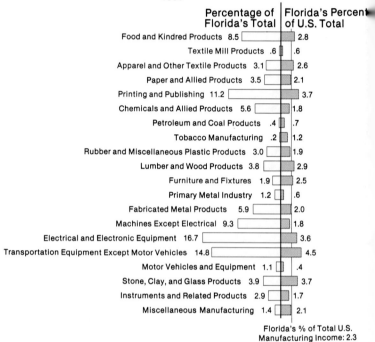

	Percentage of Florida's Total	Florida's Percent of U.S. Total
Food and Kindred Products	8.5	2.8
Textile Mill Products	.6	.6
Apparel and Other Textile Products	3.1	2.6
Paper and Allied Products	3.5	2.1
Printing and Publishing	11.2	3.7
Chemicals and Allied Products	5.6	1.8
Petroleum and Coal Products	.4	.7
Tobacco Manufacturing	.2	1.2
Rubber and Miscellaneous Plastic Products	3.0	1.9
Lumber and Wood Products	3.8	2.9
Furniture and Fixtures	1.9	2.5
Primary Metal Industry	1.2	.6
Fabricated Metal Products	5.9	2.0
Machines Except Electrical	9.3	1.8
Electrical and Electronic Equipment	16.7	3.6
Transportation Equipment Except Motor Vehicles	14.8	4.5
Motor Vehicles and Equipment	1.1	.4
Stone, Clay, and Glass Products	3.9	3.7
Instruments and Related Products	2.9	1.7
Miscellaneous Manufacturing	1.4	2.1

Florida's % of Total U.S. Manufacturing Income: 2.3

Change in Manufacturing Employment

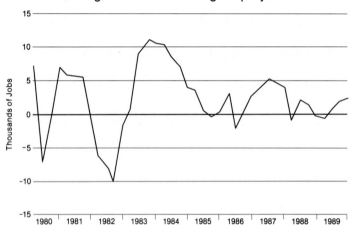

Manufacturing's Share of Nonagricultural Employment, 1989

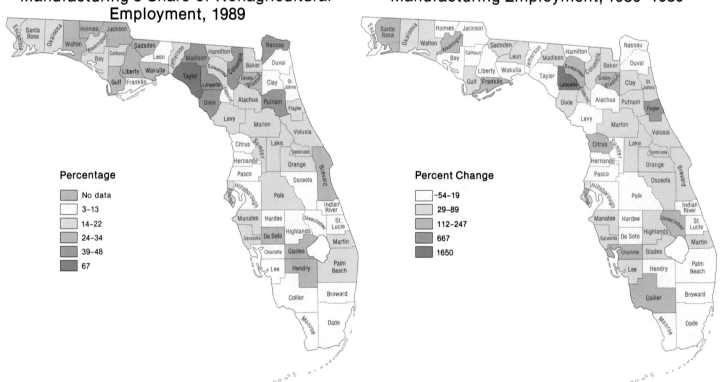

Percentage
- No data
- 3–13
- 14–22
- 24–34
- 39–48
- 67

Manufacturing Employment, 1980–1989

Percent Change
- -54–19
- 29–89
- 112–247
- 667
- 1650

Industrial Employment

Manufacturing takes place throughout the state, although it is more important in some regions than others. Certain regions also have a commanding lead in employment in particular sectors of manufacturing. Manufacturing is primarily located in the Southeast (Miami–Ft. Lauderdale–West Palm Beach) and the West Central (Tampa–St. Petersburg–Lakeland) regions. The East Central region (Orlando–Melbourne–Titusville–Cocoa), Jacksonville, and Pensacola also have a significant manufacturing base.

The majority of the state's orange groves are in central Florida. Most oranges produced in Florida are converted to orange juice concentrate. The majority of phosphate mines

are also in central Florida. A large share of the phosphoric ore is processed to remove inert material. The Northeast has unusually high shares of employment in wood products and phosphate processing. The Panhandle also has unusually high employment in manufacturing related to the region's forests, and a chemical industry in part derived from a local oil and gas field. Most of the state's textile and clothing employment is in the Southeast. Printing, principally of newspapers, also figures importantly in the Southeast. East Central Florida is the state's newest manufacturing area and owes much of its growth to the Kennedy Space Center.

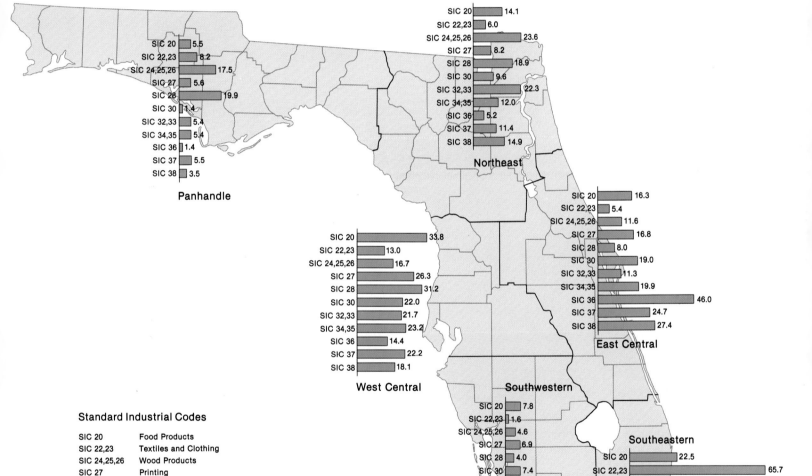

Percentage of State Total by Region, 1989

Standard Industrial Codes

SIC 20	Food Products
SIC 22,23	Textiles and Clothing
SIC 24,25,26	Wood Products
SIC 27	Printing
SIC 28	Chemicals
SIC 30	Rubber and Plastic
SIC 32,33	Processing of Stone, Clay, Glass, and Metals
SIC 34,35	Industrial Machinery and Fabricated Products
SIC 36	Electronic Equipment
SIC 37	Transportation Equipment
SIC 38	Measuring and Other Instruments

Panhandle

SIC 20	5.5
SIC 22,23	8.2
SIC 24,25,26	17.5
SIC 27	5.6
SIC 28	19.9
SIC 30	1.4
SIC 32,33	5.4
SIC 34,35	5.4
SIC 36	1.4
SIC 37	5.5
SIC 38	3.5

Northeast

SIC 20	14.1
SIC 22,23	6.0
SIC 24,25,26	23.6
SIC 27	8.2
SIC 28	18.9
SIC 30	9.6
SIC 32,33	22.3
SIC 34,35	12.0
SIC 36	5.2
SIC 37	11.4
SIC 38	14.9

West Central

SIC 20	33.8
SIC 22,23	13.0
SIC 24,25,26	16.7
SIC 27	26.3
SIC 28	31.2
SIC 30	22.0
SIC 32,33	21.7
SIC 34,35	23.2
SIC 36	14.4
SIC 37	22.2
SIC 38	18.1

East Central

SIC 20	16.3
SIC 22,23	5.4
SIC 24,25,26	11.6
SIC 27	16.8
SIC 28	8.0
SIC 30	19.0
SIC 32,33	11.3
SIC 34,35	19.9
SIC 36	46.0
SIC 37	24.7
SIC 38	27.4

Southwestern

SIC 20	7.8
SIC 22,23	1.6
SIC 24,25,26	4.6
SIC 27	6.9
SIC 28	4.0
SIC 30	7.4
SIC 32,33	10.1
SIC 34,35	5.9
SIC 36	5.6
SIC 37	6.2
SIC 38	3.6

Southeastern

SIC 20	22.5
SIC 22,23	65.7
SIC 24,25,26	26.0
SIC 27	36.2
SIC 28	18.0
SIC 30	40.6
SIC 32,33	29.2
SIC 34,35	33.6
SIC 36	27.4
SIC 37	30.0
SIC 38	32.5

Local Importance of Manufacturing Employment

Manufacturing in Florida is heavily concentrated in counties with large populations. Manufacturing as a share of total employment, however, is highest in sparsely populated north Florida counties. Raw materials govern the location of food and kindred products industries. Many counties with high employment in this sector produce large quantities of fruit and sugarcane. The forests of north Florida supply saw mills and pulp and paper plants.

Certain industries have achieved considerable local importance because of the availability of low-cost semi-skilled labor. The apparel industry has located in north Florida, where there is a large pool of native-born American labor, and in Miami, where the labor pool is mainly Hispanic. The electronics and transportation industries on Florida's east coast have attracted a skilled labor force.

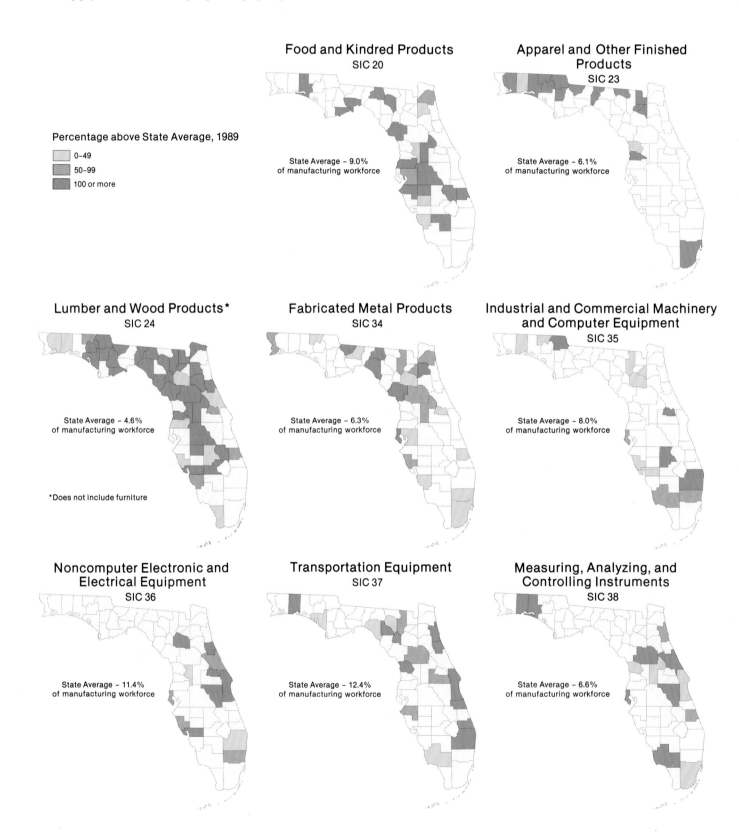

Percentage above State Average, 1989
- 0–49
- 50–99
- 100 or more

Food and Kindred Products
SIC 20
State Average – 9.0%
of manufacturing workforce

Apparel and Other Finished Products
SIC 23
State Average – 6.1%
of manufacturing workforce

Lumber and Wood Products*
SIC 24
State Average – 4.6%
of manufacturing workforce
*Does not include furniture

Fabricated Metal Products
SIC 34
State Average – 6.3%
of manufacturing workforce

Industrial and Commercial Machinery and Computer Equipment
SIC 35
State Average – 8.0%
of manufacturing workforce

Noncomputer Electronic and Electrical Equipment
SIC 36
State Average – 11.4%
of manufacturing workforce

Transportation Equipment
SIC 37
State Average – 12.4%
of manufacturing workforce

Measuring, Analyzing, and Controlling Instruments
SIC 38
State Average – 6.6%
of manufacturing workforce

High-Technology Manufacturing Employment

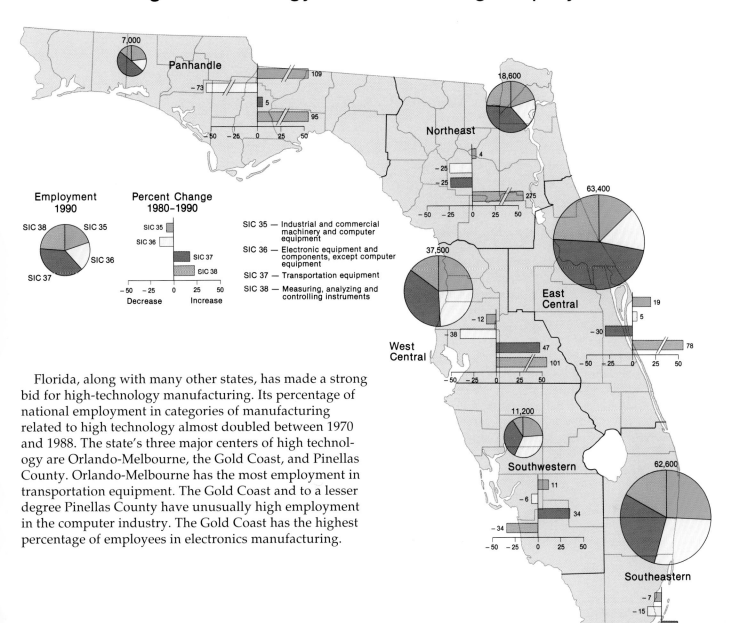

Employment 1990

SIC 38   SIC 35
SIC 37   SIC 36

Percent Change 1980-1990

SIC 35
SIC 36
SIC 37
SIC 38

−50   −25   0   25   50
Decrease   Increase

SIC 35 — Industrial and commercial machinery and computer equipment

SIC 36 — Electronic equipment and components, except computer equipment

SIC 37 — Transportation equipment

SIC 38 — Measuring, analyzing and controlling instruments

Florida, along with many other states, has made a strong bid for high-technology manufacturing. Its percentage of national employment in categories of manufacturing related to high technology almost doubled between 1970 and 1988. The state's three major centers of high technology are Orlando-Melbourne, the Gold Coast, and Pinellas County. Orlando-Melbourne has the most employment in transportation equipment. The Gold Coast and to a lesser degree Pinellas County have unusually high employment in the computer industry. The Gold Coast has the highest percentage of employees in electronics manufacturing.

Employment in High-Technology Manufacturing

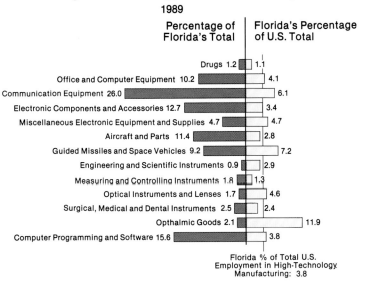

1989

	Percentage of Florida's Total	Florida's Percentage of U.S. Total
Drugs	1.2	1.1
Office and Computer Equipment	10.2	4.1
Communication Equipment	26.0	6.1
Electronic Components and Accessories	12.7	3.4
Miscellaneous Electronic Equipment and Supplies	4.7	4.7
Aircraft and Parts	11.4	2.8
Guided Missiles and Space Vehicles	9.2	7.2
Engineering and Scientific Instruments	0.9	2.9
Measuring and Controlling Instruments	1.8	1.3
Optical Instruments and Lenses	1.7	4.6
Surgical, Medical and Dental Instruments	2.5	2.4
Opthalmic Goods	2.1	11.9
Computer Programming and Software	15.6	3.8

Florida % of Total U.S. Employment in High-Technology Manufacturing: 3.8

Change in Florida High-Technology Manufacturing Employment

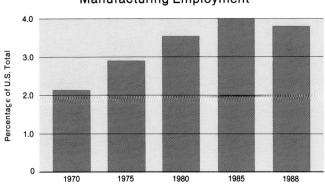

Percentage of U.S. Total

1970   1975   1980   1985   1988

Value of Construction

Florida is among the fastest growing states in the nation and has been since the end of World War II. Construction has figured far more prominently in the state's economy than in the economy of the nation as a whole. The health of the industry, however, has been uneven. In some periods its workers' share of the state's earned income has risen to over 10 percent; in other years it has fallen below 5 percent.

The cyclical nature of the construction industry is largely the result of factors outside of Florida's control. When interest rates are high or when there is a business recession, the industry declines. When developers can obtain loans cheaply, there is great expansion. The availability of venture capital and not demand sometimes stimulates construction, which has led to overbuilding. At times the number of condominiums on the market far exceeds demand. In the late 1980s an oversupply of office buildings developed, particularly in the state's central cities. Since the number of U.S. citizens entering the 60-year-old age group will decrease during the 1990s, migration to Florida is expected to slow. This may dampen enthusiasm for new residential construction.

Construction has diminished in southeastern Florida, particularly in Dade County (Miami) and to a lesser extent in Broward County (Fort Lauderdale). The construction industry remains dynamic in Palm Beach and Martin counties as well as in the Orlando area and along the southwestern coast, especially in Collier County. Despite the hopes of the region's developers, north Florida generally has not had the construction activity of peninsular Florida.

Residential Building Permits
1985–1989 Total

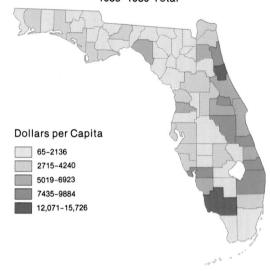

Private Nonresidential Building Permits
1985–1989 Total

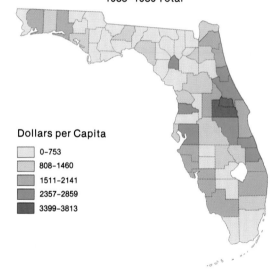

Total Building Permits by Region

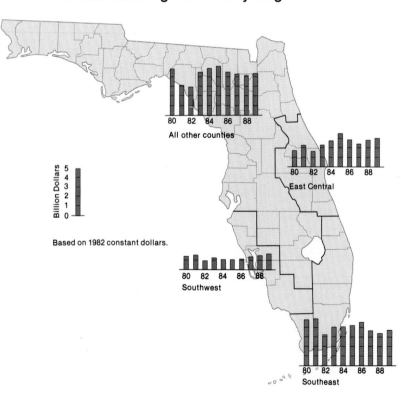

Public Building Permits
1985–1989 Total

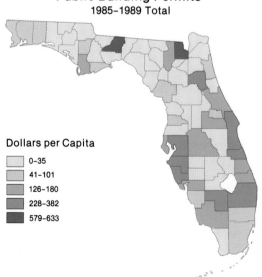

Value of Wholesale and Retail Trade

Retail trade contributes a greater percentage to personal income in Florida than to personal income in the U.S. as a whole. The state's retail establishments not only serve Floridians, but an estimated 38 million visitors each year. These visitors generate retail sales that would equal those generated by 1.5 million permanent residents. Florida's share of national employment in several retail categories—automobile dealerships, restaurants, home furnishing stores, drugstores, and building and garden supply stores—is higher than its share of total retail employment. On the other hand, it is lower in food stores, service stations, apparel stores, and department stores.

Wholesale trade's share of total employment in Florida is not as great as its share in the nation. Nonetheless, several wholesale centers have emerged, notably Jacksonville, Miami, Lakeland, Tampa, and Orlando. Jacksonville and Tampa have emerged as leaders in grocery wholesaling.

Earned Income from Retail Trade
1987

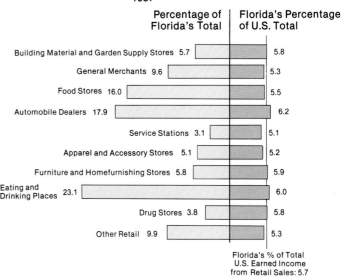

	Percentage of Florida's Total	Florida's Percentage of U.S. Total
Building Material and Garden Supply Stores	5.7	5.8
General Merchants	9.6	5.3
Food Stores	16.0	5.5
Automobile Dealers	17.9	6.2
Service Stations	3.1	5.1
Apparel and Accessory Stores	5.1	5.2
Furniture and Homefurnishing Stores	5.8	5.9
Eating and Drinking Places	23.1	6.0
Drug Stores	3.8	5.8
Other Retail	9.9	5.3

Florida's % of Total U.S. Earned Income from Retail Sales: 5.7

Wholesale Trade, 1987

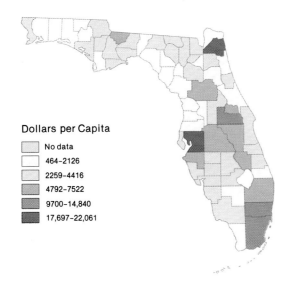

Dollars per Capita
- No data
- 464–2126
- 2259–4416
- 4792–7522
- 9700–14,840
- 17,697–22,061

Retail Trade, 1987

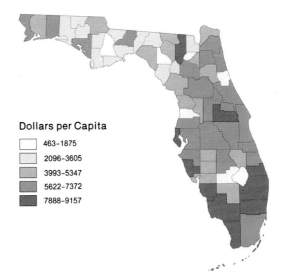

Dollars per Capita
- 463–1875
- 2096–3605
- 3993–5347
- 5622–7372
- 7888–9157

Wholesale Grocery Sales in Metropolitan Counties, 1987

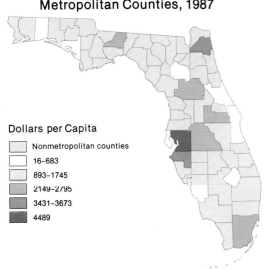

Dollars per Capita
- Nonmetropolitan counties
- 16–683
- 893–1745
- 2149–2795
- 3431–3673
- 4489

Department Store Sales, 1987

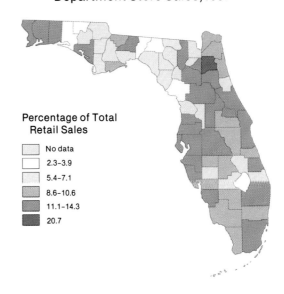

Percentage of Total Retail Sales
- No data
- 2.3–3.9
- 5.4–7.1
- 8.6–10.6
- 11.1–14.3
- 20.7

Shopping Malls

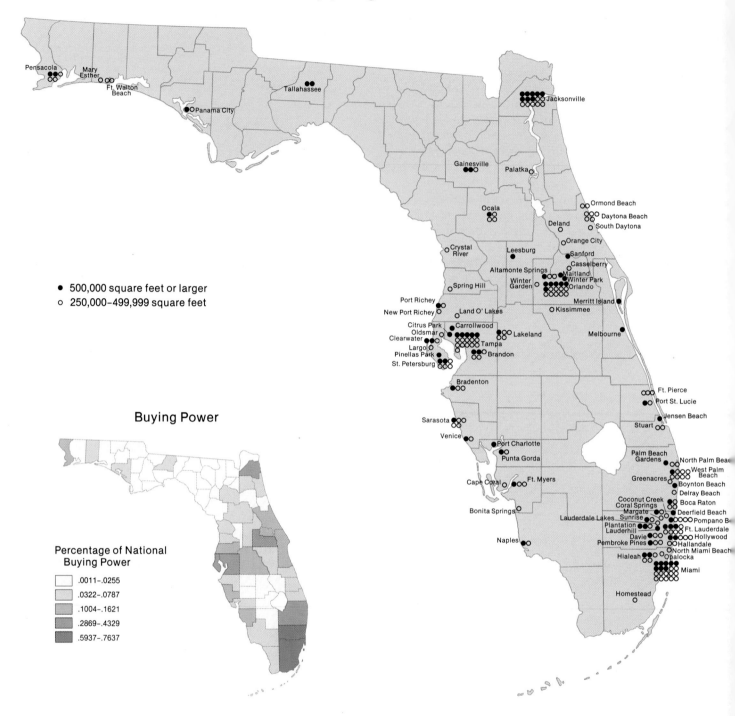

- ● 500,000 square feet or larger
- ○ 250,000–499,999 square feet

Buying Power

Percentage of National Buying Power

	.0011–.0255
	.0322–.0787
	.1004–.1621
	.2869–.4329
	.5937–.7637

Florida has grown by over 8 million people since 1960, and during that period the purchasing power of the average Floridian has risen from well below the national average to equal to it. Retailers have flocked to Florida to meet the rapidly growing demand for goods. Florida retailers like those in other states have tended to locate in malls. Malls are concentrated in high population areas where buying power is greatest: the southeastern counties, the Tampa Bay area, Orlando, and Jacksonville. In Dade and Broward counties are several regional malls that rank among the largest in floor space in the nation. In northwest Florida, large regional malls are found only in Panama City, Pensacola, and Tallahassee.

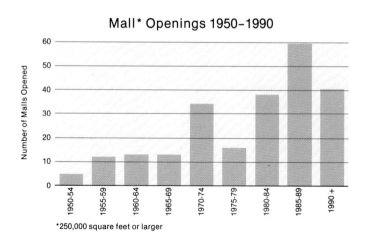

Mall* Openings 1950–1990

*250,000 square feet or larger

(Number of Malls Opened, by period: 1950-54, 1955-59, 1960-64, 1965-69, 1970-74, 1975-79, 1980-84, 1985-89, 1990+)

Transportation and Communication Employment

Motor Freight and Warehousing, 1989
SIC 42

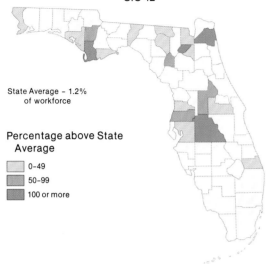

State Average – 1.2%
of workforce

Percentage above State
Average

- 0–49
- 50–99
- 100 or more

Air Transportation, 1989
SIC 45

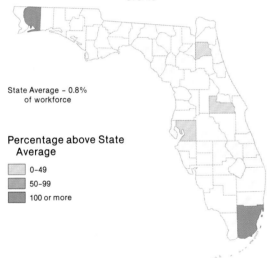

State Average – 0.8%
of workforce

Percentage above State
Average

- 0–49
- 50–99
- 100 or more

Communications, 1989
SIC 48

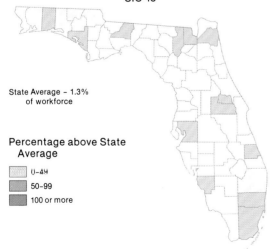

State Average – 1.3%
of workforce

Percentage above State
Average

- 0–49
- 50–99
- 100 or more

Florida's remoteness from the large population centers of the nation inhibited the growth of its economy. First ships, then trains, automobiles, airplanes, and modern communications have brought Florida closer to the rest of the nation.

More people are employed in air transportation than any other type of transportation in Florida. The majority of the state's air transportation workers are employed in Dade County. Miami International Airport has more flights per day than any airport in the state and is one of the nation's largest air freight handlers. It is also the nation's major air entry and departure point for travel and freight shipments between the U.S. and Latin America. Many airlines have service centers in Miami. Eastern Airlines was headquartered in Miami until its closure in 1991.

In Florida railroads play a relatively minor role in both the movement of freight and passengers. Much of the railroad freight consists of phosphates, transported from mine to port. Few cities have passenger train service. The only commuter railroad service in Florida was initiated in 1989 between West Palm Beach and Miami.

Most freight is moved in Florida, as well as to and from it, by truck. In earned income trucking is second only to air in the state's transportation economy. Counties in the center of the state, where citrus production is high, have a particularly large share of workers employed in motor freight.

More people are employed in communications (telephone, telegraph, radio, and television) than in any of the transportation categories. The majority of communications workers are employed by telephone companies throughout the state. Dade County has a very important radio and television industry, employing nearly a quarter of the state's workers in this category.

Earned Income from Transportation and Communication
1988

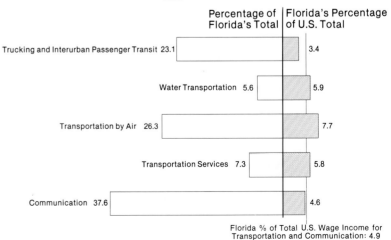

	Percentage of Florida's Total	Florida's Percentage of U.S. Total
Trucking and Interurban Passenger Transit	23.1	3.4
Water Transportation	5.6	5.9
Transportation by Air	26.3	7.7
Transportation Services	7.3	5.8
Communication	37.6	4.6

Florida % of Total U.S. Wage Income for
Transportation and Communication: 4.9

Finance, Insurance, and Real Estate

Florida absorbs hundreds of thousands of newcomers each year and is the temporary home for hundreds of thousands of others who come for prolonged periods during the winter. The sale or rental of homes, commercial property, and land has become a major economic activity. Real estate is particularly significant in total employment within Florida counties such as Orange, Charlotte, Lee, Collier, and Martin that have recently become attractive to in-migrants.

Banking employment is constant throughout the state. The insurance industry is most concentrated in Hillsborough and Duval counties. Duval County has been the headquarters of several large insurance companies for many years.

Earned Income from Finance, Insurance, and Real Estate
1988

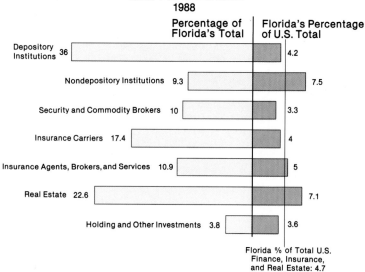

	Percentage of Florida's Total	Florida's Percentage of U.S. Total
Depository Institutions	36	4.2
Nondepository Institutions	9.3	7.5
Security and Commodity Brokers	10	3.3
Insurance Carriers	17.4	4
Insurance Agents, Brokers, and Services	10.9	5
Real Estate	22.6	7.1
Holding and Other Investments	3.8	3.6

Florida % of Total U.S. Finance, Insurance, and Real Estate: 4.7

Banking Employment, 1988
SIC 60

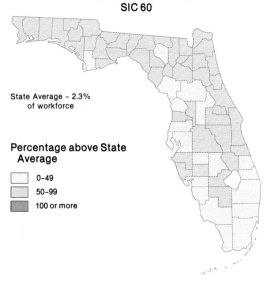

State Average – 2.3% of workforce

Percentage above State Average

- [ ] 0–49
- [ ] 50–99
- [ ] 100 or more

Real Estate Employment, 1988
SIC 65

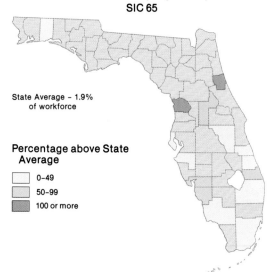

State Average – 1.9% of workforce

Percentage above State Average

- [ ] 0–49
- [ ] 50–99
- [ ] 100 or more

Insurance Employment*, 1988
SIC 63

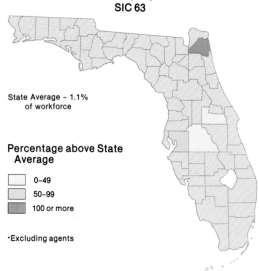

State Average – 1.1% of workforce

Percentage above State Average

- [ ] 0–49
- [ ] 50–99
- [ ] 100 or more

*Excluding agents

Banking Deposits, 1988

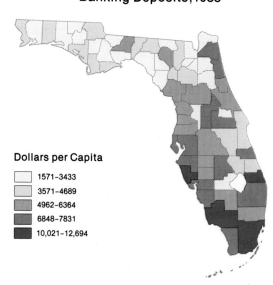

Dollars per Capita

- [ ] 1571–3433
- [ ] 3571–4689
- [ ] 4962–6364
- [ ] 6848–7831
- [ ] 10,021–12,694

Nonfinancial Services

As the home of millions of retirees and the host to 38 million visitors annually, Florida has a thriving service economy. In Florida, as in other states, medical and other health services account for the largest share of earned income from nonfinancial services.

Earned income from hotels and other lodgings as well as amusements and recreation is exceptionally high in Florida. Both categories contribute greatly to the economy of the Orlando area, the home of Walt Disney World, the state's most popular attraction, as well as several other theme parks. Tourism also contributes substantially to the economy of southwest Florida.

Florida has more lawyers per 1,000 residents than most states. This ratio is especially high in the state's largest metropolitan areas. Leon County also has a high ratio because so many lawyers are employed by the state or are engaged in administrative law or lobbying.

Receipts from All Services, 1987

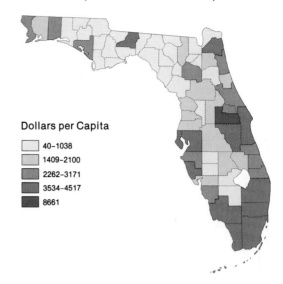

Dollars per Capita
- 40–1038
- 1409–2100
- 2262–3171
- 3534–4517
- 8661

Earned Income from Service Employment
1987

	Percentage of Florida's Total	Florida's Percentage of U.S. Total
Hotels, Rooming Houses, and Other Lodgings	5.4	8.5
Personal Services	2.9	4.3
Business Services	19.1	4.0
Automobile Services	3.0	5.0
Miscellaneous Repair	1.7	5.2
Amusement and Recreation Services	4.3	9.1
Health Services	35.6	5.4
Legal Services	8.4	5.0
Educational Services	3.3	3.1
Membership Organizations	3.3	4.8
Social Services	2.9	4.4
Other	11.1	7.0

Florida % of Total U.S.
Service Income: 5.2

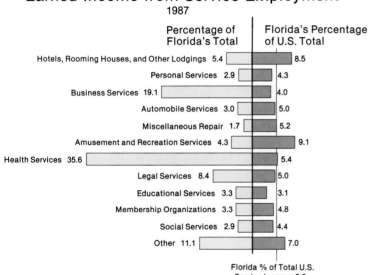

Hotel and Lodging Receipts, 1987

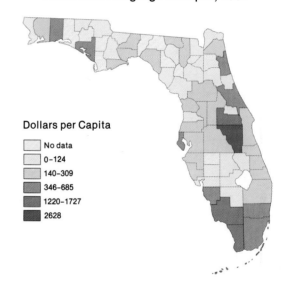

Dollars per Capita
- No data
- 0–124
- 140–309
- 346–685
- 1220–1727
- 2628

Receipts from Legal Services, 1987

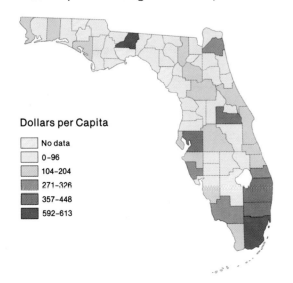

Dollars per Capita
- No data
- 0–96
- 104–204
- 271–326
- 357–448
- 592–613

Amusement and Recreation Receipts, 1987

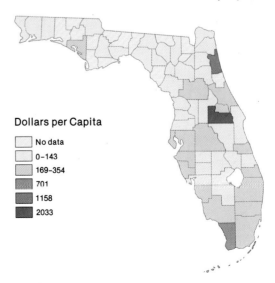

Dollars per Capita
- No data
- 0–143
- 169–354
- 701
- 1158
- 2033

Public Sector Employment

Florida has a higher proportion of military personnel among its workforce than most other states. Major military installations are located in Pensacola, Jacksonville, Panama City, Cape Kennedy, Orlando, Tampa, and Key West.

State government employment contributes more to the economy of the Big Bend than to any other part of Florida. Employment by state government—usually in prisons and state hospitals—is also significant in a number of predominantly rural counties such as Union, Bradford, DeSoto, Baker, Sumter, Jackson, and Gadsden. The University of Florida accounts for the significance of state government employment in Alachua County. Local government employment is especially important in rural counties with few other economic opportunities.

State Workers Living in Leon County

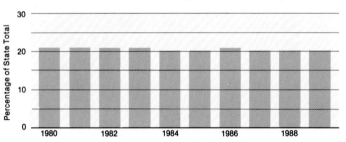

Earned Income from Government Employment
1989

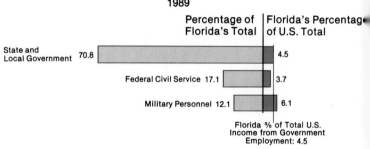

Local Government Employment, 1989

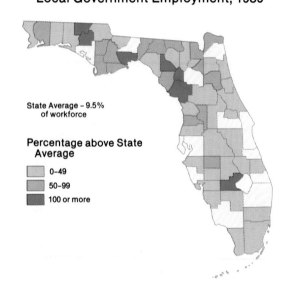

State Government Employment, 1989

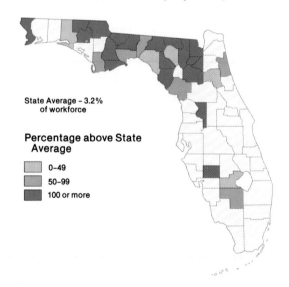

Department of Defense Civilian Employment, 1989

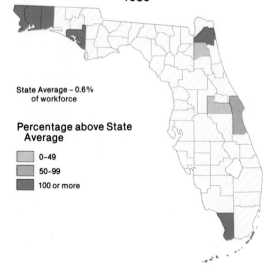

Federal Civil Service Employment, 1989*

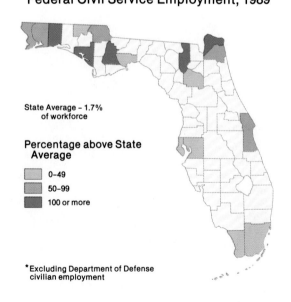

*Excluding Department of Defense civilian employment

State Government Expenditures

Florida's major sources of revenue are state sales and use taxes. Florida does not have a personal income tax, but does have gasoline, corporate income, beverage, and cigarette taxes. Funds through federal government revenue sharing were greatly reduced during the 1980s.

Education is the state's largest fiscal obligation, followed by welfare, general government, and transportation.

During the 1980s Florida's per capita appropriations for human and community service programs and law enforcement and corrections greatly increased, whereas per capita appropriations for transportation declined. Overall, in real dollars, per capita appropriations increased during the decade.

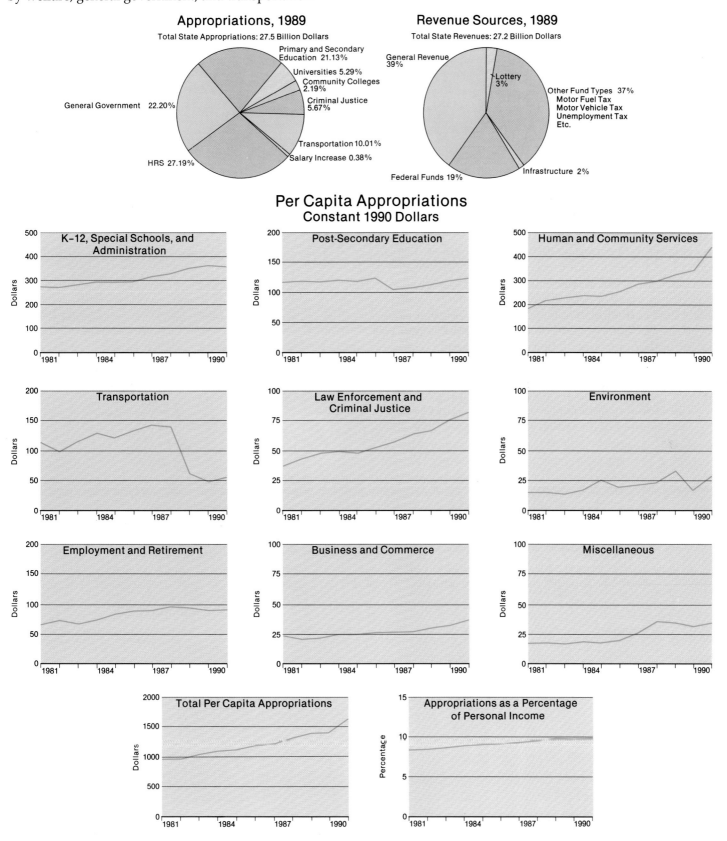

Appropriations, 1989
Total State Appropriations: 27.5 Billion Dollars

Primary and Secondary Education 21.13%
Universities 5.29%
Community Colleges 2.19%
Criminal Justice 5.67%
General Government 22.20%
Transportation 10.01%
HRS 27.19%
Salary Increase 0.38%

Revenue Sources, 1989
Total State Revenues: 27.2 Billion Dollars

General Revenue 39%
Lottery 3%
Other Fund Types 37%
Motor Fuel Tax
Motor Vehicle Tax
Unemployment Tax
Etc.
Federal Funds 19%
Infrastructure 2%

Per Capita Appropriations
Constant 1990 Dollars

K–12, Special Schools, and Administration

Post-Secondary Education

Human and Community Services

Transportation

Law Enforcement and Criminal Justice

Environment

Employment and Retirement

Business and Commerce

Miscellaneous

Total Per Capita Appropriations

Appropriations as a Percentage of Personal Income

Imports and Exports

Despite its long coastline, proximity to Latin America, and some excellent harbors, Florida has never played a major role in international trade. Nonetheless, it does make a contribution, which varies in response to national trade policies.

Oil-rich Venezuela is the destination of the largest percentage of Florida's exports. Of the top twenty nations importing products shipped from Florida, seventeen are in Latin America. During periods of economic growth in Latin America exports from Florida tend to be greater than imports. In the 1980s the reverse was true, and as a result of that area's declining economy, Florida's share in national exports decreased. Florida has become the departure point for many products from elsewhere in the United States destined for Latin America, including a huge volume of spare machinery parts.

Florida also exports its phosphate fertilizer throughout the world. The USSR, a large purchaser of this fertilizer, is usually among the top ten destinations of freight from Florida. The state's pulp and paper, and electronic and computer products are also sold overseas.

During the 1980s, the United States began to import large quantities of consumer goods from abroad. In 1990 Florida had almost 13 million people, who constitute a large internal market for these imports. Florida also receives imports to be sent elsewhere in the nation. Automobiles, primarily from Japan, but also from Europe, and recently from Korea, account for the bulk of these imports. Agricultural products, including coffee and seafood, are imported mainly from Latin America and processed within the state. All petroleum used in Florida is imported. There are no large refineries in Florida to process imported oil for state consumption. Florida has also been the port of entry of a large quantity of the nation's illegal drugs, which enter by sea and air along deserted coasts.

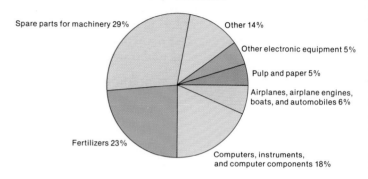

Major Export Categories, 1989
Total: 8.7 billion dollars

Spare parts for machinery 29%
Other 14%
Other electronic equipment 5%
Pulp and paper 5%
Airplanes, airplane engines, boats, and automobiles 6%
Computers, instruments, and computer components 18%
Fertilizers 23%

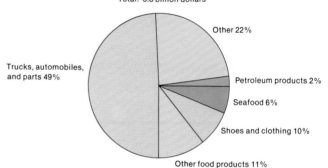

Major Import Categories, 1989
Total: 6.8 billion dollars

Other 22%
Trucks, automobiles, and parts 49%
Petroleum products 2%
Seafood 6%
Shoes and clothing 10%
Other food products 11%

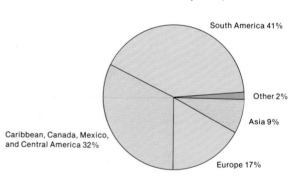

Destination of Exports, 1989

South America 41%
Other 2%
Asia 9%
Caribbean, Canada, Mexico, and Central America 32%
Europe 17%

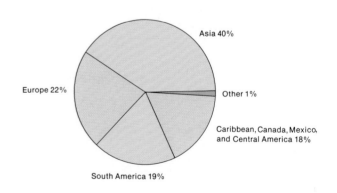

Origins of Imports, 1989

Asia 40%
Europe 22%
Other 1%
Caribbean, Canada, Mexico, and Central America 18%
South America 19%

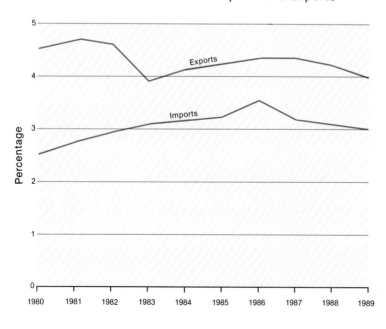

Florida's Share of U.S. Imports and Exports

Exports

Imports

Percentage

1980 1981 1982 1983 1984 1985 1986 1987 1988 1989

Foreign Trade, 1989

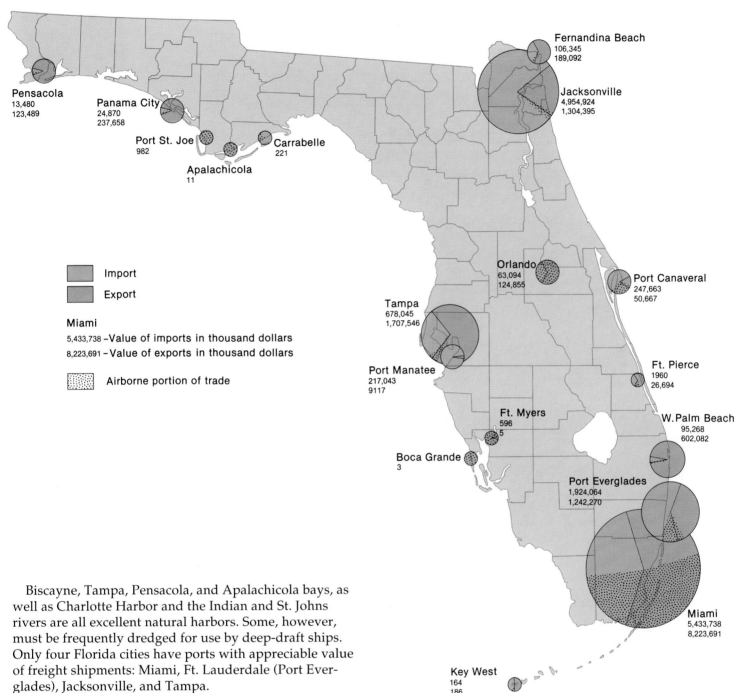

Pensacola
13,480
123,489

Panama City
24,870
237,658

Port St. Joe
982

Apalachicola
11

Carrabelle
221

Fernandina Beach
106,345
189,092

Jacksonville
4,954,924
1,304,395

Import
Export

Miami
5,433,738 – Value of imports in thousand dollars
8,223,691 – Value of exports in thousand dollars

Airborne portion of trade

Orlando
63,094
124,855

Port Canaveral
247,663
50,667

Tampa
678,045
1,707,546

Ft. Pierce
1960
26,694

Port Manatee
217,043
9117

Ft. Myers
596
5

W. Palm Beach
95,268
602,082

Boca Grande
3

Port Everglades
1,924,064
1,242,270

Miami
5,433,738
8,223,691

Key West
164
186

Biscayne, Tampa, Pensacola, and Apalachicola bays, as well as Charlotte Harbor and the Indian and St. Johns rivers are all excellent natural harbors. Some, however, must be frequently dredged for use by deep-draft ships. Only four Florida cities have ports with appreciable value of freight shipments: Miami, Ft. Lauderdale (Port Everglades), Jacksonville, and Tampa.

Miami has become one of the nation's largest air freight terminals: almost two-thirds of its exports leave by air, nearly half its imports arrive by air. In volume of exports Miami leads all Florida cities. Nearly three-quarters of the state's exports pass through Miami, most on their way to Latin America. Venezuela is the leading importer of goods from Miami. Of the top ten importers, all except the United Kingdom, are in Latin America. Spare machinery parts and manufactured and processed items produced throughout the U.S. as well as in Europe and Asia account for most of these exports. One-third of the state's imports arrive in Miami. Food, principally shellfish and coffee, as well as many types of consumer goods are imported. In nearby Port Everglades, a wide variety of commodities are exported and imported, including exports to the Bahamas and imports of oil from many nations.

Jacksonville has become one of the nation's largest importers of automobiles, a business that the city aggressively sought and won. Its initiative has made Jacksonville the state's leading importer. Jacksonville also imports large amounts of coffee, ground locally for national distribution. Jacksonville's exports primarily consist of phosphates from nearby mines, and pulp and paper from local mills. Tampa is mainly an exporter. Its major export is phosphate, mined just to its east. Since phosphates are demanded by many nations, ships leave the port for many destinations.

Foreign Investment

Floridians Employed by Foreign Firms

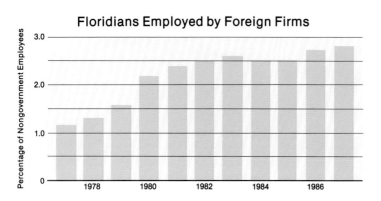

International Banks in Florida

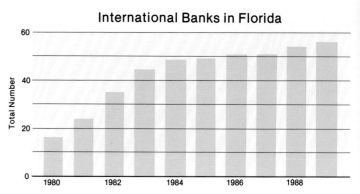

Floridians Employed by Foreign-Owned Firms, 1988
Number of Employees

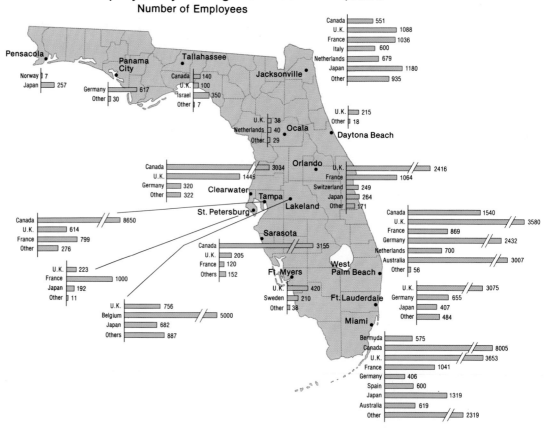

Foreign-Owned Farmland, 1989

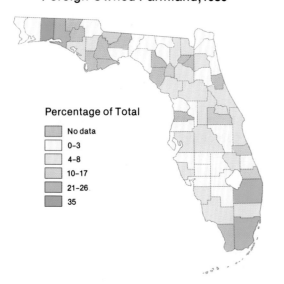

Percentage of Total

- No data
- 0–3
- 4–8
- 10–17
- 21–26
- 35

Property, Plants, and Equipment Owned by Foreign Firms

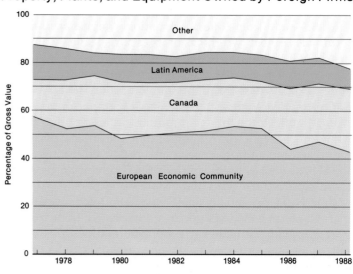

Cost of Living

Living costs have been calculated for each Florida county. The total price level index is generally highest in the coastal counties from Brevard and Pinellas counties south. To a great extent this is due to higher housing and service costs in these counties than elsewhere in the state. Health costs are particularly high there. Food is often cheaper in Florida's more populated counties than in its lightly populated rural ones. Overall, Florida's cost of living is close to the national average. It is higher than the national average in south Florida, but lower in the northern part of the state.

Cost of Living Index-First Quarter 1989
For Selected Urban Areas

Buffalo, NY	105.9
Charlotte-Gastonia-Rock Hill, NC-SC	99.8
Chicago, IL	125.5
Columbia, SC	96.0
Cleveland, OH	108.7
Dallas, TX	103.8
Denver, CO	102.2
Indianapolis, IN	99.2
Jacksonville, FL	**97.0**
Kansas City, MO-KS	96.1
Lakeland-Winter Haven, FL	**101.5**
Los Angeles-Long Beach, CA	124.4
Memphis, TN-AR-MS	94.0
Miami-Hialeah, FL	**111.1**
Milwaukee, WI	103.4
Minneapolis-St. Paul, MN-WI	101.7
Mobile, AL	97.2
Nashville-Davidson, TN	99.1
New Orleans, LA	95.9
Orlando, FL	**101.1**
Philadelphia-Wilmington-Trenton, PA-NJ-DE-MD	127.2
Phoenix, AZ	102.7
Salt Lake City-Ogden, UT	95.6
St. Louis, MO-IL	98.9
Washington, DC-MD-VA	129.8
West Palm Beach-Boca Raton-Delray Beach, FL	**107.8**

Total Price Level Index, 1990

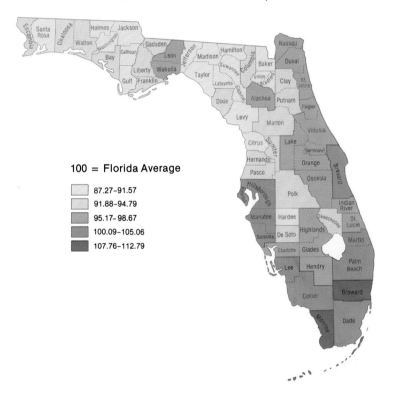

100 = Florida Average

- 87.27–91.57
- 91.88–94.79
- 95.17–98.67
- 100.09–105.06
- 107.76–112.79

Food Price Level Index, 1990

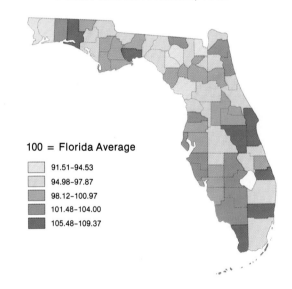

100 = Florida Average

- 91.51–94.53
- 94.98–97.87
- 98.12–100.97
- 101.48–104.00
- 105.48–109.37

Housing Price Level Index, 1990

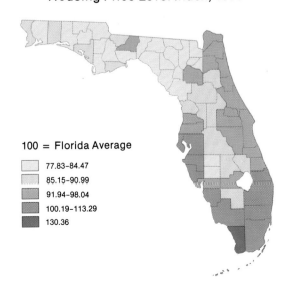

100 = Florida Average

- 77.83–84.47
- 85.15–90.99
- 91.94–98.04
- 100.19–113.29
- 130.36

Services* Price Level Index, 1990

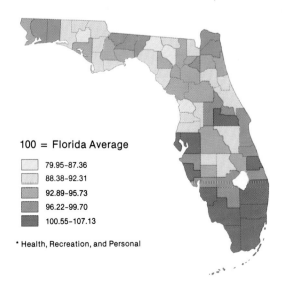

100 = Florida Average

- 79.95–87.36
- 88.38–92.31
- 92.89–95.73
- 96.22–99.70
- 100.55–107.13

* Health, Recreation, and Personal

THE BLUE UMBRELLA, Chris Nissen

TOURISM AND RECREATION

Florida, to most Americans and Canadians, and increasingly to people from other nations, is primarily a vacation destination. Beginning in the early nineteenth century its warm winters attracted visitors, and their numbers have grown ever since. Today approximately 40 million people visit Florida annually. Hundreds of thousands more come to work, or to retire, drawn by the thought of year-round outdoor recreation. The state's saltwater beaches undoubtedly are the major natural tourist resource, but its lakes, rivers, and forests provide recreational opportunities for many people as well. Commercial tourist attractions are found throughout the state, but those around Orlando are the most famous.

Economics of Tourism and Recreation

Florida's first tourists were few in number and usually content to enjoy Florida's natural environment, particularly its rivers and springs, while staying in modest accommodations. As more Americans had both the time and money to take vacations, Florida's tourist industry expanded. By 1940, 3 million tourists arrived each year. After World War II, when retirees began to flock to the state, and millions of people began to vacation there, the industry

grew to meet their needs. Today Florida has one of the most elaborate recreational infrastructures in the world, including thousands of hotels, motels, restaurants, and bars and hundreds of attractions. Some attractions are huge, like those within Orlando's Walt Disney World, whereas most are much smaller, such as the Snake-A-Torium in Panama City or the Old Jail in St. Augustine. Private golf courses abound, including extraordinary miniature ones. Tennis clubs and swimming pools are ubiquitous. There are museums to meet almost anyone's taste: large ones such as the Miami Museum of Science, and smaller ones like the Underwater Demolition Team SEAL Museum in Ft. Pierce or Potter's Wax Museum in St. Augustine. Florida also has a variety of gardens, zoos, animal farms, and historical buildings.

Spectator sports are popular with both visitors and residents. The state's national champion collegiate athletic teams draw huge crowds. There are post-season bowl games, the most famous being Miami's Orange Bowl. For decades a number of major league baseball teams have trained in Florida during the winter, playing exhibition games in the spring. Professional major league teams in football, basketball, and hockey are now located in the state, and in 1991 Miami obtained a franchise for a National League baseball team. Dog and horse tracks, as well as jai alai frontons compete for the better's money. Throughout the year communities attract visitors by holding festivals, tournaments, concerts, and other events.

Tourists spend an estimated 32 billion dollars each year in Florida. Residents, many having chosen the state for its recreational opportunities, add billions of dollars more to the tourist economy. The daily expenditures of air visitors are typically at least 60 percent higher than those of visitors who come by car. The average stay of an auto visitor, however, is over double that of one who comes by air. Winter, when about equal numbers of auto and air visitors arrive, is still the peak season to visit Florida. The spring and summer are the low seasons for air tourists. Fall is an equally low season for both visitors by air and auto. Florida's tourist industry is responsive to national economic conditions. During national recessions the tourist trade grows more slowly or even declines. The 1973 increase in gasoline prices also reduced the number of visitors.

Within the United States, Florida's most important source of tourists has been from states east of the Mississippi River, primarily the northeastern states, and those along the lower Great Lakes. Many summer visitors come from Georgia, Alabama, and Tennessee, a large share heading for the Gulf of Mexico beaches from Panama City to Pensacola. The number of foreign visitors to the state, the majority from Europe and Canada, increased throughout the 1980s and was approaching 5 million annually by the end of the decade. Almost 30 percent of all British tourists to the United States choose Florida for their vacation. Most Europeans, many on tours that include lodging and a rental car, and a visit to Walt Disney World, come in the summer. Over 2 million Canadians arrive each year to escape their nation's cold winters. The largest number go to southeast Florida.

The Economic and Demographic Research Division of the Florida Legislature has estimated that the demands of out-of-state tourists have created almost 700,000 jobs, about 13 percent of all jobs in the state. Earnings from tourist-related jobs total 10 billion dollars. More than half the jobs in restaurants and bars, hotels and motels, and amusements and attractions depend on the tourist trade. Approximately 15 percent of sales tax collected in Florida comes from sales to out-of-state tourists.

Until the end of the nineteenth century Florida's summers were considered excruciatingly hot and unhealthy to people from the northern states. Malaria, and even yellow fever outbreaks, were not unusual. Since the end of World War II a successful effort has been made to extend the tourist season. Air conditioning has contributed enormously to increasing the summer tourist trade. Also, there has been a huge investment in tourist facilities that appeal to children. During the summer typical tourists are young couples who arrive with their children, usually by car, to visit the large theme parks and the beaches. During the rest of the year most visitors are adults. Notable exceptions are the college students who pour into Ft. Lauderdale and Daytona Beach during their spring break from all over the eastern United States.

In the past thirty years the difference between the high and low tourist season has diminished greatly. Today Dade County (Miami) has no distinct tourist season. Seasonal differences are greatest on the Gulf coast between Pensacola and Panama City, as well as between Ft. Myers and Naples. North Florida is too cold in the winter to attract many northerners escaping winter. The Naples area is very popular as a resort for northerners during the winter, when it is the warmest part of the state. In the summer it is one of the hottest and most humid, and has less appeal, even to Floridians. Spring is the high season for most of the peninsula. The fall is the low season throughout most of the state.

The Distribution of Commercial Tourist Attractions

The contemporary distribution of Florida's tourist facilities differs greatly from the past. Change has been brought about by the evolution of the transportation system, the increased ability of young families to take long vacations far from home, and the immigration of large numbers of Hispanics into the Miami area. Early in the nineteenth century northern tourists reached Florida by boat, but by the end of the century rail service was established to both the Tampa area and down the east coast. Grand hotels were built by the developers of the railroads. St. Augustine was the first tourist town, but by the beginning of the twentieth century a number of tourist communities had developed along the Atlantic coast as far south as Miami. On the Gulf coast St. Petersburg, Sarasota, and Ft. Myers began to emerge as winter resorts. With the advent of the automobile, tourist facilities became less concentrated. The automobile especially increased tourism in the state's interior. By the middle of the twentieth century tourist attractions were widely distributed throughout the state.

Shortly after World War II tourist accommodations began to concentrate once more, and they have tended to do so ever since. This concentration first began with the wider use of air transportation. Miami benefited the most. Package tours to Miami became popular. They included the cost of air travel, accommodations, and a rental car. The nation's largest rental car agency, Hertz, was opened at this time in Miami. For twenty years after World War II tourism on Miami Beach boomed with opulent new hotels opening almost every year. During this period the geography of tourism was also altered by the construction of the Interstate Highway System. Automobile tourists, many of whom were young families arriving in the summer, tended to follow the new limited-access highways. Tourist facilities along the older federal and state highways suffered, and many were closed. New facilities sprung up along the exits of the interstates. An excellent example of a town whose tourist industry suffered severely following the construction of an interstate is Perry in north Florida. A town that greatly benefited was Lake City, also in north Florida, where two interstates cross.

The Cuban Revolution also precipitated change in tourism in the state. Cubans by the hundreds of thousands left the island to live in Miami, radically altering the character of the city. Many tourists, particularly from the northeastern U.S. chose other places for their vacations. Towns farther to the north on the Atlantic coast, and along the southwest coast profited from Miami's decline in tourism. The Gulf of Mexico port of Naples, a small town with fewer than 400 hotel and motel rooms at the close of World War II, now has over 5,000 rooms.

Since 1970, the Gulf coast between Panama City and Pensacola also has grown in relative importance as a tourist area. Summer visitors from the southeastern states, particularly Georgia and Alabama, have flocked to the beautiful white sand beaches of northwest Florida. First Panama City became the principal center of tourist activities, but increasingly people have chosen to vacation farther west, particularly around Destin. The beaches of northwest Florida are so popular among people of neighboring states that they are often called the "Redneck Riviera."

The Orlando Tourist Region

No single factor has altered the tourist landscape of Florida more than Walt Disney World, which opened near Orlando in 1971 on a 24,000-acre tract of land. Prior to the opening of Walt Disney World the economy of the Orlando area was primarily based on aircraft and space-related manufacturing, military installations, services to retirees, and the surrounding orange groves. There were only a handful of large tourist attractions in all of Central Florida: Silver Springs (1890), Cypress Gardens (1930), Weeki Wachee (1947), Busch Gardens (1959), and NASA Kennedy Space Center's Spaceport (1966). With the instant success of Walt Disney World the Orlando area became the state's most important tourist center. Later other theme parks were built nearby to compete with the Disney attraction. The year Walt Disney World opened Greater Orlando had 450,000 inhabitants, but by 1991 it had over 1 million. Much of that growth was due to the expansion of tourism in the region. Today the Orlando area vies with Las Vegas as having more hotel and motel rooms than any metropolitan area in the nation, including New York City. Central Florida, especially Orlando, has become such an important tourism area that it merits a detailed discussion.

Walt Disney conceived the idea to build Walt Disney World shortly after Disneyland opened in Los Angeles in 1955. Disneyland is generally regarded as the world's first theme park and was an immediate success, attendance quickly reaching 12 million. Disney wanted to build a similar park in the East. He chose the Orlando area because he wanted a large tract of inexpensive land in a place where there were warm winters, that was served by an interstate highway, and that was not too distant from the large northern cities. South Florida had warmer winters, but land costs were high. Whereas land costs were cheaper farther north in Georgia, winters were too severe to attract tourists in that season. The land transaction was made more advantageous by the Florida legislature giving Disney special governmental status over his property, in several respects making it similar to a county.

The large tract was named Walt Disney World, and within it construction began on its first theme park, the Magic Kingdom. Opened in 1971, it is larger than Disneyland in Los Angeles, but its themes are similar. The park is situated deep in the interior of Walt Disney World, and can be reached by private auto and bus. Walt Disney World today has its own hotels, and guests who stay within it can reach the Magic Kingdom by monorail. The initial success of the Magic Kingdom was even greater than Disneyland, and today between 25,000 and 75,000 people are admitted daily, depending on the season. Since the Magic Kingdom primarily has children's themes, attendance is highest during the summer, around Christmas, and during the spring school break.

Almost immediately after completion of the Magic Kingdom, the Disney Corporation began plans to build a second theme park within Walt Disney World. Whereas the Magic Kingdom was designed to meet the demands of the children of the baby boom, this new park would have themes that interested adults. Many of these adults were the now mature children of baby boom families. Named EPCOT, an acronym for Experimental Prototype Community of Tomorrow, it has two sections and resembles a world's fair. Future World was built with corporate financial support, and includes exhibitions of such multinational corporations as General Motors and Exxon. World Showcase, the second section, is a joint venture between a number of countries and Disney to display elements of each nation's history, arts, and technology. A third theme park—Disney-MGM Studios— was opened in 1989. It features a tour of stage sets of famous movies such as Casablanca, Raiders of the Lost Ark, and the Wizard of Oz, with spectacular special effects. Movies and television programs are also produced in the park, and the visitor can watch them being filmed. There is ample space for further expansion. Recently the Walt Disney Corporation opened a smaller park featuring water slides and has plans to build a fourth big park, a shopping center, more hotels, and a town where it will sell time-share apartments. Annual attendance to Disney attractions is well over 30 million. It has 35,000 employees, the largest number working for a private corporation in the state. Walt Disney World today is generally acknowledged to be the most well-attended commercial tourist attraction in the world.

Disney anticipated that his Walt Disney World would attract many competitors. One of the reasons he desired such a large tract of land was to have a buffer between his parks and the competition. Nonetheless, parks began to spring up around the Magic Kingdom. The two largest are Sea World (1973) and Universal Studios (1990). Estimated annual attendance of Sea World is approximately 5 million, and Universal Studios between 6 and 9 million. There are many smaller attractions in the Orlando area, for example Medieval Times, Mystery Fun House, Xanadu, Wet'n'Wild, and Fun'n'Wheels. The Spaceport on Cape Canaveral, Silver Springs in Ocala, and St. Augustine, the oldest continuously settled town on the North American continent, are all within easy driving distance of Orlando.

Not all theme parks in the Orlando area succeed. One large one, after trying a circus theme, and then baseball, has closed indefinitely. The Orlando area, however, is never without the promise of a new theme park. In addition to that announced by the Walt Disney Corporation, a group in 1991 was seeking money to build a large park with a Chinese theme.

A magnetically levitated railroad is scheduled for construction from the Orlando International Airport to Orlando's International Drive, where there are many large hotels. A maximum speed of several hundred miles an hour will be reached on the short run between the airport and hotels.

Although overshadowed by the giant commercial parks in the Orlando area, throughout Florida there are many private tourist attractions, each drawing hundreds of thousands or more visitors. Southeastern Florida, the so-called Gold Coast, is particularly well endowed with these attractions, including Orchid Jungle (1886), said to be the state's oldest commercial tourist attraction, the Seaquarium, Metro Zoo, Ocean World, Monkey Jungle, and Parrot Jungle in the Miami area, and Lion Country Safari near West Palm Beach. Tampa has Busch Gardens, whose annual attendance is approximately 4 million. The state's Department of Commerce publishes a catalog of Florida tourist attractions, which lists approximately 250 public and private attractions by region. Throughout Florida there are hundreds of other smaller attractions not mentioned in the catalog.

Environment-Based Tourism and Recreation

Almost everyone who lives in or visits Florida enjoys one or more of its natural amenities. During the winter few Florida residents regret not living in the cold North. Millions of visitors from the North come at that time to enjoy the state's mild to warm temperatures. The state has among the most beautiful beaches in the nation, both on the Atlantic Ocean and the Gulf of Mexico. Geologists and coastal experts in 1991 in a national poll voted Grayton Beach, located between Panama City and Ft. Walton Beach, the most beautiful in the continental United States. Many other Florida beaches have the same white-sand, rolling dunes, sea oats, tidal lakes teaming with fish, and crystal-clear blue water. For surfers, Florida's coastline might not offer the waves of California or Hawaii, but many go to Cape Canaveral and judge surfing conditions there excellent. The warm and relatively pollution-free water off all Florida beaches, however, is marvelous for swimmers. Boating , both sail and power, is also a popular pastime. Florida manufactures more pleasure boats than any state in the nation, and a large share of them are purchased by Floridians. Sportfishing from piers as well as from boats offshore is a popular recreational activity. Various communities sponsor saltwater fishing tournaments, for marlin, mackerel, bonefish, sailfish, and tarpon, among others. The intracoastal waterway is a scenic route for pleasure boats that extends for hundreds of miles along both coasts.

The appeal of Florida's coasts to both visitors and residents is so powerful that the natural amenities of its interior are often overlooked. Florida has a large number of state parks, forests, recreational areas, and wildlife management areas, many with camping facilities. The federal government maintains large national forests, estuarine and marine sanctuaries, and wildlife refuges as well as Everglades and Biscayne National parks and Big Cypress National Preserve. Within these public areas and the huge private forests owned by paper companies are lakes, rivers, and springs for boating, fishing, swimming, water skiing, and a numerous and varied wildlife to hunt or observe. North Florida's springs are particularly satisfying for summer bathing, since the subterranean water that feeds them is cool. In addition, they are extraordinarily clear, providing nearly perfect visibility for scuba diving. Many of the state's rivers are well suited for boating. Canoeists come from great distances to enjoy them. The Ichetucknee River near Gainesville has become so popular a tubing river that on some days access to it must be controlled. People float down the river on inner tubes, many with drinks attached by rope to the tube. Over a million people a year visit Everglades National Park southwest of Miami. Outside of the park, in this vast "River of Grass," others fish and hunt, or race about in airboats. Indiscriminate use of airboats has adversely affected both the wildlife and the vegetation of this wetland.

Freshwater fishing is another popular resource-based recreational activity in Florida, enjoyed by residents as well as visitors. Most lakes are well stocked with pan fish such as bluegill, perch, and bream. Largemouth and striped bass are also found throughout the state. Several lakes have acquired a national reputation for the size of their largemouth bass. Bass of record size are regularly caught in Lake Jackson, near Tallahassee, and Lake Okeechobee, in South Florida.

Conclusion

If it is true that a picture is worth a thousand words, a map must be worth several thousand. In the following pages maps portray the distribution of Florida's recreational and tourist facilities offered by government and private enterprise, as well as the impact of recreation and tourism on the state's economy. It is hoped that their perusal will prove to be enjoyable recreation in itself.

Outdoor Recreation

Florida's climate, which is warmer than that of most of the rest of the nation, is a major factor in the great popularity of outdoor recreational activities throughout the state. The coast is the state's most popular physical feature. Saltwater beach activities are the major recreational interest of both the state's residents and tourists. Saltwater fishing is another recreational activity widely enjoyed by both Floridians and tourists. The climate also offers many opportunities for swimming. Many Florida homes have swimming pools, as do most hotels and motels. Public pools operated by local governments are also numerous. Despite many lakes, particularly in the center of the state, freshwater beach activities and fishing rank rather low on the list of recreational choices of residents as well as tourists.

The state's numerous archaeological and historical sites draw many people, both residents and visitors. Golf ranks very high among tourists, although it is not in the top ten among residents. For the past two decades, at least, bicycling has been very popular among the state's residents, and since 1980 it has grown rapidly in popularity among tourists as well.

The relationship between population and public recreational acreage is not always in balance. The lightly populated panhandle has a far higher share of the state's outdoor recreational land than its share of the state's population. The reverse is true in the center of the state, which has a paucity of state-owned recreational land, but a high percentage of its population. In south Florida the two are in far better balance.

Land for Outdoor Recreation, 1988

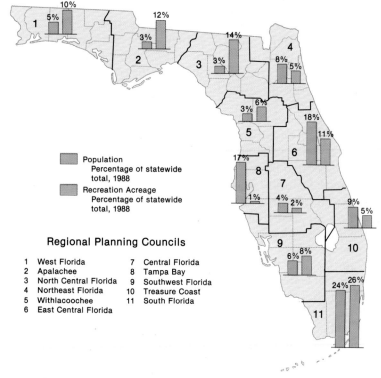

Population
Percentage of statewide total, 1988

Recreation Acreage
Percentage of statewide total, 1988

Regional Planning Councils

1 West Florida
2 Apalachee
3 North Central Florida
4 Northeast Florida
5 Withlacoochee
6 East Central Florida
7 Central Florida
8 Tampa Bay
9 Southwest Florida
10 Treasure Coast
11 South Florida

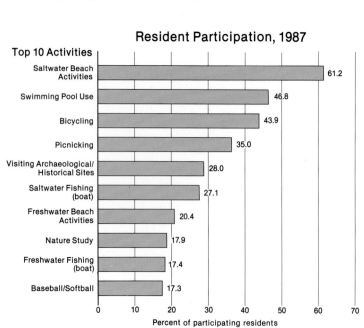

BIKE RACES, Pensacola

Resident Participation, 1987

Top 10 Activities

Activity	Percent
Saltwater Beach Activities	61.2
Swimming Pool Use	46.8
Bicycling	43.9
Picnicking	35.0
Visiting Archaeological/ Historical Sites	28.0
Saltwater Fishing (boat)	27.1
Freshwater Beach Activities	20.4
Nature Study	17.9
Freshwater Fishing (boat)	17.4
Baseball/Softball	17.3

Percent of participating residents

Tourist Participation, 1987

Top 10 Activities

Activity	Percent
Saltwater Beach Activities	50.0
Swimming Pool Use	37.5
Golf	16.8
Visiting Archaeological/ Historical Sites	15.6
Saltwater Fishing (boat)	9.8
Picnicking	8.5
Saltwater Fishing (non-boat)	7.3
Freshwater Beach Activities	6.7
Bicycling	6.4
Tennis	6.3

Percent of participating tourists

Water Recreation

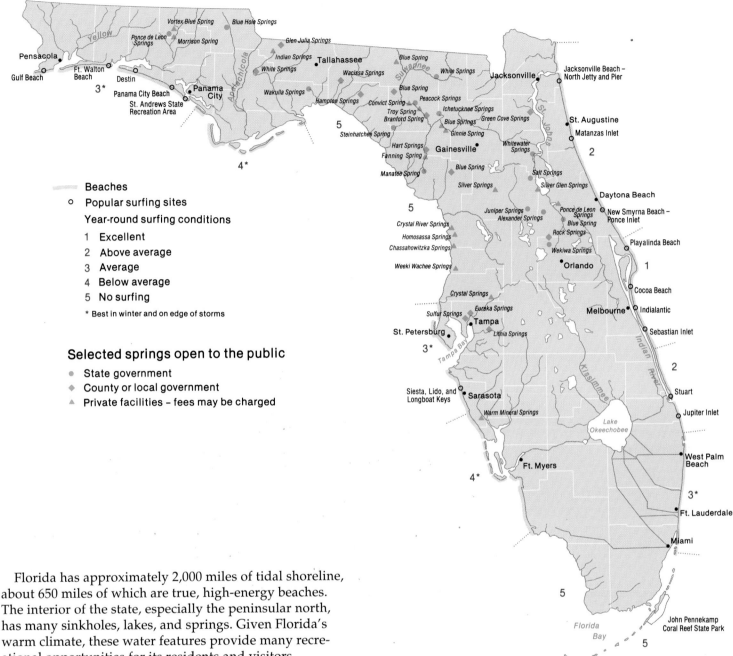

Beaches
○ Popular surfing sites
Year-round surfing conditions
1 Excellent
2 Above average
3 Average
4 Below average
5 No surfing
* Best in winter and on edge of storms

Selected springs open to the public

● State government
◆ County or local government
▲ Private facilities – fees may be charged

Florida has approximately 2,000 miles of tidal shoreline, about 650 miles of which are true, high-energy beaches. The interior of the state, especially the peninsular north, has many sinkholes, lakes, and springs. Given Florida's warm climate, these water features provide many recreational opportunities for its residents and visitors.

Saltwater recreation far exceeds freshwater recreation in popularity. The state enjoys a reputation of having many of the nation's most highly regarded beaches. Those of northwest Florida are wide with sparkling white sand. The beaches of southeastern Florida (the Gold Coast) frequently appear on television, not only to advertise Florida, but as background for many other advertisement campaigns. Many of the state's best coastal properties entered the private domain before 1950, but recently the state has begun to purchase beaches for public recreation.

To the surfer, Florida cannot compare with either California or Hawaii. Unlike the Pacific Ocean, the Gulf of Mexico and the Atlantic Ocean seldom generate large waves, sought so avidly by the surfer. Nonetheless, the state's surfers regard the coastline from West Palm Beach to Jacksonville as either excellent or above average for surfing. They often rush to the beach at the approach of a tropical depression, or even a hurricane, since they know that the unusually high winds will produce large waves.

Florida's springs were recreational attractions even before the Civil War, notably White Springs on the Suwannee River, Green Cove Springs on the St. Johns River, and Silver Springs. The state's springs are particularly appealing to local residents, who enjoy swimming in the clear and cool water. Scuba divers explore the springs, even entering underwater caverns. A number of springs have been commercialized, notably Weeki Wachee Springs, Silver Springs, and Homosassa Springs. The state's many lakes are used for both swimming and fishing.

Recreational Waterways

Florida's residents, and to an ever-growing degree its visitors, are drawn year-round to its rivers and streams. The quality of these waterways, as well as Florida's mild winters, contributes greatly to their popularity among boaters and canoeists. Although there are no opportunities for white-water rafting or canoeing, there are hundreds of miles of rivers and creeks in which a power boat owner or canoeist can leisurely navigate. Many are so seldom traveled that one can journey for long stretches without meeting another person, and see a wide assortment of wildlife, including alligators, turtles, otters, and a myriad of birds. For those in pursuit of this type of boating the

rivers of the panhandle are particularly recommended. The canals and creeks in the Everglades also provide excellent opportunities to view wildlife, but since they are close to the state's largest metropolitan area, they are more frequently visited.

The Ichetucknee River is a nationally famous "tubing" river. Tubing on the river was made popular by University of Florida students, who would launch an inner tube onto the river, and drift down it, usually with an attached bag containing cans of drinks chilling in the water. This activity now has such appeal that at some times during the year the number of tubers has to be regulated.

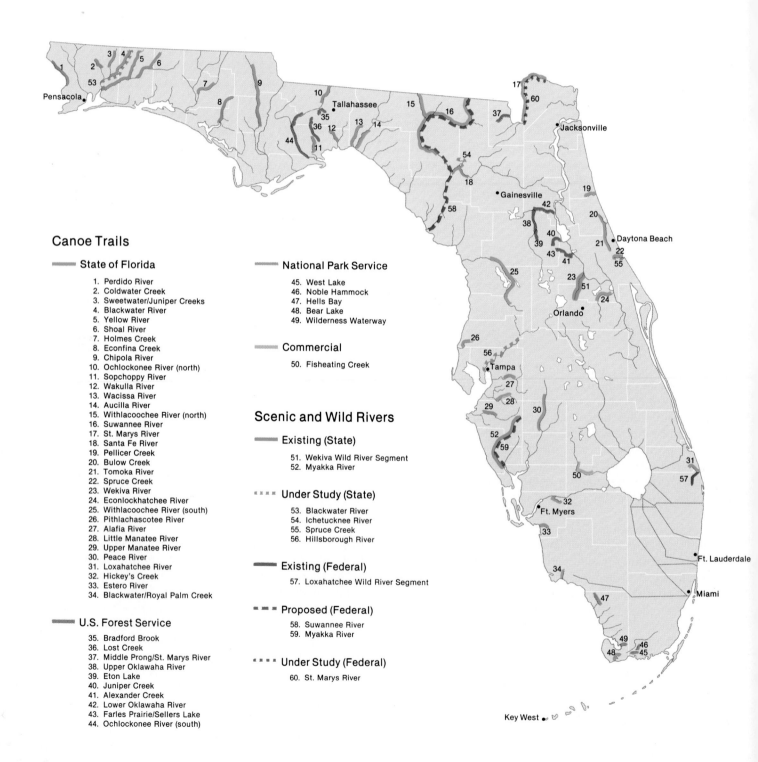

Canoe Trails

State of Florida

1. Perdido River
2. Coldwater Creek
3. Sweetwater/Juniper Creeks
4. Blackwater River
5. Yellow River
6. Shoal River
7. Holmes Creek
8. Econfina Creek
9. Chipola River
10. Ochlockonee River (north)
11. Sopchoppy River
12. Wakulla River
13. Wacissa River
14. Aucilla River
15. Withlacoochee River (north)
16. Suwannee River
17. St. Marys River
18. Santa Fe River
19. Pellicer Creek
20. Bulow Creek
21. Tomoka River
22. Spruce Creek
23. Wekiva River
24. Econlockhatchee River
25. Withlacoochee River (south)
26. Pithlachascotee River
27. Alafia River
28. Little Manatee River
29. Upper Manatee River
30. Peace River
31. Loxahatchee River
32. Hickey's Creek
33. Estero River
34. Blackwater/Royal Palm Creek

U.S. Forest Service

35. Bradford Brook
36. Lost Creek
37. Middle Prong/St. Marys River
38. Upper Oklawaha River
39. Eton Lake
40. Juniper Creek
41. Alexander Creek
42. Lower Oklawaha River
43. Farles Prairie/Sellers Lake
44. Ochlockonee River (south)

National Park Service

45. West Lake
46. Noble Hammock
47. Hells Bay
48. Bear Lake
49. Wilderness Waterway

Commercial

50. Fisheating Creek

Scenic and Wild Rivers

Existing (State)

51. Wekiva Wild River Segment
52. Myakka River

Under Study (State)

53. Blackwater River
54. Ichetucknee River
55. Spruce Creek
56. Hillsborough River

Existing (Federal)

57. Loxahatchee Wild River Segment

Proposed (Federal)

58. Suwannee River
59. Myakka River

Under Study (Federal)

60. St. Marys River

Sport Fishing

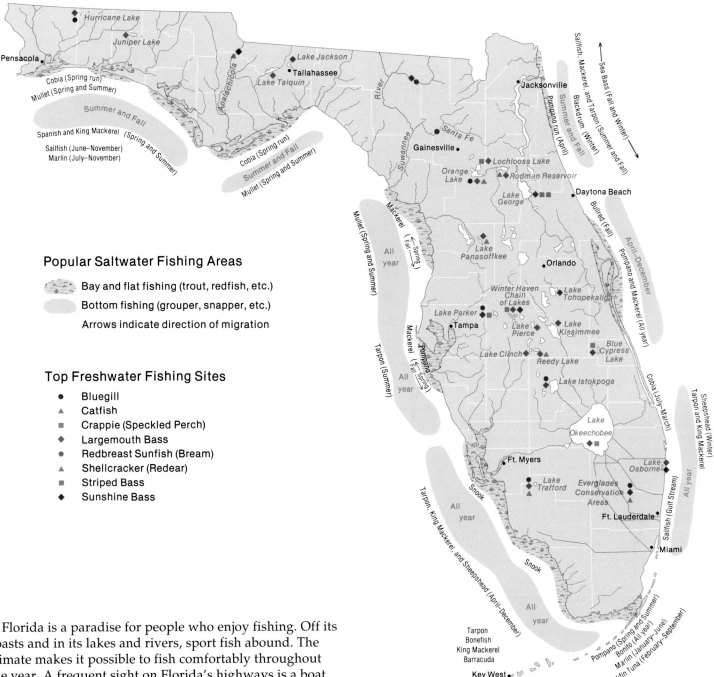

Popular Saltwater Fishing Areas

Bay and flat fishing (trout, redfish, etc.)

Bottom fishing (grouper, snapper, etc.)

Arrows indicate direction of migration

Top Freshwater Fishing Sites

● Bluegill
▲ Catfish
■ Crappie (Speckled Perch)
◆ Largemouth Bass
● Redbreast Sunfish (Bream)
▲ Shellcracker (Redear)
■ Striped Bass
◆ Sunshine Bass

Florida is a paradise for people who enjoy fishing. Off its coasts and in its lakes and rivers, sport fish abound. The climate makes it possible to fish comfortably throughout the year. A frequent sight on Florida's highways is a boat on a trailer, being towed behind a car. In many towns along the coast charter boats and party boats are available. Piers specifically for saltwater fishing are open to the public, and along many of the state's bridges there are walkways from which people can drop a line.

The waters off any point of Florida's coast provide excellent opportunities for recreational fishing, but those from Jacksonville south to the Keys and north to Tampa Bay are the most famous. Here the tarpon, perhaps Florida's most famous sport fish, is numerous. Marlin, another famous large saltwater fighting fish, though less common than the tarpon, is also frequently caught. Although tarpon and marlin are most valued, Florida deep sea fishermen are most likely to catch cobia, mullet, various kinds of mackerel, snook, bonito, grouper, snapper, and even barracuda.

Freshwater fishing opportunities abound throughout the state, from the canals of the Everglades to the lakes, reservoirs, and rivers of northern Florida. Although freshwater fish usually are smaller and less aggressive than many saltwater species, at least one Florida freshwater fish figures frequently in the record books, the largemouth bass. Largemouth bass are found in lakes from south Florida to Pensacola, but record-breaking fish are usually caught in Lake Jackson and Lake Talquin both near Tallahassee. To catch a bass may be the goal of many freshwater fishermen, but there is a much greater likelihood of returning home with a string of perch, bream, bluegill, shellcracker, and catfish.

State Recreation Sites

The Florida Department of Natural Resources manages approximately 100 sites, totaling nearly 400,000 acres. Most of these are open to the public and are visited by almost 14 million people annually. Many of these parks are open to campers.

The state's most popular recreational site is John Pennekamp Coral Reef State Park, which attracts well over 1 million visitors each year, over twice as many as the next most popular recreational site, Honeymoon Island in Pinellas County. Pennekamp is almost entirely underwater and is extremely popular with snorklers and scuba divers. "Trails" have been marked with plaques describing the natural environment for the diver.

The state owns many pre-Columbian archaeological sites as well as historical sites, including the Lake Jackson Temple Mounds, San Marcos de Apalachee, New Smyrna Sugar Mill, Kingsley Plantation, Dade Battlefield from the Second Seminole War, and Olustee and Natural Bridge battle sites from the Civil War. In the late 1980s the state purchased the grade of Florida's second railroad line, which ran from Tallahassee to St. Marks, and converted it into a bicycle trail.

Florida's most popular recreational sites are visited most frequently during the spring and summer. Maclay State Gardens in Tallahassee has the most visitors in March, when its camellias and azaleas are in bloom.

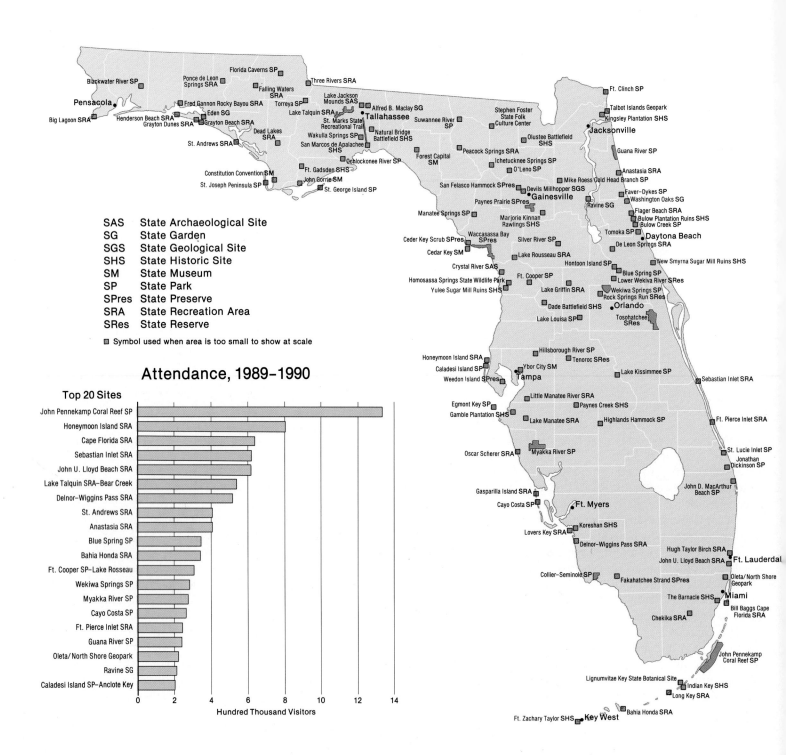

SAS   State Archaeological Site
SG   State Garden
SGS   State Geological Site
SHS   State Historic Site
SM   State Museum
SP   State Park
SPres   State Preserve
SRA   State Recreation Area
SRes   State Reserve

▪ Symbol used when area is too small to show at scale

Attendance, 1989–1990

Top 20 Sites

John Pennekamp Coral Reef SP
Honeymoon Island SRA
Cape Florida SRA
Sebastian Inlet SRA
John U. Lloyd Beach SRA
Lake Talquin SRA–Bear Creek
Delnor-Wiggins Pass SRA
St. Andrews SRA
Anastasia SRA
Blue Spring SP
Bahia Honda SRA
Ft. Cooper SP–Lake Rosseau
Wekiwa Springs SP
Myakka River SP
Cayo Costa SP
Ft. Pierce Inlet SRA
Guana River SP
Oleta/North Shore Geopark
Ravine SG
Caladesi Island SP–Anclote Key

0   2   4   6   8   10   12   14
Hundred Thousand Visitors

State Management Areas

During the nineteenth century the state of Florida sold most of the land awarded to it by the federal government to build schools, roads, railroads, and canals. Nonetheless, some land has remained under state ownership, while other properties have reverted to the state because of nonpayment of taxes. During the 1980s, the state began to purchase land under its Conservation and Recreational Lands Program, Save Our Coast Program, and others. By the beginning of the 1990s almost 100 acquisitions had been made.

To protect wildlife the state has approximately sixty wildlife management areas comprising 4.3 million acres. These consist of federal and privately owned lands in addition to state land. State land within wildlife management areas includes state forests, state wilderness areas, state wildlife and environmental areas, and state wildlife management areas. Federal lands mainly are those within the national forests, and private lands are typically large tree farms owned by paper mills. The state's Game and Fresh Water Fish Commission plays the major role in preserving the wildlife within these properties. Its principal task is to maintain a balance between preservation and recreational use. Although used primarily for hunting and fishing, Florida's wildlife management areas may also be used for hiking, nature studies, picnicking, and horseback riding.

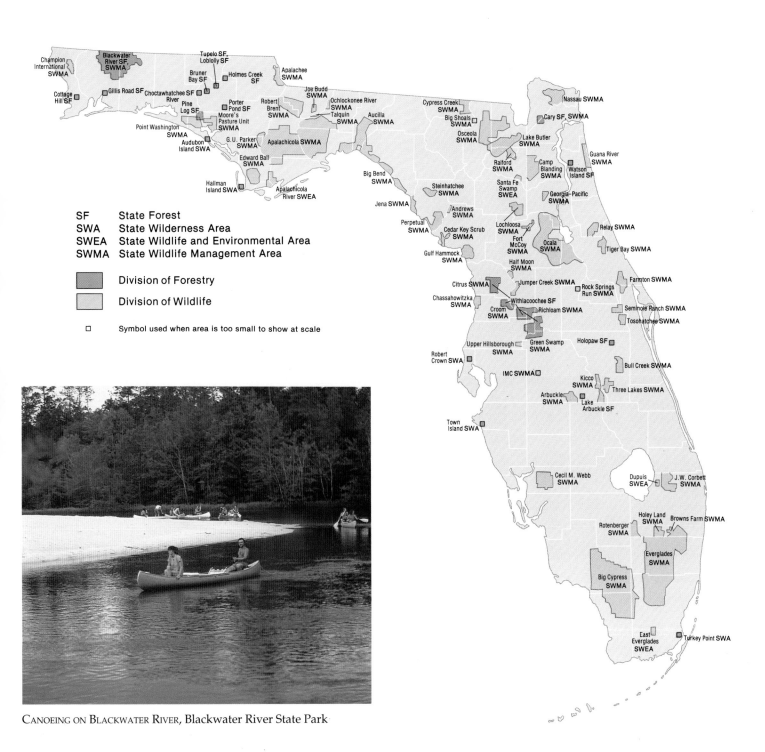

SF   State Forest
SWA   State Wilderness Area
SWEA   State Wildlife and Environmental Area
SWMA   State Wildlife Management Area

Division of Forestry

Division of Wildlife

□   Symbol used when area is too small to show at scale

CANOEING ON BLACKWATER RIVER, Blackwater River State Park

Federal Lands

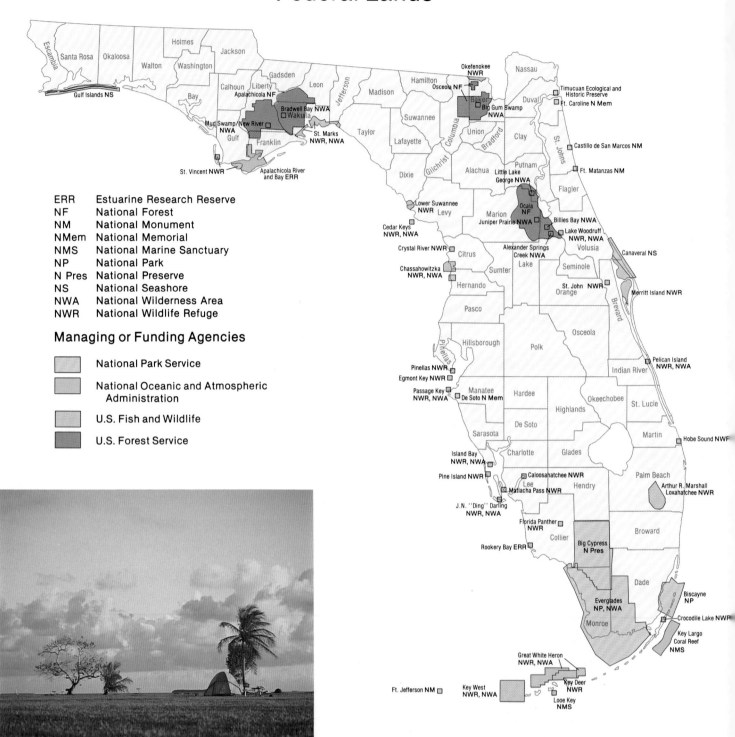

ERR   Estuarine Research Reserve
NF   National Forest
NM   National Monument
NMem   National Memorial
NMS   National Marine Sanctuary
NP   National Park
N Pres   National Preserve
NS   National Seashore
NWA   National Wilderness Area
NWR   National Wildlife Refuge

Managing or Funding Agencies

National Park Service

National Oceanic and Atmospheric
    Administration

U.S. Fish and Wildlife

U.S. Forest Service

FLAMINGO, Everglades National Park

The most famous property managed by the federal government in Florida is Everglades National Park, authorized in 1934. Encompassing nearly 1.4 million acres, including 625,000 acres of water, it is the largest remaining subtropical wilderness in the coterminous United States. In 1968 a large part (173,000 acres) of Biscayne Bay was designated a national park. The park protects interrelated marine systems, including mangrove shoreline, subtropical keys, and tropical coral reefs. Four national forests in the state are managed jointly by the federal and state governments, and are used for recreation and hunting, as well as for the harvest of trees. Other federal lands open for recreational use include Canaveral and Gulf Islands national seashores, Big Cypress National Preserve, and Timucuan Ecological and Historic Preserve, authorized in 1988.

Camping

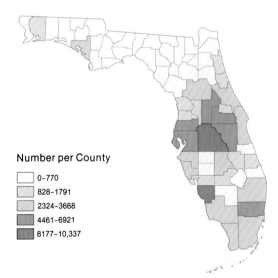

Florida has many facilities for campers. Beginning in the 1920s motorists, pulling simple trailers, began to travel to Florida. Known as "tin can" tourists, they camped at sites throughout the state and presumably ate much of their food from cans. Today recreational vehicle sites as well as sites for tents are mostly concentrated in central Florida. Recently, Florida hiking trails have been greatly expanded, and there is a proposal to complete the Florida Trail, which would run the length of the state.

Tomoka State Park, Ormond Beach

Tent Camping Sites, 1988

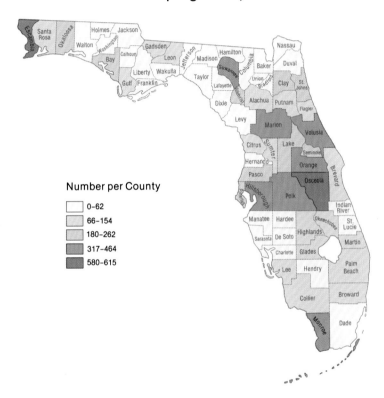

Number per County
- 0–62
- 66–154
- 180–262
- 317–464
- 580–615

Recreational Vehicle Sites, 1988

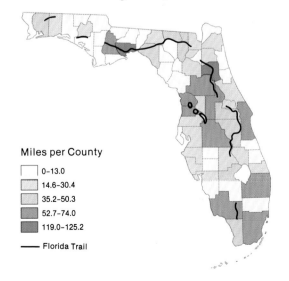

Number per County
- 0–770
- 828–1791
- 2324–3668
- 4461–6921
- 8177–10,337

Hiking Trails, 1988

Miles per County
- 0–13.0
- 14.6–30.4
- 35.2–50.3
- 52.7–74.0
- 119.0–125.2
- — Florida Trail

Boat Ramps, 1988

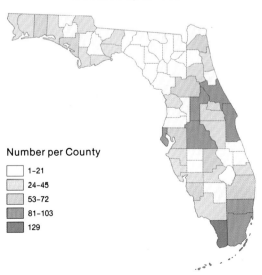

Number per County
- 1–21
- 24–45
- 53–72
- 81–103
- 129

Hunting

Wild Turkey, 1989

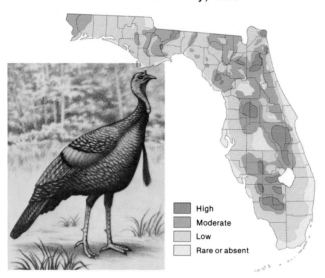

High
Moderate
Low
Rare or absent

Wild Swine, 1988

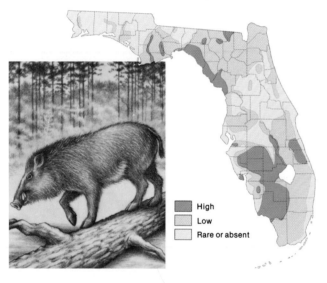

High
Low
Rare or absent

White-Tailed Deer, 1988

High
Moderate
Low
Rare or absent

In the nineteenth century Florida attained national fame among hunters. A common pastime was to shoot at animals from steamboats that plied the St. Johns and its tributaries. During the twentieth century hunting has continued to be popular, particularly in less densely populated north Florida. The Florida Game and Fresh Water Fish Commission has divided the state into three hunting regions: Northwest, Central, and South. Seasons are set aside for dog training, archery hunting, and hunting with muzzle-loading rifles. There are hunting seasons on antlered deer, antlerless deer, wild hog, wild turkey (fall and spring), quail, and bear. The squirrel and several other animals may be hunted throughout the year. Hunting of migratory birds, including ducks, doves, rails, the common moorhen, snipes, coots, and woodcocks, is regulated by the federal government. Florida ranks among the top three states, along with New York and North Carolina, in the seventeen-state Atlantic Flyway.

The Florida Game and Fresh Water Fish Commission carefully monitors the amount of game killed. In the past, populations of certain animals, notably deer, wild turkey, and bear, were allowed to decline to alarmingly low numbers. The deer population in particular has made a remarkable comeback. Even with strict control, the bear population because of great loss in habitat is much smaller than it was in the 1950s. For decades quail hunting has been popular on plantations in the Tallahassee area during late fall and winter. Wealthy landowners from the North have altered the environment to encourage large quail populations.

In 1967 Florida placed alligators on the national Endangered Species List. Protected from hunters, their population quickly grew. In September 1988 Florida had its first statewide alligator hunt in 26 years. In that year 238 hunters were permitted to harvest 3,450 alligators. Each year the number of authorized hunters has continued to be between 200 and 300, and the kill from 2,000 to 4,000. The hides of the alligators are marketed nationally, and the meat sold locally.

Alligator, 1990

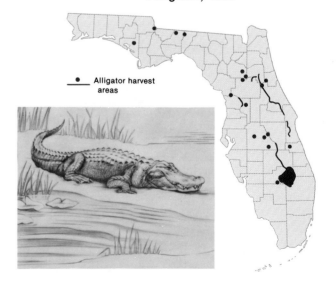

Alligator harvest areas

Hunting and Fishing Licenses

Hunting and Fishing License Revenue, 1990

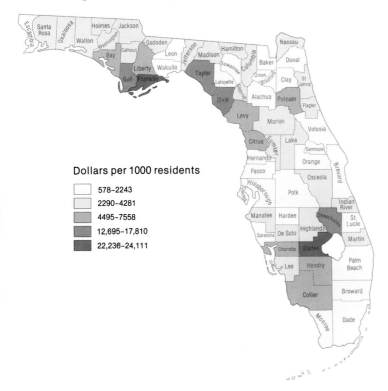

Dollars per 1000 residents

- 578–2243
- 2290–4281
- 4495–7558
- 12,695–17,810
- 22,236–24,111

Hunting Licenses, 1990

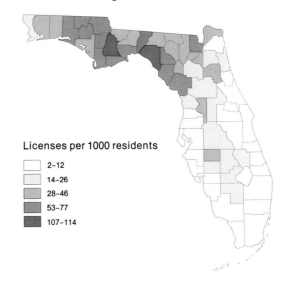

Licenses per 1000 residents

- 2–12
- 14–26
- 28–46
- 53–77
- 107–114

Freshwater Fishing Licenses, 1990

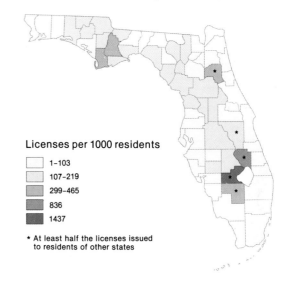

Licenses per 1000 residents

- 1–103
- 107–219
- 299–465
- 836
- 1437

* At least half the licenses issued to residents of other states

Saltwater Fishing Licenses, 1990

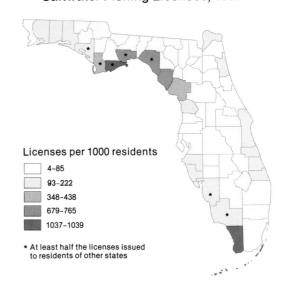

Licenses per 1000 residents

- 4–85
- 93–222
- 348–438
- 679–765
- 1037–1039

* At least half the licenses issued to residents of other states

Florida collects approximately 8 million dollars each year from the sale of freshwater fishing licenses. Forty percent of this amount comes from nonresidents who pay higher fees. About 1.5 million dollars is collected annually for hunting licenses, but only 10 percent of these fees are obtained from nonresidents. The state levies fees on freshwater commercial fishermen as well but normally collects only around 750,000 dollars each year. Trapping licenses generate under 10,000 dollars annually.

More recently the state has begun to license saltwater fishing off its coasts. These fees amount to 15 million dollars annually. Approximately 25 percent of all saltwater licenses are sold to nonresidents. The state requires a special license for crawfish (spiny lobster), snook, and tarpon. Almost half the crawfish licenses are issued in Dade and Monroe counties. Almost one-third of all snook licenses are issued in Dade, Monroe, Collier, and Lee counties, while 60 percent of all tarpon licenses are obtained in Charlotte and Pinellas counties.

Hunting is concentrated in north Florida, where there are extensive national and state forests, as well as millions of acres of commercial tree farms. Within these forests are deer, wild turkey, and other game animals. Bear is also hunted, but the season is short and the state carefully monitors the number killed.

Freshwater fishing is far more widely distributed than hunting. Game fish abound in lakes, rivers, and streams throughout the state. Okeechobee County has a particularly high per capita sale of freshwater fishing licenses because of nearby Lake Okeechobee.

Attractions

NORTHWEST

Alfred B. Maclay State Gardens, Tallahassee
Capitol Complex, Tallahassee
Florida Caverns State Park, Marianna
Gulf World, Panama City Beach
Gulfarium, Ft. Walton Beach
Historic Pensacola Village, Pensacola
Indian Temple Mound Museum, Ft. Walton Beach
Junior Museum of Bay County, Panama City
Lafayette Vineyards and Winery, Tallahassee
Miracle Strip Amusement Park, Panama City Beach
Museum of Florida History, Tallahassee
Museum of Man in the Sea, Panama City Beach
Museum of the Sea and Indian, Destin
National Museum of Naval Aviation, Pensacola
North Hill Preservation District, Pensacola
San Luis Archaeological and Historical Site, Tallahassee
Seville Historic District, Pensacola
Shipwreck Island Water Park, Panama City Beach
Snake-A-Torium, Panama City Beach
Stephen Foster State Folk Culture Center, White Springs
T.T. Wentworth, Jr., Florida State Museum, Pensacola
Tallahassee Junior Museum, Tallahassee
The 1840 House, Ltd and the Gallery, Marianna
U.S. Air Force Armament Museum, Valparaiso
Wakulla Springs State Park, Wakulla Springs
Zoo and Botanical Gardens, Gulf Breeze

Florida caverns State Park, Marianna

Castillo de San Marcos, St. Augustine

NORTHEAST

Amelia Island Museum of History, Fernandina Beach
Anheuser-Busch Brewery Tour, Jacksonville
Castillo de San Marcos, St. Augustine
Centre Street, Fernandina Beach
Florida Museum of Natural History, Gainesville
Florida Sports Hall of Fame, Lake City
Fort Caroline National Memorial, Jacksonville
Fort Clinch State Park, Fernandina Beach
Fountain of Youth, St. Augustine
Fred Bear Museum, Gainesville
Jacksonville Art Museum, Jacksonville
Jacksonville Zoological Park, Jacksonville
Kingsley Plantation State Historic Site, Jacksonville
Lightner Museum, St. Augustine
Marineland of Florida, Marineland
Marjorie Kinnan Rawlings State Historic Site, Hawthorne
Museum of Science and Industry, Jacksonville
Old Jail, St. Augustine
Oldest House, St. Augustine
Oldest Store Museum, St. Augustine
Oldest Wooden Schoolhouse, St. Augustine
Potter's Wax Museum, St. Augustine
Ripley's Believe It or Not!, St. Augustine
Riverwalk, Jacksonville
St. Augustine Alligator Farm, St. Augustine
St. Augustine's Restored Spanish Quarter, St. Augustine
Zorayda Castle, St. Augustine

GLASS-BOTTOM BOAT, Florida's Silver Springs

CENTRAL WEST

Bellm's Cars and Music of Yesterday, Sarasota
Braden Castle Park, Bradenton
Busch Gardens, The Dark Continent, Tampa
Clearwater Marine Science Center, Clearwater
Florida's Weeki Wachee, Brooksville
Gamble Plantation State Historic Site, Ellenton
Gator Jungle of Plant City, Inc., Plant City
Great Explorations, St. Petersburg
Homosassa Springs Wildlife Park, Homosassa Springs
John and Mable Ringling Museum of Art, Sarasota
Lionel Train and Seashell Museum, Sarasota
Lowry Park Zoo, Tampa
Manatee Village Historical Park, Bradenton
Marie Selby Botanical Gardens, Sarasota
Museum of Fine Arts, St. Petersburg
Museum of Science and Industry, Tampa
Pier, St. Petersburg
St. Nicholas Greek Orthodox Cathedral, Tarpon Springs
Salvador Dali Museum, St. Petersburg
Sarasota Jungle Gardens, Sarasota
South Florida Museum/Bishop Planetarium, Bradenton

SPACESHIP EARTH AND MONORAIL, Walt Disney World Resort

©The Walt Disney Company

Spongeorama Exhibit Center, Tarpon Springs
St. Petersburg Historical Museum, St. Petersburg
Suncoast Seabird Sanctuary, Inc., Indian Shores
Sunken Gardens, St. Petersburg
Tampa Museum of Art, Tampa
Tiki Garden, Indian Shores
Ybor Square, Tampa

CENTRAL

Alligatorland Safari Zoo, Kissimmee
Appleton Museum of Art, Ocala
Bok Tower Gardens, Lake Wales
Central Florida Railroad Museum, Winter Garden
Central Florida Zoological Park, Lake Monroe
Charles Hosmer Morse Museum of American Art, Winter Park
Church Street Station, Orlando
Don Garlits Museum of Drag Racing, Ocala
Elvis Presley Museum, Orlando
Florida Citrus Tower, Clermont
Florida's Cypress Gardens, Winter Haven
Florida's Silver Springs, Silver Springs
Flying Tigers Warbird Air Museum, Kissimmee
Gatorland, Orlando
House of Presidents, Clermont
Leu Botanical Gardens, Orlando
Medieval Life, Kissimmee
Mulberry Phosphate Museum, Mulberry
Old Town, Lake Buena Vista
Orlando Museum of Art, Orlando
Orlando Science Center and John Young Planetarium, Orlando
Polk Museum of Art, Lakeland
Reptile World Serpentarium, St. Cloud
Sea World of Florida, Orlando
Universal Studios Florida, Orlando
Walt Disney World Resort (Magic Kingdom, EPCOT, Disney-MGM
   Studios), Lake Buena Vista
Water Mania, Kissimmee
Wet'n' Wild, Orlando
Xanadu, Home of the Future, Kissimmee

CENTRAL EAST

Astronaut Memorial Space Science Center, Cocoa
Birthplace of Speed Museum, Ormond Beach
Boardwalk, Daytona Beach
Brevard Art Center and Museum, Melbourne
Brevard Museum of History and Natural Science, Cocoa
Casements, Ormond Beach
Daytona International Speedway, Daytona Beach
De Land Museum, De Land
Elliot Museum, Stuart
Gilbert's Bar House of Refuge, Stuart
Halifax Historical Society and Museum, Inc., Daytona Beach
Museum of Arts and Sciences, Daytona Beach
NASA Kennedy Space Center's Spaceport USA, Kennedy Space Center
Ponce de Leon Inlet Lighthouse, Ponce Inlet
Space Coast Science Center, Melbourne
St. Lucie County Historical Museum, Ft. Pierce
Underwater Demolition Team SEAL Museum, Ft. Pierce
United States Astronaut Hall of Fame, Titusville

Attractions

J.N. "DING" DARLING NATIONAL WILDLIFE REFUGE, Sanibel

SOUTHWEST

Collier County Museum, Naples
Corkscrew Swamp Sanctuary, Naples
Edison Winter Home, Ft. Myers
Everglades Wonder Gardens, Bonita Springs
Ford Winter Home, Ft. Myers
Ft. Myers Historical Museum, Ft. Myers
J.N. "Ding" Darling National Wildlife Refuge, Sanibel
Jungle Larry's Zoological Park at Caribbean Gardens, Naples
Nature Center of Lee County and Planetarium, Ft. Myers
Shell Factory, Inc., North Ft. Myers
Waltzing Waters, Ft. Myers

SOUTHEAST

American Police Hall of Fame and Museum, Miami
Ancient Spanish Monastery, North Miami Beach
Art Deco District Tours, Miami Beach
Atlantis, The Water Kingdom, Hollywood
Audubon House and Gardens, Key West
Bass Museum of Art, Miami Beach
Bayside Marketplace, Miami
Biscayne National Underwater Park Tour Boats and Canoe Rental, Homestead
Butterfly World, Coconut Creek
Charles Deering Estate, South Miami
Coral Castle, Homestead
Coral Gables House, Coral Gables
Crane Point Hammock, Marathon
Discovery Center, Ft. Lauderdale
Dolphin Research Center, Marathon Shores
Dreher Park Zoo, West Palm Beach
East Martello Museum and Art Gallery, Key West
Fairchild Tropical Garden, Miami
Flamingo Gardens, Davie
Florida Pioneer Museum, Florida City
Fruit and Spice Park, Homestead
Gold Coast Railroad and Museum, Miami
Hemingway Home and Museum, Key West
Henry M. Flagler Museum, Palm Beach
International Swimming Hall of Fame Aquatic Complex, Ft. Lauderdale
Key West Aquarium, Key West
Key West Lighthouse Museum, Key West
Lion Country Safari, West Palm Beach
Lowe Art Museum, University of Miami, Coral Gables
Metro-Dade Cultural Center, Miami
Miami Metrozoo, Miami
Miami Museum of Science and Space Transit Planetarium, Miami

MIAMI METROZOO

Miami Seaquarium, Miami
Miccosukee Indian Village and Airboat Rides, Miami
Monkey Jungle, Miami
Morikami Museum and Japanese Gardens, Delray Beach
Museum of Archaeology, Ft. Lauderdale
Museum of Art, Ft. Lauderdale
Norton Gallery of Art, West Palm Beach
Ocean World, Ft. Lauderdale
Orchid Jungle, Miami
Parrot Jungle and Gardens, Miami
South Florida Science Museum, West Palm Beach
Theater of the Sea, Islamorada
Turtle Kraals, Key West
Vizcaya Museum and Gardens, Miami
Weeks Air Museum, Miami
Wrecker's Museum (The Oldest House in Key West), Key West

Recreational Facilities

Florida's mild climate makes it attractive for golf, tennis, and swimming. Palm Beach County has become the golfing capital of the state. In 1988 it had 12 public golf courses and 120 private ones. In Naples, Ft. Myers, Cape Coral, Bradenton, West Palm Beach, Boca Raton, and Sarasota the ratio of golf courses to people is particularly high. Florida is also the home of a number of internationally ranked professional tennis players. Metropolitan areas with young populations such as Gainesville, Tallahassee, Panama City, and Ft. Lauderdale–Hollywood have particularly high ratios of tennis courts to population.

Public Tennis Courts, 1988

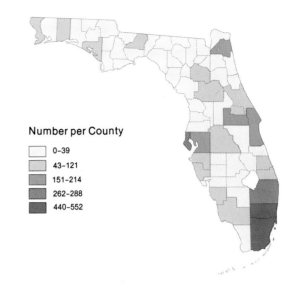

Number per County

- 0–39
- 43–121
- 151–214
- 262–288
- 440–552

Public Golf Courses, 1988

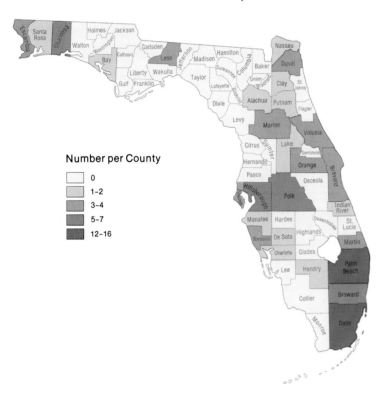

Number per County

- 0
- 1–2
- 3–4
- 5–7
- 12–16

Public Swimming Pools, 1988

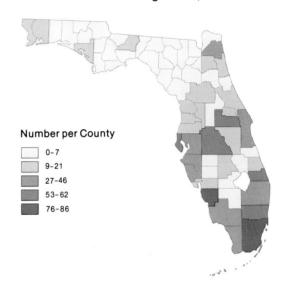

Number per County

- 0–7
- 9–21
- 27–46
- 53–62
- 76–86

Private Golf Courses, 1988

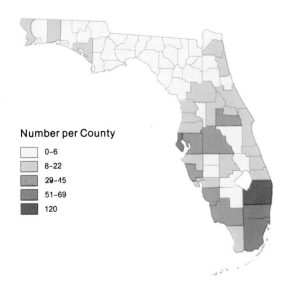

Number per County

- 0–6
- 8–22
- 29–45
- 51–69
- 120

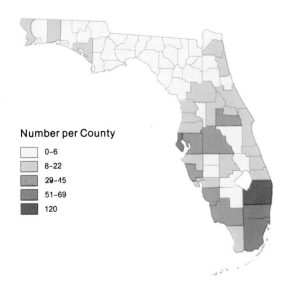

Tournament Players Club, Ponte Vedra Beach

Professional Sports

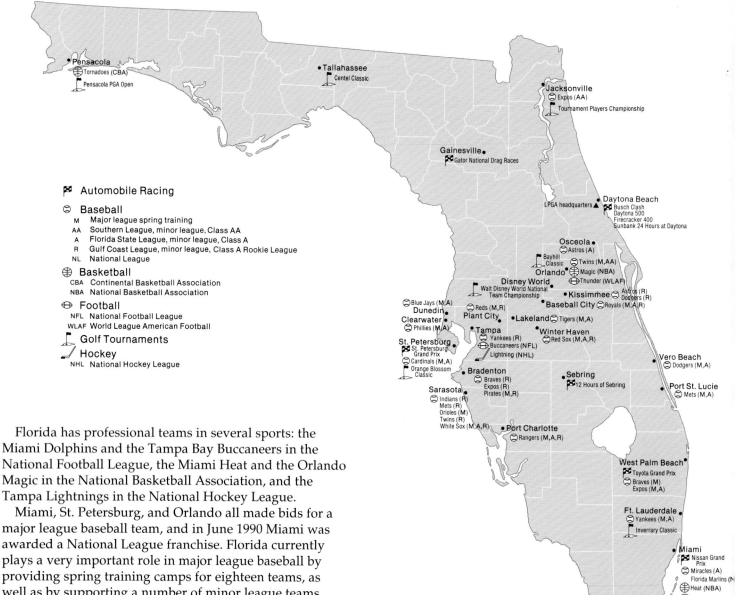

Automobile Racing

⊖ Baseball
M   Major league spring training
AA Southern League, minor league, Class AA
A   Florida State League, minor league, Class A
R   Gulf Coast League, minor league, Class A Rookie League
NL National League

⊕ Basketball
CBA Continental Basketball Association
NBA National Basketball Association

⊕ Football
NFL   National Football League
WLAF World League American Football

Golf Tournaments

Hockey
NHL National Hockey League

Florida has professional teams in several sports: the Miami Dolphins and the Tampa Bay Buccaneers in the National Football League, the Miami Heat and the Orlando Magic in the National Basketball Association, and the Tampa Lightnings in the National Hockey League.

Miami, St. Petersburg, and Orlando all made bids for a major league baseball team, and in June 1990 Miami was awarded a National League franchise. Florida currently plays a very important role in major league baseball by providing spring training camps for eighteen teams, as well as by supporting a number of minor league teams.

Several major professional golf tournaments are held in Florida, as well as several annual automobile races. The most famous automobile race is the Daytona 500, at Daytona Beach. Another famous automobile event is the endurance race held at Sebring.

BASEBALL SPRING TRAINING, N.Y. METS, St. Petersburg

DETROIT LIONS AND TAMPA BAY BUCCANEERS, November 1989, Tampa

College Sports

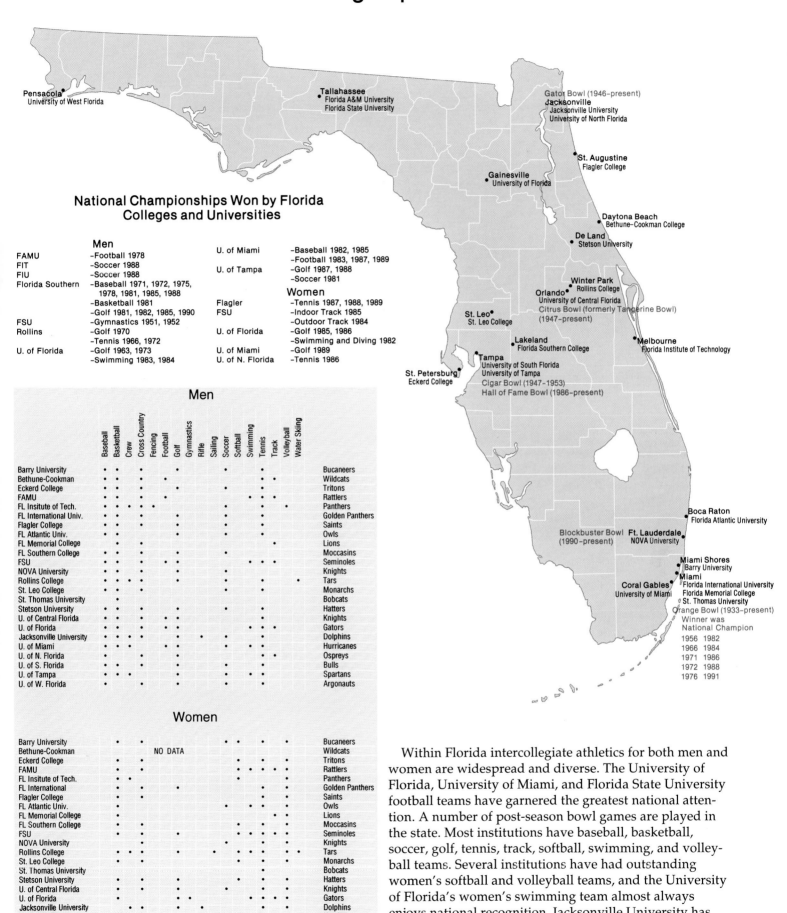

National Championships Won by Florida Colleges and Universities

Men

FAMU	–Football 1978	U. of Miami	–Baseball 1982, 1985
FIT	–Soccer 1988		–Football 1983, 1987, 1989
FIU	–Soccer 1988	U. of Tampa	–Golf 1987, 1988
Florida Southern	–Baseball 1971, 1972, 1975, 1978, 1981, 1985, 1988		–Soccer 1981
	–Basketball 1981		
	–Golf 1981, 1982, 1985, 1990		

Women

FSU	–Gymnastics 1951, 1952	Flagler	–Tennis 1987, 1988, 1989
Rollins	–Golf 1970	FSU	–Indoor Track 1985
	–Tennis 1966, 1972		–Outdoor Track 1984
U. of Florida	–Golf 1963, 1973	U. of Florida	–Golf 1985, 1986
	–Swimming 1983, 1984		–Swimming and Diving 1982
		U. of Miami	–Golf 1989
		U. of N. Florida	–Tennis 1986

Men

	Baseball	Basketball	Crew	Cross Country	Fencing	Football	Golf	Gymnastics	Rifle	Sailing	Soccer	Softball	Swimming	Tennis	Track	Volleyball	Water Skiing	
Barry University	•			•							•			•				Bucaneers
Bethune-Cookman	•	•		•		•								•	•			Wildcats
Eckerd College	•	•		•							•			•				Tritons
FAMU	•	•		•		•							•	•	•			Rattlers
FL Insitute of Tech.	•	•	•	•							•			•			•	Panthers
FL International Univ.	•	•					•				•			•				Golden Panthers
Flagler College	•	•		•			•				•			•				Saints
FL Atlantic Univ.	•	•									•			•				Owls
FL Memorial College	•			•											•			Lions
FL Southern College	•	•		•			•				•							Moccasins
FSU	•	•		•		•	•						•	•	•			Seminoles
NOVA University	•						•				•			•				Knights
Rollins College	•	•	•	•			•				•			•			•	Tars
St. Leo College	•	•		•			•				•			•				Monarchs
St. Thomas University	•										•							Bobcats
Stetson University	•	•					•				•			•				Hatters
U. of Central Florida	•	•		•		•	•				•			•				Knights
U. of Florida	•	•		•		•	•						•	•	•			Gators
Jacksonville University	•	•	•	•			•		•		•			•				Dolphins
U. of Miami	•	•		•		•	•							•	•			Hurricanes
U. of N. Florida	•	•					•				•			•	•			Ospreys
U. of S. Florida	•	•		•			•				•			•				Bulls
U. of Tampa	•	•		•							•			•				Spartans
U. of W. Florida	•			•							•			•				Argonauts

Women

	Baseball	Basketball	Crew	Cross Country	Fencing	Football	Golf	Gymnastics	Rifle	Sailing	Soccer	Softball	Swimming	Tennis	Track	Volleyball	Water Skiing	
Barry University		•		•								•		•		•		Bucaneers
Bethune-Cookman				NO DATA														Wildcats
Eckerd College		•		•								•		•		•		Tritons
FAMU		•		•								•		•	•	•		Rattlers
FL Insitute of Tech.		•	•									•		•				Panthers
FL International		•		•			•					•		•				Golden Panthers
Flagler College		•										•		•		•		Saints
FL Atlantic Univ.		•										•		•		•		Owls
FL Memorial College		•													•	•		Lions
FL Southern College		•		•								•			•	•		Moccasins
FSU		•		•								•		•	•	•		Seminoles
NOVA University		•										•		•				Knights
Rollins College		•	•	•			•					•		•		•	•	Tars
St. Leo College		•		•								•		•		•		Monarchs
St. Thomas University																		Bobcats
Stetson University		•		•								•		•		•		Hatters
U. of Central Florida		•		•			•					•		•		•		Knights
U. of Florida		•		•			•	•				•	•	•	•	•		Gators
Jacksonville University		•	•	•								•		•	•			Dolphins
U. of Miami		•	•				•							•	•			Hurricanes
U. of N. Florida		•		•								•		•				Ospreys
U. of S. Florida		•		•								•		•		•		Bulls
U. of Tampa		•	•	•										•		•		Spartans
U. of W. Florida		•		•								•		•		•		Argonauts

Within Florida intercollegiate athletics for both men and women are widespread and diverse. The University of Florida, University of Miami, and Florida State University football teams have garnered the greatest national attention. A number of post-season bowl games are played in the state. Most institutions have baseball, basketball, soccer, golf, tennis, track, softball, swimming, and volleyball teams. Several institutions have had outstanding women's softball and volleyball teams, and the University of Florida's women's swimming team almost always enjoys national recognition. Jacksonville University has men's and women's riflery teams. Rollins College has water skiing teams as well as a coeducational sailing team.

Festivals and Events

JANUARY

Annual Art Expo/Craft Show, Key West
Annual Senior Citizens Day Parade
    and Festival, Zephyrhills
Art Deco Weekend, Miami Beach
Battle of Dade, Dade Battlefield
    State Historic Site
Buskerfest, Key West
Federal Express Orange Bowl Football Classic, Miami
Festival of the Epiphany, Tarpon Springs
Florida Citrus Bowl, Orlando
Florida Citrus Festival and Polk County Fair, Winter Haven
Florida Keys Renaissance Faire, Marathon
Hall of Fame Bowl, Tampa
Homestead Frontier Days and Rodeo, Homestead
Martin Luther King Jr. Parade and Festival, Miami
Mazda Gator Bowl, Jacksonville
Pensacola Beach Snow Fest, Pensacola
Seafood Festival, Islamorada
South Florida International Wine & Food Festival, Miami Beach
Super Fine Art Festival, Bay Harbor Islands

FEBRUARY

Antique Car Parade, Palm City
Bach Festival, Winter Park
Black Hills Passion Play, Lake Wales
Edison Festival of Light, Ft. Myers
Florida Citrus Festival, Winter Haven
Florida Strawberry Festival, Plant City
Hatsume, Delray Beach
Mardi Gras Carnival, Cape Coral
Menendez Day Celebration, St. Augustine
Miami Beach Festival of the Arts, Miami Beach
Miami Film Festival, Miami
Miami International Boat Show, Miami
Nissan Grand Prix of Miami, Greater Miami
Old Island Days, Key West
Olustee Battle Festival and Civil War Re-enactment, Lake City
Seafood Festival, Grant
Silver Spurs Rodeo, Kissimmee
Sistrunk Historical Festival, Broward County
Southeast Florida Scottish Festival and Games, Miami
Speed Weeks, Daytona Beach
Swamp Buggy Races, Naples
Swamp Cabbage Festival, La Belle
Ybor City Fiesta Day & Night Parade, Ybor City

MARCH

All-Florida Championship Rodeo, Arcadia
Bike Week, Daytona Beach
Carnaval Miami/Calle Ocho Festival, Miami
Chalo Nitka Festival, Moore Haven
Conch Shell Blowing, Key West
Festival of the States, St. Petersburg
Ft. Myers Beach Shrimp Festival & Blessing of the Fleet, Ft. Myers Beach
Grand Prix Auto Race, Miami
Great American Love Affair, Boynton Beach
Italian Renaissance Festival, Miami
Kissimmee Bluegrass Festival, Kissimmee
Las Olas Art Festival, Ft. Lauderdale
Major League Baseball Spring Training
Manatee Heritage Week, Bradenton
McGuire's St. Patrick's Day Celebration, Pensacola
Medieval Fair, Sarasota
Rainbarrel Art Festival, Islamorada
Sanibel Shell Fair, Sanibel Island
Seafood Festival, Pine Island
Selby Gardens Spring Plant Fair, Sarasota
Springtime Tallahassee, Tallahassee
Suwannee River Fair and Livestock Show, Fanning Springs
Winter Equestrian Festival, Tampa
Winter Park Spring Sidewalk Art Festival, Winter Park

APRIL

Apopka Art and Foliage Festival, Apopka
Arts and Crafts Festival, Tarpon Springs
Black Gold Jubilee, Belle Glade
Bounty of the Sea Seafood Festival, Miami
Carillon Festival, Lake Wales
Celtic Art and Music Festival, Ormond Beach
Children's Art Festival, Sarasota
Cracker Festival, Ft. Myers
Dade Heritage Days, Dade County
De Soto Celebration, Bradenton
Dunedin Highland Games and Scottish Festival, Dunedin
Easter Week Festival, St. Augustine
Florida Jam, Pompano Beach
Jacksonville Film Festival, Jacksonville
Mizner Festival, Boca Raton
Pensacola Jazz Festival, Pensacola
Sand Sculpture Contest, Siesta Key Beach
Sarasota Jazz Festival, Sarasota
Seven Mile Bridge Run, Marathon
Shakespeare Festival, Orlando
St. Johns River Catfish Festival, Crescent City
William Bartram Day, Gainesville

MAY

Annual Seminole Bluegrass and Arts Festival, Seminole
Arabian Knights Festival, Miami
Blue Crab Festival, Panacea
De Soto Watermelon Festival, Arcadia
Fiesta of the Five Flags Antique Show, Pensacola
Florida Folk Festival, White Springs
Fun 'n Sun Festival, Clearwater
Hispanic Theatre Festival, Coral Gables
Isle of Eight Flags Shrimp Festival, Fernandina Beach
Old Time Havana Day, Havana
Orlando Film Festival, Orlando
Ringling Museum's Outdoor Art Carnival, Sarasota
Riverwalk Arts and Crafts Festival, Jacksonville
Sailfish Power Boat Championship, Stuart
SpringFest, Pensacola
SunFest, West Palm Beach
Sunshine-Jr. Gulf Coast Triathlon, Panama City
Sweet Corn Festival, Zellwood
Wine Fest, Sarasota
Zucchini Festival, Windsor

JUNE

Bahamas Goombay Festival, Coconut Grove
Billy Bowlegs Festival, Ft. Walton Beach
Boat-A-Cade, Kissimmee
Cross and Sword, St. Augustine
Downtown Gainesville Blueberry Bash, Gainesville
Hialeah Music Festival, Hialeah
New College Summer Music Festival, Sarasota
Panhandle Watermelon Festival, Chipley
Sarasota Music Festival, Sarasota
Sea Turtle Watch, Jensen Beach
Spanish Night Watch, St. Augustine
Summer Fest, Pompano Beach
Water Skiing Championships, Cypress Gardens
Watermelon Festival, Monticello
World's Largest Indoor Flea Market, Miami Beach

JULY

Big Bang, Pensacola
Everglades International Music and Crafts Festival, Miami
Florida's Sunshine State Games, Jacksonville
Fourth on Flagler, West Palm Beach
Hemingway Days Festival, Key West
Invitational Billfish Tournament, Panama City
Pirate Days Celebration, Treasure Island
Pops on the Bay, Key Biscayne
Shark Tournament, Naples
Speed Week, Daytona Beach
Tropical Agri Fiesta, Boca Raton

AUGUST

Boca Festival Days, Boca Raton
Dancin' in the Streets, Stuart
Days in Spain Fiesta, St. Augustine
German Beerfest, Cape Coral
Great Grunt Fishing Tournament, Islamorada
National Night-Out, Hallandale
Shark Tournament, Marco Island
Wausau Fun Day and Possum Festival, Wausau

SEPTEMBER

Beachfest, St. Petersburg Beach
Florida Native American Heritage Festival, Tallahassee
Founding of St. Augustine, St. Augustine
Great American Raft Race, Port St. Lucie
Hispanic Cultural Arts Festival and Fair, West Palm Beach
Huck Finn Day, Palm Beach County
Oktoberfest, Orlando
Osceola Art Festival, Kissimmee
Pensacola Beach Seafood Festival, Pensacola
Pioneer Florida Day, Dade County
Rivertown Festival, Deland
Sarasota Sailing Squadron Labor Day Regatta, Sarasota
Tampa's Jazzin' Jubilee, Tampa

OCTOBER

Ameliafest, Fernandina Beach
Banka-No-Hi Festival, Delray Beach
Boggy Bayou Mullet Festival, Valparaiso
Country Jubilee, Largo
Fantasy Fest, Key West
Florida Forest Festival, Perry
Florida State Chili Cookoff Championship, Naples
Great Chowder Debate, St. Augustine
Greater Jacksonville Agricultural Fair, Jacksonville
Greek Festival, Pensacola
Guavaween Extravaganza, Tampa
Hispanic Heritage Festival, Dade County
Hollywood Jazz Festival, Hollywood
Indian Summer Seafood Festival, Panama City Beach
Italian Street Festival, Orlando
Jeannie Auditions and Ball, White Springs
McGuire's Irish Billfish Tourney, Pensacola
National Jazz Festival, Jacksonville
Ocala Week, Ocala
Oktoberfest, Lake Worth
Pioneer Days Folk Festival, Orlando
Quincyfest, Quincy
Rattlesnake Festival, San Antonio
Sanibel Jazz on the Green, Sanibel Island
Southland Regatta, St. Petersburg
St. Anne's Autumn Round-Up, Pensacola
Swamp Buggy Races, Naples
Venetian Sun Fiesta, Venice
West Indian American Miami Carnival, Miami

NOVEMBER

"Harvest" and "Traditions," Miami
Blue Angels Air Show, Pensacola
Children's Day, Key West
Eustis International Folk Festival, Eustis
Florida Seafood Festival, Apalachicola
Florida State Air Fair, Kissimmee
Florida's Withlacoochee River Bluegrass Jamboree, Dunnellon
Ft. Lauderdale Film Festival, Ft. Lauderdale
Great Gulf Coast Arts Festival, Pensacola
Jensen Beach Pineapple Festival, Jensen Beach
Miami Book Fair International, Miami
Pioneer Days, Orlando
Rural Folklife Days, White Springs
Sarasota French Film Festival, Sarasota
Space Coast Art Festival, Cocoa Beach
Sportsfest, South Walton
Sunshine State Rodeo, Davie
Sunstreet Festival, Liberty City
World's Chicken Pluckin' Championship, Spring Hill

DECEMBER

Asiafest, Miami
Bok Tower Gardens Christmas Eve Recital, Lake Wales
British Night Watch, St. Augustine
Candlelight Processional, Walt Disney World
Christmas in Lantana, Lantana
Edison Home Holiday House, Ft. Myers
Festival of the Continents, Key West
Florida Tournament of Bands, St. Petersburg
Junior Orange Bowl Festival, Coral Gables
Kwanza, African Thanksgiving Celebration, Liberty City
Miccosukee Indian Arts Festival, Miccosukee Indian Village, Miami
Orange Bowl Festival, Miami
St. Johns River Boat Parade, Deland
Winter Fantasy on the Waterway, Boca Raton
Winterfest and Boat Parade, Ft. Lauderdale

BALLOON RALLY, Springtime Tallahassee, March

MEDIEVAL FAIR, Sarasota, March

BAHAMAS GOOMBAY FESTIVAL, Coconut Grove, June

Wagering

In 1988 the Florida Lottery sold its first ticket and became an instant success. It quickly gained great popularity, and today is one of the nation's most successful lotteries. There are four different games, Instant, Cash 3, Lotto, and Fantasy 5. Lotto, which offers the opportunity for the largest prize, is by far the most popular, producing nearly half of total sales. Lotto's share of total lottery sales varies by county. Usually Lotto is less popular in counties where the average income is low than in wealthier counties. Notable exceptions to this pattern are poor rural counties bordering Alabama and Georgia. People come to these counties in large numbers from neighboring states to buy Lotto tickets. In September 1990 the Florida Lottery had total sales of 301 million dollars, the result of a Lotto prize that had mounted to 106.5 million dollars. The prize was won that month and split among six people. The largest Lotto prize earned by one person was 52 million dollars. In early 1991 a bill to create a Georgia lottery was being discussed. The opening of a Georgia lottery would have a significant impact on Florida Lottery sales.

Florida has many pari-mutuel facilities throughout the state. Betting at these facilities, particularly Jai-Alai and Greyhound racing, has decreased as a result of the Florida Lottery. Thoroughbred racing in south Florida is held at Miami's new Calder Race Course, which has 136 race days each year; at Gulfstream Park in Hallandale, which has 90 days; and at Tropical Park, which has a season of 49 days. Hialeah, Florida's oldest track, had its last race day in December 1989. In 1991 it was still unclear whether racing would resume there. Tampa Bay Downs, a thoroughbred track, provides the Tampa Bay area with racing 90 days

each year. Pompano Beach has a harness track with 150 race days.

The Seminole Indians own and operate two high-stake bingo facilities on reservation land in Tampa and Hollywood. More recently the Miccosukee Indians have opened a facility on reservation land west of Miami. All these facilities are open year-round.

Pari-Mutuel Facilities

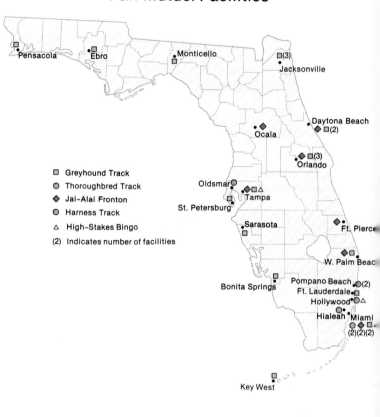

Lottery Ticket Sales, 1990

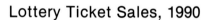
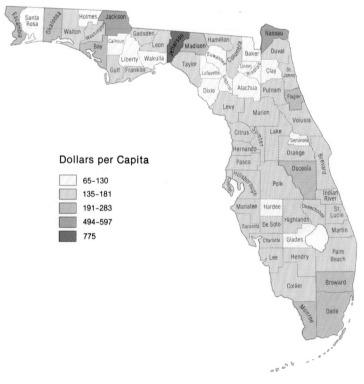

Dollars per Capita

- 65–130
- 135–181
- 191–283
- 494–597
- 775

Lottery Sales by Month

Restaurant Sales

The Florida tourist industry has always endeavored to attract visitors year-round. Before World War II this was very difficult without air conditioning. Many hotels simply closed in May and reopened in November. After World War II, but especially since the opening of Walt Disney World and other theme parks nearby, the difference between high and low seasons has diminished.

Restaurant sales are one measure of the difference between the peak and low tourist seasons. Spring is typically the high season throughout the peninsula, and summer the high season along the coast of northwestern Florida. The latter area, colloquially known as the "Red Neck Riviera," draws many summer visitors from Alabama and Georgia. A distinct fall peak occurs only in Leon County, coinciding with the Florida A & M and Florida State universities' football schedules. The difference between the peak and low season is greatest in southwestern Florida and along the northwestern Florida coast, with fall being the season of lowest restaurant sales in both areas.

When restaurant sales are measured as a percentage grocery sales, the percentage is especially high in southwestern Florida and in the Orlando area. Though not a perfect index, it does give some indication of the degree of importance tourism has to these areas. Restaurant sales as a percentage of grocery sales are also particularly high in Alachua (Gainesville) and Leon (Tallahassee) counties because of large student populations.

Peak Restaurant Sales, 1989

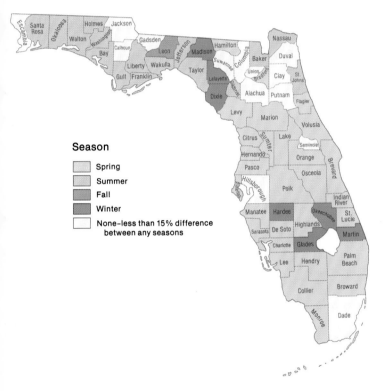

Lowest Restaurant Sales, 1989

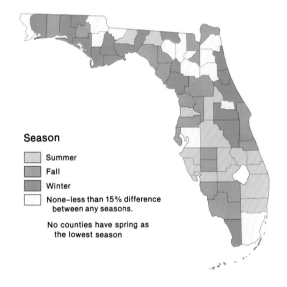

Difference between Peak and Lowest Season, 1989

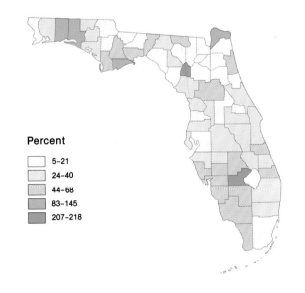

Restaurant Sales, 1989

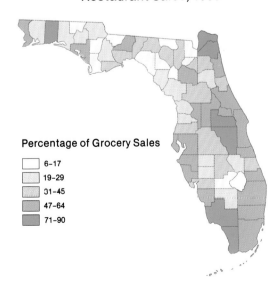

Visitor Accommodations

Hotel and Motel Rooms, 1989

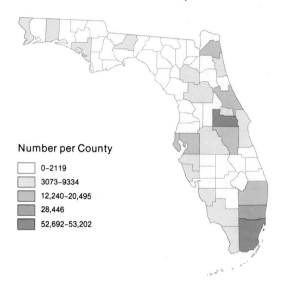

Number per County
- 0–2119
- 3073–9334
- 12,240–20,495
- 28,446
- 52,692–53,202

Hotel and Motel Rooms, 1989

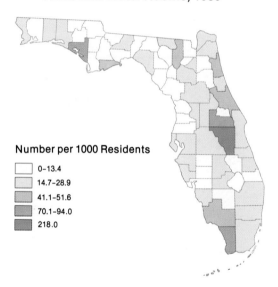

Number per 1000 Residents
- 0–13.4
- 14.7–28.9
- 41.1–51.6
- 70.1–94.0
- 218.0

Room Occupancy Rate, 1989

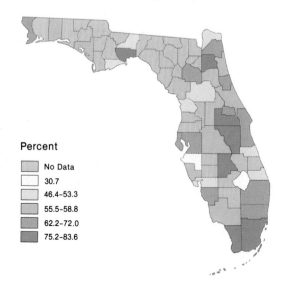

Percent
- No Data
- 30.7
- 46.4–53.3
- 55.5–58.8
- 62.2–72.0
- 75.2–83.6

Today hotels and motels are found throughout Florida. Early in this century hotels were concentrated in a few places, particularly along the Atlantic coast and the Tampa Bay region, that had railroad connections with the rest of the nation. With the building of roads, hotel and motel accommodations became more widely distributed. Since 1971, with the opening of Walt Disney World and other theme parks nearby, as well as the construction of the interstate highway system, the distribution of hotels and motels is once again more uneven. The Orlando area vies with Las Vegas, Nevada, as the metropolitan area with the most hotel and motel rooms. Considerable hotel and motel construction has also occurred in southwestern Florida, especially Naples and Marco Island.

For Florida as a whole, occupancy rates vary by the season. In the winter they are highest, and each season thereafter they fall. First quarter occupancy rates during the 1980s have varied greatly. In 1984 and 1985 they were especially low, in part due to cold weather on the southern peninsula, but also because of national business conditions.

Quarterly Occupancy Rate 1980–1990 Average

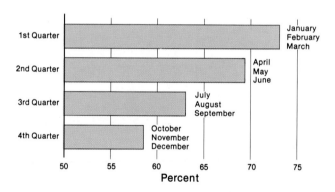

First Quarter Occupancy Rate, 1980–1990

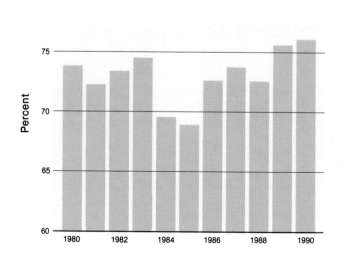

Origin of Visitors

Approximately 40 million visitors arrive in Florida each year. The number of visitors doubled during the 1980s. During the winter and fall the numbers of visitors who arrive by auto and air are about equal, but during the spring and especially in the summer automobile visitors dominate. Many parents drive to the state with their children during the summer and in the late spring. Vacation ranks high among the reasons for tourists coming to Florida especially those who arrive by car. Staying with friends and relatives also figures high as a motive for a visit.

Florida in recent years has become a magnet for visitors from abroad. For years most foreign visitors were Canadian. Throughout the 1980s, however, especially when the value of the dollar against foreign currency was low, hundreds of thousands of tourists flew from Europe to Florida. Between 1987 and 1989 the number of European tourists, predominantly from Britain and Germany, doubled to almost 1.5 million. Most foreign visitors travel on package tours, which include airfare, hotel rooms, and often the use of a rental car for a week. Many spend at least a week in the Orlando area. Previously a much larger percentage of international visitors to the state were from Latin America. The weakened economy of Latin American nations during the 1980s greatly reduced the rate of growth of visitors from the region.

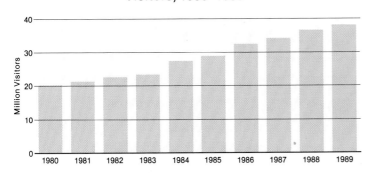
Visitors, 1980–1989

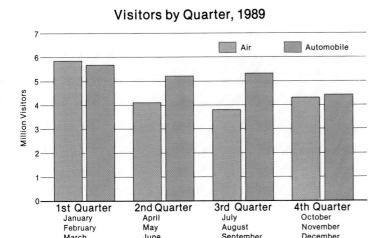
Visitors by Quarter, 1989

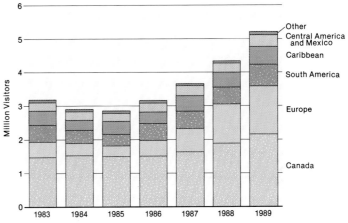
International Visitors, 1983–1989

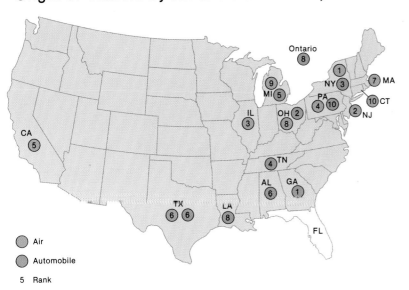
Origin of Visitors by Air and Automobile, 1989

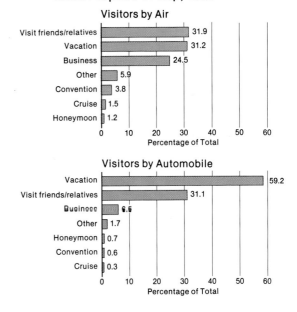
Main Purpose of Trip, 1989

Visitor Destinations

With the completion in 1971 of Walt Disney World's Magic Kingdom, the most popular destination of visitors to the state shifted from south Florida to central Florida. There is little variation in the pattern of visitor destinations throughout the year, although the northwest Florida coast draws many visitors from other southern states during the summer. People who visit Florida tend to stay longer during the winter than the summer. In most seasons visitors who come by automobile typically stay longer than those who arrive by air.

Top Ten Attractions, 1989

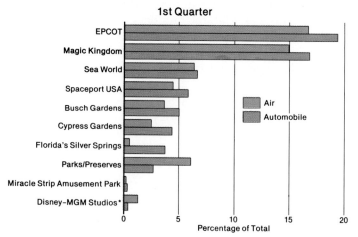

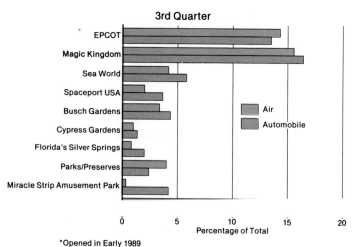

*Opened in Early 1989

Length of Visit, 1989

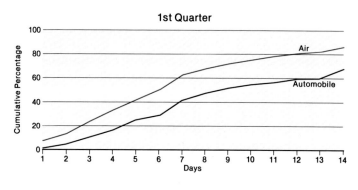

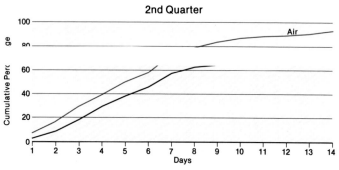

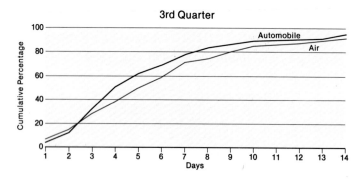

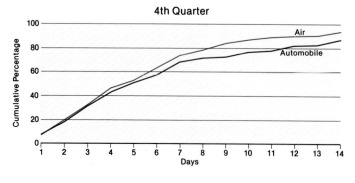

Top Ten Destinations of Visitors Surveyed 1989

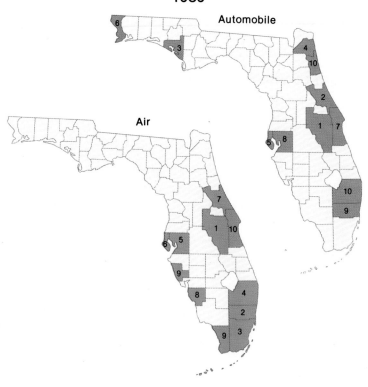

Tourism is big business to Florida and has been for many years. In 1990 around 40 million people visited the state, more than double the number of tourists for 1980. Approximately 10 percent of all purchases in the state are made by visitors. Most visitors are from east of the Mississippi River, but a growing percentage arrive from Europe.

Central Florida, with its theme parks, is today the principal destination of the majority of visitors. In most parts of the state winter is the major tourist season, although seasonal differences in numbers of tourists have diminished substantially in the past thirty years. Visitors who arrive by air constitute a far higher share of the total in southern Florida than in the northern part of the state.

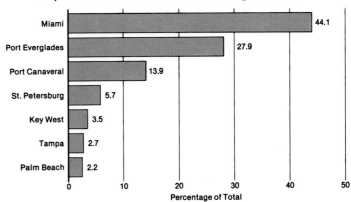

Departure Point of Cruise Passengers, 1989

Departure Point	Percentage of Total
Miami	44.1
Port Everglades	27.9
Port Canaveral	13.9
St. Petersburg	5.7
Key West	3.5
Tampa	2.7
Palm Beach	2.2

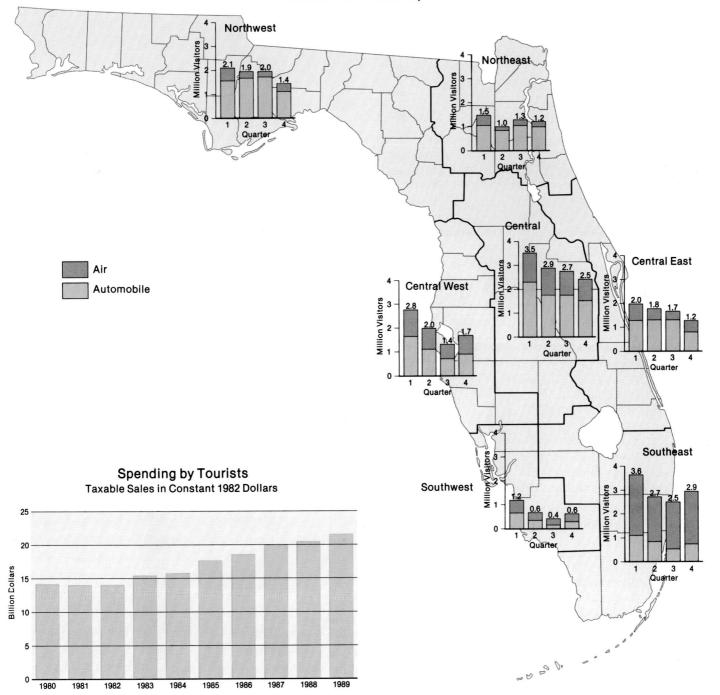

Number of Visitors, 1989

Air
Automobile

Spending by Tourists
Taxable Sales in Constant 1982 Dollars

MIAMI LINE, Rockne Krebs

INFRASTRUCTURE AND PLANNING

This section describes some of the state's growth problems and how citizens can be involved in solutions to these problems. Rapid population growth is at the root of many of Florida's infrastructure and planning problems. Each day, Florida grows by more than 700 new residents. This steady growth onslaught exceeds that of most states, and uniquely challenges citizens and businesses alike.

Florida's growth can also improve the state's economic health and well-being, if it is well planned and managed. The consequences of not doing so are evident in many forms. The state's continuing infrastructure problems are visible reminders to citizens concerned about their quality of life. In 1987, a legislative advisory committee concluded it would take roughly $53 billion to implement a state comprehensive plan adopted in 1985 by the Florida legislature, largely to pay for state and local infrastructure costs. Nearly half of the state's $35.9 billion share was for transportation needs alone.

Decades of rapid population growth have taken a toll on Florida's environment. Fifty-five percent of Florida's original wetlands have been lost to drainage and filling. One-third of the state's upland forests have been converted to agricultural and urban uses. Approximately 730 billion gallons of treated domestic and industrial wastewater are discharged annually into the state's surface waters and onto upland areas. Few problems are more serious than the need to protect Florida's water resources, the state's environmental lifeline to the future. Wise land use planning is closely tied with sound water management practices. State and local planning and growth management processes offer Florida's citizens real opportunities to address these and other aspects of their quality of life.

Population Growth

Florida is a growth state. This stark single fact characterizes much of the state's history, and helps explain many of the state's current dilemmas as well as some of its good fortunes. The state's population almost doubled between 1970 and 1990, eclipsing 10 million people in 1984 and reaching almost 13 million by 1990. Florida is projected to be home to over 15.5 million permanent residents as the twenty-first century dawns.

The state's annual population also includes as many as 40 million tourists. There are economic and social trade-offs for residents living in tourist areas, such as increased traffic on highways and larger crowds in shopping areas. Tourists also mean jobs and economic benefits to many local businesses, retail outlets, and the services industry, and tax revenues for government. Local officials must plan for greater capacities of water and sewer systems, local roads, and other public facilities and services that visitors expect. Like new residents, tourists do not bring those things with them. Counties and municipalities must plan locally for these peak seasonal demands.

Infrastructure

Infrastructure describes the major physical facilities that provide safety and convenience within communities, regions, and the state as a whole. Infrastructure is commonly associated with governmental institutions, since they chiefly provide and maintain infrastructure facilities. When it comes to planning, infrastructure means many things such as interstate highways, state and local roads, water and sewer facilities, stormwater runoff systems, solid waste disposal facilities, police and fire stations, schools, and libraries. Furthermore, citizens who value their quality of life want good roads and schools and other infrastructure items. Federal and state laws also demand minimum quality standards in building and operating public facilities such as water and sewer systems.

Adequate infrastructure is something most citizens take for granted. State and local officials who fail to address problems of congested roads, polluted lakes and rivers, flooding and drainage problems, and crowded schools often face unpopular political consequences. But providing adequate infrastructure can carry a big price tag. Further, providing it when it is needed for new development, as opposed to postponing these costs until later, creates enormous problems for fast-growing states like Florida. Past arguments that growth in Florida pays for itself were short-sighted at best, and fiscally foolish by current measures. Local officials can charge impact fees that pay some costs of new growth. By law, however, local impact fees provide no relief from infrastructure backlogs. The state faces similar problems in providing new state highways, prisons, universities, and other state facilities. A balanced state and local tax structure capable of raising adequate revenues to meet enormous state and local infrastructure needs remains one of Florida's biggest challenges.

Planning and Growth Management

In 1971, rapid population growth in south Florida collided with the state's worst drought then on record, forcing state and local leaders to confront growth and development problems. Since that time, Florida's citizenry and its leaders have addressed these issues through better state and local planning, environmental protection programs, sounder land and water management practices, acquisition of environmentally sensitive areas, and closer attention to infrastructure planning and budgeting.

Florida has become not so much a planned state as it has become a planning state, through its governmental and business leaders as well as its citizens. Florida leads the nation with state laws that call for better comprehensive planning and growth management. Environmental and infrastructure planning is a hallmark of the state's growth management system, whereby state policies guide efforts in every region as well as in every municipality and county

to plan for orderly future growth and development. In 1985 the legislature adopted a State Comprehensive Plan containing 26 general goals to help guide future growth through the end of this century. State growth policies address major questions of how to deal with urban sprawl, continued growth in sensitive coastal areas, better land and water management practices, energy conservation and efficiency measures, encouraging public transit systems, and providing affordable housing. These are carried out in large measure through regional and local comprehensive plans. All 457 of Florida's local governments have adopted comprehensive plans to help guide future growth and development in their communities, consistent with state and regional comprehensive plans.

Counties and municipalities may allow future development only when there are plans for adequate roads and bridges, water and sewage facilities, and other key infrastructure items. New growth must pay its own way under this concurrency approach. At the same time, state and local leaders are being asked to pay the bills due on unmet infrastructure needs postponed from years past.

State laws and programs governing growth and the environment address many past environmental errors and misjudgments. They require reducing the number of landfills, cleaning up toxic waste sites and underground petroleum spills, acquiring more land for environmental preservation and conservation purposes, and restoring important wetland and upland habitats. They also mandate improved water quality and restoration of many of the state's important surface waters such as Tampa and Biscayne bays, Lake Okeechobee and Lake Apopka, and the Indian River lagoon. New environmental restoration objectives also include redressing environmental damage caused by channeling and straightening the Kissimmee River, restoring the partially built Cross Florida Barge Canal into a coast–to–coast greenway, and restoring the Florida Everglades to resemble its original grandeur.

The state's environmental assets constitute a vital economic resource. Florida's sandy beaches and coastal waters, its woods and its wetlands, its natural bird and wildlife habitats, its clean rivers and lakes, its recreational fishing opportunities, and its other environmental treasures are irreplaceably linked to the state's continued economic health. These environmental assets are not easily measured in the millions and billions of dollars that they represent. They are nonetheless very real in economic and natural terms. Similar to the state's infrastructure, they can be thought of as the state's ecostructure that must be protected, nurtured, sustained, and enhanced. At times in the state's history the price of progress was often at the expense of the natural environment. Florida's land and water management policies now reflect new attitudes among the state's citizens and their elected representatives about how Florida should grow.

Population and economic growth will continue to shape Florida well into the twenty first century. State and local leaders must continue to explore new ways of providing an adequate quality of life for its citizens, while continuing to protect the natural environment. Providing infrastructure while guarding and protecting the state's ecostructure remain vital ingredients in Florida's future.

Traffic Volume

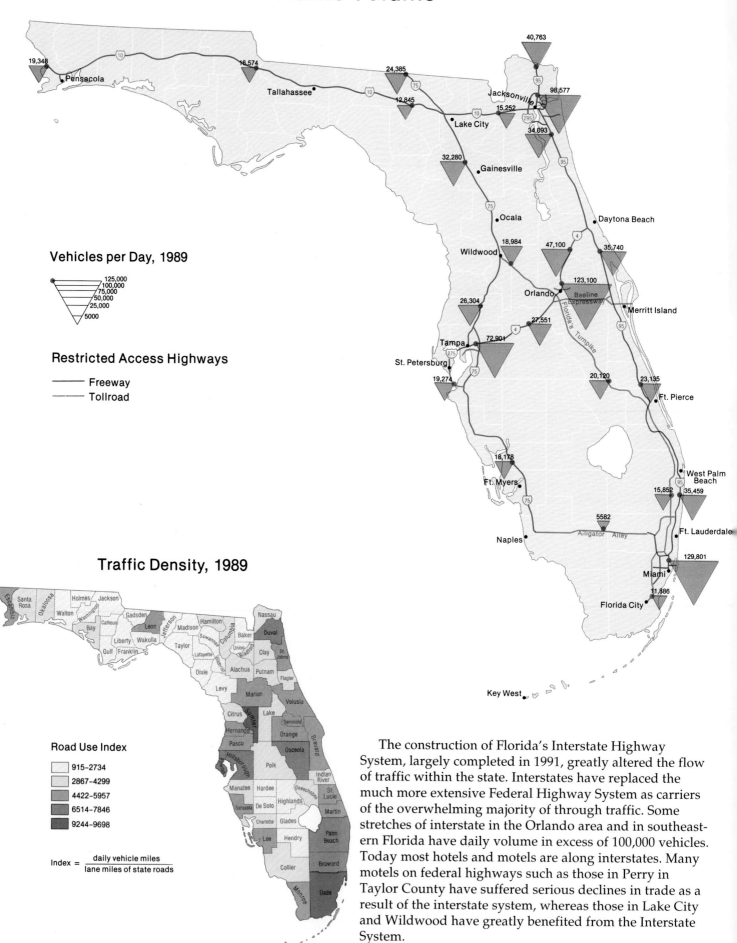

Vehicles per Day, 1989

125,000
100,000
75,000
50,000
25,000
5000

Restricted Access Highways

——— Freeway
········· Tollroad

Traffic Density, 1989

Road Use Index

915–2734
2867–4299
4422–5957
6514–7846
9244–9698

$$\text{Index} = \frac{\text{daily vehicle miles}}{\text{lane miles of state roads}}$$

The construction of Florida's Interstate Highway System, largely completed in 1991, greatly altered the flow of traffic within the state. Interstates have replaced the much more extensive Federal Highway System as carriers of the overwhelming majority of through traffic. Some stretches of interstate in the Orlando area and in southeastern Florida have daily volume in excess of 100,000 vehicles. Today most hotels and motels are along interstates. Many motels on federal highways such as those in Perry in Taylor County have suffered serious declines in trade as a result of the interstate system, whereas those in Lake City and Wildwood have greatly benefited from the Interstate System.

Travel Time and Distance

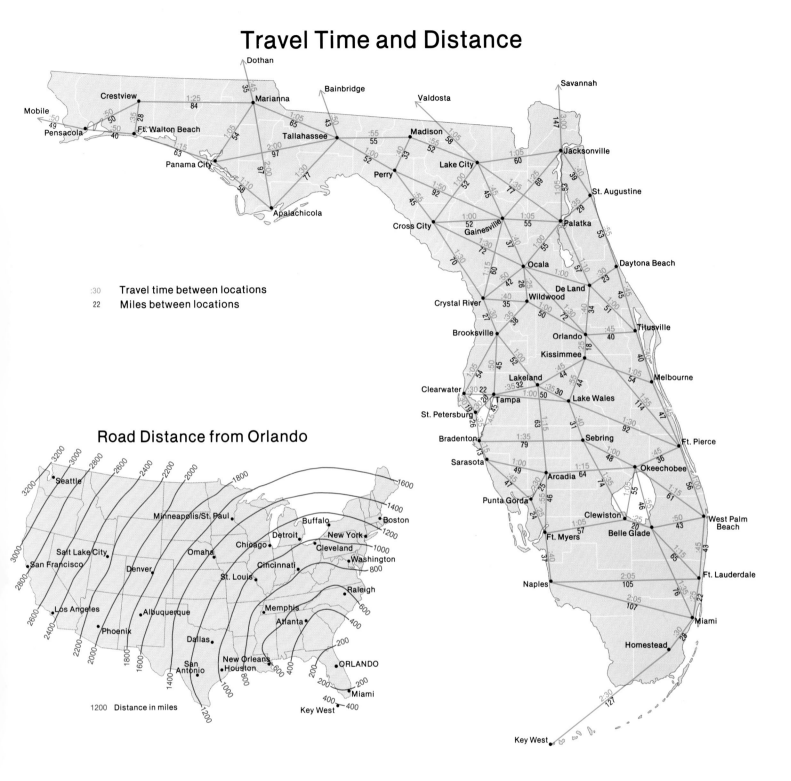

:30   Travel time between locations
22   Miles between locations

Road Distance from Orlando

1200   Distance in miles

Approximately half (53 percent) of all tourists arrive in Florida by automobile. The vast majority of the state's visitors live within 1,200 miles of Orlando. The Great Plains states are a "divide" separating visitors who tend to go to Florida from those who head toward the Southwest or California.

Few who visit Florida realize just how long it is. Pensacola is only slightly less distant from Key West than it is from Chicago, and Key West is 161 miles from Miami. Fortunately, as roads have improved the time taken to drive from one place to another has greatly diminished. In 1950 to drive from Jacksonville to Miami, a distance of 368 miles, was a long day's drive. Today, even with the conges-

tion on I-95 south of West Palm Beach, the drive is normally under seven hours.

Both mileage and travel time between principal Florida cities are shown on the Florida map. Travel time was calculated on the basis of an average speed of 55 miles per hour, taking into consideration periodic stops. Other factors to be considered in the time-distance ratio for highway travel are weather conditions, amount of limited access highway to be used, and possibility of encountering heavy traffic. Highways, even those of limited access, in certain areas such as between Miami and West Palm Beach, Orlando, and Tampa Bay all experience enormous congestion during the day.

Road Mileage and Vehicle Registration

In Florida the relationship between road mileage and population is perhaps more balanced today than in the past when some powerful north Florida legislators were accused of spending more for roads in their districts than their populations warranted. Traffic congestion is greatest in southeastern Florida and in the Tampa Bay area. A number of rural counties particularly in the north still have high percentages of unpaved roads.

Besides personalized plates, Florida issues a number of specialty plates. Each of the state universities has its own plate. Currently the most popular specialty plate com-

memorates the space shuttle *Challenger* tragedy. Sales of a more recently issued one in defense of the manatee, however, are growing much faster than sales of Challenger plates.

Specialty Licences, 1990

Type	Date Enacted	Cumulative Issued	Additional Fee
Challenger	1987	420,968	$15
Manatee	1987	84,783	$15
U. of Florida	1987	43,034	$25
Florida State U.	1987	37,992	$25
Disabled Veterans	1951	25,866	$0
Super Bowl	1987	17,556	$15
U. of Miami	1987	12,627	$25
Florida Salutes Veterans	1987	12,396	$15
Horseless Carriage	1957	9,843	$0
Amateur Radio	1949	8,036	$5
Florida A&M	1987	6,059	$25
U. of Central Florida	1987	5,016	$25
Regular Wheel Chair	1974	5,006	$0
Ex-POWs	1983	3,665	$0
Florida Panther	1990	3,427	$25
U. of South Florida	1987	3,374	$25
National Guard	1965	3,171	$0
U.S. Reserve	1983	2,302	$0
U. of West Florida	1987	1,842	$25
Florida Atlantic U.	1987	1,415	$25
Front End Plate	1984	1,068	$5
U. of North Florida	1987	1,064	$25
Pearl Harbor Survivor	1983	1,005	$0
Disabled Vets Wheel Chair	1972	644	$0
Seminole/Miccosukee Indians	1971	546	$0
Street Rod	1983	509	$0
Honorary Consular Corps	1989	269	$0
Paralyzed Vets of America	1987	156	$0
Medal of Honor	1985	23	$0

Road Mileage, 1990

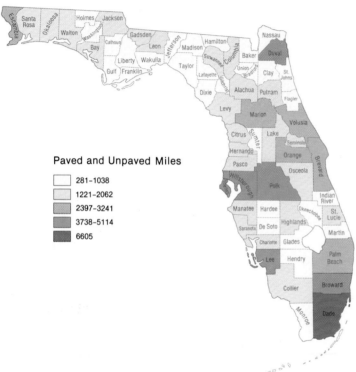

Paved and Unpaved Miles
- 281–1038
- 1221–2062
- 2397–3241
- 3738–5114
- 6605

Unpaved Road Mileage, 1990

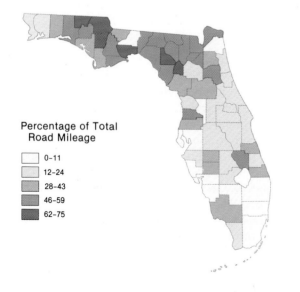

Percentage of Total Road Mileage
- 0–11
- 12–24
- 28–43
- 46–59
- 62–75

Registered Vehicles, 1990

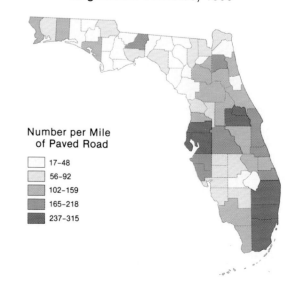

Number per Mile of Paved Road
- 17–48
- 56–92
- 102–159
- 165–218
- 237–315

Traffic Accidents and Insurance

Traffic Accidents, 1988

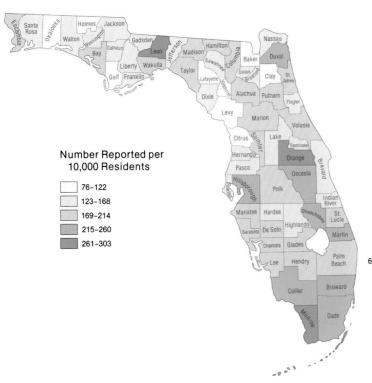

Number Reported per
10,000 Residents

	76–122
	123–168
	169–214
	215–260
	261–303

Alcohol- and Drug-Related Accidents, 1988

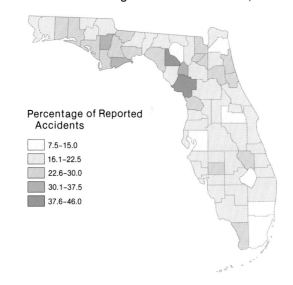

Percentage of Reported
Accidents

	7.5–15.0
	15.1–22.5
	22.6–30.0
	30.1–37.5
	37.6–46.0

Traffic Accidents, by Time of Day, 1989

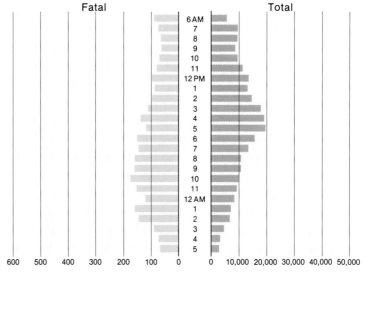

Traffic Accidents, by Day of Week, 1989

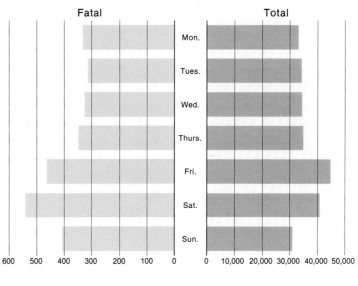

Traffic Accidents, by Month, 1989

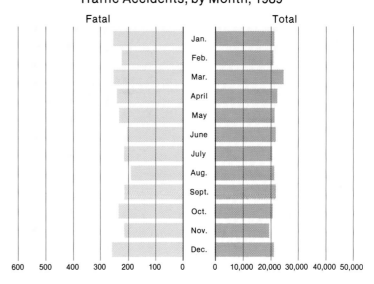

Selected Insurance Rates, 1991

City	Liability	UM	Comp.	Collision	Total
Daytona Beach	137.77	16.10	29.67	84.64	268.18
Ft. Lauderdale	176.41	39.80	57.04	120.98	394.23
Gainesville	98.67	16.10	31.74	78.66	225.17
Jacksonville	108.45	15.00	39.10	107.06	269.61
Key West	110.17	16.10	30.82	101.43	258.52
Miami	187.91	58.10	94.30	147.66	487.97
Miami Beach	244.03	58.10	86.02	169.28	557.43
Orlando	111.32	16.10	29.21	100.51	257.14
Panama City	84.41	15.00	32.89	84.64	216.94
Pensacola	106.72	15.00	37.95	103.50	263.17
Sarasota	91.77	16.10	24.61	82.11	214.59
Tallahassee	86.25	15.00	30.36	101.43	233.04
Tampa	148.58	22.50	43.01	116.61	330.70

Note: Rates are in dollars and for six months. UM is uninsured motorist coverage.
Rates are based on a 1991 Chevrolet Lumina.

Commercial Transit

Trucks carry the greatest volume of commercial goods within Florida. Volume of truck traffic is greatest in counties with large cities and those traversed by I-75. Greyhound provides the only intercity bus passenger service within Florida and to points outside the state. Rail passenger service in Florida is greatly reduced from 40 years ago. AMTRAK continues to provide service to Miami and Tampa, with stops in-between. Tri-Rail, a commuter line linking West Palm Beach with Miami's public transportation system, has ridership approaching 7,000 daily. Freight, principally phosphates, chemicals, and coal, continues to be carried by railroads.

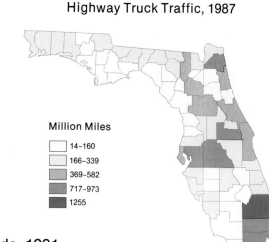

Highway Truck Traffic, 1987

Million Miles
- 14–160
- 166–339
- 369–582
- 717–973
- 1255

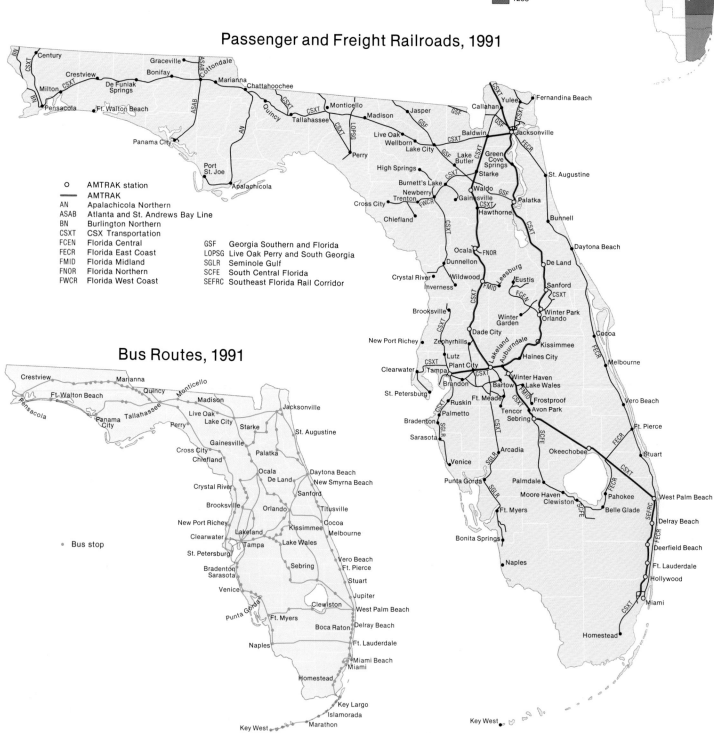

Passenger and Freight Railroads, 1991

- o   AMTRAK station
- —   AMTRAK
- AN   Apalachicola Northern
- ASAB   Atlanta and St. Andrews Bay Line
- BN   Burlington Northern
- CSXT   CSX Transportation
- FCEN   Florida Central
- FECR   Florida East Coast
- FMID   Florida Midland
- FNOR   Florida Northern
- FWCR   Florida West Coast
- GSF   Georgia Southern and Florida
- LOPSG   Live Oak Perry and South Georgia
- SGLR   Seminole Gulf
- SCFE   South Central Florida
- SEFRC   Southeast Florida Rail Corridor

Bus Routes, 1991

- • Bus stop

Ports and Waterways

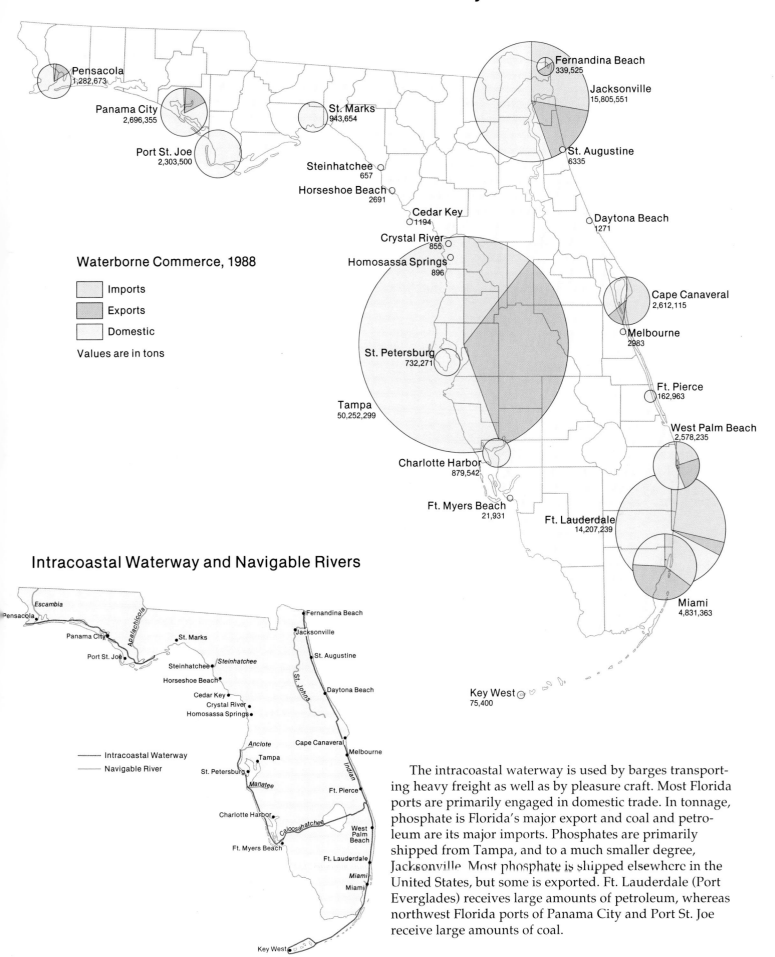

Waterborne Commerce, 1988

Imports

Exports

Domestic

Values are in tons

Pensacola
1,282,673

Panama City
2,696,355

Port St. Joe
2,303,500

St. Marks
943,654

Fernandina Beach
339,525

Jacksonville
15,805,551

St. Augustine
6335

Steinhatchee
657

Horseshoe Beach
2691

Cedar Key
1194

Daytona Beach
1271

Crystal River
855

Homosassa Springs
896

Cape Canaveral
2,612,115

Melbourne
2983

St. Petersburg
732,271

Ft. Pierce
162,963

Tampa
50,252,299

West Palm Beach
2,578,235

Charlotte Harbor
879,542

Ft. Myers Beach
21,931

Ft. Lauderdale
14,207,239

Miami
4,831,363

Key West
75,400

Intracoastal Waterway and Navigable Rivers

Escambia

Pensacola

Panama City

Port St. Joe

Apalachicola

St. Marks

Steinhatchee

Steinhatchee

Horseshoe Beach

Cedar Key

Crystal River

Homosassa Springs

Fernandina Beach

Jacksonville

St. Augustine

St. Johns

Daytona Beach

Anclote

Tampa

Cape Canaveral

Melbourne

Indian

St. Petersburg

Manatee

Ft. Pierce

Charlotte Harbor

Caloosahatchee

West Palm Beach

Ft. Myers Beach

Ft. Lauderdale

Miami

Miami

Key West

Intracoastal Waterway

Navigable River

The intracoastal waterway is used by barges transporting heavy freight as well as by pleasure craft. Most Florida ports are primarily engaged in domestic trade. In tonnage, phosphate is Florida's major export and coal and petroleum are its major imports. Phosphates are primarily shipped from Tampa, and to a much smaller degree, Jacksonville. Most phosphate is shipped elsewhere in the United States, but some is exported. Ft. Lauderdale (Port Everglades) receives large amounts of petroleum, whereas northwest Florida ports of Panama City and Port St. Joe receive large amounts of coal.

Airline Passengers

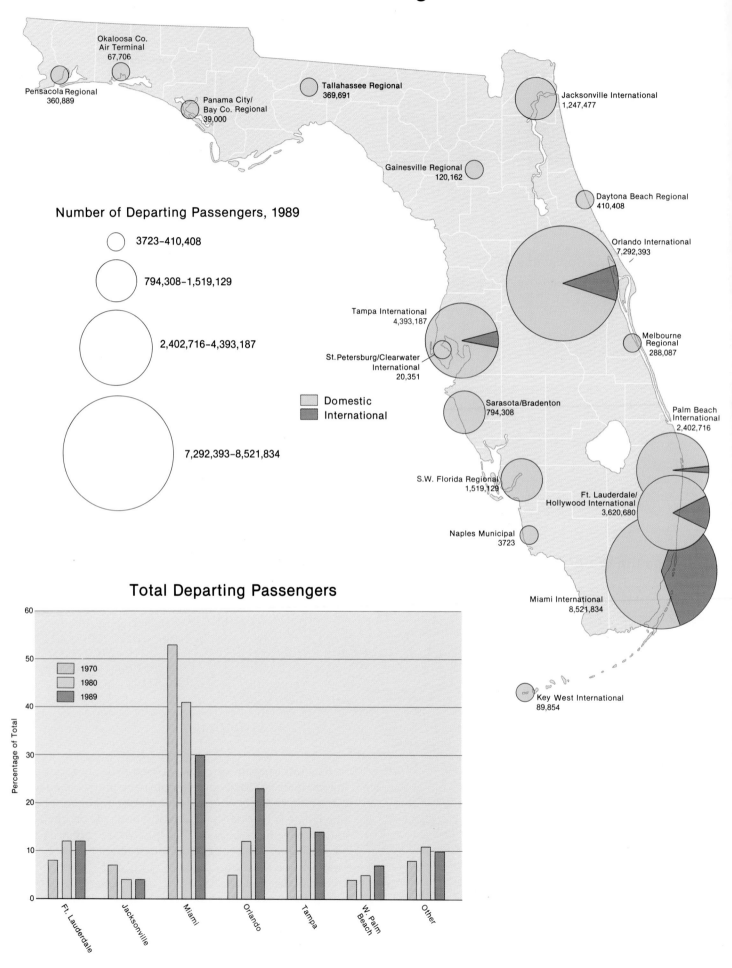

Okaloosa Co.
Air Terminal
67,706

Pensacola Regional
360,889

Panama City/
Bay Co. Regional
39,000

Tallahassee Regional
369,691

Jacksonville International
1,247,477

Gainesville Regional
120,162

Daytona Beach Regional
410,408

Orlando International
7,292,393

Number of Departing Passengers, 1989

3723–410,408

794,308–1,519,129

2,402,716–4,393,187

7,292,393–8,521,834

Tampa International
4,393,187

St. Petersburg/Clearwater
International
20,351

Melbourne
Regional
288,087

Domestic
International

Sarasota/Bradenton
794,308

Palm Beach
International
2,402,716

S.W. Florida Regional
1,519,129

Ft. Lauderdale/
Hollywood International
3,620,680

Naples Municipal
3723

Miami International
8,521,834

Key West International
89,854

Total Departing Passengers

Percentage of Total

60

50

40

30

20

10

0

1970
1980
1989

Ft. Lauderdale
Jacksonville
Miami
Orlando
Tampa
W. Palm
Beach
Other

Airports and Airfreight

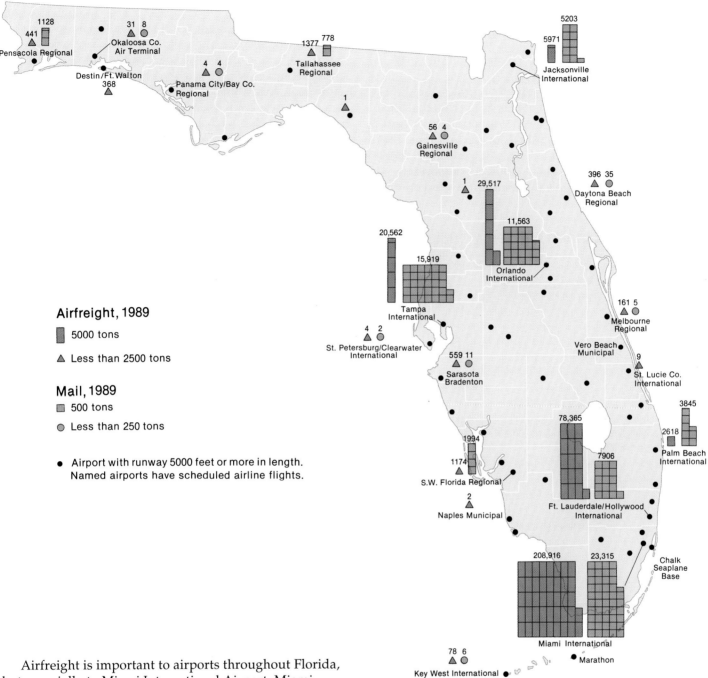

Airfreight, 1989

▉ 5000 tons

▲ Less than 2500 tons

Mail, 1989

▢ 500 tons

● Less than 250 tons

● Airport with runway 5000 feet or more in length.
Named airports have scheduled airline flights.

Airfreight is important to airports throughout Florida, but especially to Miami International Airport. Miami International Airport is usually within the top three airports in the nation in weight of airfreight. The significance of Miami as an airfreight carrier is the result of its proximity to Latin America. Large quantities of seafood, fruit, and cut flowers are imported from Latin America. A large volume of clothing from Asia is also imported.

Exports from Miami International Airport are largely to Latin America. By weight, the most common category is spare parts for a myriad of products that previously had been exported to Latin America. Miami's airfreight terminal is not entirely oriented toward foreign trade. Much airfreight is domestic, including a large share of the sportswear produced in factories near the airport and marketed throughout the nation. Nearby Ft. Lauderdale International Airport has increased its volume of airfreight but still remains far behind Miami International Airport.

Energy

Most of Florida's energy is derived from petroleum and natural gas principally from Texas and Louisiana. In 1979, the state's best year of oil production, its two oil fields produced 17 percent of the state's demand. In the early 1990s that share had fallen to about 2 percent.

Since the 1970s, as a result of high oil prices, the state has sought alternative sources of energy such as coal and nuclear. Many of the state's power stations have converted from petroleum to coal as their fuel source, and some have converted to natural gas.

Although meeting only about 6 percent of Florida's total energy demands, renewable sources have become more important. Commercial solar energy today is only in its infancy, but has potential. Of renewable energy sources, biomass, wood waste, and solid waste have expanded most dramatically since 1970. The sugar industry today uses a large percentage of its waste to generate power and heat to refine sugar. More and more communities are choosing to generate power from their solid waste rather than to put it into landfills. The state's large paper industry also uses its waste material to produce electricity for its mills.

Imports and Exports of Energy, 1988

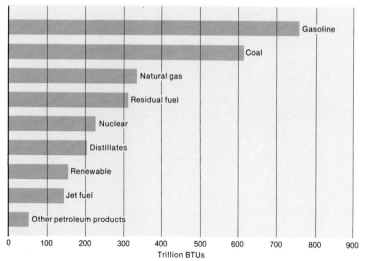

Municipal Solid Waste Combustion for Energy 1991

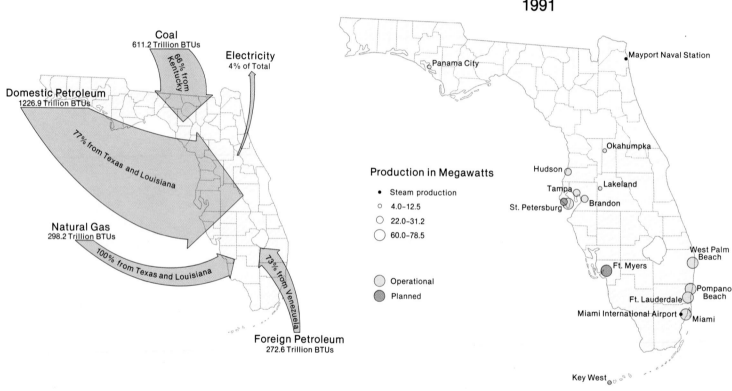

Energy Consumption, 1989

Renewable Energy Consumption, 1970–1989

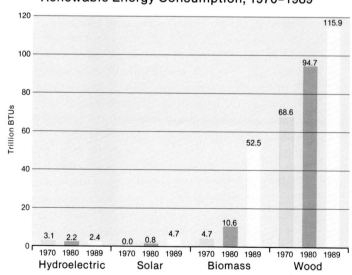

Commuting

Florida has grown rapidly only since World War II. Many of its large cities are also young. Dade County (Miami) had a population of 935,047 in 1960 and 1,937,094 in 1990. During the same period Broward County's population (Ft. Lauderdale-Hollywood) grew from 333,946 to 1,255,488, and Orange County's (Orlando) from 263,540 to 677,490. Unlike the older cities of the north, Florida's cities experienced their major growth during the automobile age and as a consequence are far less compact than many other U.S. cities. The private automobile is the dominant means of commuter transportation, and the vast majority of those who commute do so alone.

Most cities with over 50,000 inhabitants have a bus system. City buses typically serve a small number of low-income or aged people and operate on a route frequency of one bus per hour and no night service. Miami has the most complex public transit system including a modern overhead light railway that runs from Hialeah to Dadeland, via the downtown. A lighter gauge system that covers the downtown connects with it.

The percentage of commuters who use the automobile is over 80 percent everywhere in the state except in Monroe County. In Key West many people walk or ride bicycles to work. Commuters within most counties with large central cities more often drive to work alone than those who commute within less densely populated counties. Travel time to work is longest in rural counties on the periphery of large cities, for example: Liberty and Wakulla counties near Tallahassee; Baker, Bradford, and Clay counties near Jacksonville; and Walton County to the east of Pensacola.

Public Transportation Use

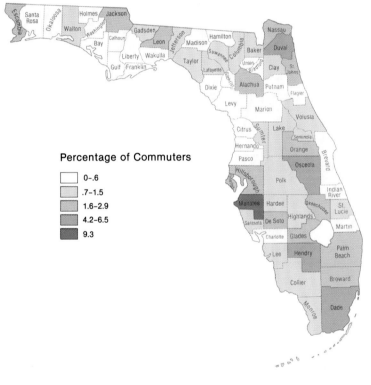

Percentage of Commuters

- 0–.6
- .7–1.5
- 1.6–2.9
- 4.2–6.5
- 9.3

Travel Time to Work

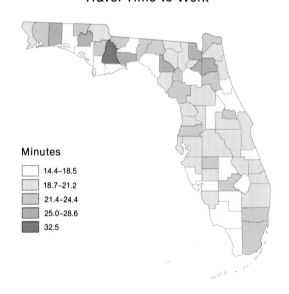

Minutes

- 14.4–18.5
- 18.7–21.2
- 21.4–24.4
- 25.0–28.6
- 32.5

Private Vehicle Use

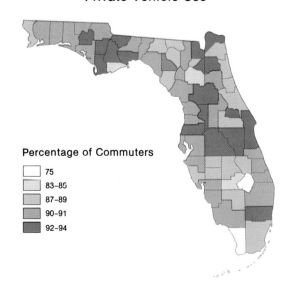

Percentage of Commuters

- 75
- 83–85
- 87–89
- 90–91
- 92–94

Private Vehicles—Single Occupant

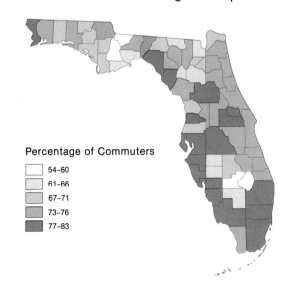

Percentage of Commuters

- 54–60
- 61–66
- 67–71
- 73–76
- 77–83

Planning Districts

Regional Planning Councils

1   West Florida
2   Apalachee
3   North Central Florida
4   Northeast Florida
5   Withlacoochee
6   East Central Florida
7   Central Florida
8   Tampa Bay
9   Southwest Florida
10 Treasure Coast
11 South Florida

Water Management Districts

1   South Florida
2   Southwest Florida
3   St. Johns River
4   Suwannee River
5   Northwest Florida

Florida's eleven regional planning councils address growth and development problems that are of greater than local concern or scope. They provide technical assistance to local governments on growth management matters, engage in areawide comprehensive and functional planning, undertake regional reviews of large-scale developments, and help carry out a wide variety of federal and state programs. Regional planning councils review and comment on local comprehensive plans prepared by counties and municipalities located within their region. They also support informal mediation processes to help resolve local planning conflicts.

Two-thirds of the voting members of each regional planning council's governing board are elected officials from local governments chosen by the cities and counties of the region. The remaining one-third are appointed by the governor. Each council must adopt a comprehensive regional policy plan containing goals and policies that address significant regional resources, infrastructure needs, or other important regional issues. In preparing a regional policy plan, regional planning councils analyze present and future trends and conditions based on forecasts of the region's population and economic growth.

Regional policy plans help implement the goals of the state comprehensive plan. As such, regional planning councils address a wide variety of issues in addition to traditional physical and growth and development concerns, such as economic development, public safety, health care, transportation disadvantaged planning, and the educational needs of citizens within the region.

Florida's five water management districts are principally responsible for planning and managing water resources within the state. Created under the Florida Water Resources Act of 1972, the districts operate under the general supervision of the Department of Environmental Regulation. They deal with water quality and quantity problems, and coordinate with the department in water pollution control, wetlands protection, and other water resource matters. The districts are managed by governing boards comprised of nine residents of each district, appointed by the governor.

Water management districts must balance competing water supply demands from commercial, industrial, agricultural, and municipal water uses. They must also protect the critical water supply needs of environmentally sensitive areas. The districts regulate land development activities that affect wetlands and floodplains, and those which cause stormwater runoff.

Water management districts engage in general water use and supply planning to help protect the state's groundwater resources, which supply approximately 90% of Florida's drinking water. The districts prepare special plans to conserve water during water shortage conditions, and to protect and restore surface waters in major lakes, rivers, and bays. They also help local governments in local land and water use planning activities.

The districts purchase land through the Save Our Rivers program for water management, supply, conservation, and protection. In 10 years since the program's inception in 1981, the districts spent $365 million to acquire approximately 450,000 acres of land, mostly in river floodplains.

Environmental Land and Water Management

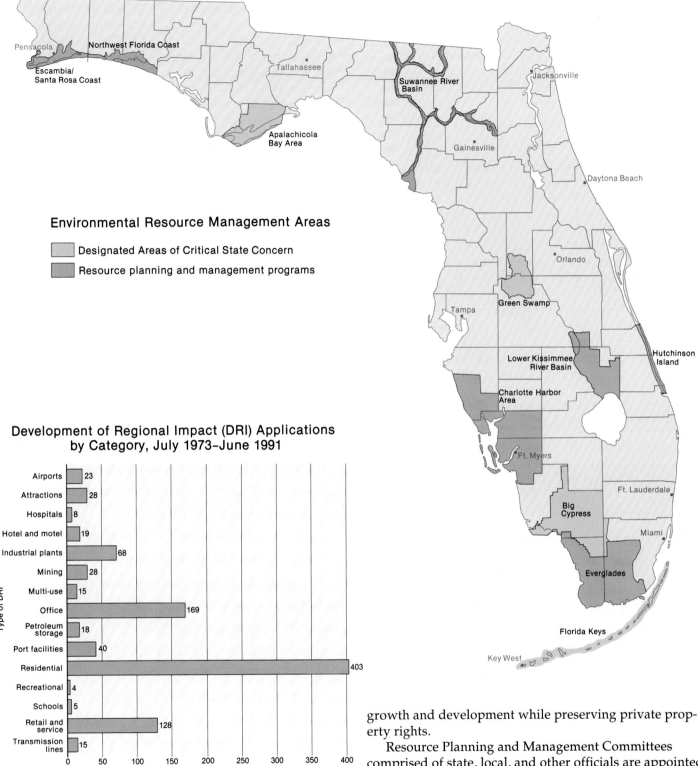

Environmental Resource Management Areas

- Designated Areas of Critical State Concern
- Resource planning and management programs

Development of Regional Impact (DRI) Applications by Category, July 1973–June 1991

Type of DRI	Number of DRIs
Airports	23
Attractions	28
Hospitals	8
Hotel and motel	19
Industrial plants	68
Mining	28
Multi-use	15
Office	169
Petroleum storage	18
Port facilities	40
Residential	403
Recreational	4
Schools	5
Retail and service	128
Transmission lines	15

Under Florida's landmark Environmental Land and Water Management Act of 1972, the Areas of Critical State Concern program focuses public attention on geographic areas whose environmental or historical uniqueness is important to protect. Administered by the Department of Community Affairs, the program is intended to establish a strong state and local government partnership to guide growth and development while preserving private property rights.

Resource Planning and Management Committees comprised of state, local, and other officials are appointed first by the governor to explore voluntary approaches to solving growth problems. An Area of Critical State Concern may be designated if this proves unsuccessful.

The Development of Regional Impact (DRI) process provides for state and regional review of developments that impact more than one county. Major residential, shopping center, office, industrial, and other types of large-scale development are subject to DRI review according to statewide guidelines and standards. The Department of Community Affairs administers the overall DRI program.

State Land Acquisition

The extraordinary population growth and development of Florida's natural areas has significantly diminished and reduced wildlife habitat, recreational areas, and many environmentally sensitive lands. Although rules and regulations can help minimize the degradation of environmentally sensitive lands, purchasing these areas is one of the most effective ways of protecting them, and is an action supported by the people of Florida and their representatives in the legislature. As a result of this, Florida has one of the largest and best-funded set of land acquisition programs in the United States. The state of Florida has spent well over $1 billion since the early 1970s to acquire more than 1 million acres of environmentally sensitive lands, recreational lands, forests, wildlife management areas, historic, archaeological, and geologic sites, and other lands for conservation and recreation.

Major state programs for purchasing environmentally important lands include the Environmentally Endangered Lands, the Save Our Coasts, the Conservation and Recreation Lands, and the Save Our Rivers programs. A new funding program introduced in 1990 called Preservation 2000 is expected to provide up to $3 billion through the end of this century for these and several other land acquisition programs. Many local governments are also now using land acquisition as a means to implement portions of their local comprehensive plans. Several nonprofit organizations also buy environmentally sensitive lands to sell or donate to the state. These include the Trust for Public Land, the Nature Conservancy, the Audubon Society, and several local land trusts throughout the state. Most of these organizations also own and manage their own environmentally sensitive lands as preserves.

Funds for state and local land acquisition programs have come from a variety of sources, including legislative appropriations, documentary stamp taxes, mineral severance taxes, federal appropriations, donations, permit sales, operating or leasing income, state or local bonds, ad valorem (property) taxes, local option sales taxes, increased millage rates, impact and mitigation fees from new development, and even the sale of license plates. Because of the high costs of purchasing land in Florida and the multi-use nature of these purchases, these various land acquisition programs are coordinated with each other as much as possible in order to buy as much high quality land as can be afforded and to use taxpayer dollars as efficiently as possible.

Besides recreation, habitat preservation, and conservation of other natural resources, land acquisition in Florida is conducted for the purposes of groundwater recharge protection, flood control, and restoration of environmentally degraded areas. State and local government land acquisition programs are an excellent example of providing for the public good through the conservation and protection of Florida's natural heritage.

Land Use Planning

Florida's present growth management system is built upon the State Comprehensive Plan. This plan provides general long-range goals and policies to help guide the state's growth and governance in many areas, including education, children, families, the elderly, housing, health, public safety, water resources, coastal and marine resources, natural systems and recreational lands, air quality, hazardous and nonhazardous materials and waste, mining, property rights, land use, downtown revitalization, public facilities, cultural and historical resources, transportation, governmental efficiency, the economy, agriculture, tourism, employment, and plan implementation.

The state comprehensive plan guides the development and implementation of other plans as required by Florida's growth management system, including state agency functional plans, comprehensive regional policy plans (prepared by the regional planning councils), and local government comprehensive plans. All of these plans must be consistent within themselves and with other plans.

Written under the guidance and direction of local citizens, planners, and decisionmakers, local comprehensive plans address a minimum of eight major planning areas or elements. These areas include capital improvements (infrastructure); future land use; traffic planning; sewage treatment, solid waste, stormwater drainage, potable water, and groundwater recharge; conservation; recreation and open space; affordable housing; and intergovernmen-tal coordination. A plan may also have additional, optional elements such as mass transit or economic development. After the draft plan is submitted to the local decision-making body for consideration and adoption, the Florida Department of Community Affairs reviews the plan for compliance with state law.

Perhaps the most dramatic requirement of Florida's growth management system is the concurrency requirement for new development. This means that infrastructure (public facilities and services) needed to support new development is required to be available concurrent with environmental, traffic, and other impacts of the development. The infrastructure can be coordinated with new development as the impacts come online; however, if the infrastructure is not available, then the local government cannot permit the development. This is a major change from the way development and infrastructure has been handled in the past, when development was assumed to pay for itself.

The future land use portion of a local comprehensive plan designates and maps future land use distribution, location, and extent for various land use categories in a planning area. The future land use portion, when combined with population forecasts and service standards for public facilities, ideally determines the placing and extent of new public infrastructure needed by the community to permit new development.

A sample representation of an adopted future land use map is shown here. This is an approximately one-mile-square portion of Pinellas County showing several categories of land use, including a segment of the U.S. 19 corridor and a segment of the Anclote River.

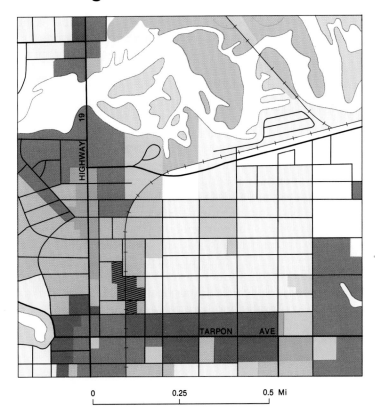

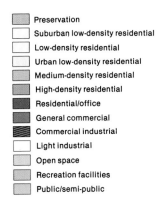

	Preservation
	Suburban low-density residential
	Low-density residential
	Urban low-density residential
	Medium-density residential
	High-density residential
	Residential/office
	General commercial
	Commercial industrial
	Light industrial
	Open space
	Recreation facilities
	Public/semi-public

The Hydrologic Cycle

Understanding the cyclical movement of water between the ocean, atmosphere, land, vegetation, and freshwater bodies is essential for the proper management of Florida's water resources. The hydrologic cycle is a relatively slow process that is driven by sunlight. Heat energy from the sun evaporates ocean water, forming clouds composed of water vapor. As this water vapor moves over the warmer land, it is heated and condenses as it rises. The vapor falls as precipitation, flowing into rivers and lakes, soaking into the ground to become groundwater, or evaporating into the air. Evaporation either occurs directly from water bodies, or after rainfall is taken up by vegetation and transpired back into the atmosphere as water vapor.

Groundwater is the source of most of the water that Floridians use for drinking, bathing, and other public water supply uses. Groundwater normally occupies the spaces found within formations of permeable rock, usually below a confining layer of impermeable soil or rock. This combination of water and permeable rock is called an aquifer. A large majority of Florida's potable, or drinkable, water is drawn from wells that pierce the Floridan aquifer underlying most of the state. The Floridan aquifer is close to the surface and quite shallow along the coasts. Here, excessive drawdown of the aquifer can allow seawater to

move into the freshwater aquifer, causing saltwater intrusion. Excessive drawdown of the aquifer in non-coastal areas from public, agricultural, industrial, and mining wells can also have harmful effects, causing lakes to disappear, sinkholes to open up, and competition for scarcer water to increase.

Water is Florida's most critical resource. That makes water resources planning one of the state's most critical activities. In Florida water has been historically treated as a commodity to be gathered from wells and waterbodies and provided for agriculture, domestic, industrial and other uses, or as a substance to drain for the purpose of agricultural or urban development (e.g. the draining of large areas of the Everglades). However, drought, pollution, saltwater intrusion, and the daily water demands of the fourth-most-populous state and its annual 40 million tourists create growing pressure to conserve and protect Florida's water resources. This means using planning and management techniques such as land use planning and regulation, restoring wetlands and floodplains altered by drainage and channelization, xeriscaping (using natural, drought-resistant plants for landscaping), and recognizing that the flora and fauna in environmentally sensitive areas have natural water rights, just as humans do.

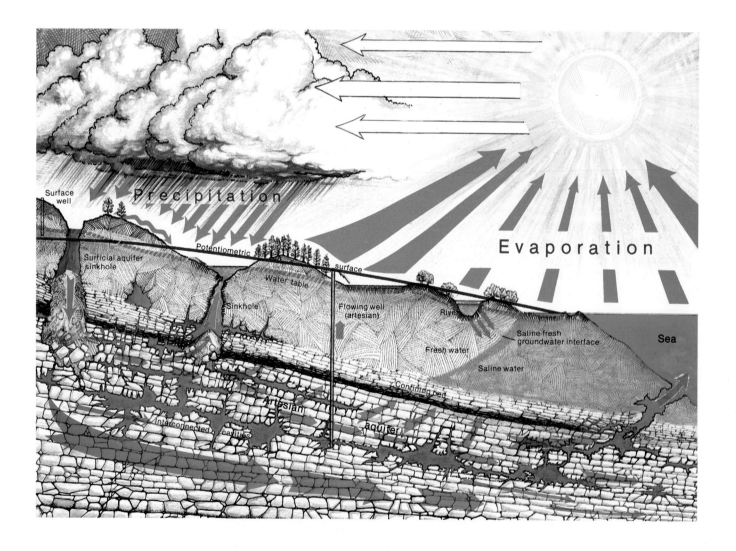

The Everglades

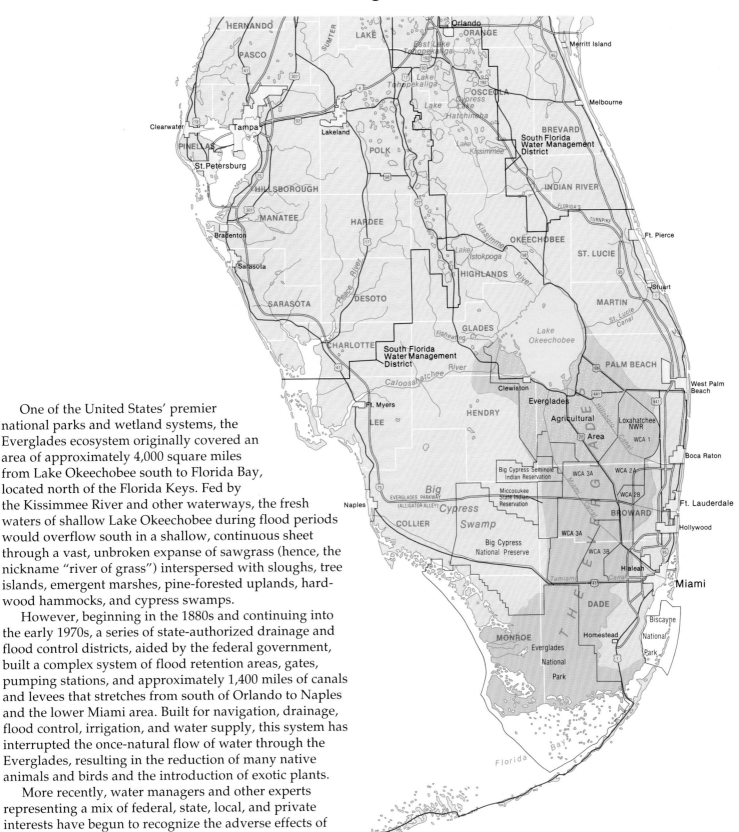

One of the United States' premier national parks and wetland systems, the Everglades ecosystem originally covered an area of approximately 4,000 square miles from Lake Okeechobee south to Florida Bay, located north of the Florida Keys. Fed by the Kissimmee River and other waterways, the fresh waters of shallow Lake Okeechobee during flood periods would overflow south in a shallow, continuous sheet through a vast, unbroken expanse of sawgrass (hence, the nickname "river of grass") interspersed with sloughs, tree islands, emergent marshes, pine-forested uplands, hardwood hammocks, and cypress swamps.

However, beginning in the 1880s and continuing into the early 1970s, a series of state-authorized drainage and flood control districts, aided by the federal government, built a complex system of flood retention areas, gates, pumping stations, and approximately 1,400 miles of canals and levees that stretches from south of Orlando to Naples and the lower Miami area. Built for navigation, drainage, flood control, irrigation, and water supply, this system has interrupted the once-natural flow of water through the Everglades, resulting in the reduction of many native animals and birds and the introduction of exotic plants.

More recently, water managers and other experts representing a mix of federal, state, local, and private interests have begun to recognize the adverse effects of impounding, channelizing, and allowing the pollution of the waters that once nourished the Everglades. Although past efforts to address these problems have not been successful for many reasons, the federal government, the state, and the South Florida Water Management District are now cooperating in the planning and implementation of improvements needed to protect the Everglades National Park and the Loxahatchee National Wildlife

Refuge. These include converting 35,000 acres of agricultural lands into a stormwater treatment area to reduce the amount of nutrients in agricultural runoff, restoring natural sheet flows, and providing adequate amounts of water for the refuge and the park.

Population Projections

Florida's population during the 1990s is predicted to grow less than in previous decades. Nonetheless, Florida will continue to be among the most rapidly growing states in the nation. Population growth during the decade is predicted to be principally on the peninsula. More retirees are expected to move to southwestern Florida and the Greater Orlando area than to the Gold Coast (Broward, Dade, and Palm Beach counties). Northwestern Florida between Destin and Panama City is also predicted to have a high rate of growth from retirees. The state's white population is expected to be even more aged by the year 2000 than in 1990. The black population, which is far more youthful than the white, will probably be as youthful in 2000 as it was in 1990.

Growth of Population, 1990–2000

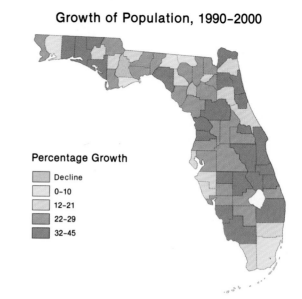

Growth of Population 0–24 Years Old

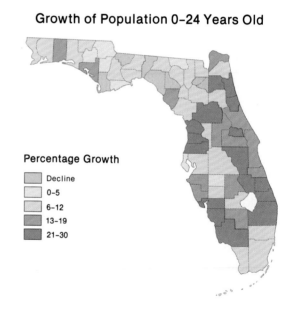

Growth of Population 65 Years and Older

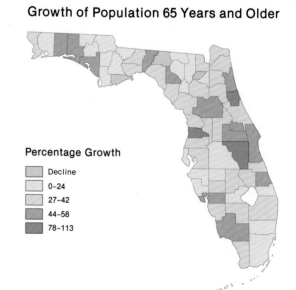

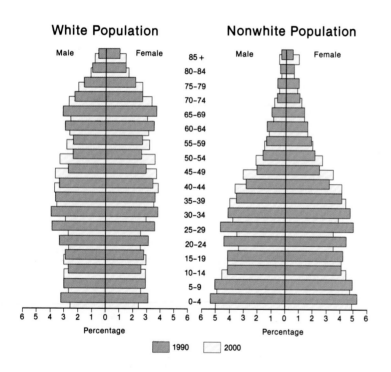

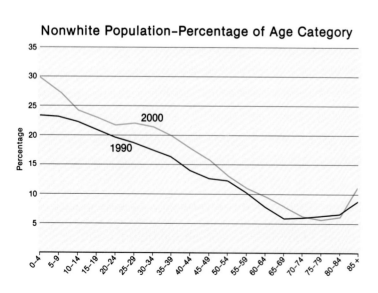

Enrollment Projections

Projected Change 1990–2000
Elementary (K–5)

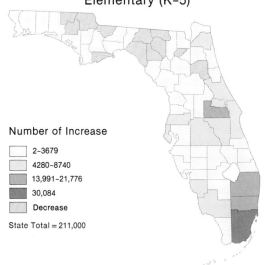

Number of Increase

- 2–3679
- 4280–8740
- 13,991–21,776
- 30,084
- Decrease

State Total = 211,000

The majority of Florida's in-migrants are younger than 55 and many have school-aged children. To provide education to this growing population places an enormous strain on the state's budget. Obviously the large cities anticipate the greatest growth in school enrollment during the 1990s. Several north Florida counties, where many young people seek opportunities elsewhere, anticipate decreases in enrollment by 2000. In K-12 Florida will need an estimated 14,600 new teachers between 1990 and 1993, and 11,500 between 1993 and 2000. Community college enrollment is predicted to grow by 142,000 between 1990 and 2000, and the State University System enrollment is expected to expand by 36,000. Currently there are nine state universities, a number with branch campuses. In 1991 money was authorized in the state budget to plan for a tenth university in southwest Florida.

Projected Change 1990–2000
Middle School (6–8)

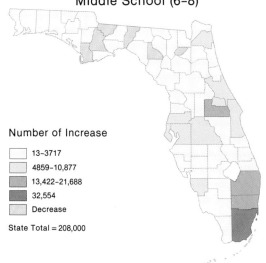

Number of Increase

- 13–3717
- 4859–10,877
- 13,422–21,688
- 32,554
- Decrease

State Total = 208,000

State University Enrollment Projections

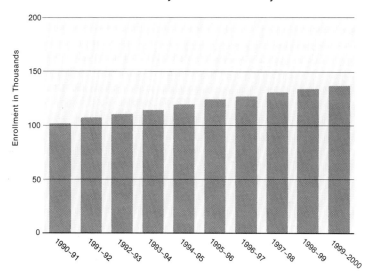

Projected Change 1990–2000
High School (9–12)

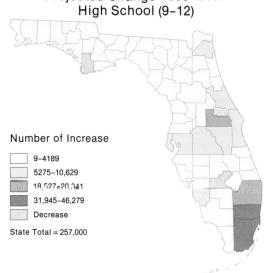

Number of Increase

- 9–4189
- 5275–10,629
- 18,527–20,041
- 31,945–46,279
- Decrease

State Total = 257,000

Community College Enrollment Projections

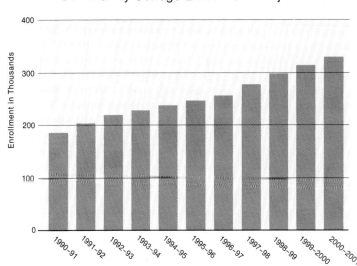

Population Dispersal

Unincorporated Population

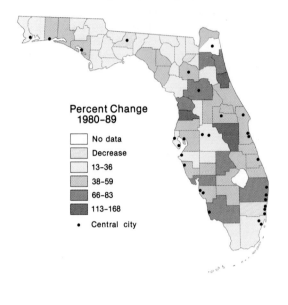

Percent Change
1980–89

- [ ] No data
- [ ] Decrease
- [ ] 13–36
- [ ] 38–59
- [ ] 66–83
- [ ] 113–168
- • Central city

Population Distribution

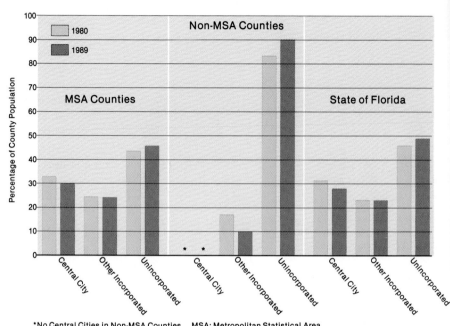

*No Central Cities in Non-MSA Counties.   MSA: Metropolitan Statistical Area

Gold Coast Population Change, 1980–89

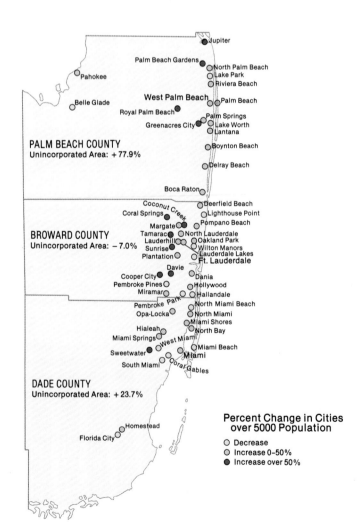

PALM BEACH COUNTY
Unincorporated Area: + 77.9%

BROWARD COUNTY
Unincorporated Area: – 7.0%

DADE COUNTY
Unincorporated Area: + 23.7%

Percent Change in Cities
over 5000 Population

- ○ Decrease
- ◐ Increase 0–50%
- ● Increase over 50%

Florida is among the most rapidly growing states in the nation. Much of this growth has been in the last fifty years, when automobiles have become widely available. As a consequence, urban growth has been far less compact in Florida's cities than in the older cities of the nation's north. The majority of Florida's growth has occurred in unincorporated areas. This "urban sprawl" has lowered the quality of life within metropolitan areas and has increased the cost of providing state and local government services.

Metropolitan expansion through urban sprawl has occurred in Dade, Broward, and Palm Beach counties. In Broward County, sprawl into the unincorporated portion of the county occurred early, and now most of these communities have been incorporated. Dade County still has large unincorporated areas, which are rapidly being developed. In Palm Beach County development in unincorporated areas is truly intense with relatively weakly controlled urban growth rapidly spreading westward from the coast.

The Governor's Task Force on Urban Growth Patterns, created in May 1988, has recommended: (1) local governments establish urban service areas and urban expansion areas in their comprehensive plans; (2) development of a state urban policy to facilitate building of new infrastructure particularly for transportation; (3) enactment of land development regulations that encourage an appropriate mix of housing, employment, shopping, as well as social and recreational opportunities; (4) development of state and local land acquisition policies to increase the stock of recreational land; (5) greater intergovernmental coordination and; (6) greater effort to encourage use of public transportation.

Transportation Networks

Florida's surface transportation system is extensive and very complex. Over 99 percent of those who travel by land to Florida do so by motor vehicle. Trucks are the major carriers of freight to and from, as well as within, the state. The road network of the state is so extensive that, during the next ten years, few new projects are being entertained. Most money devoted to highway construction will be spent in repair and road widening.

Rail systems are receiving renewed attention in Florida. Tri-Rail, a commuter railroad between West Palm Beach and Miami, began operations in the late 1980s. The world's first commercial high-speed magnetically levitated rail system was authorized in 1991 to connect Orlando Interna-

tional Airport with hotels and amusement centers at International Drive several miles from Disney World. The Florida High-Speed Rail Commission was established to study the feasibility of high-speed rail systems linking major Florida cities, using technology already successfully employed in Japan and many European countries. Systems have been proposed from Miami to Orlando, and from Orlando to Tampa. Currently the state Department of Transportation is actively studying the prospects of these systems including extending high-speed rail from these two initial systems to Jacksonville in the northeast and Ft. Myers in the southwest.

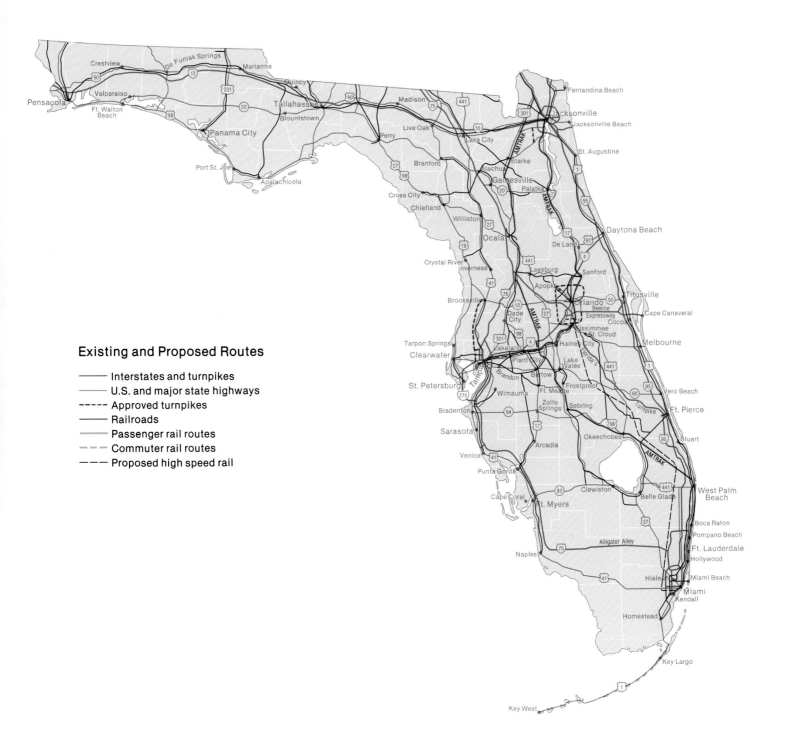

Existing and Proposed Routes

——— Interstates and turnpikes
——— U.S. and major state highways
----- Approved turnpikes
——— Railroads
——— Passenger rail routes
- - - Commuter rail routes
—·— Proposed high speed rail

Waste Management

Recycled Solid Waste
July 1, 1989–June 30, 1990

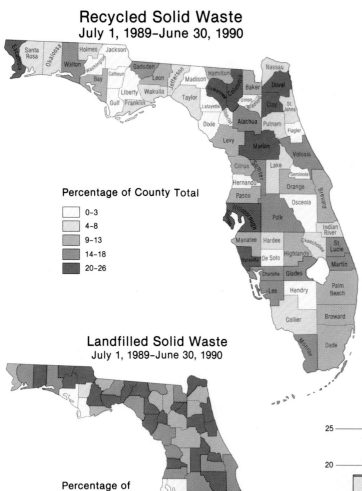

Percentage of County Total
- 0–3
- 4–8
- 9–13
- 14–18
- 20–26

In 1980 Florida had almost 500 open dumps, 1 small waste-to-energy plant, and virtually no local government recycling. By 1991 Florida had approximately 150 permitted landfills, 12 waste-to-energy plants, and one of the largest and most progressive recycling programs in the nation. Progress on such a scale was the result of the passage in 1988 of the Solid Waste Management Act, which among its many provisions required recycling of 30 percent of the solid waste generated in the state by 1995. The act also established new programs for the management of special wastes, and required training of landfill operators and full cost accounting for local government solid waste services.

Florida's recycling rate increased from an estimated 4 percent in 1988 to 15 percent in 1990 and is expected to reach 20 percent by the end of 1991. Florida is expected to reach its goal of 30 percent by 1994. If Florida meets the 30 percent recycling goal and builds all the waste-to-electricity plants permitted or under construction as of 1990, by 1995 one-third of its waste will be recycled, one-third burned for electricity, and one-third placed in landfills.

Landfilled Solid Waste
July 1, 1989–June 30, 1990

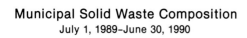

Percentage of County Total
- 9–17
- 49–64
- 74–83
- 84–92
- 93–100

Municipal Solid Waste Management Projections

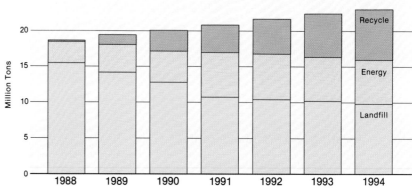

Legend: Recycle, Energy, Landfill
Y-axis: Million Tons (0–25)
X-axis: 1988, 1989, 1990, 1991, 1992, 1993, 1994

Municipal Solid Waste Composition
July 1, 1989–June 30, 1990

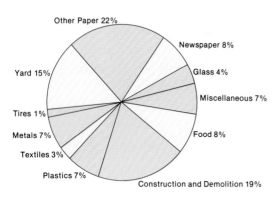

- Other Paper 22%
- Newspaper 8%
- Glass 4%
- Miscellaneous 7%
- Food 8%
- Construction and Demolition 19%
- Plastics 7%
- Textiles 3%
- Metals 7%
- Tires 1%
- Yard 15%

Hazardous Waste Production and Management, 1987 *

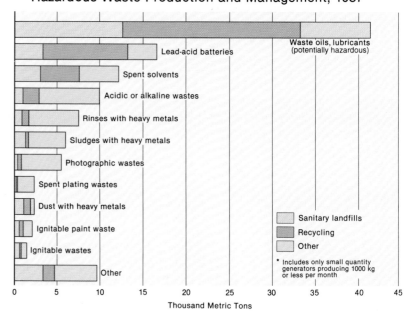

- Waste oils, lubricants (potentially hazardous)
- Lead-acid batteries
- Spent solvents
- Acidic or alkaline wastes
- Rinses with heavy metals
- Sludges with heavy metals
- Photographic wastes
- Spent plating wastes
- Dust with heavy metals
- Ignitable paint waste
- Ignitable wastes
- Other

Legend:
- Sanitary landfills
- Recycling
- Other

* Includes only small quantity generators producing 1000 kg or less per month

X-axis: 0, 5, 10, 15, 20, 25, 30, 35, 40, 45
Thousand Metric Tons

Hurricane Preparedness

Evacuation Time

Flood Zone–100-Year Storm Surge

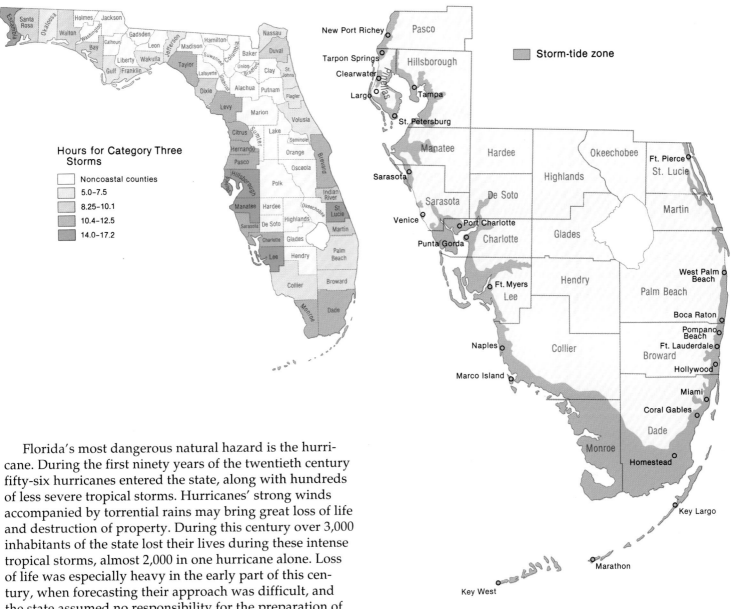

Hours for Category Three Storms
- Noncoastal counties
- 5.0–7.5
- 8.25–10.1
- 10.4–12.5
- 14.0–17.2

Storm-tide zone

Florida's most dangerous natural hazard is the hurricane. During the first ninety years of the twentieth century fifty-six hurricanes entered the state, along with hundreds of less severe tropical storms. Hurricanes' strong winds accompanied by torrential rains may bring great loss of life and destruction of property. During this century over 3,000 inhabitants of the state lost their lives during these intense tropical storms, almost 2,000 in one hurricane alone. Loss of life was especially heavy in the early part of this century, when forecasting their approach was difficult, and the state assumed no responsibility for the preparation of evacuation plans. Following a devastating hurricane that hit the Keys in 1935 and killed approximately 425 people, the state began to take a more active approach to disaster preparedness and evacuation. Since 1950 seventeen hurricanes have entered the state, but fewer than 100 people have died as a consequence. Low fatalities in recent years is a tribute to the state's Division of Emergency Management, and other federal, state, and local agencies.

The most deadly aspect of a hurricane is the storm surge, which may spread out over a large area of land. South Florida, frequently in the path of hurricanes, is especially low, and its coastal cities may be easily inundated if a large surge should arrive. A surge is a rise in sea level as the storm drives water onto the land. The height of this tide depends upon the depth of water offshore, the shape of the coastline, the forward speed of the storm, the direction and strength of the winds, the stage of the normal tide at the time of arrival, and the air pressure within the storm. Air of low pressure causes the water below it to dome upward, and the lower the pressure, the higher the dome. The worst possibility is for a fast-moving, powerful hurricane with very low pressure to reach shore at high tide along a shallow coastline and drive water directly up a bay or estuary. The September 1926 hurricane drove water up Miami's Biscayne Bay causing a surge that in several places reached 12 feet above sea level and flooded a large part of the city. Ft. Myers, Port Charlotte, and Tampa–St. Petersburg are also particularly vulnerable to surges.

Evacuation times have been calculated for Florida counties. The length of time is dependent upon the density and size of population and the road system that must be used. Key West and the Tampa Bay, Ft. Myers, Ft. Pierce, and Pensacola areas have the longest estimated evacuation times.

Health Planning

As Florida enters the last decade of the twentieth century, the state is faced with a variety of major health care issues. Demographically, the population over age 65 continues to increase at a rate higher than that of any other state. This population will have increased from 985,700 in 1970 to a projected 3,029,925 in 2000, an increase of 300 percent. The population over 85, known as the frail elderly, has nearly tripled since 1970 and will grow to 100,000 by 2000. With the aged making up an estimated 30 percent of the total population by 2000, health care for this population will be a major priority. Planners can expect an increased incidence of injuries and disabilities caused by arthritis, falls, fractures, and osteoporosis. However, the biggest problem in the 1990s will be the increased prevalence of Alzheimer's disease, a debilitating brain disease that robs the patient of memory. Alzheimer's patients require significantly more long-term-care resources than most of the aged since they must be closely monitored to prevent them from becoming lost or disoriented.

Population 65 and Older

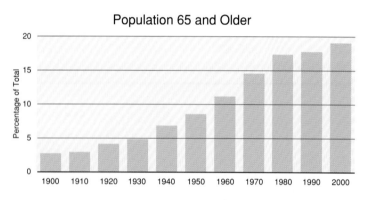

The increasing population of the aged has greatly increased the need for long-term-care services in recent years. The number of nursing home beds rose from 29,400 in 1975 to more than 64,000 in 1990. More than 8,000 beds are under construction with more planned. The rapid increase in nursing home beds has resulted in huge increases in the state's Medicaid budget, which jumped from $177 million in FY 1981-82 to $779 million in FY 1990-91. Overall, Floridians paid over $1.5 billion for nursing home care in 1990. Substantial increases in nursing home expenditures are expected during the 1990s as more nursing home beds are licensed.

Among the chronic diseases, cancer will be the major problem during the 1990s. Florida currently has the highest crude incidence and death rates for cancer of all states. About 60,000 new cases of cancer are diagnosed every year; by 2000, the number of new cases will rise to 80,000 per year. Although death rates for other chronic diseases have been declining, the cancer death rate has been increasing. By 2000, cancer will become Florida's leading cause of death.

Cancer Deaths

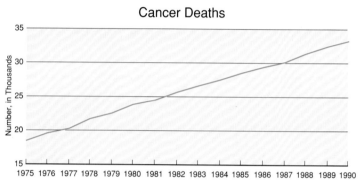

More than 65 percent of all cancer cases can be prevented by not smoking, reducing the amount of fat in the diet, reducing alcohol consumption, and avoiding excessive sun exposure. Cervical cancer can be detected by Pap smears, breast cancers by mammography, and other cancers by other screening methods, thus increasing the chances of successful treatment. Early detection and treatment significantly increases the prognosis for survival and at a much lower cost. Expansion of mass cancer screening programs such as mammography diagnostic centers is a possible solution for reducing cancer mortality.

Throughout history, as one communicable disease was eradicated, another took its place. The yellow fever and typhoid epidemics of the nineteenth century were replaced by diphtheria in the early twentieth century, measles and poliomyelitis in the mid-twentieth century, and by Acquired Immune Deficiency Syndrome (AIDS) in the late twentieth century. AIDS, caused by the Human Immunodeficiency Virus (HIV) is a debilitating disease, which destroys the immune system, allowing other opportunistic diseases to kill the patient. AIDS was unknown in Florida until 1982, but the number of cases has risen rapidly.

Medicaid Nursing Home Expenditures

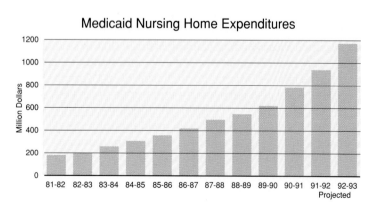

AIDS Cases

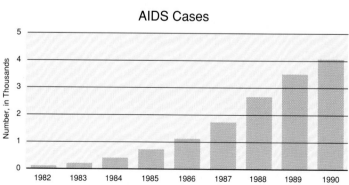

Since AIDS is almost always fatal, HIV/AIDS is now the eighth leading cause of death in Florida, and the fifth leading cause for nonwhites. Although HIV was initially spread primarily through homosexual contact, the number of individuals infected through heterosexual contact has been increasing with 14 percent of total AIDS cases attributed to heterosexual transmission in 1990. The AIDS epidemic now substantially threatens the younger, more sexually active segments of the population. With AIDS medical care costs now averaging between $70,000 and $90,000 per patient, the health care system is rapidly reaching its capacity to pay for AIDS treatment. Hospitals are incurring substantial uncompensated care costs, governments are using increasing amounts of public funds to pay for AIDS treatment and research, and employers are paying increasing premiums as health care insurance costs rise. Health care expenditures related to AIDS are projected to reach $2.4 billion in Florida by 2000.

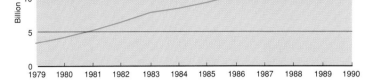

Hospital Costs

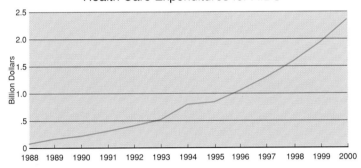

Health Care Expenditures for AIDS

Maternal and infant health care is another major problem area. One of every 12 Florida mothers receives little or no prenatal care, the fourth worst percentage in the nation. One of every 17 births is to a mother under 18, over 73 percent of them unmarried. One of every eight births to these teenage mothers is a low weight baby, resulting in increased health problems and higher infant mortality. About 1800 infants die in Florida each year before they reach their first birthday. Thousands of others must be cared for in high technology, high cost neonatal and perinatal intensive care centers, including many of the more than 4,400 newborns who are drug dependent as the result of the mother's addiction to crack cocaine or other substance abuse. Over 500 newborns per year are HIV-infected. Extraordinary costs are incurred in treating HIV-infected and substance-abused newborns.

Health care costs have become a major issue in Florida as well as the nation as a whole. Florida's total health care expenditures were estimated at $31.4 billion in 1990, more than triple the $9.4 billion in 1980 health care expenditures. By 2000, total expenditures are expected to reach $90.6 billion. Hospital costs, which account for nearly half of all health care expenditures in Florida, have risen rapidly in the last decade. Gross operating revenues increased from $3.44 billion in 1979 to $19.85 billion in 1990.

Increased health care costs result in increased insurance premiums, causing employers to reduce or eliminate health insurance benefits. Over 2.2 million Floridians are uninsured, 75 percent of them workers and their dependents. About a quarter of the uninsured are children. Many employees, especially in small businesses and service industries, cannot get health insurance from their employers and cannot afford to purchase individual policies. This situation is expected to worsen during the 1990s because Florida's job market is composed mostly of service industries, which have low-paying jobs and minimal insurance coverages.

Even for those who have health insurance or are covered by a government program such as Medicaid or Medicare, access to health care continues to be a problem in many areas. Rural hospitals are going out of business in many small counties and few are expected to survive until 2000 without assistance. Physicians are maldistributed geographically and by specialty. Ten counties have less than three primary care physicians per 10,000 population and Glades County has no resident physician. Health manpower shortage areas for physicians have been designated for 21 entire counties and portions of 33 others. There are shortages of nurses and allied health personnel in many communities, but educational institutions have been unable to expand training programs to meet needs because of budget cutbacks and some have actually reduced enrollments. Because of the length of training time required for many health professions, Florida will have to rely on in-migration of practitioners from other states to meet the state's health care needs.

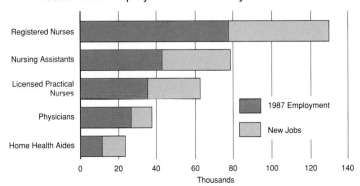

Health Care Employment Demand by the Year 2000

Taxation and Spending

State and Local Per Capita Expenditures

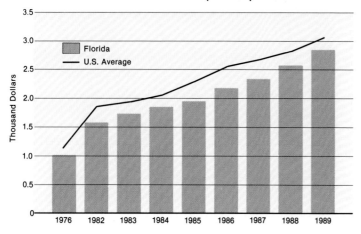

In 1990, 9.64 percent of personal income in Florida went to payment of state and local taxes, compared to a national average of 11.09 percent. State and local expenditures are also lower than the national average although they increased from 84 percent of the national average in 1976 to 93 percent in 1989. A dramatic shift in spending between levels of governments occurred between 1980 and 1990. Cities' share dropped from 21.3 percent of the total to 16.7 percent. Average city spending increased by 9 percent, whereas the average increase for county spending was 12.6 percent and 13.4 percent for state government. Differences in city and county spending as well as tax capacity are quite varied. Differences in tax capacity, however, cannot explain differences in per capita spending. The lowest spender, Holmes County, has an average tax base of 28.1 percent of the state average, whereas the spending leader, Alachua County, also has a relatively low average tax base of 51.7 percent of the state average.

Expenditures by Type of Government

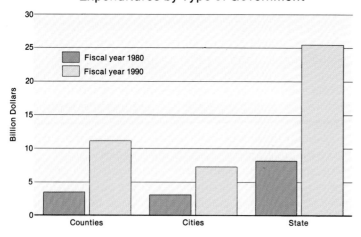

State and Local Taxes

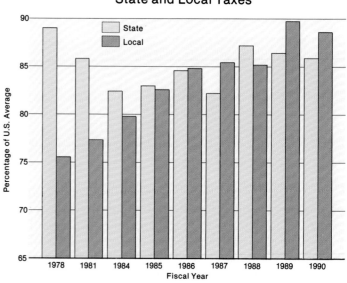

Total City and County Per Capita Expenditures

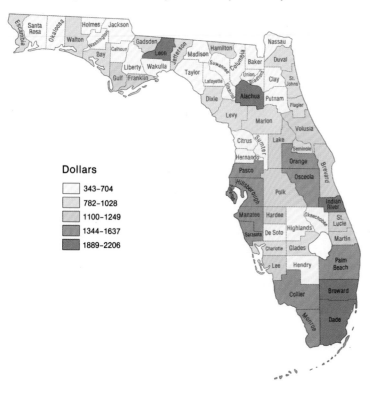

Per Capita Taxable Value

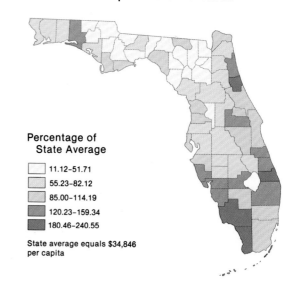

Party Registration and Political Change

Republican Registration, 1990

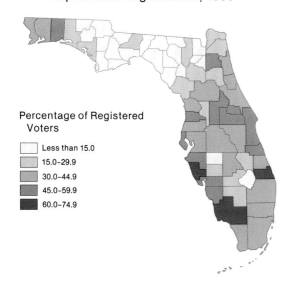

Percentage of Registered Voters

- Less than 15.0
- 15.0–29.9
- 30.0–44.9
- 45.0–59.9
- 60.0–74.9

Democratic Registration, 1990

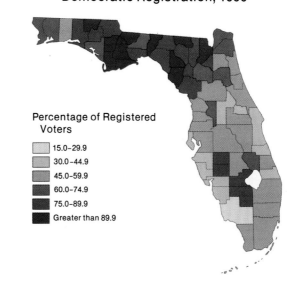

Percentage of Registered Voters

- 15.0–29.9
- 30.0–44.9
- 45.0–59.9
- 60.0–74.9
- 75.0–89.9
- Greater than 89.9

Change in Republican Registration, 1980–1990

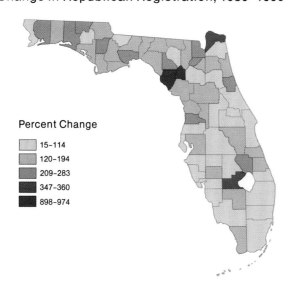

Percent Change

- 15–114
- 120–194
- 209–283
- 347–360
- 898–974

Change in Democratic Registration, 1980–1990

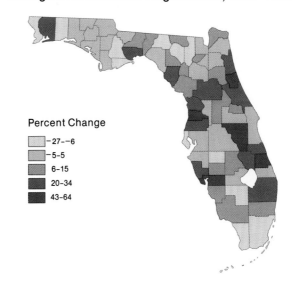

Percent Change

- −27––6
- −5–5
- 6–15
- 20–34
- 43–64

Florida's Congressional Seats from Statehood to Present

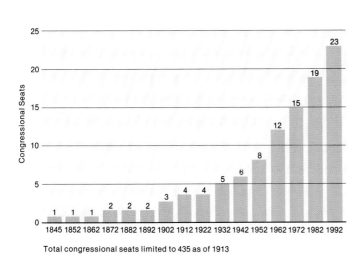

Total congressional seats limited to 435 as of 1913

Change in Congressional Seats, 1980–1990

- Increase
- No change
- Decrease

Place Names

Alachua (1824)—either Muskogee or Timucua word for sinkhole.

Baker (1861)—James McNair Baker, Judge, Fourth Municipal District, Confederate Senator.

Bay (1913)—St. Andrews Bay.

Bradford (1861)—(was New River, 1858-1861) Captain Richard Bradford, killed at Battle of Santa Rosa Island during Civil War.

Brevard (1855)—(was St. Lucia 1844-1855) Doctor Ephriam Brevard, writer of the so-called Mecklenberg (N.C.) Declaration of Independence, or Theodore Washington Brevard, state comptroller, 1854, 1855-1860.

Broward (1915)—Napoleon Bonaparte Broward, governor 1905-1909.

Calhoun (1838)—John C., U.S. Senator from South Carolina.

Charlotte (1921)—The Bay of Charlotte Harbor.

Citrus (1887)—Citrus trees.

Clay (1858)—Henry Clay, U.S. Senator from Kentucky.

Collier (1923)—Barron Collier, landowner and developer.

Columbia (1832)—Christopher Columbus, discovered America.

Dade (1836)—Major Francis L. Dade, killed at the Dade Massacre, 1835.

De Soto (1887)—Hernando de Soto, Spanish explorer.

Dixie (1921)—Lyric term for the South.

Duval (1822)—William P. DuVal, territorial governor, 1822-1834.

Escambia (1821)—Escambia River and Spanish for "barter" or "exchange."

Flagler (1917)—Henry M. Flagler, East Coast railroad builder.

Franklin (1832)—Benjamin Franklin, scientist and author.

Gadsden (1823)—James Gadsden of South Carolina, aide-de-camp of Jackson in Florida campaign of 1818.

Gilchrist (1925)—Albert W. Gilchrist, governor, 1909-1913.

Glades (1921)—Everglades.

Gulf (1925)—Gulf of Mexico.

Hamilton (1827)—Alexander Hamilton, Secretary of U.S. Treasury.

Hardee (1921)—Cary A. Hardee, governor, 1921-1925.

Hendry (1923)—Captain Francis A. Hendry, one of the first settlers.

Hernando (1843)—(was Benton, 1844-1850) Hernando de Soto, Spanish explorer.

Highlands (1921)—Highland terrain.

Hillsborough (1834)—Wills Hill, Viscount Hillsborough of England.

Holmes (1848)—Thomas J. Holmes of North Carolina who settled in the area about 1830.

Indian River (1925)—Indian River.

Jackson (1822)—Andrew Jackson, President, U.S., 1829-1837.

Jefferson (1827)—Thomas Jefferson, President, U.S., 1801-1809.

Lafayette (1856)—Marquis de Lafayette, French officer who served with Washington in the American Revolution.

Lake (1887)—The large number of lakes in the area.

Lee (1887)—General Robert E. Lee.

Leon (1824)—Juan Ponce de León, discoverer of Florida.

Levy (1845)—David Levy (Yulee), U.S. Senator, 1845-1851, 1855-1861.

Liberty (1855)—Name applied to common objective of American people.

Madison (1827)—James Madison, President, U.S., 1809-1817.

Manatee (1855)—The sea cow, or manatee.

Marion (1844)—General Francis Marion, Revolutionary War Hero.

Martin (1925)—John W. Martin, governor, 1925-1929.

Monroe (1824)—James Monroe, President, U.S., 1817-1825.

Nassau (1824)—Duchy of Nassau, Germany.

Okaloosa (1915)—Choctaw Indian words *oka* (water) and *lusa* (black).

Okeechobee (1917)—Hitchiti words *oki* (water) and *chobi* (big).

Orange (1845)—(was Mosquito, 1824-1845) Oranges.

Osceola (1887)—The Indian leader Osceola ("Singer of the Black Drink").

Palm Beach (1909)—Palms and beaches.

Pasco (1887)—Samuel Pasco, U.S. Senator, 1887-1899.

Pinellas (1911)—Pinta Pinal or Point of Pines.

Polk (1861)—James K. Polk, President, U.S., 1845-1849.

Putnam (1849)—Either for Israel Putnam, Revolutionary hero, or Benjamin A. Putnam, officer in Seminole War and unsuccessful candidate, U.S. House of Representatives, 1815.

St. Johns (1821)—St. John the Baptist.

St. Lucie (1844)—St. Lucy of Syracuse, Roman Catholic Saint.

Santa Rosa (1842)—Rosa de Viterbo, Roman Catholic Saint.

Sarasota (1921)—from Calusa Indian language, meaning not known, but perhaps "Point of Rocks."

Seminole (1913)—Seminole Indians, thought to be derived from Spanish word *cimarron*, meaning "wild" or "runaway."

Sumter (1853)—General Thomas Sumter, Revolutionary War hero.

Suwannee (1858)—is either Cherokee *sawani*, meaning "echo river," or corruption of Spanish *San Juan*.

Taylor (1856)—Zachary Taylor, President, U.S., 1849-1851.

Union (1921)—Unity.

Volusia (1854)—An English settler, Volus.

Wakulla (1843)—Probably Timucuan Indian word for "spring of water."

Walton (1824)—George Walton, Secretary, Territorial Florida, 1821-1826.

Washington (1829)—George Washington, President, U.S., 1789-1797.

OTHER SELECTED NAMES

Altamonte Springs: Seminole Co.—Altamonte is Spanish for "high hill."

Anna Maria Island: Manatee Co.—Ponce de León was said to have named the island for the queen of King Charles II, the sponsor of his expedition. Pronunciation is often disputed, most prefer Anna Mar-EE-a, but the old timers like Anna Mar-EYE-a.

Apalachicola: Franklin Co.—probably of Hitchiti *apalahchi* (on the other side) and *okli* (people), therefore "those people residing on the other side, shore, or river."

Arcadia: De Soto Co.—Named in honor of Arcadia Albritton, daughter of pioneer settlers, who baked a birthday cake for Rev. James Hendry. In appreciation he named the town after her.

Aripeka: Pasco Co.—Named after Sam Jones, a famous Miccosukee chief, who was called Aripeka or Aripeika. The name is possibly corrupted from Muskogee *abihka* (pile at the base or heap at the root), which was a contest for supremacy among warriors who piled up scalps, covering the base of the war-pole.

Belle Glade: Palm Beach Co.—Was originally known as the Hillsborough Canal Settlement. When the inhabitants requested their own post office a new name was necessary. A tourist one day said on a trip to the area that the Hillsborough Canal Settlement was "the belle of the" glades. It was later voted on and became the official name.

Bithlo: Orange Co.—Derives from the Muskogee word *pilo* (canoe). In the transliteration of this Indian language the voiceless "l" was often written as "thl-."

Blountstown: Calhoun Co.—Named for John Blount, a Seminole Indian and the distinguished chief of the Indian tribe who occupied the reservation that was just east of the area.

Boca Ciega: Pinellas Co.—Named for Boca Ciega Bay. Literally the Spanish word for *boca* (mouth) and *ciega* (blind). This may have been a reference to what it looked like at the entrance of the river.

Boca Raton: Palm Beach Co.—The Spanish words *Boca de Ratones* mean rat's mouth, a term used by seamen to describe a hidden rock that a ship's cable might rub against.

Bonifay: Holmes Co.—Named for a prominent old family in the vicinity.

Brandon: Hillsborough Co.—Named by John Brandon, who moved his family and all their possessions to Florida. The settlement is named for his family.

Brooksville: Hernando Co.—Named after Congressman Preston Brooks of South Carolina.

Cape Canaveral: Brevard Co.—Canaveral is the Spanish word for "a place of reeds or cane."

Cedar Key: Levy Co.—Named for the abundant growth of cedar trees that originally covered the island.

Chattahoochee: Gadsden Co.—The name was taken from the well-known river in Georgia. The name itself is from Muskogee *chato* (rock) and *huchi* (marked).

Chipley: Washington Co.—Named in honor of Colonel William D. Chipley, a railroad official.

Clearwater: Pinellas Co.—The town was first called Clear Water Harbor, because of a spring of water that bubbles up in the Gulf of Mexico close to shore, making the water in the vicinity clear. The harbor was later dropped from the name.

Cross City: Dixie Co.—Two public roads crossed at this point, one coming from Perry to old Archer and the other from Branford to Horseshoe. W.H. Matthis, who decided the name, wanted the location to be thought of as more than a crossroads.

Crystal River: Citrus Co.—The correct translation of the name is *weewahiiaca* which is derived from Seminole-Creek Indians *wiwa* (water), *haiyayaki* (clear, shining).

Dade City: Pasco Co.—Named for Maj. Francis Langhorne Dade, a U.S. Army officer killed by Seminoles. The Dade Massacre triggered the start of the Second Seminole War.

Daytona Beach: Volusia Co.—Named after its founder Mathias Day.

DeFuniak Springs: Walton Co.—Colonel Fred Defuniak, an official of the Louisville and Nashville Railroad, gave his name to the town.

Fenholloway: Taylor Co.—The source of Fenholloway (finalui) is Muskogee *fina* (footlog) and *halwi* (high) giving you "high footlog."

Fernandina Beach: Nassau Co.—Fernandina was the early name of Cuba. Fernandina claims to be the oldest city in the United States.

Flagler Beach: Flagler Co.—Name honors Henry M. Flagler.

Floridatown: Santa Rosa Co.—One of the oldest place names in this state. The town was a trading post in the Spanish days.

Fort Dade: Pasco Co.—Named for Maj. Francis Langhorne Dade.

Fort Lauderdale: Broward Co.—Named for Maj. William Lauderdale.

Fort Myers: Lee Co.—Named for Gen. Abraham Charles Myers, a distinguished officer in the U.S. Army.

Fort Pierce: St. Lucie Co.—Named for Lt. Colonel Benjamin Kendrick Pierce, the brother of President Franklin Pierce, the fort was the headquarters of the Army of the South under General Jesup.

Fort Walton Beach: Okaloosa Co.—Named after the fort that was established here during the Seminole Wars.

Frostproof: Polk Co.—It was named by cowboys who brought cattle to the region during the winter months because of the absence of frost.

Gainesville: Alachua Co.—Named for Gen. Edmund Pendleton Gaines, who led the capture of Aaron Burr.

Green Cove Springs: Clay Co.—The St. Johns River curves here and is sheltered by trees that are perennially green.

Groveland: Lake Co.—Originally called Taylorville, it was renamed Groveland due to the large number of citrus groves in the region.

Haines City: Polk Co.—It was first known as Clay Cut but the name was later changed to Haines City, in honor of a railroad official named Colonel Henry Haines.

Hialeah: Dade Co.—Of Muskogee origin *haiyakpo* (prairie) and *hili* (pretty).

High Springs: Alachua Co.—It was named this because a spring was located atop a hill within the town. The spring no longer exists.

Hillsborough River or Locktsapopka: Hillsborough Co.—The Indian name of the stream came from the Muskogee *lokcha* (acorns) and *papka* (eating place)—the place where the acorns are eaten.

Hollywood: Broward Co.—It was established Hollywood-by-the-Sea by its founder, Joseph W. Young of California.

Homosassa: Citrus Co.—Muskogee *homo* (pepper) and *sasi* (is there)—the place where the wild pepper grows.

Indian Rocks Beach: Pinellas Co.—A number of large rocks along the shore gave the community its name.

Inverness: Citrus Co.—Named by a Scotch settler for the ancient capital of the Scottish Highlands.

Islamorada: Monroe Co.—It is Spanish for "purple island."

Jacksonville: Duval Co.—Two of the Spanish names for the area can be translated as "pass of San Nicolas." It was also called "the place where the cows cross" by the Timucuan Indians.

Jasper: Hamilton Co.—Named in memory of Sgt. William Jasper Revolutionary War hero, who rescued the American flag during the British assault on Ft. Sullivan, now Ft. Moultrie.

Key West: Monroe Co.—It is the westernmost island extending from the Florida peninsula. It was originally called Bone Island by the early Spanish explorers because they found large quantities of human bones.

LaBelle: Hendry Co.—Named by Capt. Francis Ausbury Hendry for his two daughters, Laura and Belle.

Lacoochee: Pasco Co.—A shortened form of the river (Withlacoochee) where the town is located.

Lake Butler: Union Co.—Named for Colonel Robert Butler, who received the surrender of East Florida from the Spanish.

Lake City: Columbia Co.—The name was renamed from "Alligator" by an act of the legislature to its present form because of the myriad of lakes that surround the area.

Lakeland: Polk Co.—So named because of the nineteen lakes within the city limits.

Largo: Pinellas Co.—Named for Lake Largo nearby. Largo is the Spanish word for "big" or "long."

Longboat Key: Sarasota Co.—The exact origin of this name has been lost but a longboat is the largest boat carried by a merchant sailing vessel.

Macclenny: Baker Co.—Named after H.C. Macclenny, who owned large tracts of land in the vicinity.

MacDill A.F.B.: Hillsborough Co.—Named in honor of Colonel Leslie MacDill, who was killed in an air crash near Washington, D.C.

Maderia Beach: Pinellas Co.—Named for Maderia, Portugal's wine producing island off of Africa. The word itself means "wood."

Madison: Madison Co.—First called Hickstown, after the Seminole Indian chief John Hicks; later known as Newton. But the mail kept coming addressed to Madison C.H. (meaning the courthouse of Madison Co.) so they dropped the C.H. and used Madison as the name of the town.

Marianna: Jackson Co.—Named for the daughters of the original owners of the site, the Beveridges.

Masaryktown: Hernando Co.—Named by the editor of a Czech newspaper in New York, who was its founder, after the first president of Czechoslovakia.

Mayo: Lafayette Co.—Named after James Mayo, a colonel who had been in charge of the Confederate Army. He delivered a speech in the area on the Fourth of July and the settlers were so impressed by him that they named the community after him.

Miami: Dade Co.—Comes from Mayaimi (a lake—now Lake Okeechobee) which means "very large."

Micanopy: Alachua Co.—Head chief of the Seminoles in the Seminole War; it means "head chief."

Miccosukee: Leon Co.—From Hitchiti *miki* (chief) and *suki* (hogs)—"chiefs of the hog clan."

Monticello: Jefferson Co.—Named for the historic Virginia home of Thomas Jefferson.

Moore Haven: Glades Co.—Named for its founder, James A. Moore.

Naples: Collier Co.—Named for Naples, Italy.

Ocala: Marion Co.—The literal meaning of this Indian word is "heavily clouded," perhaps beyond discovery.

Opa Locka: Dade Co.—Refers to a hammock located within the present limits of the city. The source is Muskogee *opilwa* (swamp) and *lako* (big), though the usual combination is *opillakpo*.

Orlando: Orange Co.—There are several different versions to the origin of Orlando's name, however, the official story is that it is named in honor of Orlando Reeves. Orlando Reeves was on sentinel duty for a camping party. While they were sleeping, an Indian attempted to penetrate the camp, but Reeves saw him and fired on him, but not before the Indian shot an arrow killing Reeves.

Palatka: Putnam Co.—Its name is derived from the Muskogee word *pilotaikita* which means "ferry", "ford", or "crossing." Palatka was a major trading post on the St. Johns River.

Panama City: Bay Co.—George West, the original developer of the town, named it Panama City because it is in a direct line between Chicago and Panama City, Panama.

Panasoffkee: Sumter Co.—derived from the Muskogee *pani* (valley) and *sufki* (deep)—deep valley.

Pass-a-Grille Beach: Pinellas Co.—The name referred to the practice of fishermen, who, using this point to cross over the island, would stop here to cook or grill their meals.

Pensacola: Escambia Co.—Most likely derivation of the name is from a tribe called Pansfalaya or long-haired people in Choctaw.

Ponte Verde: St. Johns Co.—Named for the city in Spain.

Punta Gorda: Charlotte Co.—The Spanish words for "wide point" or "fat point," which was in reference to the arm of land jutting into Charlotte Bay near the present city.

Quincy: Gadsden Co.—Named in honor of John Quincy Adams who was Secretary of State of the U.S. at the time of establishment.

Sanibel: Lee Co.—The name is thought to be a combination of health and beauty.

Sebring: Highlands Co.—Named for George Sebring, a pottery manufacturer of Sebring, Ohio.

Silver Springs: Marion Co.—Named for the celebrated spring, Florida's largest, whose crystal clearness inspired its name.

Sopchoppy: Wakulla Co.—The name has been corrupted from *Lockchoppe*, the former designation of the stream in Wakulla Co. Muskogee *lokchapi* which signifies the (red) oak; the word is composed of *lokcha* (acorn) and *api* (stem.)

St. Augustine: St. Johns Co.—The oldest continually settled city in the U.S. It was named by its founder, Pedro Menéndez de Avilés, for St. Augustine, the Bishop of Hippo.

St. Petersburg: Pinellas Co.—Called the "Sunshine City" but it was named after one of the coldest, great cities of the world—Russia's St. Petersburg, now Leningrad.

Starke: Bradford Co.—It was named after Gov. Starke Perry of Florida or after Thomas Starke, a slaveholder who purchased the land around the area.

Steinhatchee: Taylor Co.—The name is derived from the Muskogee *ak* (down) *isti* (man) and *hatchee* (creek)—Dead man's creek.

Stuart: Martin Co.—Named for Samuel C. Stuart, first telegraph operator and station agent, when the Florida East Coast Railroad was built across the St. Lucie River.

Tallahassee: Leon Co.—The name is derived from a Muskogee word meaning "old town."

Tarpon Springs: Pinellas Co.—The name was said to have come from a remark from Mrs. Ormond Boyer, who while standing on the shore saw many fish leaping from the water, and exclaimed "see that tarpon spring," henceforth the name. However the fish was not a tarpon, but a mullet.

Temple Terrace: Hillsborough Co.—Named for the temple orange.

Titusville: Brevard Co.—Established just after the Civil War by Colonel Henry T. Titus, who had been a fierce antagonist of John Brown in the struggle over Kansas which preceded the war.

Trenton: Gilchrist Co.—Named after Trenton, Tennessee by Ben Boyd, who served in the Confederate Army and who established a sawmill there.

Tyndall A.F.B.: Panama City—Named for Lt. Frank B. Tyndall, a World War I ace who was killed in the line of duty near Mooresville, N.C.

Valparaiso: Okaloosa Co.—Name taken from that of the city in Indiana, which in turn was named for the famous Chilean port. The word is Spanish for valley of paradise.

Venice: Sarasota Co.—Named by Franklin Higel, an early settler who felt that the blue waters of the bays, rivers, and Gulf gave the place a resemblance to the famous Italian city.

Wauchula: Hardee Co.—The name may be derived from the Muskogee *wakka* (cow) and *hute* (house or tank).

Weeki Wachee Springs: Hernando Co.—From the Muskogee words *wekiwa* (spring) and *chee* (little). Therefore you get little spring.

Wewahitchka: Gulf Co.—This complex name believed to be derived from an unknown Indian language and meaning "water eyes." A perfect pair of eyes is formed by two oblong lakes along the edge of town; these are separated by a pronounced ridge that corresponds to the bridge of the nose.

Winter Haven: Polk Co.—It was so called because it was considered a haven from the severe winters of the north. Also known as the City of a Hundred Lakes.

Winter Park: Orange Co.—It was named by Loring Chase and Oliver Chapman who were designing a town in the style of the New England town. They chose this name because the area was a "veritable park in winter."

Yeehaw: Indian River Co.—A corruption of Muskogee *yaha* which means wolf.

Zellwood: Orange Co.—Named for Colonel T. Elwood Zell, publisher of Zell's Cyclopedia; Zellwood was his home and the community adopted the name in his honor.

Zephyrhills: Pasco Co.—The name calls attention to the cooling breezes that blow over the hills in this section of the state.

	Population 1990	Population 1980	Percent Change 1980–1990	Percent White 1990	Percent Black 1990	Percent Hispanic Origin 1990	Percent 65 years and older 1990
Alachua	181,596	151,369	20.0	77.5	19.0	3.7	9.3
Baker	18,486	15,289	20.9	84.3	15.0	1.1	8.0
Bay	126,994	97,740	29.9	86.3	10.8	1.8	12.0
Bradford	22,515	20,023	12.5	78.6	20.2	1.9	12.1
Brevard	398,978	272,959	46.2	89.8	7.8	3.1	16.6
Broward	1,255,488	1,018,257	23.3	81.7	15.4	8.6	20.8
Calhoun	11,011	9,294	18.5	83.2	15.1	1.1	14.5
Charlotte	110,975	58,460	89.8	95.0	3.8	2.5	33.8
Citrus	93,515	54,703	71.0	96.7	2.4	1.8	31.3
Clay	105,986	67,052	58.1	92.2	5.2	2.6	8.5
Collier	152,099	85,971	76.9	91.4	4.6	13.6	22.7
Columbia	42,613	35,399	20.4	80.8	18.0	1.5	13.3
Dade	1,937,094	1,625,509	19.2	72.9	20.5	49.2	14.0
De Soto	23,865	19,039	25.4	80.2	15.6	9.6	19.4
Dixie	10,585	7,751	36.6	90.6	8.7	0.9	14.7
Duval	672,971	571,003	17.9	72.8	24.4	2.6	10.7
Escambia	262,798	233,794	12.4	76.6	20.0	1.9	11.9
Flagler	28,701	10,913	163.0	90.0	8.2	4.4	25.6
Franklin	8,967	7,661	17.1	86.7	12.4	0.7	18.0
Gadsden	41,105	41,674	-1.4	40.6	57.7	2.3	12.6
Gilchrist	9,667	5,767	67.6	90.6	8.5	1.6	13.8
Glades	7,591	5,992	26.7	78.9	12.1	8.0	19.6
Gulf	11,504	10,658	7.9	80.4	18.8	0.7	15.3
Hamilton	10,930	8,761	24.8	59.0	38.9	2.7	11.4
Hardee	19,499	20,357	-4.2	84.0	5.3	23.4	15.2
Hendry	25,773	18,599	38.6	72.1	16.7	22.3	11.0
Hernando	101,115	44,469	127.4	95.0	3.9	2.9	30.7
Highlands	68,432	47,526	44.0	87.3	10.0	5.1	33.5
Hillsborough	834,054	646,939	28.9	82.8	13.2	12.8	12.2
Holmes	15,778	14,723	7.2	93.4	5.0	1.1	15.7
Indian River	90,208	59,896	50.6	90.3	8.5	3.0	27.3
Jackson	41,375	39,154	5.7	72.7	26.2	2.4	14.9
Jefferson	11,296	10,703	5.5	56.1	43.4	1.2	14.8
Lafayette	5,578	4,035	38.2	83.0	14.1	4.1	10.9
Lake	152,104	104,870	45.0	89.2	9.3	2.8	27.5
Lee	335,113	205,266	63.3	91.4	6.6	4.5	24.8
Leon	192,493	148,655	29.5	73.6	24.2	2.5	8.2
Levy	25,923	19,870	30.5	86.2	12.4	1.9	19.0
Liberty	5,569	4,260	30.7	80.9	17.6	1.9	11.3
Madison	16,569	14,894	11.3	57.6	41.7	1.4	14.1
Manatee	211,707	148,445	42.6	90.0	7.7	4.5	28.1
Marion	194,833	122,488	59.1	85.8	12.8	3.0	22.2
Martin	100,900	64,014	57.6	91.3	6.0	4.7	27.4
Monroe	78,024	63,188	23.5	92.1	5.4	12.3	16.0
Nassau	43,941	32,894	33.6	88.9	10.3	1.1	10.2
Okaloosa	143,776	109,920	30.8	87.1	9.0	3.1	9.3
Okeechobee	29,627	20,264	46.2	84.3	6.4	11.8	16.2
Orange	677,491	470,865	43.9	79.6	15.2	9.6	10.6
Osceola	107,728	49,287	118.6	89.3	5.5	11.9	13.9
Palm Beach	863,518	576,758	49.7	84.8	12.5	7.7	24.3
Pasco	281,131	193,661	45.2	96.3	1.9	3.3	32.3
Pinellas	851,659	728,531	16.9	90.5	7.7	2.3	26.0
Polk	405,382	321,652	26.0	84.4	13.4	4.9	18.6
Putnam	65,070	50,549	28.7	79.9	18.3	2.6	18.0
St. Johns	83,829	51,303	63.4	90.1	8.7	2.3	16.5
St. Lucie	150,171	87,182	72.3	81.3	16.4	4.0	21.0
Santa Rosa	81,608	55,988	45.8	93.6	4.0	1.5	9.5
Sarasota	277,776	202,251	37.3	94.6	4.3	2.1	32.2
Seminole	287,529	179,752	60.0	88.2	8.5	6.5	10.3
Sumter	31,577	24,272	30.1	82.6	16.2	2.4	22.4
Suwannee	26,780	22,287	20.2	84.1	14.7	1.6	16.9
Taylor	17,111	16,532	3.5	80.6	18.0	1.0	13.3
Union	10,252	10,166	0.9	75.1	23.2	3.3	7.5
Volusia	370,712	258,762	43.3	88.6	9.0	4.0	22.8
Wakulla	14,202	10,887	30.5	86.1	12.9	0.6	11.6
Walton	27,760	21,300	30.3	91.1	6.8	0.9	16.5
Washington	16,919	14,509	16.6	82.9	14.5	1.1	17.6
Florida	12,937,926	9,746,961	32.7	83.1	13.6	12.2	18.3

	Birth Rate per 1000 1989	Death Rate per 1000 1989	Per Capita Personal Income Average 1989	Largest City	Largest City Population	Crime Rate per 100,000 Persons 1990	Persons per Square Mile 1990
Alachua	14.9	6.3	14,719	Gainesville	84,770	9,792	207.7
Baker	16.4	7.7	11,670	Macclenny	3,966	3,398	31.6
Bay	14.9	7.5	13,524	Panama City	34,378	6,062	166.3
Bradford	14.6	9.2	10,029	Starke	5,226	5,675	76.8
Brevard	13.2	8.4	16,445	Palm Bay	62,480	7,114	391.7
Broward	14.5	11.5	21,898	Ft. Lauderdale	149,377	8,737	1038.5
Calhoun	13.9	10.3	9,243	Bountstown	2,404	781	19.4
Charlotte	10.1	15.4	16,600	Punta Gorda	10,747	2,810	160.0
Citrus	10.2	14.8	12,559	Inverness	5,797	3,281	160.2
Clay	15.0	6.2	15,785	Orange Park	9,488	4,871	176.3
Collier	15.5	10.7	23,322	Naples	19,505	6,335	75.1
Columbia	15.6	9.1	11,947	Lake City	10,005	5,558	53.5
Dade	17.8	10.0	17,963	Miami	358,548	13,587	996.2
De Soto	17.1	11.7	11,712	Arcadia	6,488	4,221	37.4
Dixie	17.4	9.6	9,690	Cross City	2,041	3,464	15.0
Duval	18.5	8.0	16,074	Jacksonville	635,230	9,642	869.6
Escambia	15.4	7.7	13,375	Pensacola	58,165	7,269	396.0
Flagler	13.0	12.4	13,506	Flagler Beach	3,820	4,487	59.2
Franklin	14.9	13.9	12,100	Apalachicola	2,602	579	16.8
Gadsden	17.3	8.7	10,445	Quincy	7,444	4,216	79.6
Gilchrist	19.0	10.1	12,947	Trenton	1,287	606	27.7
Glades	11.1	10.3	8,776	Moore Haven	1,432	3,623	9.8
Gulf	14.7	8.9	10,824	Port St. Joe	4,044	1,731	20.4
Hamilton	17.8	9.3	10,733	Jasper	2,099	3,624	21.2
Hardee	21.0	8.5	12,128	Wauchula	3,253	5,187	30.6
Hendry	22.2	8.7	13,728	Clewiston	6,085	5,304	22.4
Hernando	10.3	13.8	12,676	Brooksville	7,440	5,661	211.4
Highlands	12.5	13.6	13,932	Sebring	8,900	5,640	66.5
Hillsborough	16.4	8.2	16,044	Tampa	280,015	9,280	793.6
Holmes	10.1	9.3	10,096	Bonifay	2,612	1,265	32.7
Indian River	11.1	11.2	20,880	Vero Beach	17,350	5,361	179.3
Jackson	11.8	9.7	11,205	Marianna	6,292	2,406	45.2
Jefferson	15.2	10.9	10,628	Monticello	2,573	4,560	18.9
Lafayette	12.5	6.3	11,554	Mayo	917	527	10.3
Lake	13.8	13.7	17,698	Leesburg	14,903	4,884	159.6
Lee	13.2	11.2	18,063	Cape Coral	74,991	5,160	417.0
Leon	14.5	5.6	15,724	Tallahassee	124,773	10,750	288.7
Levy	14.5	13.6	10,884	Williston	2,179	5,174	23.2
Liberty	17.4	11.2	12,110	Bristol	937	880	6.7
Madison	18.5	11.0	10,934	Madison	3,345	2,899	23.9
Manatee	14.7	14.0	18,482	Bradenton	43,779	8,149	285.6
Marion	14.4	11.7	12,669	Ocala	42,045	7,492	123.4
Martin	13.2	11.9	23,832	Stuart	11,936	5,007	181.6
Monroe	12.2	8.9	17,986	Key West	24,832	12,963	78.2
Nassau	15.4	6.9	15,316	Fernandina Beach	8,765	3,710	67.4
Okaloosa	15.3	5.5	13,619	Ft. Walton Beach	21,471	3,530	153.6
Okeechobee	18.2	10.6	11,193	Okeechobee	4,943	5,009	38.3
Orange	17.4	7.3	18,083	Orlando	164,693	9,527	746.5
Osceola	16.8	9.0	17,596	Kissimmee	30,050	9,593	81.5
Palm Beach	14.5	11.2	24,319	West Palm Beach	67,643	9,621	424.5
Pasco	11.1	14.8	13,710	New Port Richey	14,044	4,484	377.4
Pinellas	11.7	14.2	21,255	St. Petersburg	238,629	7,866	3039.5
Polk	15.3	9.6	14,246	Lakeland	70,576	9,098	216.2
Putnam	14.7	11.8	11,304	Palatka	10,201	8,672	90.1
St. Johns	12.8	9.7	18,436	St. Augustine	11,692	6,417	137.7
St. Lucie	16.1	10.7	13,349	Port St. Lucie	55,866	7,573	262.3
Santa Rosa	18.7	7.8	14,023	Milton	7,216	4,578	80.3
Sarasota	10.3	14.6	24,039	Sarasota	50,961	7,446	485.8
Seminole	14.9	6.4	16,316	Altamonte Springs	34,879	5,949	932.9
Sumter	14.3	12.1	11,517	Wildwood	3,421	4,131	57.9
Suwannee	12.2	11.4	11,225	Live Oak	6,332	3,921	38.9
Taylor	16.0	8.8	11,700	Perry	7,151	3,480	16.4
Union	13.2	7.8	9,452	Lake Butler	2,116	907	42.7
Volusia	12.7	12.4	15,364	Daytona Beach	61,921	7,154	335.2
Wakulla	14.6	8.0	11,438	Sopchoppy	367	1,929	23.4
Walton	11.7	10.1	10,245	De Funiak Springs	5,120	1,933	26.2
Washington	12.4	12.5	10,741	Chipley	3,866	761	29.2
Florida	15.0	10.3	17,715	Jacksonville	635,230	8,539	239.6

Photo Credits

208   *The Blue Umbrella*, courtesy of Barbara Gillman Gallery.

212   *Bike Races,* Florida Department of Commerce, Division of Tourism.

217   *Canoeing on Blackwater River*, by James Gaines, Florida Department of Commerce, Division of Tourism.

218   *Flamingo*, by Karen Aldhizer, Florida Department of Commerce, Division of Tourism.

219   *Tomoka State Park*, Florida Department of Commerce, Division of Tourism.

222   *Florida Caverns State Park*, by James Gaines, Florida Department of Commerce, Division of Tourism.
       Castillo de San Marcos, Florida Department of Commerce, Division of Tourism.

223   *Glass-Bottom Boat*, Florida Department of Commerce, Division of Tourism.
       Spaceship Earth and Monorail, ©The Walt Disney Company, courtesy of the Walt Disney World Resort.

224   *Miami Metrozoo* and *J.N. "Ding" Darling National Wildlife Refuge*, Florida Department of Commerce, Division of Tourism.

225   *Tournament Players Club*, by Don Burk, Florida Department of Commerce, Division of Tourism.

226   *Baseball Spring Training*, by Robert Overton, Florida Department of Commerce, Division of Tourism.
       Detroit Lions and Tampa Bay Buccaneers, by Paul R. Baker, Florida Department of Commerce, Division of Tourism.

229   *Balloon Rally*, courtesy of Springtime Tallahassee, Inc.
       Bahamas Goombay Festival, Greater Miami Convention and Visitors Bureau.
       Medieval Fair, courtesy of the John and Mable Ringling Museum of Art.

236   *The Miami Line*, neon lights and photo by Rockne Krebs, courtesy of Metro-Dade Art in Public Places.

250   Loxahatchee River, by Clyde Butcher, ©1991.

Sources

The principal sources for the graphics and text are listed by section. The particular map or graph for which the source was used is in parentheses at the end of the reference. When sources pertain to the entire page, individual graphics are not separately identified. Sources used more than once are referenced to their original citation by page number.

Page

INTRODUCTION

1–2   Winsberg, Morton D. *Florida Weather*. Orlando: University of Central Florida Press, 1990.

1–7   Derr, Mark. *Some Kind of Paradise*: *A Chronicle of Man and Land in Florida*. New York: William Morrow and Company, Inc., 1989.

6–7   U.S. Department of Commerce, Bureau of the Census. Census of Population, 1990. (maps)

NATURAL ENVIRONMENT

Unless otherwise noted climate maps were drawn from data from 86 stations, over 90 percent of which have recorded climatic observations for at least 30 years.

14   Data from U.S. Geological Survey and U.S. Coast and Geodetic Survey.

15   Adapted from White, W.A. *Geomorphology of Florida*. Bulletin 51. Tallahassee: Florida Department of Natural Resources, Bureau of Geology, 1970. (physiography map)
       Data from U.S. Geological Survey. (relief map)

18   U.S. Department of Agriculture, Soil Conservation Service. *Atlas of River Basins of the United States*. 2d ed. Washington, D.C.: U.S. Government Printing Office, June 1970. (drainage basins and divides map)

19   Adapted from Coastal and Oceanographic Engineering Department, University of Florida. *Coastal Newsletter*. June, 1981. (coastal information stations map)
       Data from National Oceanic and Atmospheric Administration. (weather stations map)
       Data from U.S. Geological Survey. (stream gauging stations and groundwater monitoring stations)

20   Adapted from Vernon, Robert O., and Harbass S. Puri. *Geologic Map of Florida*. Map Series 3. Tallahassee: Florida Department of Natural Resources, Bureau of Geology, 1964. (map)
       Chart modified by Thomas Scott, Florida Geological Survey, 1991.

21   Thomas Scott. (stratigraphic nomenclature chart)

22   Adapted from Barnett, Richard S. "Basement Structure of Florida and Its Implications." *Transactions of Gulf Coast Association of Geological Societies* 25 (1975): 126. (basement structural geology map)

Adapted from Vernon, Robert O. *Geology of Citrus and Levy Counties of Florida*. Tallahassee: Florida Department of Natural Resources, Bureau of Geology, 1951; Vernon and Puri (p. 20). (principal structures map)
Adapted from Wicker, Russell A., and Douglas L. Smith. "Florida Basement: An Isometric View." *Bulletin of the American Association of Petroleum Geologists* 61 (1977): 2143. (basement geology map)

23   Barnett (p. 22). (generalized basement structure)
       Vernon and Puri (p. 20). (tertiary detail)

24   Bryant, W.R., A.A. Meyerhoff, N.K. Brown, Jr., M.A. Furrer, T.E. Pyle, and J.W. Antoine. "Escarpments, Reef Trends and Diapiric Structures, Eastern Gulf of Mexico." *Bulletin of the American Association of Petroleum Geologists* 53 (1969): 2506-2542. (cretaceous map)
       McElhinny, M.W. *Paleomagnetism and Plate Tectonics*. Cambridge, Massachusetts: University Press, 1973. (paleolatitudes map)
       Puri, Harbass S., and Robert O. Vernon. *Summary of the Geology of Florida and a Guidebook to the Classic Exposures*. Special Publication 5. Tallahassee: Florida Geological Survey, 1964. (middle miocene map)

25   Adapted from Spencer, Steven M., comp. *The Industrial Minerals Industry Directory of Florida*. Information Cir. 105. Florida Geological Survey, 1989. (economic geology map)
       Florida Department of Natural Resources, Bureau of Geology. Environmental Map Series 78, 79, 80, 84, 85, 88, 89, 90, 93, 97, 99, 100, 101. Tallahassee, Florida, 1975-1981. (environmental geology map)

26   Adapted from King, Elizabeth R. "Regional Magnetic Map of Florida." *Bulletin of the American Association of Petroleum Geologists* 43 (1959): 2844-2854.

27   U.S. Geological Survey. *Composite Magnetic Anomaly Map of U.S.* Map GP-954-A. 1982.

28   Adapted from American Geophysical Union and U.S. Geological Survey. *Bouguer Gravity Anomaly Map of the United States*. Washington, D.C., 1964.

29   Simpson, R.W., R.C. Jachens, R.W. Saltus, and R.J. Blakely. *Isostatic Residual Gravity, Topographic, and First-Vertical-Derivative Gravity Maps of the Conterminous United States*. Map GP-975, Sheet 2 of 2, Map D. U.S. Geological Survey, 1986.

30   Adapted from Tanner, W.F. "Florida." In *World Shorelines*, edited by Eric Byrd and Maurice Schwartz. Stroudsburg, Pennsylvania: Dowden, Hutchinson and Ross, Inc., 1980. (depth to 100 degrees celcius map)
       Adapted from Tanner, W.F. "Geothermal Exploration from Deep Well Data." *Transactions of Gulf Coast Association of Geological Societies* 26 (1976): 65-68. (geothermal gradient map)

Stover, C.W., B.G. Reagor, and S.T. Algermissen. *Seismicity Map of Florida*. Miscellaneous Field Studies Map 1056. Washington, D.C.: U.S. Geological Survey, 1979. (seismic activity map)

31   Data from U.S. Geological Survey and Florida Department of Natural Resources, Bureau of Geology.

32   Peddie, Norman W., and Audronis K. Zunde. *The Magnetic Field in the United States, 1985, Declination Chart*. Map GP-986-D. U.S. Geological Survey, 1988. (magnetic declination map)
_____. *The Magnetic Field in the United States, 1985, Inclination Chart*. Map GP-986-I. U.S. Geological Survey, 1988. (magnetic inclination map)

33   Peddie, Norman W., and Audronis K. Zunde. *The Magnetic Field in the United States, 1985, Horizontal Intensity Chart*. Map GP-986-H. U.S. Geological Survey, 1988. (horizontal magnetic intensity map)
_____. *The Magnetic Field in the United States, 1985, Vertical Intensity Chart*. Map GP-986-Z. U.S. Geological Survey, 1988. (vertical magnetic intensity map)
_____. *The Magnetic Field in the United States, 1985, Total Intensity Chart*. Map GP-986-F. U.S. Geological Survey, 1988. (total magnetic intensity map)

34   Adapted from *National Atlas of the United States of America*. Washington , D.C.: U.S. Geological Survey, 1970. (types of tides map)
National Oceanic and Atmospheric Administration, National Weather Service. *Hurricanes, Florida and You*. Washington, D.C.: U.S. Government Printing Office, 1977. (storm surge map, hundred-year storm-tide zone map)

35   *National Atlas of the United States of America* (p.34). (sea surface temperature maps, sea surface salinity maps).

36   Adapted from Ginsburg, Robert N., ed. *South Florida Bottom Sediments*. Miami, Florida: University of Miami, 1972; U.S. Geological Survey. "Atlantic Continental Shelf and Slope of the U.S.—Texture of Surface Sediments from New Jersey to Florida." Professional Paper 529-M. Washington, D.C.: U.S. Government Printing Office, 1973. (texture of bottom sediments)
Adapted from Tanner. "Florida." (p. 30). (wave height and wave energy density)

37   Tanner. "Florida." (p. 30).
Winker, Charles D. "Plio-Pleistocene Paleography of the Florida Gulf Coast Interpreted from Relic Shorelines." *Transactions Gulf Coast Association of Geological Societies* 27 (1977): 409-420.
Winker, Charles D., and James D. Howard. "Correlation of Tectonically Deformed Shorelines on the Southern Atlantic Coastal Plain." *Geology* 5 (1977): 123-127.

38–39   Stapor, F.W. "Coastal Sand Budgets and Holocene Beach Ridge Plain Development, Northwest Florida." Ph.D. dissertation, Florida State University, 1973.
Stapor, F.W., and Tanner, W.F. "Late Holocene Mean Sea Level Data from St. Vincent Island and the Shape of the Late Holocene Mean Sea Level Curve." In *Proceedings, Coastal Sedimentology Symposium*. Florida State University, Department of Geology, 1977.
Tanner, W.F., and F.W. Stapor. "Precise Control of Wave Run-Up in Beach Ridge Construction." *Zeitschrift fur Geomorphologie* (1972): 393-399.

40   Adapted from U.S. Department of Commerce, Environmental Science Services Administration. *Climate Atlas of the United States*, 1988. (January map, July map)

42   Adapted from Marsh, William M. *Earthscape: A Physical Geography*. New York: John Wiley & Sons, Inc., 1987, p. 103. (surface temperature chart)
Winsberg, Morton D. *Florida Weather*. Orlando: University of Central Florida Press, 1990. figs 1:4a, p. 7 and 1:4b, p. 8. (maximum daily temperature map, minimum daily temperature map)

43   Winsberg (p. 42). fig. 2:6, p. 36. (days with minimum temperature below 40° map)
_____. p. 48. (most severe cold wave map)
_____. table D:9, p. 160, table D:10, p. 161. (average temperature extremes map)
_____. fig. 4:3, p. 80. (days with maximum temperature 88°F or

higher map)

44   Winsberg (p. 42). fig. 2:3, p. 30. (winter days temperature exceeds 75°F map)
_____. fig. 2:2, p. 29. (beginning of winter map)
_____. fig. 5:1, p. 107. (beginning of fall map)
_____. fig. 4:1, p. 77. (beginning of summer map)
_____. fig. 3.2, p. 54. (beginning of spring map)

45   Data from National Oceanic and Atmospheric Administration, National Weather Service. (maps)

46   Winsberg (p. 42). fig. 2:4, p. 34. (January days with 0.1+ rainfall map)
_____. fig. 3.3, p. 56. (April days with 0.1+ rainfall map)
_____. fig. 4:7a, p. 92. (July days with 0.1+ rainfall map)
_____. fig. 5:3, p. 109. (October days with 0.1+ rainfall map)
_____. fig. 4:5, p. 90. (beginning of summer rainy season map)

47   Adapted from McKnight, Tom L. *Physical Geography: A Landscape Appreciation*. 2nd ed. Englewood Cliffs: Prentice-Hall, Inc., 1987, p. 111. (types of atmospheric uplifting and precipitation drawings)
Fernald, Edward A., and Donald J. Patton, eds. *Water Resources Atlas of Florida*. Tallahassee: Florida State University, Institute of Science and Public Affairs, 1984, p. 26. (maximum rainfall in 24 hours map)
_____. p. 27. (diurnal variation in rainfall charts)
_____. p. 29. (average September rainfall from storms)

48   Data from National Oceanic and Atmospheric Administration. (Bermuda High map)
Fernald and Patton (p. 47). p. 32. (extended dry periods chart)

49   Visher, F.N., and G.H. Hughes. *The Difference between Rainfall and Potential Evaporation in Florida*. rev. ed. Map Series 32. Tallahassee: Florida Department of Natural Resources, Bureau of Geology, 1969. (rainfall and evaporation map)

50   Adapted from U.S. Department of Commerce (p. 40). pp. 65-66. (average percentage of total possible sunshine maps)
Adapted from U.S. Department of Commerce. pp. 67-68; Doesken, Nolan, and William P. Eckrich. "How Often Does it Rain Where You Live?" *Weatherwise* 40 (1987): 200-203. (average total hours of sunshine, January, July)

51   Data from National Oceanic and Atmospheric Administration. (wind direction maps)

52   Adapted from Holzworth, George C. *Mixing Heights, Wind Speeds, and Potential for Urban Air Pollution Throughout the Contiguous U.S.* Washington, D.C.: U.S. Environmental Protection Agency, 1972.

53   U.S. Department of Commerce. *Monthly Normals of Temperature, Precipitation, and Heating and Cooling Degree Days 1951–1980, Florida*. Asheville, N.C.: National Climatic Center, Climatography of the United States No. 81, 1982.

54   Winsberg (p. 42). fig. 3:1, p. 53. (comfort zones map)

55   Patton and Fernald (p. 47). p. 28. (thunderstorm maps)
Winsberg (p. 42). fig 3:6, p. 69. (tornado map)

56   Adapted from Anthes, Richard A., Hans A. Panofsky, John J. Cahir, and Albert Rango. "Hurricanes." In *The Atmosphere*. Columbus, Ohio: Charles E. Merrill Publishing Company, 1975, fig. 6.6, p. 157. (cross section of a hurricane)

57   *Miami Herald*, September 5, 1988. (Florida hurricanes in the 20th century)
U.S. Department of Commerce. *Some Devastating North Atlantic Hurricanes of the 20th Century*. Washington, D.C.: National Weather Center, NOAA/PA Publication 77019, 1977.
Recent data from Florida Department of Community Affairs, Division of Emergency Management. (selected hurricanes table 1926-89)

58   Adapted from Hampson, Paul S. *Wetlands in Florida*. Map Series 109. Tallahassee: Florida Department of Natural Resources, Bureau of Geology, 1984; Snell, L.J., and W.E. Kenner. *Surface Water Features of Florida*. Map Series 66. Tallahassee: Florida Department of Natural Resources, Bureau of Geology, 1974. (surface water map)
Florida Department of Natural Resources, Bureau of Geology. *Map of Karst Areas of Florida*. Open File Report. Tallahassee, Florida, 1965; Data from National Speleological Society, 1980. (karst terrain map)

59   Adapted from Anderson, Warren. *Temperature of Florida Streams.* Map Series 43. Tallahassee: Florida Department of Natural Resources, Bureau of Geology, 1975. (stream temperature map)

Fernald and Patton (p. 47). p. 59. (discharge of major Florida rivers table, discharge of selected Florida rivers and major world rivers diagram)

Rumenik, Roger P. *Runoff to Streams in Florida.* Map Series 122. Tallahassee: Florida Department of Natural Resources, Florida Geological Survey, 1988. (annual runoff map)

60   Adapted from Florida Department of Natural Resources, Division of Recreation and Parks. *Florida Environmentally Endangered Lands Plan.* Tallahassee, Florida, 1975; Hyde, Luther W. *Principal Aquifers in Florida.* rev. ed. Map Series 16. Tallahassee: Florida Department of Natural Resources, Bureau of Geology, 1975. (map)

61   Adapted from Barr, G.L. *Potentiometric Surface of the Upper Floridan Aquifer in Florida, May 1985.* Map Series 119. Tallahassee: Florida Department of Natural Resources, Florida Geological Survey, 1987. (potentiometric surface map, decline in potentiometric surface map)

Adapted from Healy, Henry G. *Potentiometric Surface and Areas of Artesian Flow of the Floridan Aquifer in Florida, May 1974.* Map Series 73. Tallahassee: Florida Department of Natural Resources, Bureau of Geology, 1975. (potentiometric surface map)

Adapted from Klein, Howard. *Depth to the Base of the Potable Water in the Floridan Aquifer.* rev. ed. Map Series 42. Tallahassee: Florida Department of Natural Resources, Bureau of Geology, 1975. (depth to the base of potable water map)

Adapted from Vernon, Robert O. *Top of the Floridan Artesian Aquifer.* Map Series 56. Tallahassee: Florida Department of Natural Resources, Bureau of Geology, 1973. (Floridan aquifer map)

62   Adapted from Marella, Richard L. *Freshwater Withdrawals and Water-Use Trends in Florida, 1985.* Map Series 123. Tallahassee: Florida Department of Natural Resources, Florida Geological Survey, 1989. (freshwater withdrawals map and graphs)

Data from Carlisle, Victor W., Professor of Soil Science, University of Florida. (soil drainage map)

63   Adapted from Kaufman, Matthew I. *Generalized Distribution and Concentration of Orthophosphate in Florida Streams.* Map Series 33. Tallahassee: Florida Department of Natural Resources, Bureau of Geology, 1975. (chemical quality of stream water map, maximum orthophosphate concentration in streams map)

Adapted from Shampine, William J. *Chloride Concentration in Water from the Upper Part of the Floridan Aquifer in Florida.* Map Series 12. Tallahassee: Florida Department of Natural Resources, Bureau of Geology, 1975. (chloride concentration in upper aquifer map, water hardness of upper aquifer map)

64   Data from U.S. Department of Agriculture, Soil Conservation Service.

66–69   Davis, John H. *General Map of Natural Vegetation of Florida.* Cir. S-178, Institute of Food and Agricultural Sciences. Gainesville: University of Florida, 1967, 2nd printing, 1980.

Florida Natural Areas Inventory and Department of Natural Resources. *Guide to the Natural Communities of Florida.* Tallahassee: Florida Natural Areas Inventory and Office of Land Use Planning and Biological Services, Florida Department of Natural Resources, 1990.

Myers, R.L., and J.J. Ewel, eds. *Ecosystems of Florida.* Orlando: University of Central Florida Press, 1990.

Nature 2000 Task Force. *Preserving Florida's Biodiversity* . Draft Report. Tallahassee, Florida: Governor's Office of Environmental Affairs,1990.

U.S. Department of Agriculture, Soil Conservation Service. *26 Ecological Communities of Florida.* Fort Worth: Texas, 1981.

72   Carr, Archie F., and C.J. Goin. *Guide to the Reptiles, Amphibians, and Freshwater Fishes of Florida.* Gainesville: University of Florida Press, 1955.

Koukoulis, A. *Poisonous Snakes of Florida.* Silver Springs, Florida: Dukane Press, Inc., 1972.

Moler, Paul. *A Checklist of Florida's Amphibians and Reptiles.* Florida Game and Fresh Water Fish Commission, 1988, revised 1990.

Rare and Endangered Biota of Florida. 4 vols. Gainesville: University Presses of Florida, 1978.

Stevenson, Henry M. *Vertebrates of Florida.* Gainesville: University Presses of Florida, 1976.

73   *Rare and Endangered Biota of Florida* (p. 72).
74   Carr and Goin (p. 72).

Lee, David S., Carter R. Gilbert, Charles H. Hocutt, Robert E. Jenkins, Don E. McAllister, and Jay R. Stauffer, Jr., eds. *Atlas of North American Freshwater Fishes.* North Carolina Biological Survey Publication 1980-12. Raleigh: North Carolina State Museum of Natural History, 1981.

Rare and Endangered Biota of Florida (p. 72)

Stevenson (p. 72).

75   Hall, F.W. *Birds of Florida.* St. Petersburg, Florida: Great Outdoors Publishing Company, 1979.

Rare and Endangered Biota of Florida (p. 72).

Sprunt, Alexander. *Florida Bird Life.* New York: Coward-McCann, Inc. and the National Audubon Society, 1963.

Stevenson (p. 72).

76–77   *Rare and Endangered Biota of Florida* (p. 72)

Stevenson (p. 72).

HISTORY AND CULTURE

82-83   Map Collection, Strozier Library, Florida State University.
84   Data from Miller, James J., Florida Department of State, Division of Historical Resources, Bureau of Archaelogical Research. (map)

Milanich, Jerald T., and Charles Fairbanks. *Florida Archaeology.* New York: Academic Press, 1980.

Wisenbaker, Michael. "Florida's True Natives." *Florida Naturalist* (Spring 1988): 2-5.

85   Cline, Howard F. *Florida Indians II.* New York and London: Garland Publishing Inc., 1974.

Fairbanks, Charles. *Florida Indians III.* New York and London: Garland Publishing Inc., 1974.

Hudson, Charles M., ed. *Four Centuries of Southern Indians.* Athens: University of Georgia Press, 1975.

Lorant, Stefan, ed. *The First Pictures of America Made by John White and Jacques Le Moyne and Engraved by Theodore de Bry with Contemporary Narratives of the French Settlements in Florida, 1562-1565 and the English Colonies in Virginia, 1585-1590.* rev. ed. New York: Duell, Sloan & Pearse. (drawing)

Milanich, Jerald, and Susan Milbrath. *First Encounters: Spanish Explorations in the Caribbean and the United States, 1492-1570.* Gainesville: University of Florida Press and Florida Museum of Natural History, 1989.

Swanton, John R. *The Indian Tribes of North America.* Washington, D.C.: Smithsonian Institution Press, 1952. (map)

86–87   Davis, T. Frederick. "Juan Ponce de Leon's Voyages to Florida." *Florida Historical Quarterly* 14 (1935-36): 1-70; Hudson, Charles, Chester B. De Pratter, and Marvin T. Smith. "Hernando de Soto's Expedition through the Southern United States." In Milanich and Milbrath (p. 85); Hudson, Charles, Marvin T. Smith, Chester B. De Pratter, and Emilia Kelly. "The Tristan de Luna Expedition, 1559-1561." In Milanich and Milbrath (p. 85). (Spanish exploration map)

Marx, Robert F. *Spanish Treasure in Florida's Waters: A Billion-Dollar Graveyard.* Boston: Mariners Press, 1979; Marx, Robert F. *The Treasure Fleets of the Spanish Main.* Cleveland: World Publishing Company, 1968. (Spanish treasure fleet map and text)

Milanich and Milbrath (p. 85).

Tebeau, Charlton W. *A History of Florida.* rev. ed. Coral Gables: University of Miami Press, 1971, 7th Printing, 1980.

U.S. Congress. *Final Report of the United States De Soto Expedition Commission.* 76th Congress, First Session, House Document 71, 1939.

U.S. Department of the Interior, National Park Service, Office of Archaeology and Historic Preservation. *Cultural Resources Evaluation of the Northern Gulf of Mexico Continental Shelf.* vol.

2, Historical Cultural Resources. (Spanish treasure fleet map)
West, Robert C., and John P. Augelli. *Middle America: Its Lands and Peoples.* Englewood Cliffs, N.J.: Prentice-Hall, Inc., 1966.
Wright, James Leitch, Jr. *Anglo-American Rivalry in North America.* Athens: University of Georgia Press, 1971.

88-89   Boyd, Mark F., Hale G. Smith, and John W. Griffin. *Here They Once Stood.* Gainesville: University of Florida Press, 1951.
Gannon, Michael V. *The Cross in the Sand: The Early Catholic Church in Florida, 1513-1870.* Gainesville: University of Florida Press, 1965.
Hann, John H. *Apalachee: The Land between the Rivers.* Gainesville, Florida: University Presses of Florida, 1988. (text, map, drawing)
Milanich and Milbrath (p.85).

91   Florida Department of Natural Resources, Bureau of State Lands, Land Records Division. *Florida Tract Books.* Tallahassee, 1824-1850; *Public Lands.* American State Papers, vol. 4. Washington, D.C.: Gales and Seaton, 1950. (land distribution map)
Whitfield, James Bryan. *Political and Legal History of Florida.* Atlanta: Harrison Company, 1943.
Vanderhill, Burke G., and Frank A. Unger. "The Georgia-Florida Land Boundary: Product of Controversy and Compromise." *West Georgia College Studies in the Social Sciences* 18 (1979): 59-73. (Georgia-Florida boundary map and text)

92   Bureau of American Ethnology. *Eighteenth Annual Report.* pt. 2. Washington, D.C.: U.S. Government Printing Office, 1899.
Mahon, John K. *The Second Seminole War.* Gainesville: University of Florida Press, 1968.
McReynolds, Edwin. *The Seminoles.* Norman: University of Oklahoma Press, 1957.
Remini, Robert V. *Andrew Jackson and the Course of the American Empire 1767-1821.* New York: Harper and Row, 1977.
Weisman, Brent Richards. *Like Beads on a String: A Culture History of the Seminole Indians in Northern Peninsular Florida.* Tuscaloosa: The University of Alabama Press, 1989.

93   Bruff, J. Goldsborough. *The State of Florida.* Washington, D.C.: Washington War Department, U.S. Army Corps of Engineers, 1846; Florida Statutes, 1821-1845. (map)

94   Adapted from Paisley, Clifton. *The Red Hills of Florida.* Tuscaloosa: The University of Alabama Press, 1989, pp. 121, 125, 134, 143, 148. (map)
Derr, Mark. *Some Kind of Paradise: A Chronicle of Man and Land in Florida.* New York: William Morrow and Company, Inc., 1989.
Paisley, Clifton. *From Cotton to Quail: An Agricultural Chronicle of Leon County, Florida, 1860-1967.* Tallahassee: University Presses of Florida, 1968.
Smith, Julia Hering. *Slavery and Plantation Growth in Antebellum Florida.* Gainesville: University of Florida Press, 1973.
Tebeau (p. 86-87).

95   Boyd, Mark F. "The Battle of Marianna." *Florida Historical Quarterly* 29 (1950-51): 225-242.
Boyd, Mark F. "The Federal Campaign of 1864 in East Florida." *Florida Historical Quarterly* 29 (1950-51): 3-37.
Boyd, Mark F. "The Joint Operations of the Federal Army and Navy near St. Marks, Florida, March 1865." *Florida Historical Quarterly* 29 (1950-51): 96-124. (map)
Davis, William Watson. *The Civil War and Reconstruction in Florida.* New York: Columbia University Press, 1913. (map)
Dodd, Dorothy. "Florida in the War, 1861-1865." In *The Florida Handbook, 1959-1960.* Tallahassee: Peninsular Publishing Company, 1959.
Itkin, Stanley L. "Operations of the East Coast Blockade Squadron in the Blockade of Florida, 1862-1865." Masters thesis, Florida State University, 1962.
Johns, John E. *Florida During the Civil War.* Gainesville: University of Florida Press, 1963.
Tebeau (p. 86-87).
Thurston, William Nathaniel. "A Study of Maritime Activity in Florida in the Nineteenth Century." Ph.D. dissertation, Florida State University, 1972.

96-97   U.S. Department of Commerce, Bureau of the Census. Census of Population, 1830-1960.

98-99   Ordinance of 1821; Florida Territorial Acts, 1822-1845; Florida Statutes.

100   Adapted from Davis, John H. *General Map of Natural Vegetation of Florida.* Cir. S-178, Institute of Food and Agricultural Sciences. Gainesville: University of Florida, 1967, 2nd printing, 1980. (forestry map)
Adapted from Neel, Earl Myers. "The Economic Geography of the Ridge and Highlands Citrus District of Florida." Ph.D. dissertation, University of Tennessee, 1963. (citrus maps)
Derr (p. 94).
Tebeau (pp. 86-87).
Weeks, Jerry Woods. "Florida Gold: The Emergence of the Citrus Industry 1865-1895." Ph.D. dissertation, University of North Carolina at Chapel Hill, 1977.

101   Blakey, Arch F. *The Florida Phosphate Industry: A History of the Development and Use of a Vital Mineral.* Cambridge: Wertheim Committee, Harvard University, 1973.
Fuller, R.B. "The History and Development of the Mining of Phosphate Rock." In *Manual on Phosphate in Agriculture*, edited by Vincent Sauchelli. Baltimore: The Davidson Chemical Corporation, 1951.
Mealor, W. Theodore Jr., and Merle C. Prunty, "Open-Range Ranching in Southern Florida." *Annals of the Association of American Geographers* 66 (1976): 360-376.

102   Blake, Nelson M. *Land into Water—Water into Land: A History of Water Management in Florida.* Tallahassee: University Presses of Florida, 1980.
Mueller, Edward, Director of Transportation Planning, Reynolds, Smith and Hills, Jacksonville. (map)
Thurston, William Nathaniel. "A Study of Maritime Activity in Florida in the Nineteenth Century." Ph.D. dissertation, Florida State University, 1972.

103   Derr (p. 94).
Frisbie, Louise K. *Florida's Fabled Inns.* Bartow, Florida: Imperial Publishing Co., 1980.
Vanderhill, Burke G. "The Historic Spas of Florida." *West Georgia College Studies in the Social Sciences* 12 (1973): 59-77.

104   Adapted from Johnson, Dudley Sady. "The Railroads of Florida, 1865-1900." Ph.D. dissertation, Florida State University, 1965. (map)

105   Adapted from Bruff, J. Goldsborough. *The State of Florida.* Washington, D.C.: Washington War Department, U.S. Army Corps of Engineers, 1846; and *Johnson's Florida.* New York: A.J. Johnson, 1863. (19th-century map)
Adapted from *Road Map, State of Florida, 1917.* State Road Department Florida; *Pan-Am Official 1928 Road Map of Florida.* Chicago: H.M. Gousha Company. (basic highway network map)
Adapted from *Progress Map, Florida Interstate System.* Florida Department of Transportation, Division of Transportation Planning, December 1964. *Official Transportation Map, Florida.* Florida Department of Transportation, 1990. (limited access highway map)

106   Adapted from Florida Department of Administration, Division of State Planning. *Final Report on the Special Project to Prevent Eutrophication of Lake Okeechobee.* Tallahassee, 1976. (map and text)
Blake (p. 102).
Trustees of the Internal Improvement Fund. *Map of Everglades Drainage District of Florida.* Tallahassee, 1911.

107   Data from U.S. Department of Commerce, Bureau of the Census. Census of Agriculture, *1925, 1930, 1935, 1940, 1945, 1950, 1954, 1959, 1964, 1969, 1974, 1978, 1982*; U.S. Department of Commerce, Bureau of the Census, *Twelfth Census of the United States, 1900, Thirteenth Census of the United States, 1910, Fourteenth Census of the United States, 1920*; and the sixth through the twentieth biennial reports on agriculture in Florida, issued until 1910 by the Commissioner of Agriculture of the State of Florida and thereafter by the Department of Agriculture of the State of Florida, and covering the period from 1899 through 1928. (vegetable graphs)
Data from Salley, George H. *A History of the Florida Sugar Industry.* Florida Sugarcane League, 1984, p. 46. (sugarcane

graph)

The area shown to be in sugarcane production in 1955 was specifically produced for this atlas by Joseph R. Orsenigo of Sci-Agri, Inc., Belle Glade, Florida. The two greatly enlarged sugarcane areas shown on the same map have been adapted from *Cane Growing Areas 1972*. Map. Florida Sugar Cane League, Inc.; *Cane Growing Areas, 1985*. Map. Sugar Cane League, Inc.

108   Campbell, Archer Stuart. *The Cigar Industry of Tampa, Florida*. Gainesville: Bureau of Business and Economics Research, University of Florida, 1939.

Derr (p. 94).

Harner, Charles E. *A Pictorial History of Ybor City*. Tampa: Trend Publications, 1975.

Rivero Muñiz, José. *The Ybor City Story (1885-1954)*. Tampa: (n.p.), 1976.

West, Robert C., and John P. Augelli. (p. 86-87).

Westfall, L. Glenn. "Don Vicente Martinez Ybor: The Man and His Empire: Development of the Clear Havana Industry in Cuba and Florida in the Nineteenth Century." Ph.D. dissertation, University of Florida, 1977.

Westfall, L. Glenn. *Key West: Cigar City, U.S.A.* Key West: Historic Key West Preservation Board, 1984.

Zach, Paul, ed. *Insight Guides: Florida*. 7th ed. Singapore: APA Publications, 1990.

109   Comnemos, Caroline. "Florida's Sponge Industry: A Cultural and Economic History." Ph.D. dissertation, University of Florida, 1982.

Derr (p. 94).

Durrell, Lawrence. *The Greek Islands*. New York: Viking Press, 1978.

Frantzis, George T. *Strangers at Ithaca: The Story of the Sponges at Tarpon Springs*. St. Petersburg: Great Outdoors Publishing Company, 1962.

Petrof, John Vasil. "A Study of Florida's Natural Sponge Industry." Ph.D. dissertation, University of Florida, 1987.

Rozee, Eileen. *Sponge Docks, Tarpon Springs, Florida: America's Sponge Diving Birthplace*. Tarpon Springs: Rozee, Eileen and Lon, 1973.

Stevely, John, Sea Grant Extension Agent, Florida Cooperative Extension Service, Palmetto, Florida, 1991. (map)

Zack, Paul (p. 108).

110   Burnham, Walter Dean. *Presidential Ballots 1836-1892*. Baltimore:
–111   Johns Hopkins University Press, 1955.

Florida Office of the Secretary of State. *Official Votes in General Elections*. Report of the Secretary of State of the State of Florida. Tallahassee, 1848-1988. (table)

Robinson, Edgar Eugene. *The Presidential Vote 1896-1932*. Stanford: Stanford University Press, 1934.

116   Lamme III, Ary J., and Raymond K. Oldakowski. "Vernacular
–117   Areas in Florida." *Southeastern Geographer* 22 (1982), p. 106. (map)

Zelinsky, Wilbur. *The Cultural Geography of the United States*. Englewood Cliffs, N.J.: Prentice-Hall, Inc., 1973, 118. (map)

120   Data from Florida Department of State, Division of Cultural Affairs, and Metropolitan Dade County Art in Public Places Program.

121   Florida Department of State, Bureau of Folklife, Florida Folklife Archives.

122   Data from Department of Commerce.
–123   *Musical America, International Directory of the Performing Arts*. New York: Musical America Publications, 1991.

1991 Professional Theatre Directory. West Palm Beach: Florida Professional Theatres Association.

Thielen, Thomas E., ed. *1991 Florida Dance Directory*. Florida Dance Association.

124   Quinn, Bernard, ed. *Churches and Church Membership in the United States, 1980*. Atlanta: Glenmary Research Center, 1982.

125   Adapted from Carver, Craig M. *American Regional Dialects: A Word Geography*. Ann Arbor: University of Michigan Press, 1987. (dialect regions map)

Data from U.S. Department of Commerce, Bureau of the Census. Census of Population, 1980. (Florida maps and table)

POPULATION

All data from the U.S. Department of Commerce, Bureau of the Census, Census of Population (years noted on graphic) unless otherwise indicated.

139   Data from Florida Department of Health and Rehabilitative
–141   Services, Office of Vital Statistics.

143   Data from Internal Revenue Service. (migration by U.S. region map)

U.S. Immigration and Naturalization Service. *Annual Reports (1986-1989)*. (immigration)

150   Data from Seminole, Miccosukee, and Poarch Creek tribes. (reservation and trust lands map and table)

151   Shermyen, Anne H., ed. *1990 Florida Statistical Abstract*. 24th ed. Gainesville: University Presses of Florida, 1990.

157   Data from Executive Office of the Governor, Office of Planning and Budgeting.

158   Mittan, J. Barry, ed. *1991 Florida Health Care Atlas*. Florida
–161   Department of Health and Rehabilitative Services, Office of Comprehensive Health Planning, and Florida State University, 1990.

162   Data from Florida Department of Education.
–163

164   Florida Department of Education. "Designated Area Vocational Education Schools and Area Vocational—Technical Centers." In *1989-90 Florida Educational Directory*. (vocational-technical schools map)

Shermyen (p. 151). (community colleges and colleges and universities)

165   Florida Board of Regents. *Fact Book 1989-90*. (map, state university table)

Peterson's Guide to Graduate and Professional Programs: An Overview 1991. 25th ed. Princeton, N.J.: Peterson's Guides. (professional programs table)

166   Florida Department of Law Enforcement. *Crime in Florida*. Annual Reports; U.S. Department of Justice, Federal Bureau of Investigation. *Uniform Crime Reports for the United States*.

167   Florida Department of Corrections. Annual Reports. (state prison population graph)

Florida Department of Law Enforcement (p. 166). U.S. Department of Justice (p. 166). (arrests map and graphs)

ECONOMY

172   Executive Office of the Governor, Office of Planning and Budgeting. *Florida's Ten-Year Summary of Appropriations, Data 1980-81 through 1989-90*. vol. 12. (comparisons of Florida's economic sectors with U.S. graphs)

U.S. Department of Commerce, Bureau of Economic Analysis. *Survey of Current Business*. 1989. (earned income by economic sectors graph)

173   U.S. Department of Commerce, Bureau of the Census. *County Business Patterns*. 1989. (maps)

174   Shermyen, Anne H., ed. *1988 Florida Statistical Abstract*. 22nd ed. Gainesville: University Presses of Florida, 1988. (maps, pie chart)

U.S. Department of Commerce, Bureau of Economic Analysis. *Survey of Current Business*. 1980-89. (graphs)

175   Shermyen (p. 174). (per capita income maps)

"Survey of Buying Power." *Sales and Marketing Management* (August 13, 1990): C-36–C-38. (household income extremes map)

U.S. Department of Commerce (p. 174). (graph)

176   Shermyen, Anne H., ed. *1990 Florida Statistical Abstract*. 24th ed. Gainesville: University Presses of Florida, 1990. (map)

177   Data from Florida Department of Labor and Employment Security. (graph, maps)

180   Data from U.S. Department of Commerce, Bureau of the Census. Census of Agriculture, 1984-87. (maps, graph)

181   U.S. Department of Agriculture, Economics, Statistics, and Cooperative Service. *State Farm Income Statistics*. 1987. (graph)

U.S. Department of Commerce, Bureau of the Census. Census of Agriculture, 1987. (maps)

182   Data from Florida Department of Agriculture and Consumer
−185   Services, Florida Crop and Livestock Reporting Services.
        (maps, graphs)

186   U.S. Department of Commerce (p. 181). (maps)

187   Bradley, James T. *Freeze Probabilities in Florida*. Bulletin 777.
        Gainesville: University of Florida, Institute of Food and
        Agricultural Sciences, 1975. (mean date of first freeze and last
        freeze maps)
        Data from Florida Department of Agriculture and Consumer
        Services, Florida Crop and Livestock Reporting Services.
        (graphs)

188   Data from Florida Department of Agriculture and Consumer
        Services, Florida Crop and Livestock Reporting Service.
        (maps)
        U.S. Department of Agriculture, Economics, Statistics, and
        Cooperative Service. *State Farm Income Statistics*. 1984-88.
        (graph)

189   Data from Florida Department of Natural Resources, Bureau of
        Geology. (locations of oil and natural gas)
        Data from Tootle, Charles H., Florida Geological Survey.
        (volume of oil and natural gas)
        Florida Department of Administration. *Florida Energy Resources*.
        1989. (Florida crude oil production graph)
        U.S. Department of the Interior. *Minerals Yearbook*. 1989.
        (mineral deposits map, mineral production graph)

190   Data from Florida Department of Natural Resources. (map,
        graphs)

191   Data from Florida Department of Agriculture and Consumer
        Services, Division of Forestry. (maps, graphs)

192   Adapted from West, Carol Tayler. "Manufacturing Faces a
        Rockier Road." *Florida Trend* (June 1990): 13. (change in
        manufacturing employment graph)
        Shermyen, Anne H., ed. *1989 Florida Statistical Abstract*, 23d ed.
        Gainesville: University Presses of Florida, 1989. (maps)
        U.S. Department of Commerce (p. 174). (earned income from
        manufacturing graph)

193   Shermyen (p. 174). (maps and graphs)
-195

196   University of Florida, Bureau of Economic and Business
        Research. *Building Permit Activity in Florida, 1980-89*. (maps)

197   U.S. Department of Commerce, Bureau of the Census. Census of
        Wholesale Trade, 1987; Census of Retail Trade, 1987. (maps)
        U.S. Department of Commerce, Bureau of the Census. *County
        Business Patterns, 1987*. (graph)

198   National Research Bureau. *1990 Directory of Shopping Centers in
        the United States*. 30th ed. Chicago: The National Research
        Bureau, 1989. (shopping malls map, graph)
        "Survey of Buying Power" (p. 175). (buying power map)

199   Shermyen (p. 192). (maps)
        U.S. Department of Commerce 1988. (p. 174). (graph)

200   Shermyen (p. 174). (maps)
        U.S. Department of Commerce (p. 174). (graph)

201   U.S. Department of Commerce (p. 174). (graph)
        U.S. Department of Commerce, Bureau of the Census. Census of
        Service Industries, 1987. (maps)

202   Data from Florida Department of Labor and Employment
        Security, Bureau of Labor Market Information. (Leon County
        graph).
        Shermyen (p. 192). (maps)
        U. S. Department of Commerce (p. 174). (earned income graph)

203   Executive Office of the Governor. *Florida's Ten-Year Summary of
        Appropriations*; Florida Senate Committee on Appropriations.
        Florida's Fiscal Analysis in Brief-1990. (appropriations and
        revenue pie charts)

204   U.S. Department of Commerce, Bureau of the Census. *U.S.
        General Imports, 1988; U.S. General Exports, 1988; U.S. Merchan-
        dise Trade, 1988*. (pie charts, graph)

205   U.S. Department of Commerce. Transportation Series. Micro-
        fiche. 1989. (map)

206   Florida Department of Commerce. *Directory of International
        Manufacturing and Commercial Operations in Florida*. June 1989.
        (maps, graphs)

207   Executive Office of the Governor, Office of Planning and

        Budgeting, Revenue and Economic Analysis Unit. *The Florida
        Price Level Index*. 1990. (maps)

TOURISM AND RECREATION

212   Florida Department of Natural Resources, Division of Recre-
        ation and Parks. *Outdoor Recreation in Florida-1989*. October
        1989.

213   *Outdoor Recreation in Florida-1989* (p. 212). (beaches)
        Rosenau, Jack C., Glen L. Faulkner, Charles W. Hendry Jr., and
        Robert W. Hull. *Springs of Florida*. Bulletin 31. Tallahassee:
        Florida Department of Natural Resources, Bureau of Geology,
        1977. (springs)

214   *Outdoor Recreation in Florida-1989* (p. 212).
        Data from Florida Game and Fresh Water Fish Commission.
        (freshwater fishing)

215   *Outdoor Recreation in Florida-1989* (p. 212). (saltwater fishing)

216   *Outdoor Recreation in Florida-1989* (p. 212).

217   Data from Florida Game and Fresh Water Fish Commission.
        Outdoor Recreation in Florida-1989 (p. 212).

218   Data from U.S. Department of the Interior, National Park
        Service; U.S. Department of Agriculture, Forest Service; and
        Florida Department of Natural Resources, Division of
        Recreation and Parks.

219   *Outdoor Recreation in Florida-1989* (p. 212).

220   Data from Eichholz, Neal, Florida Game and Fresh Water Fish
        Commission, Wild Turkey Management Program. (wild
        turkey map)
        Data from Florida Game and Fresh Water Fish Commission.
        (alligator map)
        U.S. Department of Commerce, Bureau of the Census. *Feral/Wild
        Swine Populations 1988*. Map. (wild swine map)
        U.S. Department of Commerce, Bureau of the Census. *White-
        Tailed Deer Populations 1988*. Map. (white-tailed deer map)

221   Data from Florida Game and Fresh Water Fish Commission.

222   Florida Department of Commerce, Division of Tourism. *Florida
−224   Vacation Guide 1990-91*. Miami Lakes, Florida: Worth Interna-
        tional Communications Corporation, 1990.

225   Data from Florida Department of Natural Resources, Division
        of Recreation and Parks.

226   Data from Florida Department of Commerce, Florida Sports
        Foundation.

227   *The 1990-91 National Directory of College Athletics*. Women's
        edition. Amarillo, Texas: Ray Franks Publishing Ranch, 1990.
        The 1989-90 National Directory of College Athletics. Men's edition.
        Cleveland, Ohio: Collegiate Directories Inc., 1989.

228   Data from Florida Department of Commerce, Division of
−229   Tourism.

230   Data from Florida Department of Business Regulation, Division
        of Pari-Mutuel Wagering. (pari-mutuel facilities map)
        Data from Florida Department of Lottery. (lottery ticket sales
        map, lottery sales graph)
        Data from Florida Governor's Council on Indian Affairs.
        (Indian bingo)

231   Florida Department of Revenue. *Sales Tax Collection by Counties*,
        1989.

232   Data from Florida Department of Business Regulation, Division
        of Hotels and Restaurants. (maps)
        Data from Florida Hotel and Motel Association. (graphs)

233   Florida Department of Commerce, Division of Tourism. *Florida
−234   Tourist Study*. 1983-1989.

235   *Florida Tourist Study* (p. 233-34). (cruise passengers graph, map)
        Trager, Kenneth. *The Impact of Fiscal Year 1988-89 Out-of-State
        Tourism on the Florida Economy*. The Florida legislature.
        (spending by tourists graph)

INFRASTRUCTURE AND PLANNING

236   Executive Office of the Governor. *Investing in Florida 1992-1996*.
−237   January 1992.
        The State Comprehensive Plan Committee. *Keys to Florida's
        Future: Winning in a Competitive World*. Final Report, vol. 2.
        June 1987.
        Executive Office of the Governor, Office of Planning and
        Budgeting. (population figures)

Executive Office of the Governor, Office of Planning and Budgeting, Environmental Affairs. *Facing Florida's Environmental Future.* April 1990.

238   Data from Florida Department of Transportation. (maps)

239   Florida Department of Transportation. *Florida Official Transportation Map.* 1991. (map)

240   Data from Florida Department of Highway Safety and Motor Vehicles, Division of Florida Highway Patrol. (road mileage and unpaved road mileage maps)

Data from Florida Department of Highway Safety and Motor Vehicles, Division of Motor Vehicles. (registered vehicles map, specialty license table)

241   Data from Florida Department of Highway Safety and Motor Vehicles, Division of Florida Highway Patrol. (maps, graphs)

242   Data from Florida Department of Transportation. (truck map)

Florida Department of Transportation. *The Florida Transportation Plan.* 1991. (railroad map)

Greyhound Trailways Timetable. Folders No. 66 and No. 81. January 1991. (bus map)

243   Data from U.S. Maritime Administration. (coastal waterway and navigable rivers map)

U.S. Department of Commerce. *Waterborne Commerce of the U.S. 1988.* (ports and waterways map)

244   Data from Florida Department of Transportation, Office of Aviation. (map and graph)

245   Data from Florida Department of Transportation, Office of Aviation; Florida Department of Transportation, Office of Aviation. *Florida Airports 1989.* (map)

246   Berg, Sanford V., and Prakash Loungani. *Forecasts of Energy Consumption in Florida: 1987–2006.* Public Utility Research Center, University of Florida. April 1989; Salazar-Carrillo, Jorge, and Maria Dolores Espino. *Sources of Energy in Florida: Supply and Distribution.* Center of Economic Research, Department of Economics, Florida International University. November 1989. (imports and exports of energy map)

Florida Department of Environmental Regulation. *Solid Waste Management in Florida.* 1990 Annual Report. March 1991. (solid waste combustion energy map)

Governor's Energy Office. *Florida Energy.* 1989. (energy and renewable energy consumption graphs)

247   Data from Florida Department of Transportation, Division of Planning and Engineering. (maps)

248   Data from Cleary, Ruark, Florida Department of Environmental Regulation. (text)

249   Data from Florida Department of Community Affairs, Division of Resource Planning and Management. (map, graph)

250   Land Acquisition Selection Committee. *Florida Statewide Land Acquisition.* July 1986.

251   "Florida Watershed." *National Geographic* 178 (1990): 100-01.; Florida Department of Transportation. (p. 239). (Everglades map)

Florida Department of Environmental Regulation. *Signal* 4 (1991): 1-3. (text)

252   Fernald, Edward A., and Donald J. Patton, eds. *Water Resources Atlas of Florida.* Tallahassee: Florida State University, Institute of Science and Public Affairs, 1984.

253   Pinellas County Property Appraiser's Office. *Future Land Use Map of Pinellas County, Florida.* 1989. (land use map detail)

254   Florida Consensus Estimating Conference. *State of Florida Population and Demographic Forecast.* Book 3: Executive Summary, vol. 6. Spring 1990. (maps, graphs)

Shermyen, Anne H., ed. *1990 Florida Statistical Abstract.* 22d ed. Gainesville: University Presses of Florida, 1990. (maps, graphs)

255   Data from Florida Department of Education. (maps)

Florida Board of Regents. *State University System of Florida Master Plan, 1988-89 through 1992-93.* 1988. (university graph)

Data from Florida Department of Education, Florida State Board of Community Colleges. (community college graph)

256   Data from U.S. Department of Commerce, Bureau of the Census. Census of Population, 1990; *Florida Governor's Task Force on Urban Growth Patterns: Final Report.* June 1989. (maps, graph)

257   *The Florida Transportation Plan* (p. 242). (map)

258   Florida Department of Environmental Regulation (p. 246). (solid waste maps, chart, graph)

Herndon, R.C., J.E. Moerlins, E.B. Jones, V.W. Lambou and J.D. Koutsandreas. "Small-Quantity-Generator Hazardous-Waste Production and Management in Florida." *Waste Management and Research* 7 (1989): 165-175. (hazardous waste chart)

259   Florida Department of Community Affairs, Division of Emergency Management. *Florida Hazards Analysis.* October 1984. (evacuation time map)

National Oceanic and Atmospheric Administration, National Weather Service. *Hurricanes, Florida and You.* 1977. (storm surge map)

260   Mittan, J. Barry, ed. *1990 Florida Health Care Atlas.* Florida
–261   Department of Health and Rehabilitative Services, Office of Comprehensive Health Planning, and Florida State University, 1990. (graphs)

262   Data from Taxation and Budget Reform Commission. (graphs, maps)

263   Data from Florida Department of State, Division of Elections. (Florida maps)

Data from U.S. Department of Commerce, Bureau of the Census. (graph)

U.S. Department of Commerce, Bureau of the Census. *Statistical Abstract of the United States: 1991.* 111th ed. Washington, D.C., 1991. (change in congressional seats map)

PLACE NAMES

264   Bloodworth, Bertha E., and Alton C. Morris. *Places in the Sun.*
-267   Gainesville: University Presses of Florida, 1978.

Morris, Allen. *Florida Place Names.* Coral Gables, Florida: University of Miami Press, 1974.

Patrick, Rembert W., and Allen Morris. *Florida Under Five Flags.* Gainesville: University of Florida Press, 1967.

Read, William A. *Florida Place Names of Indian Origin.* Baton Rouge: Louisiana State University Press, 1934.

Index